International
Trade
Statistics

WILEY PUBLICATIONS
IN STATISTICS

Walter A. Shewhart, Editor

Mathematical Statistics

HANSEN, HURWITZ, and MADOW · Sample Survey Methods
  and Theory, Volume II
DOOB · Stochastic Processes
RAO · Advanced Statistical Methods in Biometric Research
KEMPTHORNE · The Design and Analysis of Experiments
DWYER · Linear Computations
FISHER · Contributions to Mathematical Statistics
WALD · Statistical Decision Functions
FELLER · An Introduction to Probability Theory and Its Applications, Volume I
WALD · Sequential Analysis
HOEL · Introduction to Mathematical Statistics

Applied Statistics

COCHRAN · Sampling Techniques
WOLD and JURÉEN · Demand Analysis
HANSEN, HURWITZ, and MADOW · Sample Survey Methods
  and Theory, Volume I
CLARK · An Introduction to Statistics
TIPPETT · The Methods of Statistics, *Fourth Edition*
ROMIG · 50-100 Binomial Tables
GOULDEN · Methods of Statistical Analysis, *Second Edition*
HALD · Statistical Theory with Engineering Applications
HALD · Statistical Tables and Formulas
YOUDEN · Statistical Methods for Chemists
MUDGETT · Index Numbers
TIPPETT · Technological Applications of Statistics
DEMING · Some Theory of Sampling
COCHRAN and COX · Experimental Designs
RICE · Control Charts
DODGE and ROMIG · Sampling Inspection Tables

Related Books of Interest to Statisticians

ALLEN and ELY · International Trade Statistics
HAUSER and LEONARD · Government Statistics for Business Use

International Trade Statistics

Edited by

R. G. D. ALLEN
London School of Economics

and

J. EDWARD ELY
Bureau of the Census
U. S. Department of Commerce

New York · John Wiley & Sons, Inc.
London · Chapman & Hall, Limited

Foreword

STATISTICS ARE VIEWED BY THE GENERAL PUBLIC EITHER AS PROVing everything or as being completely untrustworthy. International trade statistics are looked upon as an unusually esoteric variety of data. Few people who benefit from the use of such data have any knowledge of them. But the same can be said for most data used either by pure scientists or by other workers with specialized knowledge. Nevertheless, the need to "measure" accurately the forces that mold our world was never more clear than it is today.

The disruption of world trade by World War II had many facets. For example, unrestricted submarine warfare destroyed large quantities of shipping, and much of the wartime construction was inefficient for postwar use. Japanese and German merchant fleets were either destroyed or transferred to other owners. Another facet of the disrupted trade was the limitation during the war on production for markets abroad, similar to the restrictions on production for home use. After the war, the resumption of production, particularly of goods for foreign trade, was an important objective in all parts of the world. The amazing fact is that production and trade have recovered as quickly as they have. Three years after the cessation of fighting the physical volume of trade had become as large as that of the prewar period. However, the character of the trade, the sources of supply, and the distribution of markets had completely changed.

The "abnormal" character of this postwar world trade grew out of the destruction during the war of both productive facilities and business organization. In the United States and some other countries, productive facilities had been expanded, whereas destruction had taken place in much of Europe and Asia. In many places the businesses that had carried on foreign trade were reduced to shells of their former selves. Government corporations and bureaus had achieved large stature in carrying on the former activities of private businesses. Where private business still functioned, it was under government control.

Export and import statistics became a necessity of "recovery." These statistics were so important that when they could not be had directly they had to be estimated by a variety of indirect methods. The result of all this work showed itself in the growing awareness of the shortcomings of the raw data.

v

The need for trade information on which to base balance-of-payments estimates was supplemented by the related need for the trade data as a component of national-income or gross-national-product statistics. The interest in the data used for estimating these important summaries of national well-being has grown steadily in recent years. Trade data are so common in work dealing with taxation or national budget estimates that to mention their use is to stress their importance.

These two technical uses for foreign trade data relate to the governmental tasks of today; the data have become increasingly important in the world of business. Estimates of the size and character of foreign markets depend increasingly on the quality of the data. The figures which have been available have been useful, but they have had large margins of error. The men responsible for the collection of the data have been more aware of the shortcomings than those who have used them. In estimating possibilities of foreign markets and in making possible a real knowledge of the size of trade in particular commodities, the data that the governments make public have become increasingly useful to businessmen.

This volume provides a more adequate appraisal of the statistics of the countries of the world than has previously been available. It is intended for persons who use these data for purposes such as those noted in the preceding paragraphs, as well as for other purposes.

The book starts with the recognition that statistics on international trade are a type of information frequently not well understood by those using them and that they are frequently treated either with undeserved confidence on the one hand or a puzzled lack of confidence on the other. It is also recognized that, because trade statistics are constructed from the point of view of the nation doing the compiling, the portrayal of the same international transaction in two nations' statistics may differ substantially.

The objective of the volume, then, is so to describe and appraise the principles and practices under which the statistics are compiled that the user of the statistics will recognize the limitations of the data and take advantage of their strong points. In achieving this objective it is necessary to indicate how trade statistics are compiled. The development of methods of compiling international trade statistical information so that it will be most useful is a field in which much work remains to be done. However, it is being given increasing attention with the growing need for improved and comparable trade statistics among nations.

THOMAS C. BLAISDELL, JR.

University of California, Berkeley

Acknowledgments

OUR FIRST ACKNOWLEDGMENT IS TO THE AUTHOR-CONTRIBUTORS TO this joint undertaking. They have been responsible not only for the chapters to which their names are attached but also for valuable advice and criticism of other chapters.

In addition, there are others whose names do not appear but who have contributed in various degrees, and often in quite substantial ways, to the production of the volume. The manuscripts of various chapters were read by numerous experts, and improvements were made by the authors and editors as a result of the suggestions made. These included officials in the British Board of Trade and Colonial Office, in the Dominion Bureau of Statistics of Canada, and in several government organizations in the United States, notably, Samuel J. Dennis, Howard C. Grieves, Morris H. Hansen, Donald C. Horton, Mary D. Keyserling, Roy V. Peel, and Donald C. Riley. Comments on the whole manuscript from Willard L. Thorp and Walter F. Shewhart were particularly useful. This acknowledgment is but a poor recognition of the contributions made.

The late Bruce L. Jenkinson undertook much of the heavy work of final editing. He took the original manuscripts and turned them into the more finished product which is now published.

The authors and the editors have made their contributions to the volume as individuals. Any views expressed are their own, and they do not necessarily coincide with those of the organizations with which they are associated.

R. G. D. A.
J. E. E.

Contents

FOREWORD, by Thomas C. Blaisdell, Jr.

x CONTENTS

Contributors

R. G. D. ALLEN, Professor of Statistics, London School of Economics, University of London.

THOMAS C. BLAISDELL, JR., Professor of Political Science, University of California, Berkeley; formerly Assistant Secretary of Commerce, Washington.

C. D. BLYTH, International Trade Statistics Division, Dominion Bureau of Statistics, Ottawa.

E. DANA DURAND, Member of the Tariff Commission, Washington; formerly member of the League of Nations Committee of Statistical Experts.

J. EDWARD ELY, Foreign Trade Division, Bureau of the Census, Department of Commerce, Washington.

WALTER R. GARDNER, Balance of Payments Division, International Monetary Fund, Washington.

EARL HICKS, Statistics Division, International Monetary Fund, Washington.

D. H. JONES, Research and Development Division, Dominion Bureau of Statistics, Ottawa.

L. A. KANE, External Trade Branch, Dominion Bureau of Statistics, Ottawa.

V. S. KOLESNIKOFF, Division of Statistical Standards, Bureau of the Budget, Washington; consultant to the United Nations Statistical Office in the development of the Standard International Trade Classification.

WILLIAM R. LEONARD, United Nations Statistical Office, New York.

JOHN A. LOFTUS, Bureau of Near Eastern, South Asian, and African Affairs, Department of State, Washington; Lecturer in International Economics, School of Advanced International Studies, Washington.

PATRICK J. LOFTUS, United Nations Statistical Office, New York.

A. MAIZELS, Commercial Relations and Exports Division, Board of Trade, London; formerly with Economic Commission for Europe, Geneva.

HERBERT MARSHALL, Dominion Statistician, Ottawa.

J. M. MATON, Statistics Division, Board of Trade, London.

NICHOLAS M. PETRUZZELLI, Office of International Trade, Department of Commerce, Washington; author of a volume on international trade statistics.

JOHN B. ROTHROCK, Inter-American Statistical Institute, Pan American Union, Washington.

W. F. SEARLE, Statistics Department, Colonial Office, London.

L. A. SHACKLETON, International Trade Statistics Division, Dominion Bureau of Statistics, Ottawa.

J. STAFFORD, Director of Statistics, Board of Trade, London.

AMOS E. TAYLOR, Department of Economic and Social Affairs, Pan American Union, Washington; formerly Director, Bureau of Foreign and Domestic Commerce, Department of Commerce, Washington.

H. VAUTHIER, Research and Planning Division, Economic Commission for Europe, Geneva; formerly Adminstrateur de l'Institut de Statistique francais.

MURIEL VENNING, Statistics Division, Board of Trade, London.

IRVING WEISS, Foreign Trade Division, Bureau of the Census, Department of Commerce, Washington.

CHAPTER 1

Introduction

R. G. D. ALLEN
London School of Economics

J. EDWARD ELY
Bureau of the Census,
U.S. Department of Commerce

Never before have statistics of international trade been so important and so widely used. The World War of 1939–1945, spreading destruction far and wide, disrupted both the composition and the direction of international trade. In the subsequent period of recovery, individual business men were compelled to re-assess their foreign markets and sources of supply. At the same time national governments were faced with the problems of the stresses and strains in their domestic economies arising from international developments. Many countries were forced to concentrate on achieving, or on maintaining, national solvency in a disturbed world. Systems of import quotas were designed to restrict payments to other countries; export targets were set with consequent limitations on production for home uses, to increase receipts of foreign exchange. Statistics of international trade are vital in this work, both in their detail and in the general context of the balance of payments and national income accounts.

Each country, then, has recognized increasingly the scope and relevance of its trade statistics in any analysis of its domestic economy. This is not all; international trade statistics are essential to the consideration of other than purely domestic questions. Political and economic factors have become so inter-related that such economic data as trade statistics are needed in the determination, evaluation, and implementation of foreign policy. National security is being supplemented by systems of regional security; hence regional statistics on the direction of merchandise trade have taken on a new importance. The determination and allocation of economic and military aid by the United States to other countries depend on the availability of statistics of the balance of payments of various countries. More detailed statistics are required in assessing the commodity restrictions and embargoes imposed on trade between the Western Powers and communist countries, *e.g.*, East-West trade in Europe and trade with

1

China. Sources of oil and vital materials, in the Near East, South-East Asia, and elsewhere, need to be protected; statistics of trade with these areas are among the data which must be assembled.

Since many economic problems are of an international character, schemes have been developed to solve them on an international basis. Among them are the schemes for international allocation of raw materials, schemes for the development of such areas as those coming under " Point Four " and the Colombo Plan, and the planned expansion of European resources of coal, steel, and other commodities, through such agencies as the Economic Commission for Europe (ECE) and the Organization for European Economic Co-operation (OEEC). All attempts at international co-operation on these lines make use of international trade statistics; indeed, they depend on the availability of statistics in comparable form. There is therefore an increasing pressure for standardization so as to obtain the greatest degree of comparability in handling the statistics of different countries, and in aggregating the data in their international uses.

International trade statistics, then, have current uses which are as diverse as they are important, and they are likely to become even more vital in the future. This does not mean, however, that the need for the statistics has suddenly, or only recently, arisen. For centuries past there has been a special emphasis on international transactions, at first in the countries where industries developed early, and later in practically all nations of the world. The important influence of foreign trade on the domestic economy has long been realized. Accordingly governments maintained records, and later compiled regular statistical series, of the trade with other countries. The earliest economic statistics are usually those concerned with merchandise trade.

Though the influence of foreign trade was recognized, its economic nature and interpretation have been variously explained over the centuries. In 1664, John Muir of the East India Company expressed the view that foreign trade was " the ordinary means to increase our wealth," so that " we must ever observe this rule: to sell more to strangers yearly than we consume of theirs in value." This was the Mercantilist view which, despite the criticism of later economists, has survived in one form or another to this day. Economists have never failed to study international trade theory; they have simply taken different views. The classical economists thought that a continued export surplus was impossible since correcting factors, through the movements of gold and price changes, come into play. Keynes' explanation also involved correcting factors, but different ones— through changes in output and employment, incomes, and saving. Modern concentration on the balance of trade—and wider problems of international economics—owes much to Keynes and his approach to " what for centuries has been a prime object of practical statecraft."

The compilation of foreign trade statistics has been, at least in part, with the object of providing an essential tool in " practical statecraft." In addition, the more routine needs of administration have made it desirable to maintain the statistics. From quite early times, the sovereign authority in each country has exacted a customary tribute on the consumption of certain basic commodities. In the course of time, these " customs " duties were imposed mainly on imports—to make the " foreigner " pay. At times, moreover, regulations required that goods be carried in national vessels, so that the development of the export trade and the expansion of the merchant fleet went hand in hand. For these and other reasons, imports and exports alike came under close scrutiny, and scrutiny means records and statistics.

In these ways, international trade statistics came to be compiled, separately and individually, by every important country in the world. Although possessing much the same basic features, the different national compilations display an infinite variety in detail as a result of variations in the historical development and the politico-economic backgrounds of the different nations of the world.

It is only realistic to recognize that trade statistics are primarily government statistics. Because they are compiled as a by-product of other government operations and reveal information about each nation's relations to other nations, they frequently reflect national political, economic, and administrative needs and policies. The form and content of the statistics may therefore be affected by a nation's belief as to how the information may be used to its own advantage or disadvantage—its attitude toward the use of its statistics as commercial intelligence by other countries, its belief as to whether its trade figures will support its credit standing, its need to obtain other trade statistics on a reciprocal basis, its desire to conceal information for military, political, or economic reasons. With the growth of quotas, embargoes, exchange controls, and other government restrictions on trade, and with greater government participation in the trade itself, the pressures affecting the information publicly disclosed are certainly greater than prior to World War II.

The description of international trade statistics provided in this volume is divided into the following main divisions:

Part I, Basic Characteristics of the Statistics;
Part II, Important Derived Uses of the Statistics;
Part III, Statistics of Individual Countries.

A description of each of these main divisions follows.

Part I. All compilations of trade statistics provide information on the international movement of goods, but exactly what goods are included and what goods are excluded (the coverage of the statistics) depend on the particular practices followed. All countries show details of the different types of commodities moving in international trade, but how the detail is presented depends on the principles followed in establishing the system of commodity classification used in the compilation. All countries provide information on the values of their trade in terms of the separate national currencies; in doing so they must convert foreign currencies to national currency equivalents—again a matter involving the principles and practices followed. Finally, all countries group their trade statistics according to where export goods are bound for and import goods are received from—this classification also depending on the definitions adopted and the practices followed in obtaining the data from those who supply the information.

These five aspects—coverage, commodity classification, valuation, exchange conversion, and country designation—are the basic characteristics of international trade statistics. They are the topics taken up in the central chapters of Part I (Chapters 3 to 7 inclusive). They are all greatly dependent on two technical matters: (1) the procedures followed in recording the information and (2) the ways in which the data are presented and published to meet the various uses of the statistics. What goods are included in the statistics, what commodity and country classifications are used, and what valuation definition and practices are followed—all these are directly influenced both by how the information is obtained and by the use to be made of the information and the form in which it is to be published. Accordingly, Part I opens with a chapter on techniques and practices in compilation of the statistics (Chapter 2) and concludes with a chapter on publication and use of the national data (Chapter 8).

Part II. A working knowledge of international trade statistics requires a comprehension of some of the more important ways in which the basic data, as assembled and published, can be used to derive other data useful for economic analysis.

Part II (Chapters 9 to 12 inclusive) gives some account of four applications of international trade statistics for this purpose. The first of these describes how foreign trade statistics are fitted to the needs of statistics of the balance of international payments. The second concerns the way in which the statistics are used to derive index numbers of quantum and unit value—volume and price—and of the terms of trade. The third application considers the need to bring together the statistics of international trade of individual countries in the perspective of their domestic setting. A full knowledge of the relationship of a nation's imports and exports to the domestic economy, in its many and various aspects, is not readily obtainable; perhaps it can only be obtained by the professional economist. Certainly, it lies beyond the limited scope of the present volume. However, users of the statistics can be given some familiarity with the manner in which external trade statistics are related to those on domestic production, income, etc. Finally, foreign trade statistics of the individual trading countries are used to derive comparable statistics on the trade of groups of countries or to derive aggregate data for all countries combined—the problem of international comparisons and standardization. Since all the topics covered in the four chapters of Part II—the derived uses of international trade statistics—involve theoretical points of complexity, Part II, as a whole, is a little more difficult than the rest of the volume.

Part III. Users of international trade statistics must have more than a general knowledge of the basic characteristics described in Part I. An acquaintanceship with, or an ability to refer to, the detailed practices followed by the various trading nations of the world is essential if users are to make full and adequate application of the statistics of different countries.

Nations having similar foreign trade statistics are not necessarily grouped on a geographic basis. Common practices in compiling trade statistics have been developed among the widely scattered British Colonies. Certain practices have also been developed in common by the British Dominions, although to a lesser extent than among the Colonies. Similarly, the statistics of the world-wide dependencies of European countries have much in common with those of the mother countries. Also the different nations of Europe, with so many points of contact, share many practices in the compilation of trade statistics. Among Latin American countries, trade statistics tend to have similar features within a group of countries which are also concentrated geographically. In the countries of the Near and Far East (outside the British Commonwealth and the dependents of European countries), it is difficult to find many common threads in the methods of compiling such trade statistics as exist.

In Part III (Chapters 15 to 19 inclusive), the characteristics of the trade statistics of each of these groups of countries are described in turn. Their strong and weak points are appraised and their uses and limitations described. In addition, Part III contains separate chapters on the trade statistics of the United States (Chapter 13) and the United Kingdom (Chapter 14), the world's two largest trading nations. The statistics of these two countries are probably used to a greater extent than those of others, and they each merit more detailed consideration than those of any other single country. Though the various chapters of Part III contain many illustrations of the application of principles, they are primarily intended for detailed reference—along with the publications of the countries concerned—by the users of the statistics of individual countries.

The volume has been planned as a co-operative effort in which the experience and knowledge of experts in a number of countries and in international organizations have been enlisted. Each contributor deals authoritatively with his own subject and he has been free, within very modest limits, to adopt the method of exposition he has considered most suitable. It follows that there is some overlapping, since one contributor may need to refer, more or less briefly, to a topic discussed at greater length by another. However, each chapter is thereby relatively complete in itself, and the volume is therefore valuable, not only to the reader who wishes to pursue a course from beginning to end, but also to those users of trade statistics who may need only a few particular chapters, perhaps only one chapter.

The book as a whole is intended to provide the general user of international trade statistics with practical guidance and an adequate comprehension of their general scope and limitations. But no one should expect to find in these pages any detailed guidance on the application of published data to a particular problem. The applied economist or administrator can only learn for himself, and by bitter experience.

PART I

Basic Characteristics
of the Statistics

CHAPTER 2

Compilation

L. A. KANE
Dominion Bureau of Statistics,
Ottawa

IRVING WEISS
Bureau of the Census,
U.S. Department of Commerce

THE FLOW OF DOCUMENTS

Introduction. Because of the great complexity and detail of the international trade statistics compiled by the nations of the world, effective use of the data requires at least some rudimentary knowledge of how the information was derived. There are probably each year in the neighbourhood of 50,000,000 shipments of merchandise from one country to another of the world. Each of these transactions is recorded at the place the shipment starts and at the place it finally is completed. In addition, records may be kept of the shipments at the time the goods move through intermediate countries either as in-transit shipments or by reconsignment. These individual records are voluminous, detailed, and in the true sense of the word are merely raw data from which orderly and usable information must be extracted.

This chapter tells in broad outline how international trade statistics are compiled from this source material. Since each country has its own individual variations in compiling techniques only generalized procedures are described.   However, these procedures are quite universally followed by compiling countries.

Since the objective is primarily to give the user of international trade statistics a sufficient grasp of the compiling process to enable him to make more effective use of the statistics, many relatively minor parts of the compiling work are not described.   Likewise and with the same objective in mind, no description is provided of certain operations frequently carried out in the same offices as those which compile the regular import and export statistics, namely, the compilation of information on products of domestic fisheries, separate statistics on entrances and clearances of vessels, statistics on in-transit trade, etc.

Source of Information.   Foreign trade statistics are, almost without exception, compiled from copies of export and import documents which are prepared by exporters, importers, or their brokers or agents at the time goods enter or leave a country.   For statistical purposes, the essential information on the documents is the description of the commodity, the net quantity, the value, and the country from which received or to which shipped.   Frequently, the documents are copies of forms required for other governmental purposes, *e.g.*, the levying of duties, the control of import quotas, the control of exports of commodities, etc.   Invoices are often filed with the statistical copies for checking purposes, particularly in the case of import entries where a close examination of the transaction is made for duty-collection purposes.   Invoices are also filed occasionally with export entries, particularly in those cases where export duties are assessed or where some form of export control, *e.g.*, exchange, quantitative, etc., is enforced.   Copies of the basic export document for United States exports and the most frequently used basic document for Canadian imports are reproduced here as Figures *A* and *B* respectively.

How the documents flow to collectors of Customs.   In the case of exports the exporter or his agent generally files a number of copies of the export declaration with the Collector of Customs at the Custom House at the port or point of exportation.   The Collector examines the document for completeness and accuracy and occasionally examines the invoices before approving the shipment.   One copy of the form is usually kept in the Customs office and is used as the official Customs copy.   Another copy is used for the compilation of the foreign trade statistics.   Occasionally, an additional copy will be required to facilitate the physical examination of the merchandise by a Customs official at the pier or border point of export, which may be at a considerable distance from the Customs House.

For import documents the procedure is quite similar.   In most countries the import and export forms are also checked against the manifests (rail, vessel, air, etc.), which are also filed with Customs by the carrier and which describe the cargo carried on the train, vessel, or airplane. The export and import documents instead of the manifests are used for the compiling work because manifests contain only general information with less detail for commodities, quantities, and values than that shown in the export and import documents. For exports, the cargo manifest is prepared by the carrier from copies of his bills of lading and sometimes from copies of export declarations which are transmitted to him by the exporter after approval by Customs. When the export declaration is used in preparing the manifest, the carrier verifies that a document is filed for all cargo. This procedure therefore essentially gives the carrier the responsibility of insuring that a declaration has been prepared for all cargo laden on the vessel, rail car, etc. There is a similar check of the import entries against the cargo manifest, but this is normally done by the Customs Service, not by the carriers. This verification by Customs officials that an import entry is filed for all merchandise being unladen (termed " liquidation of the manifest ") takes the place of transmitting an approved import document to the carrier for his use in verifying that an entry form is filed for all cargo.

PROCESSING DOCUMENTS

Processing documents for statistical purposes. Where compilation is performed in the central statistical office, the documents are edited and coded after being received from ports or border points and recorded. If the number of shipments is large the editing and coding procedure usually takes the form of translating the items of information shown on the export and import forms into numeric codes. The principal numeric codes used are a commodity code, a country code, a code for the Customs port of import or export, a " type of transaction " code (domestic produce, foreign produce, warehouse entry, etc.), and sometimes a " method of transportation " and a " flag of vessel " code. The coding consists of writing on the document itself, or on a special transcription form, the information which is to be punched on a machine tabulation card. Each country uses its own series of codes to satisfy its particular needs. In the United States the commodity code for exports consists of 2700 items and that for imports consists of 5500. The country code includes 130 items, and the United States Customs port code includes 300 items. In Canada the commodity code for exports includes 1100 items, for imports 2500 items. The country code includes 125 items; the Canadian port code, 215 items.

Commodity coding is the most complicated process in the coding of the document. In contrast the coding of the domestic ports is relatively

Form 7525-V (Rev. Nov. 1948)   U. S. DEPARTMENT OF COMMERCE
Export Control   BUREAU OF THE CENSUS—OFFICE OF INTERNATIONAL TRADE
Foreign Commerce
Statistical Regulations   SHIPPER'S EXPORT DECLARATION
(See Instructions on Reverse Side)
OF SHIPMENTS TO FOREIGN COUNTRIES OR NONCONTIGUOUS TERRITORIES OF THE UNITED STATES

FORM APPROVED.
BUDGET BUREAU NO. 41-R397.2.

READ CAREFULLY THE INSTRUCTIONS ON BACK TO AVOID DELAY AT SHIPPING POINT   Clearance will not be granted until shipper's declaration has been filed with the Collector of Customs. This declaration shall not be used to effect any exportation after the expiration date of the export license referred to herein, except as specifically authorized by export regulations.
DECLARATIONS SHOULD BE TYPEWRITTEN OR PREPARED IN INK; INDELIBLE PENCIL IS NOT PERMISSIBLE.

CONFIDENTIAL (See Instruction 2(h) on reverse side.)

Do Not Use This Area

Do Not Use This Area

District	Port	Country (For customs use only)	FILE NO. (This Space for Use of Customs)

1. Exporting Carrier (*if vessel, give name, flag and pier number*)   2. From (*U. S. Port of Export*)

3. Exporter (*Principal or seller—licensee*)   Address (*Number, street, place, State*)

4. Agent of Exporter (*Forwarding agent*)   Address (*Number, street, place, State*)

5. Purchaser or Ultimate Consignee   Address (*Place, country*)

6. Intermediate Consignee   Address (*Place, country*)

7. Foreign Port of Unloading (*For vessel and air shipments only*)   8. Place and Country of Ultimate Destination (*Not place of transshipment*)

(9) Marks and Nos.	(10) Number and Kind of Packages, Description of Commodities, Export License Number, Issuance Date, Expiration Date (or General License Symbol) (Describe commodities in sufficient detail to permit classification according to Schedule B. Do not use general terms. Insert required license information on line below description of each item)	(11) Shipping Weight— (*Gross weight in pounds*) Not required for truck, rail, and mail exportations	(12) Specify "D," or "F,"	(13) Schedule B Commodity No.	(14) Net Quantity in schedule B units (*State unit*)	(15) Value at Time and Place of Export (Selling price or cost if not sold, including inland freight, insurance and other charges to place of export) (*Nearest whole dollar; omit cents*)

16. WAYBILL OR MANIFEST NO. (*of Exporting Carrier*)

17. DATE OF EXPORTATION (*if Vessel, Date of Clearance*)

18. THE UNDERSIGNED HEREBY AUTHORIZES _____ (Name and address—Number, street, place, State)
TO ACT AS FORWARDING AGENT FOR EXPORT CONTROL AND CUSTOMS PURPOSES. (DULY AUTHORIZED
EXPORTER _____ BY OFFICER OR EMPLOYEE) _____

▶ 19. I DECLARE THAT ALL STATEMENTS MADE AND ALL INFORMATION CONTAINED IN THIS EXPORT DECLARATION ARE TRUE AND CORRECT.

SIGNATURE _____ (Duly authorized officer or employee of exporter or named (forwarding agent)

20. Subscribed and sworn to before me on _____, 19____

FOR _____ (Name of corporation or firm and capacity of signer, e. g., secretary, export manager, etc.)

ADDRESS _____

(TITLE OR DESIGNATION) Notary Public, etc., or those authorized to administer oaths under Sec. 486, Tariff Act of 1930.

Do Not Write in This Area

▲ Declaration should be made by duly authorized officer or employee of exporter or of forwarding agent named by exporter.
* If shipping weight is not available for each Schedule B item listed in column (13) included in one or more packages, insert the approximate gross weight for each Schedule B item. The total of these estimated weights should equal the actual weight of the entire package or packages.
ᵇ Designate foreign merchandise (reexports) with an "F" and exports of domestic merchandise produced in the United States or changed in condition in the United States with a "D".
NO AUTHENTICATED DECLARATION RELATING TO ANY COMMODITY REQUIRING AN EXPORT LICENSE MAY BE ALTERED, CHANGED OR AMENDED WITHOUT PRIOR WRITTEN AUTHORIZATION FROM THE COLLECTOR OF CUSTOMS OR FROM SUCH OTHER PERSON AS MAY BE EMPOWERED BY EXPORT REGULATIONS TO GIVE SUCH WRITTEN AUTHORIZATION. (See also Instruction 2 (e).) 16—56693-2

FIG. A.

B. 1

3,000,000—1-51

Port of...19..........

Arriving per.....................................

Imported by....................................

Goods exported to Canada Direct from............

Via..................................

(Country through which carried in transit if any)

CUSTOMS, CANADA

ENTRY FOR

HOME CONSUMPTION

Sending Port Numbers of Manifests:

Report No..........

Entry No..........

Outport..........

Port..........

Marks and Numbers	Number of Packages	Description of Goods	Quantity	Value for Duty in Dollars	Rate of Duty or Free	Total Customs Duty	Duty Paid Value	Sales Tax	Rate of Excise Tax	Excise Tax	Tariff Item Applied
						$ c.	$ c.	$ c.		$ c.	

Show hereunder the invoiced price of the goods in the currency of settlement and unless already included add all charges (freight, etc.), payable to non-residents.

Currency........................ Amount........................

Cheques, etc., must be made payable to the Receiver General of Canada.

The spaces below this line are reserved for Customs–Excise Officers' use only, and must not be filled in by the Importer.

INITIALS

DUTY	
SALES TAX	
EXCISE TAX	
TOTAL	

Sales Tax Licence No.........................

Power of Attorney No.........................
which has been checked by me against this entry
is registered in the name of the importer.

CUSTOMS–EXCISE CLERK

FIG. B.

simple since clear definitions of the boundaries of the domestic ports are readily available. The coding of country is also a simple clerical operation since boundaries of countries are defined clearly. Of course, the resulting statistics may be inaccurate in terms of the country definition in view of the difficulty of obtaining accurate country information as described in Chapter 7. The commodity code, however, requires more deliberation since clear definitions of the contents of each commodity classification cannot be readily determined. Despite this greater difficulty of the commodity coding operation, it is carried out at a rate of approximately 75 to 100, or even more, items per clerk hour in countries which have a large volume of import and export transactions.

In some countries, coding manuals have been prepared to facilitate the commodity coding process. These manuals show the classification of the more common items. (A description of coding manuals designed for international use being prepared by the Inter American Statistical Institute and the United Nations Statistical Office is given in Chapter 4.)

Most countries insert this code for the first time as part of their statistical compiling operations. However, the United States and a few other countries, including France, require the exporter to insert on the export document the statistical commodity code number. To determine this commodity code number the exporter refers to the official commodity classification. The correctness of the exporter's assignment of the commodity number is verified by the Collector of Customs at the time the document is presented to him for approval. When the documents are received in the central statistical office, this code number is again verified by the statistical coding or editing clerk against the description shown on the document.

Where incomplete information is shown on the export declaration, with the result that the document cannot be properly coded, the document is returned to the exporter for more complete information. To reduce expenses, only a minimum number of declarations will be so returned; hence occasional shipments for which questionable information is provided by the shipper will be included in the statistics, particularly if the shipments are relatively small and statistically unimportant. Where documents covering a particular group of commodities contain a large number of incorrect or incomplete items of information, an educational program may be instituted to call the attention of exporters to the necessity for showing correct information. This educational program is particularly important at a time when a change is made in the commodity classification.

The processing of import documents is quite similar. The country and port codes are usually the same for exports and imports. The commodity codes, however, frequently differ. Since most countries collect import commodity information separately on all items having different rates of duty, it is possible to obtain information on duty collections from the statistical data, a type of information not as frequently required for exports.   Because of this and in view of the differing nature of an individual country's export and import trade, a common commodity code is not ordinarily used.

Punch-card processing.   Where mechanical methods of compilation are used the coded information on the documents is then perforated into cards.   A specimen copy of the punch card used by Canada in compiling the foreign trade statistics is shown as Figure *C*.

The items on the punch card are usually arranged in the same order as the items on the source document, *i.e.*, the exporter's or importer's entry form.   The document in turn has probably been arranged to facilitate the punching or perforating operation, taking into account also the shipper's convenience in preparing the form.   Thus, the items referring to all the commodities shipped are shown at the beginning of the card; such as month, port, entry number, and country; the items referring to individual commodities are shown at the end of the card, such as classification (commodity designation), quantity, and value.   This arrangement is necessary since commonly more than one commodity is reported on a document, necessitating the preparation of more than one punch card for each import or export form.

Except for the need to facilitate the punching operation itself, however, the order in which items of information appear in the punch card is of little or no importance.   Once the cards have been punched, they may be sorted and tabulated for different items of information (commodity, country, quantity, value, etc.) in any arrangement, irrespective of where each item is punched in the card.   The cards may be tabulated in commodity-by-country arrangement whether the commodity code precedes that for country or not, or whether the two codes are adjacent or widely separated.   Similarly, quantity totals may precede value totals in the tabulation, even though in the punch card they may be in reverse order.

After the documents are punched, a verification of the operation is made, either by a key-punch operation or by listing the cards and reading back from the listing to the information shown on the documents.   When the cards have been completely punched and verified they are sorted and tabulated.   In Canada, each day's transactions for each port are tabulated on the tabulating machine and are verified back to the documents.   A new tabulation is prepared at the end of the month, listing all the transactions for the month.   The daily listing and reading back not only performs the function of verification of the punching operation but also verifies the coding operation since the clerks who perform this operation are also the

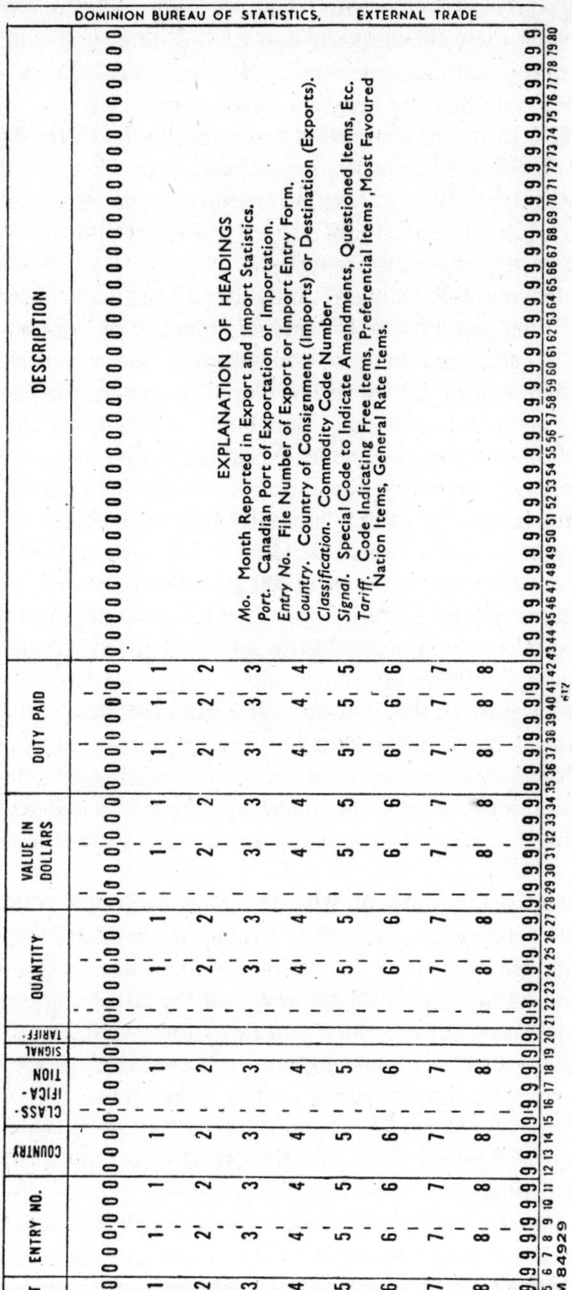

DOMINION BUREAU OF STATISTICS, EXTERNAL TRADE

DESCRIPTION | DUTY PAID | VALUE IN DOLLARS | QUANTITY | TARIFF | SIGNAL | CLASSIFICATION | COUNTRY | ENTRY NO. | PORT | MO.

EXPLANATION OF HEADINGS

Mo. Month Reported in Export and Import Statistics.

Port. Canadian Port of Exportation or Importation.

Entry No. File Number of Export or Import Entry Form.

Country. Country of Consignment (Imports) or Destination (Exports).

Classification. Commodity Code Number.

Signal. Special Code to Indicate Amendments, Questioned Items, Etc.

Tariff. Code Indicating Free Items, Preferential Items, Most Favoured Nation Items, General Rate Items.

IBM 84929

FIG. C.

coding clerks who are familiar with the codes used. After this verification listing, the cards are held until the end of the month, at which time a combined monthly listing is prepared. In the United States and many other countries only this one monthly listing is prepared.

The complete listing of a month's cards usually takes the form of an arrangement in commodity order, *i.e.*, all the cards for each commodity are grouped together. Within each commodity the codes are further sub-grouped into order of countries of export or import and usually, finally, the domestic port of export or import.

This complete monthly listing not only lists all the items but also shows totals for (*a*) each commodity, (*b*) each commodity by country summarization, and (*c*) each commodity by country by domestic port summarization. It is then scrutinized by review clerks for errors which may have been made in the previous coding, punching, or listing operations. The review operation is normally done by checking the unit price of a total for each commodity as shown on the listing against unit prices for previous months. Price ranges for each commodity may be maintained for reference. For instance, in the United States, a monthly total of all exports of automobiles should range between $1000 and $3000 per unit. If the unit price of the total exports of automobiles for a month does not fall within this range it is necessary to examine the list of the individual items to find the item which is outside the range and, therefore, probably incorrect. The document reporting this item is pulled from the files, and any necessary correction is made in the listing. Similarly, errors in the coding or punching of country codes are detected by the review clerks on the basis of their knowledge of the type of commodities traded by various countries, and by comparison of current figures with those for previous months or years.

Another tool used in some countries in the review is that of checking the array of cards within each commodity-by-country-by-district listing. The cards are arranged in value order, within the three-way grouping, *i.e.*, the shipment smallest in value is shown first, and the larger shipments follow in order of increasing value. Net quantities are shown in these listings for those commodities where a unit of quantity is available. Since the values are arrayed by size, the quantities (if they are correct) should also be generally arrayed by size. The documents for any items which fall outside this array are pulled from the files, and corrections are noted and made on the listing.

In some countries including Canada, another operation is performed to verify the accuracy of the figures. This is a comparison of the monthly commodity totals for the current month with the corresponding totals for the previous month and for the cumulative year-to-date period. Any unusual transactions found as a result of this comparison are re-examined for accuracy, and appropriate changes are made when necessary.

When this review operation has been completed a summary card is prepared for the total of each commodity exported to an individual country from an individual domestic Customs port. These summary cards are either prepared by a mechanical card-punching procedure as part of the machine listing procedure or by a subsequent manual punching of summary cards. In 1949 the average number of monthly cards summarizing the exports and imports by commodity, by country, and by port was as follows, in Canada and in the United States:

	United States	Canada
Exports	77,000	17,000
Imports	22,000	45,000
Total	99,000	62,000

The summary cards are then used as a basis for preparing all the subsequent tabulations. The basic tabulations are (a) an arrangement in commodity order with quantity and value totals shown for each country, and (b) an arrangement by country with totals shown for each commodity. In addition to these two basic arrangements other supplementary tables are prepared for special purposes such as port arrangements with detail by commodity and by country, economic class arrangement, *i.e.*, arrangement by degree of manufacture, consumer and durable goods arrangements, etc. These arrangements can easily be prepared from the summary cards since they are merely combinations of other items of information already shown on the cards. Thus the economic class arrangement can be obtained by punching into the summary card a new code representing a combination of a number of individual commodities. Other special codes such as the United Nations commodity classification (the SITC, described in Chapter 4), can be processed in the same way.

The processes involved in verifying that the totals shown on one table equal the totals shown in another are termed " balancing operations." These consist of planning the tables in such a way that each will contain a common set of summary totals which can be compared from table to table. Thus, to balance a commodity-by-country arrangement against the country-by-commodity arrangement the balancing technique consists of comparing the commodity group totals in the commodity-by-country table with the commodity group totals of all the countries combined in the country-by-commodity table. Any discrepancies between these commodity group totals are further localized by an examination of the individual commodity items included within each commodity group. In some cases it may be necessary to re-sort and re-tabulate the cards representing a particular commodity group to locate the error.

In addition to the monthly tabulations, tabulations are also usually prepared on a quarterly basis, on a cumulative quarterly basis, and on a calendar year basis. These tabulations are prepared from the same summary cards used for the monthlies and consist of the re-tabulation of the cards for the required period into this new form. Where the volume of cards is large, it is sometimes necessary to prepare a new summary card for the new period, particularly where a number of tabulations are required for this new period. Thus, for the annual tabulations, a new annual commodity-by-country-by-port card is usually prepared since a number of different annual tables will be required.

The above procedures are those used to obtain foreign trade information through the use of the punch-card technique. Similar information can be obtained by manual procedures. The manual compilation procedures are advantageous only in those cases where (a) the initial volume of transactions is small and (b) where the subsequent rearrangements and tabulations of the information are few. A more complete description of hand techniques is given below.

Alternative methods of compiling figures at ports. The procedure outlined previously describes the compilation of statistics in a central statistical office. An alternative method followed in many countries including India, Pakistan, USSR (at least until about 1944), and China, is that of having the first compilation operations carried out at the individual ports within a country. These compilations are then transmitted to a central statistical office for either mechanical or manual summarization of the port figures into aggregates of the country's trade. Even where punch cards are in general use a manual compiling procedure may be followed for part of the statistics. For example, the United States follows this procedure for statistics on shipments from Puerto Rico to the United States. In this case the procedure for the filing of export declarations is similar to that followed in the United States for exports to foreign countries. The documents, however, are not transmitted to a central United States statistical office, i.e., the United States Bureau of the Census, but instead are coded and processed manually in the Puerto Rican Customs Office. The editing and coding processes are similar except that the code numbers are not inserted by the exporter. In lieu thereof the clerk in the Customs office assigns the commodity code numbers to the documents. Ledger sheets are then prepared for each commodity on a daily basis. At the end of the month the individual shipments listed on these commodity ledger sheets are totalled and the total of shipments of commodities to the United

States are summarized and transferred to a form which lists each of the commodities with columns for quantity and value totals. These data are shown separately in the United States statistics; they are not included in the total figures of trade of the United States with foreign countries. Similar procedures are followed in many countries that compile their trade statistics on a manual basis.

The procedure of compiling the figures at the individual ports has a number of advantages. (1) Since the information compiled represents transactions within the port only, it is easier to get additional information on incomplete documents since the shippers are located within the port; (2) the port and country statistics may be obtained earlier since the volume of documents for any one port is smaller than for the country as a whole and since it is easier to transmit the few total figures to the central statistical office for summarization into national figures.

The disadvantage of this system of compiling figures in the individual ports for later summarization are: (1) The classification of commodities may vary from port to port (the use of a simple common coding manual in each port would act to reduce this variation); (2) reporting of quantities and values may vary among ports; the resulting non-comparability of information cannot be readily eliminated; (3) the advantages of having over-all supervision of a statistical operation are not as readily achieved; (4) Laborious hand procedures may be required because local compilation does not permit the efficient use of machine compilation techniques.

OTHER COMPILATION PROCEDURES

Problem of corrections in previously issued reports. Despite the checks and balances, described previously, in compiling the foreign trade statistics of a country, problems of making corrections in previously issued reports still arise. Corrections arise because (1) the information originally shown on the document is later corrected by the importer or exporter or by the Collector of Customs as a result of his checking of the shipment for duty or other purposes; (2) verification procedures have not been completely followed and subsequent use, or a subsequent inquiry from users of the statistics, may reveal an error.

The method of showing these post-facto corrections, *i.e.*, the corrections found after the original statistics have been published, presents a number of problems. *First*, many arrangements of information may have been published (*i.e.*, in commodity order with country detail, in country order with commodity detail, etc.). The making of one correction may change the information in each of these arrangements. *Second*, the correction of imports of coffee from Brazil will not only change that particular figure but also the figure on total imports of coffee, total imports of foodstuffs, or the total of any other groupings of commodities shown in the table. The grand total is also changed unless the error is compensated. If the number of corrections is very large, the amount of work involved in making all the corrections in all the pertinent tabulations will be very time consuming. It would therefore be a sizable burden for users of the statistics to carry the corrections into copies of all of the reports.

There are two basic methods of making corrections. The first is that of preparing a notice revising figures previously issued. This change notice is attached to reports issued for subsequent months. Users of the statistics can make these changes manually in the previously issued reports to obtain the corrected totals. The agencies doing the compiling work will, in addition, reperforate their punch cards as necessary and make certain that the punch cards in retabulating have been properly changed for the corrections made. The problem here is that revisions may be numerous, may affect a number of previous months' data, and may change many totals in the tabulations, causing an expenditure of considerable effort as described above.

Another method frequently followed by countries is to include in the current cumulative year-to-date figures revisions to the monthly figures previously issued. The figures for the individual months are not corrected under this system. However, some countries do correct the totals in the appropriate months for large corrections and make the smaller changes only in the cumulative totals. Where machine methods are used, the corrections to the cumulative figures are made by inserting a new addition or subtraction card to make the proper correction in the cumulative figures. This method of correcting, on a cumulative basis only, results in the previously issued uncorrected monthly figures not totalling to the corrected cumulative year-to-date figures as indicated previously. This will also affect any cumulative figures which are not on a calendar year basis, such as crop year (June to June; August to August; etc.) figures on agricultural commodities, since the corrected figures are practically always on a calendar year cumulative basis.

A third method of carrying these corrections into the reports is a modification of the first, namely, to carry in important corrections on a current basis and to carry only the relatively unimportant ones into the cumulative calendar year issue of the tabulations. This eliminates some of the work required to keep the data up to date without substantially affecting the correctness of the figures.

It can be seen that any of these procedures presents difficulties to the user of the statistics, particularly those who need statistics on an individual commodity (or small group of commodities) where corrections may change the originally issued statistics to a substantial degree. Users of total figures or totals by countries or of large groups of commodities can frequently ignore revisions with little or no loss in the accuracy of the data.

Recording date of export or import. The problem of determining when to record a particular shipment in the statistics is one faced by the compiler whether the compiler is the Customs agency itself or a separate statistical agency. As described previously, documents must flow from the Customs operation to the statistical compiling point where the statistics are prepared. This flow of documents is not strictly in chronological order. The record of a shipment made on the first of the month may arrive at the statistical compiling point before records of shipments made on the twenty-eighth of the preceding month. In addition, the documents may take several days or even several weeks to reach the compiling point. This period of delay may be even more substantial if documents are not sent to the compiling point until all Customs formalities, such as appraisement and final determination of duty, have been completed. Furthermore, shipments from nearby ports may normally reach the compiling point earlier than shipments from other, more distant, ports.

The statistical compiling agency then faces the problem of determining which documents for which periods should be included in the report of the trade for a particular month. Most countries include in the statistics for a particular month all documents received at the compiling point during that calendar month. This means that the statistics compiled for a particular month may include shipments made from the 15th of one month to the 14th of the following month for some ports, whereas at other ports the compilation may be from the 25th to the 24th. As a result the statistics may include, say, only 80 per cent of the transactions for the current month, with the remaining 20 per cent representing transactions made during the previous month.

Some countries, however, attempt to make the " statistical month " correspond as closely as possible to the month in which the shipments were actually made. In doing this they include, in a month's statistics, documents received after the end of the month if they represent shipments made during the month. A variation of this procedure occurs in some countries where the " statistical month " represents all (or about all) shipments actually made during an arbitrary 30-day period such as from the 24th of one month through the 23rd of the following month.

It follows that the statistics, say for the month of January for a particular country, may in some cases represent data for practically all shipments made during January or may represent shipments made during a period extending, perhaps, from December 15 to January 14 or during some other " statistical month." For many countries it is not too clear what period is actually represented by the statistics for a particular month. These varying " statistical months " increase the difficulty of comparing one country's statistics with those of another.

Procedure for checking statistics of one country against the statistics of another. In an ideal situation where a common set of definitions is used, where coverage principles are the same, where the time period is the same, etc., the statistics compiled by country A for its exports to country B should agree with country B's statistics on its imports from country A. In actual fact the statistics of pairs of countries most frequently do not agree for reasons described in greater detail in other chapters. In many cases discrepancies between the statistics of pairs of countries remain inexplicable even after allowance is made for all known differences in definitions and practices between the countries. If for whatever reason the objective in such cases is to locate the true reason for the discrepancies, it is usually necessary to compare the two countries' actual recording of individual selected shipments represented in each of their sets of figures.

This calls for the mutual exchange of the information shown on the original source documents used by each of the two countries in the compilation of their statistics to discover just how each country recorded the same shipments. This method has been successfully used by a number of pairs of countries in discovering the reasons for discrepancies between their statistics. In order to throw more light on the reasons for discrepancies the Inter American Statistical Institute (IASI), through its Committee on Improvement of National Statistics (COINS), at its June 1951 meeting, included the following statement and recommendation as part of its findings on the subject of international trade statistics:

The Committee felt that considerable light would be thrown on the causes of lack of comparability if an investigation could be made of the transactions between given pairs of countries having substantial unexplained discrepancies in their mutual foreign trade statistics. The reasons for such differences might reside in definitions of content of trade, methods of valuation, methods of recording country and destination, or in other similar factors. Such an investigation would be based on a selected sample of the transactions taking place in a given period. It would probably be found that the main sources of noncomparability lay in the treatment of a limited number of commodities. The different treatment of such commodities in the statistics of the two countries would then be investigated by comparing how the individual transactions were recorded by each of the countries. Such investigations would provide information on the reasons for the lack of comparability and guidance for the standardization of definitions and practices for foreign trade statistics.

IN THE LIGHT OF THE FOREGOING. The Committee on Improvement of National Statistics recommends (*a*) that the Inter American Statistical Institute select (taking into account suggestions of member nations) a limited number of cases in which two American countries have substantial unexplained discrepancies in statistics covering their mutual trade, and request those countries to investigate the reasons for these discrepancies by determining how a sample of important shipments were recorded in the statistics of each of the countries, (*b*) that the results of these studies be transmitted by IASI to members of COINS and to the United Nations for use in developing standard definitions and practices.

A meeting of European statisticians in Geneva in September 1951 took note of this recommendation of COINS and considered that this recommendation would form the basis of similar investigations in Europe. The meeting stated that it believed that the Economic Commission for Europe was the most suitable body to carry out this work.

Special reports issued on a fee basis. Despite the detail provided by most countries in the publication of their foreign trade statistics occasions arise where the published arrangements of the data do not fully meet the users' needs. These include cases where the commodity information shown is not in the detail required by the user. In instances of this sort the user may normally obtain the statistics he needs on a fee basis, the cost being that involved in pulling the original export or import declarations from the files and preparing a compilation of the more detailed information shown on the source documents. This cannot always be done, however, because the source documents may not have information in the fine detail called for by the special inquiry. Another type of special report is required where the information is available but has not been published because of the limited number of people interested in this type of information. This type of inquiry includes requests for information on a commodity, country, and domestic-port basis where the common type of information published is only on a commodity and country basis. In addition, some people are interested in summarization of some of the figures issued in published form. This information could be obtained by the inquirer by recompiling the information. He may have the compiling agency do the work for him, partly in order to make certain that the information is complete and accurate, particularly insofar as corrections subsequent to publication are concerned. Special arrangements for the preparation of the data in the form needed may usually be made on payment of the cost of the work to be done.

Low-value shipments. Since the number of foreign trade transactions is so voluminous, many countries have found it desirable, for budgetary reasons, to place more emphasis on important shipments and less on small-value shipments in the processing of the information. Most countries either use some informal method of summarizing low-value shipments, or exclude them entirely, in order to facilitate processing while still providing adequate data on international trade.   Many countries, for example, exclude information on mail shipments to foreign countries or in some cases use estimates to record the trade.

The United States has put special emphasis on this problem since it must record data on some 20 per cent of the number of transactions entering into the world's trade.   In order to compile information on this voluminous number of transactions, special studies have been made of the dollar value of individual imports or exports to differentiate between shipments having an important effect in the final statistics and those having a comparatively unimportant effect.   This study, which is more fully described in a United Nations paper (E/CN.3/128, April 10, 1951) entitled *Decrease of Work on Low-Value Shipments in the Compiling of United States Foreign Trade Statistics*, indicated generally that export shipments valued under $100 represented almost 50 per cent of the total number of shipments but had a total value of only about 1 per cent of the total export trade.   In view of this distribution the United States has minimized its compiling expenditure for these low-value shipments.   Briefly the procedure has involved summarizing these shipments to show country detail only, eliminating commodity data completely.   In the over-all, the summary totals are not affected at all since these shipments are included. The commodity data, however, for some commodities are incomplete and, in a relatively few cases, substantially reduced in usefulness.   Some few commodity classifications having a high percentage of low-value shipments had to be deleted completely.   The savings resulting from the adoption of these procedures, however, were substantial, with comparatively little effect on the usefulness of the statistics.   Some of this saving was used to provide for more accurate information on the really important shipments. Thus, only 3 per cent of the total number of shipments were at the time valued over $10,000 each, but accounted for 65 per cent of the total export trade of the United States.   These high-value documents are examined very carefully and processed through a number of additional steps to insure a very high degree of accuracy.

Related problems of legislative authority, etc.   It is apparent that in any particular country the compiling work and the accuracy of the statistics produced may be substantially influenced by a number of important factors such as the type and adequacy of the legislative authority for obtaining the import and export information included in the statistics, the effectiveness of the co-operation between Customs officers and the compiling office, the clarity of regulations and instructions issued to importers and exporters, the degree to which importers and exporters may feel free to ignore statistical requirements, the effect of tariff and other controls of exports and imports on the accuracy of the statistical information, the degree to which the release of export and import information may affect national political interests and military security, etc. These factors may be very important to the accuracy of the statistics compiled by many countries and must be taken into account in any appraisal of the effectiveness of the compiling operation in producing adequate external trade statistics.

CHAPTER 3

Coverage

A. MAIZELS
Board of Trade, London

INTRODUCTION

Statistics of foreign trade are intended to relate to the flow of physical goods across national frontiers. This statement, simple though it appears, has in practice led to many difficulties, which are discussed in some detail below. These are varied in kind and complexity, but most of them have their origin in two major difficulties of definition.

The first of these difficulties is the way in which the purpose of the foreign trade statistics is conceived, and two opposing tendencies can often be discerned. The first conceives of the trade statistics as a complete record of the *actual* flow of goods across national frontiers, whereas the second would treat the trade statistics as an adjunct of the balance of payments accounts, and would—on the extreme view—include only those flows of goods for which *payment* is made. For most countries, there is no comprehensive logical statement of the purpose to be served by their trade statistics, and a decision on particular cases is frequently taken on *ad hoc*—possibly legal—grounds. The result has been that no country adheres completely to either aim, deviations being quite common for one reason or another. However, viewed logically, the main purpose of the trade statistics has been generally agreed to be to show the addition to—

or deduction from—the currently available supply of goods within particular countries; in other words, the statistics should give a complete record of the actual total flows of goods into and out of a country. This basic aim must always be borne in mind when considering particular items. It is not necessarily inconsistent with the aim of distinguishing the trade in goods for which payment is made, but this latter purpose is a subsidiary one and is on a par with distinguishing between other categories of trade, such as trade according to means of transport (road, rail, sea, or air), and according to the trading agency concerned (public or private).

The second prime cause of difficulty has been the definition of a " frontier " for purposes of the trade statistics. Different treatments of what a frontier is have led to varying practices in the recording of important items of trade, and the logic of the different methods adopted must be more closely examined.

There are, however, certain flows of goods which can properly be treated as being outside the scope of foreign trade statistics, even accepting the definition of purpose given above. Nonetheless, actual practice in statistical recording varies widely from country to country, even on these items. In addition, there is a whole series of items which should clearly be included if the statistics were to serve the purpose outlined above, but which are excluded by many countries from their published foreign trade statistics. Finally, there are borderline cases on which it is possible to argue either way, and where again national practices vary widely.

It is most convenient, for purposes of exposition, to group the various problems into two categories: *first*, the problems concerning the coverage of particular commodities; and *second*, the problems arising from the different ways of combining the various flows of trade.

COMMODITY COVERAGE

General. There is a variety of commodities for which the practice of statistical recording differs—often very widely—from country to country. The importance of any particular item also varies widely, and a commodity which may be statistically of marginal importance for one country may be of vital importance in the trade of another country. It is therefore essential, especially in using the trade statistics of small countries, to investigate the precise commodity coverage of the figures before any analysis or interpretation is attempted. This can frequently be done by consulting the notes to the trade statistics of particular countries, though many countries do not publish adequate information on this subject. Actual current practice in the coverage of particular countries is summarized in later chapters. Here we are concerned essentially with the logic behind the inclusion or exclusion of particular commodities from the foreign trade statistics, since it is only from an examination of the logical problems involved that an assessment can be made of the advantages or disadvantages of the particular methods of treatment adopted by the different trading countries.

For this purpose, the various commodities involved have been grouped here into 5 classes: trade in monetary reserves; extra-territorial and similar trade; government trade; trade presenting difficulties of statistical recording; and a miscellaneous category of other items presenting classification difficulties. As was mentioned above, the importance of each of these classes of trade varies enormously among the different countries of the world. It is undoubtedly true, however, that for the major industrial countries these categories would normally represent only a small proportion of their total trade, though even in these cases the treatment of particular classes of trade (*e.g.*, government trade) may make a considerable difference to the published statistics for particular commodities or commodity groups.

Monetary reserves. For most countries which do not produce gold themselves, the movement of gold bullion and specie is entirely a movement in their monetary reserves, and as such is more properly treated as a movement on capital account. Such movements of monetary reserves may well have an important *indirect* influence on the supply of currently available goods, but they do not, as reserves, represent part of that supply. They therefore fall outside the scope of the foreign trade statistics which are, for this reason, often referred to as statistics of " merchandise " trade. The movement of non-monetary gold, such as gold for use by the jewellery industry should, of course, logically be included in the foreign trade statistics. India is an example of a non-gold-producing country importing gold for consumption (*e.g.*, in jewellery), though such imports are recorded separately as " treasure " and are not included in the accounts for merchandise trade.

For countries that produce gold, the shipment abroad of *newly mined* gold is also clearly a commodity movement and not a movement in reserves. The same applies also to all other shipments, from gold-producing countries, which are not offset by changes in the national monetary gold reserves, *e.g.*, shipments from private stocks.

In practice, however, it is extremely difficult to distinguish the monetary from the non-monetary movement of gold,[1] and therefore all gold movements between countries are normally recorded separately. Many countries, however, such as Finland and Spain, include all gold movements in their trade accounts, but in many other countries, such as the United

---

[1] The principles underlying the definitions of monetary and non-monetary gold and the difficulties of distinguishing between them are examined in detail in Chapter 9.

States and the United Kingdom, a separate account of the trade in gold bullion and specie is kept and published separately.

The position of silver bullion and specie is different from that of gold, since silver is not an acceptable international standard of value. The price of silver is determined by the play of market forces so that even silver bullion must be regarded as a commodity no different from any other when it appears on the international market. However, most countries have traditionally treated silver bullion and specie as being in much the same category as gold, and have excluded it altogether from their statistics of international trade. Separate statistics of the movement of silver bullion and specie are usually available, but the importance of such movements is nowadays relatively very small, though before the war there were some big movements from China to the United States, partly via the United Kingdom.

Securities and bank notes (in circulation) should be treated in the same way as gold. Securities are claims on capital and should, accordingly, be excluded throughout; this is also true for bank notes. On the other hand, bank notes exported after printing or engraving should be included in exports of printed or engraved paper at their commercial value (and not at face value).

Extra-territorial and similar trade. Embassies of foreign governments established in any country have traditionally the freedom to import goods for their own use without payment of duty and usually without declaration to the Customs authorities. This is because they are regarded as part of the territory of the country they represent. Such shipments are, therefore, normally excluded from the statistics of the country exporting goods to its embassies abroad and from the statistics of the country to which the goods are shipped. Trade between countries and their embassies abroad is, of course, normally negligible, but the principle of extra-territoriality can be extended legitimately to government military forces abroad. This extension is of great importance since it means that the exports of all military equipment to national forces abroad escape Customs record. Conversely, the country in which such military forces are situated[2] would not include such military equipment among its imports, since the importing agency would be held to have extra-territorial rights or their equivalent. Shipments of United States military equipment for United States forces abroad, for example, are excluded altogether from the United States export statistics; and during World War II the imports of such equipment into the United Kingdom were also excluded from the United Kingdom import returns, and they are excluded from the 1952 returns.

[2] Assuming that this country is an ally of the first. If a state of war exists, the question does not arise for the second country, though it does for the first.

Fish. A further extension of the principle of extra-territoriality can legitimately be made for fishing vessels. Such vessels, sailing from home ports, can be regarded as part of the national capital equipment and their catch of fish as part of total national production. It follows that landings of fish from national fishing vessels are not " imports " as are landings of fish from foreign vessels. This distinction is, in fact, followed by practically all countries. A different distinction is, however, made by Japan, France, and the Netherlands. These countries include in their imports only those landings of fish which are consigned from a port in another country; fish landed directly from vessels arriving from the high seas is excluded, irrespective of whether national or foreign vessels are concerned.

A complication is also introduced by the mobile nature of a " national frontier " if defined so as to include national fishing vessels, since it follows that any purchases they make in foreign ports are, strictly speaking, " imports " and any sales they make are " exports." The purchases in this case are relatively small (bunkers and other ships' stores) and would normally be excluded from the import statistics of all countries because of the difficulties of statistical recording. The sales, however, can be very considerable for countries having large fishing fleets, and the treatment of fish may make a considerable difference in the recorded export totals. Canada, Denmark, and Iceland include such sales in their export statistics; sales of fresh fish in foreign ports direct from Icelandic fishing vessels account for some 90 per cent of the total recorded exports of that country. The export statistics of other important maritime countries, however, such as Norway, the United Kingdom, and the Netherlands, exclude such sales altogether.

A further complication arises from the treatment of fishing grounds within territorial waters; these are traditionally within the national frontier, so that fish caught in territorial waters by foreign vessels and landed directly abroad could, strictly speaking, be regarded as exports. Similarly, fish caught by national vessels in the territorial waters of other countries could be regarded as " imports " rather than as national production. On the other hand, it could also be argued that fish caught by national vessels are properly regarded as national production irrespective of the location of the fishing ground concerned; on this view, territorial waters would be outside the national frontier for trade statistics purposes. Whichever view is taken on the logical position, it is clear that the systematic inclusion in the trade statistics of fish caught in territorial waters by vessels of foreign nationality would generally be uneconomic in terms of cost of collecting the necessary information. Both Mexico and Costa Rica, however, include in their export figures fish caught by United States ships in their territorial waters and landed in United States ports. The United States, however, does not regard such fish landed by United States boats as imports, but rather as part of the total production of United States fisheries. It follows that a discrepancy exists on this account between exports of fish to the United States from Mexico and Costa Rica, as recorded by Mexico and Costa Rica, and imports of fish into the United States from those countries, as recorded in the United States statistics. In 1949, for example, Mexican fish exports to the United States were recorded at about $36·4 million as against only $13·6 million shown in the United States import statistics. It might be noted that a small part of this discrepancy may be caused by the United States practice of excluding from its import statistics imports on entries having a value less than $100, but the major reason for the discrepancy is the different concept of national production implied in the United States and Mexican trade statistics.

The United Kingdom and Norway, as well as other countries, maintain large fleets of whaling vessels in Antarctic waters. Logically, these can be treated in the same way as fishing vessels, and imports of whale oil from national whalers can be excluded from the import statistics. This is the Norwegian position, though the Norwegian export figures should, to maintain consistency, include sales of whale oil direct from Norwegian whaling vessels to foreign countries; such sales are, however, excluded. The United Kingdom treatment of whale oil is different, landings from British whalers being treated as " imports " and not as home production. The difference in the British treatment of fish and of whale oil is due to the legal provisions of the Act governing Customs entry, which specifically exempts fish of British taking but not whale oil.

Ships and aircraft. The basic difficulty in the treatment of sales and purchases of ships and aircraft for trade statistics purposes is their continual movement from one country to another. It follows from this that two alternative lines of argument are possible. The first would regard shipping and aircraft movements as movements *between* but not *across* national frontiers, thus implying that all merchant shipping (including national shipping) lies outside the national frontier. The second would consider all national ships as being within the national frontier at all times. These two lines of argument can result in completely different methods of statistical recording, so that the implications of each require further examination.

The first view (that *all* shipping in the foreign trade lies outside the national frontier) would clearly exclude all sales and purchases of *old* ships (except old ships bought for breaking up) from the scope of the trade statistics. Moreover, new ships purchased abroad for the national shipping fleet would have to be excluded from imports, whereas both newly built ships transferred to purchasers abroad and ships newly built for *national* owners would have to be regarded as exports. No country, in fact, includes ships built for national owners as " exports," but otherwise many countries appear to conform to this point of view. The United Kingdom, for example, records as exports newly built ships departing from the United Kingdom for transfer or delivery to overseas buyers, and excludes any sales and purchases of old ships from both the import and export statistics and purchases of new ships from the import statistics. It is doubtful, however, whether even this degree of conformity has arisen from any serious considerations of the logic behind the treatment of such sales and purchases; the exclusion of certain types of trade (*e.g.*, purchases of new ships and sales and purchases of old ships) seems more likely to have arisen from practical difficulties of recording.

The second view (that all national ships lie within the national frontier) also raises difficulties of recording, especially if the sale or purchase takes place when the vessel is in a foreign port. The United States records sales of ships on this basis, sales of United States vessels when they are in foreign ports, for example, being included in the export totals. Norway and Portugal use this system also. The treatment of such sales as " exports " (and the corresponding purchases as " imports ") is, however, rather awkward in many respects, particularly when the transaction relates to vessels in the cross-trades, *i.e.*, trading wholly between foreign ports.

Many countries fall somewhere between these two main procedures and exclude *all* transactions in ocean-going ships, as do, for example, India, South Africa, Chile, and Greece. Had purchases of ships by Greece—a large shipowning country—been included in 1937 and 1948, they would have accounted for a further 10 and 7 per cent, respectively, of the total value of imports as recorded.

A further corollary of the view that all national ships and aircraft should be considered as within the national frontier for trade statistics purposes is that *equipment purchased* and *repair work* done on such ships and aircraft abroad should be regarded as " imports," and repairs done on foreign vessels in home ports as " exports." New equipment purchased abroad may be subject to import duty, so that—under this system of recording—strict Customs control of such expenditure abroad is necessary. The United States includes such expenditure in its import totals, but similar expenditure by foreign vessels in United States ports is not regarded as " exports," presumably because no duty is involved. The United Kingdom, which excludes from its trade statistics altogether the sale or transfer of secondhand ships, also excludes ships' expenditures on equipment and repairs.

Ships' stores including bunkers. The logical treatment of stores taken on board by vessels in the foreign trade depends on the view taken of the status of foreign trade shipping for trade statistics purposes. As we saw above, two views are possible. The first treats *all* such shipping as being outside national frontiers; to be consistent with this, sales of stores to all foreign trade ships, whether national or foreign, should, strictly speaking, be regarded as " exports." However, countries (such as the United Kingdom) which exclude sales and purchases of old ships from their trade statistics also exclude the trade in ships' stores. Many of them enforce a statutory recording of bunker loadings (easily the most important item in this category), and these figures are published together with, though they are not included in, the export statistics. The United Kingdom, indeed, distinguishes in the statistics between coal bunkers loaded on British vessels and those loaded on foreign vessels, but a similar distinction is not made for oil bunkers, though these are almost as large and the distinction would be just as useful, for most purposes, as that made for coal bunkers.

The second view of the status of foreign trade shipping (treating all national ships as being within national frontiers) would have as a logical corollary the treatment of ships' stores and bunkers loaded by foreign ships at national ports as " exports," and such loadings by national ships at foreign ports as " imports." No country, however, follows this procedure entirely. Some countries, such as Italy and Egypt, include as " exports " ships' stores and bunkers loaded by foreign ships in national ports, but do not obtain returns from their own ships of stores and bunkers loaded at foreign ports; the difficulty is, apparently, one of obtaining the statistical information. The Netherlands makes a further distinction, as regards bunker loadings on foreign ships, between bunkers of national origin (recorded as exports) and those of foreign origin (recorded as transit trade).[3] At the other extreme, there are a few countries, such as South Africa and Uruguay, which include *all* loadings of ships' stores and bunkers in their ports among their " exports," irrespective of whether loaded by national or foreign ships.

The statistical recording of bunkering by aircraft operating on international routes is more obscure than that for ships. Few countries state in their trade statistics just how this item is treated, and it seems probable that the oil bunkers of aircraft escape record in most cases.

A further difficulty arises from the shipment of coal and fuel oil to bonded stores at particular ports for use as bunker fuel. Where the trade statistics do not include arrivals at such bonded stores among the imports, nor bunker loadings from bond among the exports, the whole of this trade may escape record,[3] or may be excluded from the trade statistics

[3] See the discussion of warehouse and transit trade below.

proper. It is therefore important, in any study of the trade in bunkers, to examine carefully any separate Customs warehouse or transit trade accounts; Spain, for example, records bunker loadings as " warehouse trade," whereas the Netherlands practice of recording loadings of foreign bunker fuel on foreign ships as " transit trade " has already been noted.

The treatment of ships' stores and bunkers in the different national statistics differs widely from country to country and has in most cases little logical justification. Difficulties of obtaining comprehensive statistical recording are part only of the reasons for the present glaring non-comparability of national statistics in this field. It is not, therefore, possible to obtain comprehensive data on bunker loadings in most overseas trading countries from published trade statistics. Some special studies of the problems involved have, however, been made, using the available trade statistics data and other information which can be collected.[4]

Special arrangements. In some countries there are foreign companies operating under special treaties or other arrangements that give the companies diplomatic privileges as regards imports and exports. In such cases, the privileged companies are treated as " extra-territorial " for trade statistics purposes. Thus, in Iran, petroleum exported by the Anglo-Iranian Oil Company was excluded from the main export trade statistics; in 1948 for example, the value of oil exports was about ten times the recorded export total.[5] Caspian Fisheries (a joint Iranian-Soviet corporation) also has special arrangements with the Iranian Government, and exports of fish by this organization are excluded from the official export figures, though this trade is relatively quite small. Details of both the oil and fish exports are, however, given separately in the Iranian trade volumes. Similarly, petroleum exported *via* pipeline from Iraq to the Mediterranean coast is excluded from the Iraqi export figures, since the Iraqi Petroleum Company's agreement with the Iraqi Government allows it to dispose freely of its oil exports. The value of oil exports from Iraq has been estimated at about half as much again as the official export total (for 1948).[6] Similarly, at the other end of this pipeline, the crude petroleum entering Syria-Lebanon is excluded from the import statistics of these countries.

Government trade. In addition to " extra-territorial " trade, many governments buy and sell commercially both military and non-military goods and the treatment of these for trade statistics purposes needs to be considered.

---

[4] See, for example, *The Energy Resources of the World*, United States State Department, 1945.

[5, 6] *Balance of Payments Yearbook*, 1948, International Monetary Fund.

The non-military trade by governments comprises mainly the import of foods, feeding stuffs, and raw materials of many kinds, and is especially important where the whole of the import trade in a given commodity is monopolized by the government. The whole of this trade should clearly be included in the trade statistics, if these are correctly to represent the net addition to, or depletion of, the physical supplies of goods in each country. For some purposes, it may, of course, be useful to present separate statistics of government trade, especially where government trade is competing with private trade, but even if this is so, there is no valid reason for excluding government trade from the ordinary trade statistics; the logic is, rather, to show such trade under separate headings therein. Some countries exclude government " civil " trade altogether from their trade statistics (Peru, Nicaragua, and Hong Kong are in this group); their inclusion in the ordinary trade statistics is, in fact, the normal procedure of most countries, the practice being usually to include government trade with the total trade in individual commodities. The trade reports of British Colonial territories show Government imports and exports separately, for individual commodities; few of the more economically advanced countries do this, since in these countries government trade has been traditionally confined to goods necessary for military and other strictly governmental purposes. The growth in government trade in " commercial " commodities during and since World War II has, however, necessitated some revision of this practice, and some countries compile detailed commodity tabulations of trade by government agencies in addition to their normal trade statistics. In the United States, which compiled such figures for part of 1944, the year 1945, and part of 1946, imports by United States Government agencies[7] accounted for about 30 per cent of total imports in 1944 and 1945, but by the early part of 1946 this had fallen to between 15 and 20 per cent.

A wartime and post-war development has been the suppression for security reasons of statistics of trade in fissionable materials. Neither the United States nor the United Kingdom show imports of these materials; exports from the Belgian Congo to both countries were, however, included in the export statistics of the Belgian Congo up to 1948, but have been excluded since then. Canada classifies her exports of fissionable materials to the United States in a miscellaneous category in the published statistics where they cannot be separately distinguished.

[7] The definition of " imports by a government agent " must be carefully examined before any use is made of such figures. In the United States statistics, for example, the figures relate to imports to which a United States Government agency held title at the time of importation; imports by private importers on government behalf, for example, are excluded from the definition, as are also United States Government agency imports for account of a foreign government.

For similar security reasons, many countries exclude imports and exports of military equipment from the published statistics, or include them only in categories where details cannot be distinguished. United States exports of military-type items are comprised within export totals in the statistics but without classification by commodity or by country of destination; the only information given is a figure for total dollar value. For a few other commodities, such as aviation motor fuel, the total of exports is shown in the statistics but without segregation by country of destination. Exports of military equipment from the United Kingdom have generally been recorded in detail in the British statistics as published, but imports of military equipment from the United States under the Mutual Defence Assistance Agreement are not recorded by the United Kingdom for trade statistics purposes.[8]

A special case of government trading—both in military and non-military goods—arises when sales or purchases of stocks held abroad take place. Situations where government stocks of non-military goods held abroad arise because many governments currently act as trading bodies so as to secure their minimum requirements of particular foods or raw materials. In acting this way, they are in the same category as private trading organizations, from the trade statistics point of view, and sales and purchases made abroad should not be included in their national trade statistics; such commodity transactions abroad are, however, relevant to a balance of payments account in which it may be preferable to include such transactions with other commodity transactions *vis-à-vis* the rest of the world.

The end of World War II saw, moreover, considerable accumulations abroad of surplus military goods and equipment owned by Allied governments. In many cases, such equipment was sold to the governments of the countries where the equipment was. Now, we saw above that government exports of military equipment to national forces abroad can legitimately be regarded as extra-territorial and therefore are not regarded as " exports " at the time of shipment. It follows that, if such equipment is later sold (or transferred) to another government, it can at that date be included in the export statistics of the selling country. Conversely, the receiving country could legitimately regard the transaction as an " import." Much of this military equipment was originally shipped from the United States for use of United States armed forces abroad; these shipments were not regarded as exports and were not included in the United States export figures. When sold to other governments after the war, they should have been included in the United States export statistics at that time, but the practical difficulties of getting information on such

[8] See also Chapter 14.

transfers prevented this from being done. At the receiving end, purchases of United States (or other) military equipment already in their countries by the governments of Finland, Iran, Iraq, and New Zealand—among others—were recorded as imports, but similar purchases by France, Italy, Canada and the Philippines were not. A special position was adopted by Norway, such purchases being included in the import statistics if intended for civilian use, but not if for use by the Norwegian military forces.

Finally, there is a miscellaneous assortment of government transfers, grants, and aid in kind, some—but not all— of which is given free. These are in quite a separate category from the government trade in civil and military goods. The most important examples in this third category are shipments by the United Nations Relief and Rehabilitation Administration (UNRRA), Lease-Lend, Reverse Lend-Lease, Mutual Aid and Reciprocal Aid, government relief shipments, and war reparations and war restitutions. Again, these should, logically, be included in the total trade figures, though many countries (*e.g.*, the United States) also keep separate accounts for these special types of shipment. Lend-Lease and similar imports into the United Kingdom were included in the import totals for the relevant years, but it was not found possible to keep a separate record of them.

Some countries, however, have excluded such shipments altogether from their trade statistics on the grounds presumably, that they are of a special, non-commercial character. Thus, the import statistics of Czechoslovakia, Greece, Hungary, Finland, and the Netherlands, for example, excluded all UNRRA imports, though UNRRA shipments to those countries were recorded as among the exports of the United Kingdom, the United States, and Canada.

War reparations in kind have, for some countries, been a heavy drain on current output (or on the existing stock of capital equipment) and, again, should be included in the export totals. Since World War II these have been important only for Finland, Germany, and Italy. Reparations deliveries in kind from Finland to the USSR are recorded separately by the Finnish Customs, and separate details of these goods are published; total Finnish exports in 1949, for example, amounted to 77·8 billion Finnish marks, of which 12·2 billion marks (or 16 per cent) were in respect of war reparation deliveries. It should also be noted that Finland's export totals include the value of former German assets transferred to the USSR.[9] Reparations deliveries from western Germany are not, however, included in the export statistics of that country, though when these goods arrived in the United Kingdom, for example, they were treated as imports.

---

[9] These amounted to 1·1 billion marks in 1949. For balance of payments purposes, the more useful concept is exports exclusive of reparations and transfer of German assets.

Omissions due to recording difficulties. The published trade returns of most countries are defective, to a greater or lesser extent, because of the omission of items presenting important difficulties of statistical recording. *Contraband trade* is the most obvious exclusion, and the importance of this varies enormously from one country to another. Contraband trade can now be assumed to be negligible in most—though not all—of the economically developed countries, but a thriving trade in smuggled goods is carried on in some of the more backward countries.[10] The recorded trade statistics for 1948 of China, Iraq, Uruguay, and Bolivia, for example, should be increased by approximately the following percentages to allow for smuggled goods escaping Customs record.[11]

	Exports	Imports
	Per cent	Per cent
China*	40	15
Iraq	16	3
Uruguay	9	7
Bolivia	—	5

* The figures for China also include an allowance for the undervaluation of trade in the official statistics.

In some countries, *land frontiers* are very difficult to patrol, and trade across them may be completely excluded from the trade statistics. Thus, the statistics of both India and Pakistan relate only to the seaborne and airborne trade and exclude all trade across their land frontiers. In 1950, for example, the Indian import statistics were deficient by about 7 per cent as a result of the exclusion of the land frontier trade, which consists mainly of imports of raw jute from Pakistan. Among other countries excluding trade with neighbouring states are Thailand (trade with Burma), Egypt (trade with the Sudan), and Panama (which excludes exports to the Panama Canal Zone, though—inconsistently—imports from that Zone are included in the Panamanian statistics).

An important item frequently omitted because of the difficulty of collecting comprehensive information is the trade in *diamonds* and other precious stones. The difficulty arises because diamonds are frequently sent by registered letter post, and are also carried by private persons, and many consignments would escape the notice of the Customs. In any

[10] Especially where import duties are high and the frontiers are not too difficult to cross by means escaping Customs notice.

[11] These percentages are based on the estimates for contraband given in the International Monetary Fund's *Balance of Payments Yearbook*, 1948.

event, the Customs would have little opportunity of an effective valuation check, since this could be done only by an expert valuer. The United Kingdom, for example, included diamonds and other precious and semi-precious stones in its import statistics up to 1949, insofar as they were declared on Customs entries, but no record was kept of their export. Since this record of imports covered only a small part of the trade, diamonds and other precious stones have been excluded altogether since the beginning of 1949. A very approximate picture of the diamond import of the United Kingdom can be built from the statistics of the main diamond-exporting countries. Since diamonds are an important export from South Africa, Gold Coast, Angola, Brazil, and other producing countries, these exports are made under close government control, and for these countries the statistics of quantity (though not of value) can probably be taken as reasonably accurate. There is an important diamond-processing industry in the Netherlands, but diamonds are excluded from the published Netherlands statistics of trade with individual countries, though separate totals for this trade are published.

Sales of gas and electricity by one country to another are of great local importance in many frontier areas. Often the supplies are sent in both directions as, for instance, when one country supplies electric current to another during the summer and receives current during the winter. In nearly every case, such sales are not recorded by the Customs for trade statistics purposes, but they are, nevertheless, a real import and export of commodities, in this case, of energy. The difficulty of recording imports of electric current is obvious when there are thousands of domestic consumers being supplied by a power station in an adjacent foreign country. However, to obtain a complete record of merchandise trade an addition of some 4 per cent to the Austrian export figures must be made on this account. Similarly, additions must be made to both the import and export figures of Czechoslovakia and the United States, among other countries, to cover the gas and electricity trade.[12] France, on the other hand, includes electricity both in imports and in exports.

Another item which is frequently omitted from the trade statistics is *parcel post*. The difficulty here is that parcels are handled by the post office organizations rather than by the Customs, who would be interested only in incoming parcels containing dutiable goods. Many countries, therefore, record as imports dutiable goods entering *via* the parcel post; countries with a general tariff would in this way cover all imports by parcel post, but exports may be excluded from the trade statistics because no export tax is levied. Ecuador, Iraq, and Venezuela are cases in point.

---

[12] See *Balance of Payments Yearbook*, 1948, International Monetary Fund, for details of some of the necessary additions.

Even when there is a general tariff on imports, gift parcels may be free of duty, and imports of such parcels would probably be excluded from the import statistics (as in Germany).   The United Kingdom and other Commonwealth countries include all parcel post in their import and export totals, but only the goods liable for duty (imports) or for payment of drawback (exports) are classified to their proper commodity headings; the rest are all lumped together as parcel post.   Another group of countries, among them the United States, includes only those parcels containing goods valued above a stated figure.   Thus, the United States includes imported parcels if valued at $100 or more, and exported parcels if valued at $25 or more and shipped from one business concern to another.   Care must therefore be taken, in the case of countries which exclude certain postal shipments from their commodity statistics, in the use of the statistics for those non-dutiable commodities which are expensive, light in weight and non-bulky, and are therefore likely to be shipped by parcel post. Examples are exports from the United Kingdom of lenses and spectacles and exports of books, where possibly only about half the real exports are shown under the appropriate United Kingdom commodity headings.   For the United States, the value of parcel post exports which were excluded from the statistics in 1948, for example, amounted to $154 million (1·2 per cent of the total recorded value of exports).[13]

Other items presenting classification difficulties. *Temporary trade.* Goods are sometimes exported with the intention of subsequent re-import. Examples are the shipment of paintings for exhibition abroad or of race-horses for racing abroad. It can be argued that such purely temporary flows are not part of a country's foreign trade proper, and they could therefore be legitimately excluded from the foreign trade statistics.   If this view is taken, then clearly some assurance must be given on export that the goods *will* later be re-imported (or on import, that re-export is intended).   Where the goods are dutiable, such assurance would take the form of a Customs bond on import, and the whole movement can then be controlled. Where no duty is chargeable, however, temporary trade of this kind could not easily be excluded from the statistics unless special Customs arrangements were adopted.   This view seems to be generally taken by the United States. Horses imported into the United States from Canada, for example, for breeding, exhibition, or competition may be imported without payment of duty provided their stay does not exceed 6 months, and this move-ment is excluded altogether from the United States import and export statistics.

In many other countries the opposite view is taken, *viz.*, that the passage of goods in temporary trade is no different, logically, from ordinary trade

[13] See Chapter 5 for a discussion of the difficulties in the *valuation* of parcel post trade.

movements. Moreover, it could be argued that even though the *intention* of the exporter may be to re-import the goods subsequently, there is no *guarantee* at the time of export that this in fact will happen. This appears to be the line of thought behind the inclusion in the foreign trade statistics of the United Kingdom and of the Irish Republic of the important temporary trade in racehorses and greyhounds between the two countries. In 1950, for example, horses " exported temporarily " from Ireland were valued at £2,775,000 and temporary imports of horses at £2,744,000. Though this trade is largely with the United Kingdom, the United Kingdom does not similarly subdivide its trade in horses into " temporary trade " and " other." Moreover, the United Kingdom does not treat all temporary trade consistently; although the trade in live animals is included, that in articles exported or imported solely for temporary exhibition in galleries or museums is excluded altogether from the trade statistics.

Temporary trade must be distinguished from *re-imports* of goods previously exported. Goods returned by foreign customers are best considered as re-imports, *i.e.*, as not having, in effect, left the country; most countries would, therefore, cancel the original export entries. A special—and important—example of re-import arose after the last war when considerable shipments of battle scrap were made both to the United States and the United Kingdom. In both cases, they were recorded as imports, though the scrap shipped to the United States almost certainly originated largely from United States war material.

Gifts and other borderline items. The procedures adopted by different countries in the classification of government grants and aid in kind were discussed above. Much the same differences exist also in the treatment of gifts sent by private organizations or individuals. *Private gift parcels* to national armed forces abroad were sent on a very large scale during and immediately after World War II, and shipments of Red Cross and other privately gathered aid (clothing, drugs, food, etc.) is still carried out on some scale from such countries. Gift parcels exported from the United States and the United Kingdom, for example, are counted as exports by those countries (if above the value limits mentioned previously), but some of the receiving countries, such as Italy, do not count them among their imports. Generally speaking, this trade is negligible in relation to commercial imports and exports, though in abnormal circumstances private gifts may be of importance, *e.g.*, Red Cross supplies to some countries during or immediately after the war.

Many countries exclude from their trade statistics *personal baggage and household effects* brought in, or taken out, by passengers; other countries include only the dutiable portion; still others apply value limits as criteria for inclusion in their trade accounts. It is unlikely, however, that the excluded trade is of great significance, except for countries having a big tourist trade, or where migration is taking place on a big scale and the migrants take their personal property with them. Both the United States and the United Kingdom currently exclude all personal and household effects from their trade statistics,[14] since only a small proportion of these goods were, in fact, being recorded on the normal Customs entry forms.

There remain a variety of miscellaneous items on which the practice of statistical recording may vary from country to country. These include frontier trade, such as local produce sold between specified limits in the neighbourhood of a land frontier; salvaged goods; and goods of no commercial value (*e.g.*, ballast). The effect of differences in the treatment of these miscellaneous items on the comparability of foreign trade statis-- tics, however, could normally be neglected.

GENERAL AND SPECIAL TRADE SYSTEMS

Flows of trade. We have so far been concerned with the problem of which commodities should, and which should not, be included in the statistics of foreign trade. Having defined the purpose of the statistics, and their consequent scope in terms of particular commodities, we can now turn our attention to the classification of the various flows of trade into and out of each trading country. The problem here arises because goods are imported not only for use or consumption in the importing country, but also for onshipment—either with or without transformation of some kind—to other countries.

The principal trade flows are depicted on Figure *A*. The outer circumference is intended to represent the national frontier; the inner represents Customs clearing points. All goods arriving in the country either (1) pass through the Customs—duty being paid on the dutiable portion—and are then at the free disposal of the importer, or (2) remain under Customs control in one form or another.

In the first category (goods passing through the Customs) are goods intended for merchanting without any further processing being performed, for direct consumption, and for further processing. These movements are shown as letters *b*, *c* and *d* on the figure.

In the second category (goods remaining under Customs control) are the following:

---

[14] This exclusion took effect as from 1st January, 1950 for the United States. For the United Kingdom, dutiable goods imported by passengers were excluded as from 1st May, 1947; prior to that date, they were included, but non-dutiable personal and household effects were excluded.

MAIN FLOWS OF FOREIGN TRADE.

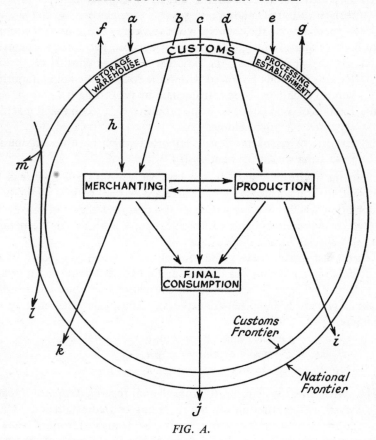

FIG. A.

(i) Imported goods entering bonded[15] storage warehouses (*a*); these
goods are subsequently either exported (*f*) or withdrawn for home
consumption after payment of duty (*h*).

(ii) Imported goods entering bonded[15] processing establishments, *e.g.*,
where petroleum is refined in bond (*e*); these goods are processed
in bond because the finished product is sold abroad, so that complications of duty-payment and drawback are thus avoided. The
export of the finished product is shown as (*g*) on the figure.[16]

---

[15] The term " bonded " relates to a warehouse or processing establishment under
Customs control.

[16] There will also normally be sales of by-products and waste as well as, possibly,
sales of finished products, to buyers in the home market, but this movement is relatively
extremely small (except for a few commodities like petroleum, metals, and sugar) and
is neglected here.

(iii) Imported goods entered for transit or transhipment to another
foreign country (*l* and *m*).

Of the goods leaving the country, we have already accounted for exports
from bond (*f* and *g*) and goods in transit between two foreign countries
(*l* and *m*).   Apart from these, the export trade proper consists of:

(i) Exports of goods produced within the country, including imported
goods which have been transformed by processing (*i*).

(ii) Exports of used goods or waste products, *e.g.*, secondhand machinery, used cars, used clothes (*j*).

(iii) Exports of goods previously imported which have undergone no
processing within the country (*k*).

From the figure it is easy to see how the various trade flows can be
combined for statistical purposes.   There are, in fact, various methods of
combination which have been used in the past, but they can mostly be
reduced to two main systems of classification, known as the " general "
and the " special " trade systems.

General and special trade.   The general trade system is a record of *all*
goods entering the country as imports and *all* goods leaving as exports,[17]
but a distinction is made between exports of national produce and exports
of goods previously imported (re-exports).   Thus, using the lettering on
the figure,

$$\text{General imports} = a + b + c + d + e$$
$$\text{Domestic exports} = g + i + j$$
$$\text{Re-exports} \qquad = f + k$$

The *special trade* system, on the other hand, regards *clearance through
the Customs* as the criterion for the recording of trade statistics.   Thus,
although the *general trade* system regards the " statistical frontier " as the
port or other point of entry into a country, the *special trade* system puts
the " statistical frontier " at the clearance point of the Customs authorities.   Special imports are therefore defined as imports cleared through
the Customs (having paid duty if dutiable) *plus* goods withdrawn for home
consumption or use from Customs warehouses (and likewise having paid
duty).   Similarly, special exports consist of exports of national produce
plus exports of imported goods which have been " nationalized " by
having been cleared through the Customs.

A particular difficulty arises from the processing of imported goods in
bond and their re-export after processing.   Thus, in France crude oil is
imported for refining in bonded refineries, whereas in Belgium non-ferrous
metals are smelted in bond and then re-exported.   If the rules of the
special trade system were strictly applied, such trade would not be

---

[17] *I.e.*, all goods considered as genuine merchandise trade with other countries.

recorded at all because the goods had not been cleared through the Customs. It is clear, however, that processing in bond is no different, from an economic point of view, from processing out of bond, though indeed the legal position is different. For this reason, the 1928 convention relating to economic statistics (League of Nations) specifically recommend- ed the inclusion of this bonded " improvement " trade in the record of special trade. Such improvement trade (which also includes the repair trade in some cases) is currently included by most countries concerned, though many excluded it prior to 1930.

In terms of the Figure A lettering, we can now define the special trade categories as follows:

$$\text{Special imports} = b + c + d + e + h$$
$$\text{Special exports} = g + i + j + k$$

Comparisons of general and special trade categories. There are some important differences between the concepts of general and special import trade. In most countries with high import duties, large stocks of dutiable goods are held in Customs warehouses (as well as in bonded manufacturing establishments under Customs control) and the stock change between the beginning and end of a period may be very substantial. In such cases there will be a significant difference between the *general* and the *special* record of imports for the particular commodities affected. A further reason for differences between the two methods of recording imports arises when significant quantities of particular commodities imported into Customs warehouses are subsequently re-exported therefrom, since such re-exports are not recorded at all in the *special* trade system.[18] The United States is one of the few countries that record imports on both the *general* and *special* systems, so that each of the different flows can be readily identified.

Although special imports aim at recording those goods intended, at the time of importation (or clearance through Customs), for national use or consumption, general imports clearly include goods which will subse- quently be shipped on to other countries without any intermediate pro- cessing. An approximation to the concept of " imports for national use or consumption " can, however, be obtained under the general trade system by deducting such re-exports from total imports, the residue being known as *retained imports*.

The figures of retained imports are not, however, equivalent to those of special imports,[19] and they must be used with care when individual com- modities are dealt with. The deduction of re-exports from total imports

---

[18] The difference between *general* and *special* imports $(a - h)$ is the stockchange in bonded warehouses $(a - f - h)$ *plus* re-exports from those warehouses (f). Such re-exports are treated as goods in transit in the *special* trade system.

[19] The difference between retained imports and special imports is $(a - h) - (f + k)$.

causes two difficulties. There is, first, a time lag between importation and subsequent re-exportation, which may in some cases exceed a year; thus the deduction in any year may relate to imports made in the preceding year, and this sometimes results in negative figures for retained imports for particular commodities. A further difficulty results from the higher value which goods have on re-exportation than their value when imported, the difference arising from internal warehousing, merchanting, insurance, and transport charges. Thus, even if the goods were re-exported in the same period as they were imported, the value (though not the quantity) of retained imports would be lower than that of special imports.

Special exports differ from total general exports (*i.e.*, domestic exports plus re-exports), insofar as special exports exclude re-exports from bonded storage warehouses, but such re-exports are relatively small for most countries. It should be noted, however, that some countries, such as Switzerland, also publish separate accounts of the exports of " nationalized goods " (*k*), and keep the term " special exports " to refer only to domestically produced goods. Special exports in this narrower sense are equivalent to domestic exports in the general trade system.

Domestic exports and re-exports. It is often extremely difficult to distinguish accurately between domestic exports and re-exports (or, on the special trade system, between national and " nationalized " goods). *Re-exports* can be defined as goods exported in essentially the same physical condition as when they were previously imported. *Domestic exports*, on the other hand, cover two main categories; first, goods wholly produced within the national boundaries and exported, and second, imported goods which have undergone a process of transformation and which have then been exported. The process of transformation can be a simple one, such as the assembly of imported parts (*e.g.*, of machines or automobiles) or the production of furniture from imported wood, or it can be more elaborate and consist of many stages of production, such as the use of imported ore in the production of machinery. The use of an imported component as a part of another commodity is also, logically, a " transformation." For example, if a small electric motor is imported and incorporated in a home-produced loom which is then exported, the export counts entirely as " domestic."

The *degree* of transformation of imported goods can therefore vary widely, and where only simple operations are performed the demarcation between domestic exports and re-exports becomes rather blurred. For example, the blending of tea is carried on in the United Kingdom on a large scale, and a substantial proportion of the tea blended is subsequently exported. The blending process is regarded by the United Kingdom authorities as not essentially altering the character of the import (*i.e.*, unblended tea), though in fact the process requires the use of machinery for cutting as well as for blending. If, however, two different commodities were blended (such as butter and margarine) then the result can justifiably be called a " new " commodity and shipments abroad can be included in domestic exports. Other borderline cases are bottling, cleaning (*e.g.*, the scouring of greasy wool), and repair work.

Transit trade. At the other extreme, re-exports also merge into goods in transit. The transit trade covers two distinct cases, which were defined as follows in the 1928 convention relating to economic statistics (League of Nations):

(1) " *Direct transit* relates to goods passing through a country for purposes of transport only, without being placed at the free disposal of the importers, or warehoused." This category covers both goods transferred from one vessel ot another at the same port (*m* on the figure) and goods shipped from one port to another under Customs bond (*l*).

(2) " *Indirect transit* relates to goods arriving from abroad, warehoused, and subsequently exported without being placed at the free disposal of the importers and without having undergone transformation, repair, or supplementary treatment other than re-packing, sorting or blending "; (*f* and part of *a*).

It is clear that there is no real difference between indirect transit and re-export from Customs warehouse; the difference arises solely from the method of classification. Under the general trade system, goods arriving from abroad and deposited in a Customs warehouse are necessarily recorded as imports, so that they must be recorded as re-exports when they are shipped abroad again. The special trade system, however, recognizes neither movement as relevant, so that they are, by default, part of the country's transit trade. It is only when such goods become exempt from duty for any reason that they might escape record as " transit " and be included in the trade statistics. Most of such cases of " disguised transit " are, however, usually detected and removed from special trade figures. " Disguised " transit can arise even under the general trade system. In the United Kingdom, for example, the pre-war import and re-export figures included free goods in transit on through bills of lading, this movement being no different, logically, from the ordinary transit trade.[20]

Because of the similarities in the physical movement of many re-exported goods and goods in transit, the abolition of an import duty may result in the importer entering transit goods in the normal way (*i.e.*, as imports) so

[20] In 1938, the United Kingdom imports and re-export total included about £9 million of free goods in transit on through bills of lading. The practice of giving through bills of lading has been discontinued since the beginning of World War II.

as to avoid the Customs formalities applied to goods in transit. Non-dutiable goods in transit tend, therefore, to appear more frequently in the import and re-export statistics than in the transit statistics. Care must therefore be taken when using the re-export statistics in case any imposition or abolition of import duties has resulted in a change in the method of Customs entry for goods in transit.

CONCLUSION

The detailed discussion in this Chapter of the coverage aspect of national trade statistics has amply demonstrated the wide diversity of existing national practices as regards the scope of the published statistics. This diversity is generally of greater importance in the statistics of particular commodities than in the trade aggregates of imports and exports, and is especially notable in the case of " borderline " items, such as ships, aircraft and government trade. It is therefore a necessary precaution to study any notes on coverage published with national trade statistics before any comparisons are made between the statistics of trade in individual commodities, as compiled by different countries. In many cases, it is preferable to use the statistics published by international agencies or associations, since these statistics are usually presented in as comparable a form as possible, together with any important qualifications.

Much progress has been made, since the establishment of the Statistical Commission of the United Nations after World War II, in achieving greater comparability of national statistics. The task of improving the coverage aspect of international comparability is, however, complicated by the logical difficulties discussed in the earlier parts of this Chapter. Moreover, even if international agreement is reached on the logical position, the administrative difficulties of improvement in international standards of comparability are formidable, a major factor in many countries being the methods of Customs administration, which are often laid down by law. This is particularly true of the use of the general and special systems of trade classification, which normally fit in closely with the types of Customs apparatus and of tariff system in use. Improvements in international comparability in the coverage of trade statistics may therefore be rather more difficult to achieve than improvements in other aspects, but they are nonetheless essential to strive for to enhance the value of the published figures for interpretive purposes.

CHAPTER 4

Commodity Classification

V. S. KOLESNIKOFF

U.S. Bureau of the Budget

BASIC CONCEPTS

Introduction. The purpose of this chapter is to explain the classification of commodities entering international trade. The explanation will cover the definition of classifications, the principles and rules for the development of classifications, and illustrations taken from the actual practice of various countries.

Theoretically, classification is a logical method by which the complete universe of items to be classified is divided, according to certain selected principles, into classes or kinds, which in turn may be divided and subdivided into the smaller and more detailed homogeneous classes. Classification starts by facing a disorderly mass and in the end reduces this mass to an orderly system in which there is a place for everything and everything is in its place.

Practically all users of international trade statistics require the availability of information on the commodities moving in the trade. Any change in the volume or value of an individual country's imports or exports whether in over-all total or in the trade with individual countries raises the question of what the commodities were that caused the change.

Any analysis of balance of payments information requires commodity information if the reasons for changes are to be understood. Any extensive analysis of the relationship between a country's imports and exports and its own production or consumption must be carried out on a commodity basis at least in part.

To provide this needed commodity detail some consistent categorization of the individual items must be carried out if useful statistical information is to be obtained.   With millions of international trade transactions every year, and with these transactions involving many hundreds of thousands of differently named items, a classification, i.e., a method of reducing multitudes of items to a limited number of categories, is necessary.

The results are very dramatic.   In the classification of commodities exported from the United States 55,000 individual commodity names appearing on invoices and other commercial papers are reduced to 11 major groups with some 2900 subdivisions.   In the Standard International Trade Classification (SITC) of the United Nations, *all commodities* entering world trade are classified into 10 major sections, which in turn are divided into 52 divisions, with 150 subdivisions and 570 subsequent sub-subdivisions known as " items."   The " Minimum List of Commodities for International Trade Statistics," promulgated by the League of Nations, has 17 sections, divided into 50 chapters with 456 subsequent items, of which 125 have been subdivided into 2 or more subitems each.   In all other classifications, the same situation could be observed: the limitless becomes limited.

It can be noted that it is very seldom that theoretical or scientific classification, referred to as natural classification, is applied.   Usually any convenient artificial arrangement of items into definite groups is called classification.   It would be also helpful to remember that, in the actual practice of compiling and tabulating trade statistics classes and their subdivisions, individual classified items are quite frequently referred to as " classifications."   The exact meaning of such sentences as " the French list has 6500 classifications," " the United States export list has 2900 classifications," should not escape us at any time.

In general, the large trading nations of the world provide statistical information on from 2000 to 3000 commodity items in their export and import trade.   Some commodity classifications, such as those for French imports and exports and United States imports, may run as high as 5000 or more items.   For smaller trading nations the number of commodity items may be only a few hundred.

Uses of commodity information.   The essential value of commodity classifications is to provide information in sufficient detail to permit the user to know the characteristics of the commodities entering the trade in important volume, but not in the detail of minute physical specifications. Before discussing the principles and practices of constructing commodity classifications for trade statistics, we should look at the uses to which the commodity information is put. These uses are of two types.

The first type of use is that by someone interested in relatively detailed commodity information. An illustration would be the user who is interested only in the statistics on refined copper. For such a person there is no essential difficulty involved if copper, specifically defined to meet his needs, is listed as a separate heading or as a subheading (or a sub-sub-heading) under a major heading of crude materials, or of metals, or of semi-manufactured products, or of basic materials for further manufacture. He would not be inconvenienced if copper were in fact listed under the letter C in an alphabetical list of commodities. Except for any possible minor inconveniences in locating his item he would be satisfied if copper were separately listed somewhere in the system.

It is when this user of the statistics on copper wishes to broaden his interest beyond a narrowly defined category of " refined copper " to include other non-ferrous metals or other related products that he becomes interested in the whole commodity classification. He might be interested, for example, in obtaining totals of the imports or exports of all non-ferrous metals combined. In this case he would be interested in having the statistics on imports and exports of copper grouped with the statistics on imports and exports of other non-ferrous metals. His interests might be broadened in a different way to include certain manufactures of copper, such as copper wire. In this event he would be interested in having the statistics on copper adjacent to or related with the statistics on copper wire and perhaps other manufactures of copper. However, from the point of view of the user of the statistics interested in only one or a few. products, the over-all outline of commodity classification would be of no great consequence. Even more, he might say that he did not want any classification, that he wanted merely to be certain that the products in which he was interested were separately enumerated. To look at the matter in another way: the user of detailed commodity information in import and export statistics is primarily interested in seeing that sufficient detail is shown in the statistics. As a result of the combined need for detailed information for many different products, the trade statistics of the large trading nations show substantially detailed classifications with numerous commodity items.

The other type of use of commodity information is that by a person interested in the over-all picture of the trade of an individual country or group of countries. This type of user is very much concerned with how commodities are grouped or classified, since in analysing the over-all trade of the country or group of countries he wants to deal with a relatively few commodity classes.   For this reason he wants the commodity information in broad groupings, generally no more than a few hundred at the outside, and frequently a much smaller number, as few as two on occasion.   It is obvious that this use of import and export statistics raises most of the problems as to how commodities are to be classified.   The type of commodity classification may differ substantially, depending upon the type of analysis which is to be made of the foreign trade of a country or a group of countries.   One analyst will be interested in segregating trade in raw materials, semi-manufactured materials, and manufactured products; another will be interested in trade as between consumers goods and producers goods.   One person may be interested in separating products of mining from manufactures, another in segregating products of agriculture, of fisheries, or of forestry.

This broad use of commodity information for imports and exports does at times develop into an interest in detailed commodity classifications. For example, the analysis of a country's imports and exports on an over-all basis may indicate that the trade in a certain class of commodities has increased or decreased substantially.   The next question is which particular commodity within the class caused this change.   If, for example, there is a substantial change in an over-all class called metals, the question will be what the particular items were which caused the change.   A further breakdown of this over-all class may indicate a change which has occurred only in non-ferrous metals.   Such analysis may go into even greater detail and locate the fact that the increase or decrease actually took place in copper.

At this point, then, the interest of the user in the over-all classification of commodities for a broad analysis of a country's trade overlaps the needs of the user interested in the commodity details.   In other words both now have an interest in the commodity detail and in the commodity classification structure itself.   A conflict between the two will, however, be created if the user of the detailed information, of copper let us say, wishes to have the statistics of related products such as copper ore, or copper wire, or other non-ferrous metals presented adjacent to or in combination with statistics on copper itself.   The over-all user of the statistics may, in contrast, wish to have copper wire presented in the electrical manufactures group of commodities and the copper ore placed in the category of crude materials rather than that of metals.

The commodity classification which each country constructs for its export and import statistics represents a resolution of this conflict of interests.   For most countries, some middle ground has been worked out where the commodity classification fits reasonably well the needs of most users of the statistics. It is undoubtedly true, however, that no commodity classification of any country fits precisely all the needs of all the users of its statistics. It is also undoubtedly true that a particular classification will not best meet the needs at a different time or under different circumstances. Technological changes, language differences, industrial organization, and market situation in various countries always affect a classification.

Commodities: what they are; the number of commodities. One of the basic rules for development of classification, of *any* classification we would say, prescribes that before we start the classification job it is necessary to determine what it is that we want to classify : commodities, industries, occupations, books, flowers, or something else? The same rule also requires that the material to be classified must be clearly defined.

In international trade we define commodities as materials and articles movable and procurable. They are movable, and as such differ from real estate property. They are procurable because they have an exchange value and therefore are the subject of commercial transactions.

More difficult, and sometimes rather confusing, is the concept of " commodity items," or the idea of " number of commodities." Egypt, for example, in its export statistics lists nine varieties of raw cotton. *Question :* How many commodities are there in this example: one or nine?

Another example: cotton fabrics may be subdivided into unbleached, bleached, printed, and dyed. Is it one commodity or four? A third example: pencils may be of various colours and degrees of hardness of graphite. How many commodities do we have? One, a dozen, or sixty? Whether an answer can be given to such questions depends on two vital points related to the technique of classification.

1. Classification is a method by which the complete universe of items (say, commodities) is divided according to certain selected principles into classes which in turn are subdivided into subclasses, and subclasses into sub-subclasses and so on, until we reach a desirable degree of detail in the classification process. In the natural sciences the higher level of classification is termed " genus " and the subclass subordinated to it is " species."

2. In the process of classifying " commodities" in the social sciences we aim at grouping products which are homogeneous as to unit prices, economic uses, market conditions, etc. In this process we create new " species " by increasing the degree of detail in the information. The term " commodities " may be applied to the finest detail or to

homogeneous groupings of the detailed classifications.   Or these
classifications may be called products, or commodity items, or commodity headings, etc.   There is therefore really no firm answer as to
whether " fabrics," or " cotton fabrics," or " printed cotton fabrics "
are " commodities."   The answer depends on the use to be made of
the classification and thus depends on whether the products are
sufficiently homogeneous in price, economic use, market, etc., to fit
the needs of the classification.   Given the proper market conditions,
proper differentiations in use and material of which the product is
made, a separately defined and minutely detailed product may be
looked upon as a " commodity."   The problem really becomes one
of nomenclature.

The absence of established terminology and of universally recognized
standards makes all problems of nomenclature extremely difficult to
handle.   In actual practice some degree of common understanding might
be attained if instead of " number of commodities " we refer to the
" number of items " or " headings " with appropriate numeric notations
assigned to them.

Principles.   The next point is that of the principles under which classifications may be developed.   In our " classification of classifications," we
recognize two types: (*a*) single-principle classification and (*b*) multi-
principle classification.   The distinction is very clear.   In the first, a single
principle is selected and used throughout.   The list of such possible
principles from which one may be selected is practically inexhaustive—
nature of material, origin of material, natural characteristics, use, economic
characteristics, state of production, etc.   In the second, two or more
characteristics are used either in combination or in the appropriate segregation in different sections of the field to be classified.

Here are a few examples of the application of a single principle: In
classifying furniture according to material, we would have such classes as
wood furniture, metal furniture, etc. In providing further detail, we might
classify wooden furniture according to the species of the wood (pine, oak,
etc.), or according to the degree of hardness (softwood, hardwood).
Classifying according to origin, we would have the classes of domestic
furniture and imported furniture.   In the same manner, furniture classified according to expected use would be grouped as household furniture,
office furniture, store furniture, restaurant furniture, etc.   Household
furniture according to the same principle of expected use would permit
such sub-classes as kitchen, living-room, dining-room, and bedroom
furniture.

If we take not a separate class, but the complete universe of commodities, the application of various principles would give a number of classifications. In classifying by material, we would have animal, vegetable, and mineral products. In classifying according to origin, we might have domestic and foreign goods, or products of agriculture, forestry, mining, fishing, and hunting. In classifying according to economic characteristics, we would have producers goods versus consumers goods, materials versus end products, and durable versus non-durable. It is not difficult to establish the principles of classification when the list of such principles is very limited and comprehensive (food and non-food; producers and consumers goods; durable—non-durable; crude—semi-manufactured—manufactured). The problem becomes more difficult when the principle selected is not clearly defined. Example: the principle of use. Such categories as food, apparel and transport equipment are clear and understandable, as classes established according to use in satisfying our needs in nourishment, clothing, and transport. However, if we decide to apply this principle to the complete universe of commodities, the problem becomes practically insoluble; in order to get satisfactory results, we should provide for a complete classified list of all our needs. And this is extremely difficult to do.

An examination of attempts to develop a commodity classification according to a single principle shows that the results are rather disappointing. The complete field of commodities is so wide, the population of this field so dense, and essential characteristics so different, that to follow through the complete list of commodities using only one principle is simply impossible. A material concept is very useful and applicable for classification of materials, either crude, processed, or manufactured. However, the application of this concept to the classification of finished articles ready for use (so-called " manufactured end-items ") is extremely difficult and not satisfactory in all those instances where material used in processes of manufacturing either is not important or is not traceable; and where functional characteristics are more important and more obvious. Any attempt to classify automobiles, radio receiving sets, or scientific instruments according to the material (or even the chief material) used in manufacturing, certainly would not produce satisfactory results.

The principles applied to the development of classification determine the *type of classification structure*. If we select a material concept and try to use it through all the classification structure, we have a so-called *vertical* classification. In this type, all commodities are divided into material sections and the classification then follows through all stages of transformation from crude to finished articles. So we have, say, raw cotton, cotton semi-manufactures, cotton yarn, cotton fabrics, and finally, finished articles made of cotton. As previously stated, the vertical type is hardly applicable for the classification of finished end-products. A sharp contrast to this type is presented by the *horizontal* type, where basic stages of transformation (crude, semi-manufactured, manufactured) constitute major primary sections with subsequent subclassifications according to the principle most suitable for each major section. A third type is the *industrial* classification. Here all commodities are arranged according to the classification of industries. This type of commodity classification has no independent status and always depends on the industrial classification selected for the purpose.

Countries in developing their commodity classifications have been most successful when they have selected for each particular category of commodities the principles and the type of classification which most nearly reflect the normal way in which such commodities are traded, *i.e.*, the commercial practice in dealing with the commodities. Under this procedure products are classified in a way most likely to serve the majority of users of the statistics. This is not to say that difficulties are always avoided. Thus, the manufacturers of ceramics may look upon porcelain electric insulators as a product of their industry properly to be classified with other ceramic products. At the same time, manufacturers of electrical equipment may believe such insulators can only be properly classified as parts of electrical equipment. Since both viewpoints may truly represent the normal commercial practice in each industry, the problem of where to classify porcelain electric insulators is not solved by attempting to conform to usual commercial practice. For most products, however, usual commercial practice does provide a reasonably clear answer as to where products should be classified to serve best the majority of uses of the statistics.

Principles followed in constructing the Standard International Trade Classification (SITC). The points can be illustrated, not only by the classification systems of individual countries, but also by the selection of classification principles which went into the construction of the Standard International Trade Classification (SITC), adopted by the United Nations in 1951 to increase comparability in commodity classification among the nations of the world. (For a history of efforts to achieve international uniformity of commodity classification including the adoption of the SITC, see Chapter 12.)

In general, the United Nations Statistical Office and their expert consultants believed that they were following predominant world commercial practice in setting up the SITC. In the SITC the universe of commodities entering international trade is divided into 10 major sections, which are divided into 52 divisions, which are subdivided into 150 groups, which in turn are divided into 570 commodity items. The classification into sections and divisions is given herewith.

STANDARD INTERNATIONAL TRADE CLASSIFICATION
(SITC)
(Section and Division Classification)

Section Code	Division Code	Title Description
0		FOOD
	00	Live animals, chiefly for food.
	01	Meat and meat preparations.
	02	Dairy products, eggs, and honey.
	03	Fish and fish preparations.
	04	Cereal and cereal preparations.
	05	Fruits and vegetables.
	06	Sugar and sugar preparations.
	07	Coffee, tea, cocoa, spices, and manufactures thereof.
	08	Feeding stuff for animals (not including unmilled cereals).
	09	Miscellaneous food preparations.
1		BEVERAGES AND TOBACCO
	11	Beverages.
	12	Tobacco and tobacco manufactures.
2		CRUDE MATERIALS, INEDIBLE, EXCEPT FUELS
	21	Hides, skins and fur skins, undressed.
	22	Oil-seeds, oil nuts and oil kernels.
	23	Crude rubber, including synthetic and reclaimed.
	24	Wood, lumber, and cork.
	25	Pulp and waste paper.
	26	Textile fibers, not manufactured into yarn, thread or fabrics, and waste.
	27	Crude fertilizers and crude minerals, excluding coal, petroleum, and precious stones.
	28	Metalliferous ores and metal scrap.
	29	Animal and vegetable crude materials, N.E.S.
3		MINERAL FUELS, LUBRICANTS, AND RELATED MATERIALS
	31	Mineral fuels, lubricants, and related materials.

STANDARD INTERNATIONAL TRADE CLASSIFICATION
(SITC)—*continued.*

(Section and Division Classification)

Section Code	Division Code	Title Description
4		ANIMAL AND VEGETABLE OILS AND FATS
	41	Animal and vegetable oils (not essential oils), fats, greases, and derivatives.
5		CHEMICALS
	51	Chemical elements and compounds.
	52	Mineral tar and crude chemicals from coal, petroleum, and natural gas.
	53	Dyeing, tanning, and colouring materials.
	54	Medicinal and pharmaceutical products.
	55	Essential oils and perfume materials, toilet, polishing, and cleansing preparations.
	56	Fertilizers, manufactured.
	59	Explosives and miscellaneous chemical materials and products.
6		MANUFACTURED GOODS CLASSIFIED CHIEFLY BY MATERIAL
	61	Leather, leather manufactures, N.E.S., and dressed furs.
	62	Rubber manufactures, N.E.S.
	63	Wood and cork manufactures (excluding furniture).
	64	Paper, paperboard, and manufactures thereof.
	65	Textile yarn, fabrics, and made-up articles and related products.
	66	Non-metallic mineral manufactures, N.E.S.
	67	Silver, platinum, gems, and jewelry.
	68	Base metals.
	69	Manufactures of metals.
7		MACHINERY AND TRANSPORT EQUIPMENT
	71	Machinery other than electric.
	72	Electric machinery, apparatus, and appliances.
	73	Transport equipment.

Section Code	Division Code	Title Description
8		MISCELLANEOUS MANUFACTURED ARTICLES
	81	Prefabricated buildings, sanitary, plumbing, heating, and lighting fixtures and fittings.
	82	Furniture and fixtures.
	83	Travel goods and handbags, and similar articles.
	84	Clothing.
	85	Footwear.
	86	Professional, scientific, and controlling instruments; photographic and optical goods, watches and clocks.
	89	Miscellaneous manufactured articles, N.E.S.
9		MISCELLANEOUS TRANSACTIONS AND COMMODITIES, N.E.S.
	91	Postal packages.
	92	Live animals, other than for food.
	93	Returned goods and special transactions.

In the arrangement of Section 0, *Food*, the United Nations classification disregards stage of production in all instances when the trade does not recognize this feature as an essential characteristic of commodities. As a result, for example, Division 02, Dairy Products, Eggs, and Honey, includes fresh milk, which in some countries is raw and in some countries is pasteurized; butter and cheese which are manufactured products; and eggs in the shell and natural honey which are not manufactured products. Such listing is made in recognition of universally accepted practices of trade. In the same fashion, raw and refined sugar, inedible molasses, edible syrup and molasses, and other sugars and syrups whether manufactured or not, are recognized as equal members of the same class, Sugar and Sugar Preparations, Division 06.

Section 1, *Beverages and Tobacco*, is separated from the *Food* section since these items are not usually classified as food. Beverages and tobacco are grouped together in recognition that both are grocery items, and in actual trade transactions they quite frequently are handled through the same channels of distribution.

Section 2, *Crude Materials, Inedible, Except Fuels*, includes also manufactured materials which, according to the usual trade practices, are handled as crude materials. Hence, synthetic rubber is classified in the same category as crude natural rubber. Similarly, wood in the round, wood shaped, and lumber (rough, planed, or dressed) are listed in this section, as well as pulp and other paper stock. Synthetic fibers which are products of chemical manufacturing plants are included in this section with other crude fibers. Again it was recognized that, for actual handling of items by crude materials distributors, stage of production has no significance as long as commodities remain in the form of materials to be used for further manufacturing. Here again, mill waste, as well as scrap materials, is classified in relation to the original crude items. Waste and used leather is classified in the group of undressed hides and skins, and waste and scrap rubber is classified with crude rubber. Iron and steel scrap, in view of its extreme commercial and strategic importance, is established as a separate group in the division covering metalliferous ores and scrap.

In Section 3, *Mineral Fuels, Lubricants, and Related Materials*, functional characteristics of commodities receives primary recognition in preference to the principle of stage of production. Therefore, anthracite, bituminous, and lignite coal are listed together with coke and briquettes; the classification for gas includes both natural gas and manufactured gas as commodities intended for the same use and for distribution by the same method.

Section 4, *Animal and Vegetable Oils and Fats*, is established as a separate major section outside of Section 5, *Chemicals*, in view of the importance of oils and especially in view of the great variation in methods of producing oils and fats in various countries. By providing for a separate Section 4, it is recognized that in some countries oils, especially vegetable oils, are products of primitive crushing and compressing operations; in other countries oil mills are recognized as an integral part of the highly developed chemical industry.

Section 5, *Chemicals*. It is apparent that the divisions set up within the section for chemicals reflect usual commercial practice in trade in these products. For example, Division 54 for medicinal and pharmaceutical products includes such subclasses as (1) vitamins; (2) bacteriological products, sera, and vaccines; (3) penicillin, streptomycin, tyrocidine, and other antibiotics; (4) opium alkaloids, cocaine, caffein, quinine, and other alkaloids, salts and their derivatives; and (5) medicinal and pharmaceutical products, N.E.S.

Sections 6, 7, and 8. After the classification of food, crude materials, fuel oils, and chemicals was established, the United Nations undertook the difficult problem of the classification of manufactured articles. It was first of all apparent that manufactured goods are produced at many points in the gradual process of manufacturing operations, and that there is a continuous and never-ending process of change in manufacturing organization. There are manufactured goods which are identified and quite frequently even named according to the materials used in their manufacture. Leather goods, dressed furs, rubber tires, veneers, plywood, paper bags, textile fabrics, cement, glass, glassware, and all metals are examples of such commodities. For such commodities, it appeared appropriate to establish a special Section 6, *Manufactured Goods Classified Chiefly by Material*. At one point consideration was given to the proposal that this section become two sections: *first*, a section for manufactured materials requiring, or at least capable of, further manufacture, such as leather, partly manufactured rubber materials, veneer, plywood, and paper (this group is frequently called semi-manufactured, simply manufactured, partly manufactured or fabricated materials); *second*, a section for commodities which cannot be subjected to further manufacture but are themselves end items, such as paper bags, rubber tires, cooperage, glassware, pottery, jewelry, and cutlery (these are commonly called finished manufactures). This segregation was, however, recognized as of questionable practical value in the statistics and not in accordance with normal trade practice. As a corollary it was felt that the distinction would be difficult to comprehend internationally. It should be noted that this distinction is made in the United States Standard Commodity Classification (1943) and also by India (1947), Japan (1950), and Canada (1951), in their national standard commodity classifications.

All manufactured goods, other than those of Section 6, defy any attempt at classification according to material used in the process of manufacturing and can more successfully be classified on the basis of functional characteristics, the basis on which commercial trade is carried out. Consequently, Sections 7 and 8 are established on this basis.

Section 7, *Machinery and Transport Equipment*, takes care of commodities which are classified, sold, and bought as capital equipment. Power generating equipment; agricultural machinery and implements; all other types of specialized machinery and their components; communication equipment; and transport equipment such as railway vehicles, road motor vehicles, road vehicles except motorized, aircraft, and ships and boats are all included.

Section 8, *Miscellaneous Manufactured Articles*, includes commodities for which a basic material concept is not applicable, which are not exclusively items of capital equipment, and for which the functional characteristics and expected use are indicated by their name. This section includes such classes as prefabricated buildings; plumbing, heating, and lighting fixtures and fittings; furniture; travel goods; clothing; footwear; instruments; optical goods; musical instruments; and printed matter.

Section 9 is reserved for postal packages which are handled by the trade (irrespective of their contents), returned goods, and special transactions.

The approach here described was followed not only in setting up the major sections and divisions in the SITC, but was carried over into the construction of the more detailed 150 groups and 570 items. This description is not necessarily intended, however, to be representative of the processes which have been followed in setting up the foreign trade commodity classifications of individual trading nations of the world. It is intended, rather, as an illustration of the types of considerations entering into the construction of any commodity classification. Also, it illustrates the point that successful classification must generally be based on the usual commercial practices in producing, selling, and trading in commodities.

Commodity classifications in actual use. At the time of writing this chapter (1952) it became known that a number of countries (Norway, Denmark, some members of the British Commonwealth of Nations) decided to use the SITC as their national classification for external trade statistics as well as for a classification for preparation of reports on their export-import trade to be transmitted to the United Nations Statistical Office; that other countries expressed their desire to use the SITC for reports to United Nations, keeping national classifications for their domestic uses; and that still other countries were in the process of examining classification problems. The description of existing national commodity classifications that follows may therefore be changed substantially in coming years.

Apart from a few countries without any foreign trade statistics or with statistics of commodities arranged in alphabetical order, most countries follow one of the three promulgated international standards: the Brussels Convention of 1913, the Draft Customs Nomenclature (1931, revised 1937), or the Minimum List of the League of Nations (1938). It is therefore appropriate to describe each of these three international lists in order that the user of trade statistics may be able to recognize their basic type of classification and employ the statistics more profitably.

Brussels Convention of 1913. Prior to 1900 practically every country in the world with some list of commodities, exported and imported, showed only the items of considerable importance and interest to that particular country. Furthermore, they were listed in some fashion or order desirable for the national office. No consideration was given to the desirability that such listings be made somewhat similar to, or comparable with, the lists of other countries. Any attempt to draw a world picture of commodities moving from country to country would have been impossible. In recognition of this disturbing situation, an International Customs Conference was called in 1900 after several years of preliminary diplomatic conversations. It was recommended that a common statistical classification be developed covering the more important items of international trade. Ten years later, at the International Statistical Conference in Brussels, a tentative classification was drawn up; and in 1913 it was officially signed by 24 countries in the form of an international treaty known as the Brussels Convention of 1913. This Convention influenced the national commodity classification of a number of countries, including some in Europe and many trading areas in the British Empire.

The Brussels classification had 186 items arranged in 5 major sections, as shown herewith.

BRUSSELS CONVENTION (1913) CLASSIFICATION
1. Live animals.
2. Food and beverages.
3. Crude materials or materials simply prepared.
4. Fabricated products (manufactured goods).
5. Gold and silver.

Draft Customs Nomenclature. Soon after the publication of the 1913 Brussels Convention, the inadequacies of the classification, and especially the very limited number of minor classes, became apparent, and it was felt that the classification was hardly adequate either for the analysis of international trade or as a standard nomenclature. This is probably the reason why the World Economic Conference in 1927 recommended the introduction of simplicity and uniformity into the nomenclature of Customs tariffs. The problem was referred by the Council of the League of Nations to the Economic Committee, which established a Subcommittee of Experts to make suitable proposals and suggestions for giving effect to the recommendations of the World Economic Conference. As a result of the work of the Subcommittee of seven (with the membership from Czechoslovakia, Belgium, France, Germany, Hungary, Italy, and Switzerland), the Draft Customs Nomenclature was published in 1931 and in revised form in 1937. The Draft contained 991 items arranged in 21 major sections with 86 divisions, as shown herewith.

DRAFT CUSTOMS NOMENCLATURE
(Section Classification)
I   Live animals and products of the animal kingdom.
    (5 divisions with 39 items)
II Products of the vegetable kingdom.
    (9 divisions with 60 items)

DRAFT CUSTOMS NOMENCLATURE—*continued*
(Section Classification)

III Fatty substances, greases, oils, and their cleavage products; prepared edible fats; waxes of animal or vegetable origin.
(1 division with 16 items)

IV Products of the food industries; beverages, alcoholic liquids, and vinegars; tobacco.
(9 divisions with 57 items)

V Mineral products.
(3 divisions with 39 items)

VI Chemical and Pharmaceutical products; colours and varnishes; perfumery; soap, candles, and the like; glues and gelatines; explosives; fertilizers.
(8 divisions with 136 items)

VII Hides, skins, leather, fur skins, and goods made therefrom.
(3 divisions with 21 items)

VIII Rubber and articles made of rubber.
(1 division with 11 items)

IX Wood and cork and articles made thereof; goods made of plaiting materials.
(3 divisions with 35 items)

X Paper and its applications.
(3 divisions with 26 items)

XI Textile materials and textile goods.
(8 divisions with 159 items)

XII Footwear, hats, umbrellas, and parasols; articles of fashion.
(4 divisions with 28 items)

XIII Wares of stone and other mineral materials; ceramic products; glass and glassware.
(3 divisions with 54 items)

XIV Real pearls, precious stones, precious metals, and wares made thereof; coin (specie).
(2 divisions with 14 items)

XV Base metals and articles made thereof.
(9 divisions with 124 items)

XVI Machinery and apparatus; electrical material.
(2 divisions with 59 items)

XVII Transport material.
(3 divisions with 29 items)

XVIII Scientific and precision instruments and apparatus; watchmakers' and clockmakers' wares; musical instruments.
(3 divisions with 43 items)

XIX   Arms and ammunition.
     (2 divisions with 6 items)
  XX   Miscellaneous goods and products not elsewhere classified.
     (4 divisions with 29 items)
 XXI   Works of art and collectors' pieces.
     (1 division with 6 items)

This Draft Customs Nomenclature influenced the commodity classifications of Italy, many other European countries, Egypt, Brazil, and other non-European countries.

Minimum List of the League of Nations. Before the Draft Customs Nomenclature was revised in 1937, a Committee of Statistical Experts (with a membership from Denmark, France, Norway, Poland, Switzerland, the United Kingdom, the United States, the International Institute of Agriculture, and the International Labour Office) was organized by the League of Nations as an outgrowth of the International Convention Relating to Economic Statistics in 1928. This Committee was directed by the Economic Committee of the League of Nations to develop a classification of commodities for international trade statistics.

The Committee of Statistical Experts reached the conclusion that so far as practicable the principle of classification by nature of material should be dominant, and where this principle is least applicable the principle of use should ordinarily dominate. This conclusion was responsible for the general structure of the Minimum List, which appears as a classification of commodities of the type known as vertical. At this time, many economists and statisticians were of the opinion that, for statistical reporting, it would be quite sufficient to develop a classified list of commodities taken from the tariff list. After considerable and prolonged debate in and out of the Committee of Statistical Experts, the Minimum List of Commodities for International Trade Statistics was prepared in 1935, and published in final form in 1938. In the Minimum List the entire field of commodities was divided into 17 major sections, which in turn were divided into 50 chapters (divisions) as shown herewith.

LEAGUE OF NATIONS MINIMUM LIST
(Section Classification)

   I   Food products, beverages, tobacco.*
     (13 divisions (chapters) with 86 items)
  II   Fatty substances and waxes, animal and vegetable.
     (2 divisions with 27 items)

---

* Excluding certain oils and fats which may be used either for food or for other purposes.

LEAGUE OF NATIONS MINIMUM LIST—*continued*
(Section Classification)

III   Chemicals and allied products.
(4 divisions with 33 items)
IV   Rubber.
(1 division with 6 items)
V   Wood, cork.
(1 division with 21 items)
VI   Paper.
(1 division with 12 items)
VII   Hides, skins, and leather, and manufactures thereof, N.E.S.
(3 divisions with 9 items)
VIII   Textiles.
(4 divisions with 56 items)
IX   Articles of clothing of all materials and miscellaneous made-up textile goods.
(4 divisions with 18 items)
X   Products for heating, lighting and power, lubricants and related products, N.E.S.
(1 division with 17 items)
XI   Nonmetallic minerals and manufactures thereof, N.E.S.
(4 divisions with 31 items)
XII   Precious metals and precious stones, pearls, and articles made of these materials.
(1 division with 7 items)
XIII   Base metals and manufactures thereof, N.E.S.
(4 divisions with 48 items)
XIV   Machinery, apparatus, and appliances, N.E.S., and vehicles.
(3 divisions with 31 items)
XV   Miscellaneous commodities, N.E.S.
(2 divisions with 48 items)
XVI   Returned goods and special transactions.
(1 division with 2 items)
XVII   Gold and specie.
(1 division with 4 items)

There was a close chronological coordination between the Draft Customs Nomenclature and the Minimum List. The first and revised editions of the Minimum List followed respectively the first and revised editions of the Draft Customs Nomenclature. The Minimum List as finally revised in 1938 presents a telescoping of the greater list of items in the Draft Customs Nomenclature into a limited number of items.

Primarily because of the outbreak in 1939 of World War II, the Minimum List had less influence on national commodity classifications than the Brussels or the Draft Customs Nomenclature Lists. However, many countries compiled supplemental tabulations in terms of the Minimum List, and some countries, including Norway and Denmark, adopted it for their national classifications.

In the later work by the United Nations on the SITC starting in 1947 (described above), invited expert consultants (from Belgium, Canada, Ecuador, India, Netherlands, New Zealand, Norway, the United Kingdom, and the United States) approached the problem from a somewhat different point of view; they tried to develop a classification for statistical purposes without the handicap of the necessity of following tariff patterns.

The complete world catalog of national external trade classifications would include many variations. These range from simple lists of items arranged in alphabetical order without any identification symbols to the most complex list of more than 6000 classes; from a single classification for all purposes to differing systems for imports, exports, re-exports, economic analysis, statistical requirements, control requirements, etc. Some countries use a single classification for tariff, statistical, and other purposes; other countries use one for tariff, one for statistical, and one or more for analytical purposes.

In general, as stated earlier, most countries follow the three international lists of 1913, 1937, or 1938, or are in process of adopting the new SITC of the United Nations. Some, however, such as Argentina which groups commodities into " Products of cattle ranches, products of agriculture, products of forestry, etc.", have national classifications not apparently related to any of the international lists.

Supplementary classifications. For practical reasons, specifically the cost of compiling trade statistics, virtually all countries compile the statistics in one primary classification. In addition, the need for other groupings of commodities leads many countries to recompile the statistics in broad categories differing from the primary classification.

Canada. The primary classification lists commodities in the following broad groups in which nature of the material is the predominant classification concept:

Agricultural and vegetable products.
Animals and products.
Fibers and textiles.
Wood and paper.
Iron and its products.
Non-ferrous metals.
Non-metallic minerals.

Chemical and allied products.
Miscellaneous commodities.

Annual trade statistics are recompiled into the following supplementary classifications:

1. Degree of manufacture (raw materials, partly manufactured, fully or chiefly manufactured).
2. Origin (farm, wildlife, marine, forest, mineral, and mixed origin).
3. Purpose (producers' materials; producers' equipment; fuel, electricity and lubricants; transport; auxiliary materials for commerce and industry; consumers goods; munitions and war stores; live animals for food; unclassified).

United States.   The primary classification is in the following 11 groups:

Animals and animal products, edible.
Animals and animal products, inedible.
Vegetable food products and beverages.
Vegetable products, inedible, except fibers and wood.
Textile fibers and manufactures.
Wood and paper.
Non-metallic minerals.
Metals and manufactures, except machinery and vehicles.
Machinery and related products.
Miscellaneous.

The statistics are recompiled into the following supplementary classification termed " economic classes ":

Agricultural crude materials.
Non-agricultural crude materials.
Agricultural crude foodstuffs.
Non-agricultural crude foodstuffs.
Agricultural manufactured foodstuffs and beverages.
Non-agricultural manufactured foodstuffs and beverages.
Agricultural semi-manufactures.
Non-agricultural semi-manufactures.
Agricultural finished manufactures.
Non-agricultural finished manufactures.

Italy.   The basic list of exports and imports has 8 sections:

Live animals, food, beverages, tobacco.
Oil seeds, animal and vegetable oils.
Textile fibers and their products.

Metallic minerals, common metals, products of metallurgical industries, instruments, machinery, and vehicles.
Stones, non-metallic minerals, products of ceramic industries.
Wood, lumber, and their manufactures.
Chemicals, medicinal and related products.
Miscellaneous.

These are divided into 52 categories with more than 2500 items listed consecutively. In addition, Italy has a supplemental classification into 4 economic groups:

Live animals.
Food and materials for its preparations.
Products of non-food industries and materials therefor.
Auxiliary materials.

France. For reporting external trade statistics, France uses the " General Nomenclature of Products " developed and used by the Custom House Administration. This nomenclature classifies all merchandise into 27 sections, principally determined by nature of products.

In addition, for analytical purposes and for construction of index numbers of foreign trade, there is an auxiliary classification according to the expected use of products with 4 major sections:

A. Products of agriculture and of fishing: (1) products determined for direct or indirect use as food; (2) primary materials for industrial use; (3) products for agricultural production.
B. Crude and semi-manufactured materials of industrial origin: (1) for power, including coal, petroleum, and electricity; (2) for agriculture; (3) for industry and other community activities.
C. Equipment in form of finished manufactured goods: (1) for agriculture; (2) for industry.
D. Finished consumers goods: (1) durable; (2) nondurable.

Other countries find it desirable to follow similar practices. It is apparent that commodity information, after compilation on a particular primary classification, cannot be recompiled into quite different groupings both with complete accuracy and at low cost, especially when such groupings are developed at a later date. For example, a primary classification with a major group for foods would have within this broad classification an " all other food " category in which many different kinds of food might be grouped without separate categorization. A supplementary classification according to origin would require that the " all other food " category be split between products of agriculture and fishing. Since the " all other food " categories might contain many food preparations of mixed origin, such a split would be difficult to make. Also, the split might run counter to the guiding principle of having the primary classification reflect usual commercial practice. The preferable procedure, then, is to construct the primary classification so that the " all other " categories are kept small. If this is done, the recompilation into a supplementary classification of the statistics first compiled on the basis of the primary classification is subject to the minimum of error in terms of volume of trade; that is, the inability to reclassify the " all other " categories into the supplementary classifications is encountered to a lesser extent. If the classification is so constructed that the " all other " categories are large, they could be further subdivided to increase comparability. If the volume of trade in these categories, or any other categories which are not convertible, is kept small, the figures for such trade may be more or less arbitrarily assigned to one or another of the broad supplementary categories with only a small loss of accuracy. Since the recompilation in terms of supplementary classification is primarily for the purpose of uncovering changes in the broad content of trade, generally over a relatively long period, this small loss of accuracy is of negligible importance.

Somewhat the same principle applies to the procedure followed by a number of nations in reporting statistics on their trade in terms of the SITC, as recommended by the United Nations. Some countries in fulfilling their responsibilities under the United Nations recommendation do not believe it desirable to adopt the SITC for their primary trade tabulations. For any of a number of reasons they may wish to retain their existing classification for primary compilation and to prepare supplementary tabulations in terms of the SITC. If they exercise care that items in the primary classification which do not closely fit into the SITC contain a small volume of trade, the conversion to the SITC classification by supplementary retabulation may be carried out with only a relatively unimportant loss of accuracy compared to that which would have resulted if the SITC had been adopted as the primary classification.

It should be noted that the League of Nations Minimum List provided for supplementary regrouping of its classifications by stage of manufacture and by use. The more recently developed SITC of the United Nations has been constructed without as yet providing for supplemental classification, but work is going forward to develop such supplemental codes.

It is obvious that any supplementary classification to an international standard must be done by all reporting countries in the same manner if the resulting statistics are to be comparable. Without an internationally prescribed method each country is likely to prepare supplementary tabulations in a different way. In recompiling into broad classes of, let us say, raw materials, semi-manufactured or manufactured materials, and finished products, one country may put cotton fabrics, for example, in manufactured materials. Another may put them in finished products since the fabrics are ready for use in the home. It is clear that the concept of finished products should be clearly defined, as well as those of stages of transformation and of economic characteristics of commodities.

Tariff classification. We have so far made little or no reference to the problem of commodity classification for tariff [1] or duty collection purposes. The commodity structure of the tariff has had an important effect on the classification used in compiling foreign trade statistics, since most countries assess customs duties which differ from commodity to commodity, and since trade statistics are called upon to provide information on the operations of the tariff, the amounts of duty collected on different commodities, the effect of tariffs on the trade, etc. Furthermore, the fact that trade statistics are frequently obtained as a by-product of tariff administration tends to affect the type and accuracy of the commodity information included, apart from the effect on the statistical commodity classification itself.

The characteristics of the tariff type of commodity classification make it clear that the classification is not desirable for most statistical purposes. In setting up a commodity classification for duty collection purposes the main emphasis is on defining specifically, and usually in great detail, the commodities on which a duty is to be assessed.

The selection of commodities on which duties are to be assessed at all, or at differing rates, is frequently made on the basis of political considerations of foreign policy, of the desire to be independent of foreign sources of supply, or for protection of domestic industries, of the likelihood of the burden of either an import or export duty falling upon a foreign supplier or consumer, etc. In establishing tariff rates, countries also consider the degree of industrial development, the available supply of materials, the ability of domestic industry to compete with the outside world, reciprocal reductions and retaliations, and political motives for encouraging or suppressing certain lines of industries. It should be noted that, in the process of intergovernmental tariff negotiations, new categories of commodities are frequently invented.

The character of commodity classifications designed for tariff purposes may be illustrated at least in part by a description of the commodity classification set up in the United States Tariff Act of 1930. The primary objective was to enumerate the commodities on which duties were to be collected. The classification includes 15 schedules of " tariff com-

---

[1] The term comes from the name of the town Tariffa in the southern part of Spain near Gibraltar. This town was named for a conquering Moor named " Tariff-Ebn-Malick " who established a post there for collecting tribute from passing ships according to the quantity and kind of goods.

modities," together with Schedule 16, which describes the items on the free list; namely, those not dutiable. Since not all the articles which might be included under the general headings of the first 15 schedules are actually subject to a rate of duty, many of the commodities in Schedule 16 might well have been classified under some of the first 15 schedules if commodity classification criteria alone had been followed. They are not so classified and this is due, not to physical or other characteristics, but simply to the fact that the commodities are free of duty. It is obvious that this is a commodity classification specifically designed to enumerate articles subject to duty or not subject to duty. It is not a comprehensive classification for general statistical purposes. These generalizations from the United States tariff commodity classification are applicable to a greater or lesser degree to similar classifications of other countries.

In order to reduce confusion among traders as regards commodity descriptions for tariff purposes, the Brussels European Customs Union Study Group has been working for several years in developing a common nomenclature for goods in Customs tariffs. A common nomenclature has been worked out on the basis of the customs tariff requirements of European countries. Although this tariff nomenclature puts commodities under a number of headings which have many of the characteristics of a statistical classification of commodities, the classification suffers from the one great defect, from the statistical point of view, namely, that it attempts to provide a common classification of commodities for duty or tariff description purposes and is designed primarily to meet the needs of European countries. It can be concluded, therefore, that since the *Tariff Nomenclature* of 1950 has been developed as a modern document of tariff nomenclature, it is not desirable for statistical purposes. This conclusion is agreed to by the European countries as a whole; they look upon SITC as superior to the *Tariff Nomenclature* for use in compiling import and export statistics.

It is obvious that countries (primarily European countries) may find it desirable to adopt the Brussels tariff nomenclature in order to avoid confusing traders who are required to classify commodities for tariff purposes. As a result, the primary statistical commodity classification may then be in terms of the Brussels list. At the same time such countries have a responsibility to report their trade statistics in terms of the SITC. In recognition, or more appropriately, in anticipation, of this situation, the Brussels group and the United Nations Statistical Office from the very beginning of their work on tariff nomenclature and trade classification have established a very close coordination of effort. After considerable study and a great amount of labor, the two documents, statistical and tariff, have been coordinated so that each of the 570 items on the Standard

International Trade Classification is expressed in terms of the Brussels tariff nomenclature. In turn, each item in the Brussels tariff nomenclature is referred to the corresponding items in the SITC.

Although some countries may use their own tariff commodity list for their primary statistical classification (and therefore perhaps must prepare supplementary tabulations for statistical purposes for their own national needs even if the responsibility for reporting on the basis of the SITC did not exist), it is not essential that the primary classification be in terms of the tariff commodity list. In the United States import statistics, for instance, the primary commodity classification is designed for statistical purposes. Much of the classification at least down to a level of approximately 100 broad groups of commodities and generally in greater detail is in fact comparable with the commodity classification used for export statistics where there is no tariff consideration. Within the statistical classification of imports, individual categories are, almost without exception, brought out in sufficient detail to allow retabulation in terms of sections and paragraphs of the Tariff Act described above. In a relatively few cases complete convertibility from the statistical to the tariff commodity classification would require that the statistical classification provide very clumsy categories in areas where the volume of trade is very small. In such cases complete convertibility is sacrificed but at a relatively negligible loss of accuracy in the conversion from the statistical to the tariff classification.

It is, however, still true that the statistical commodity classification of United States imports is substantially influenced by the complexities of the tariff. Chapter 13 on United States trade statistics describes the effect of the tariff (and the reciprocal trade agreements program) on the United States import statistics commodity classification.

This conflict between tariff and statistical needs creates difficulties in establishing a classification useful for all purposes. The conflict can apparently be resolved in either of two ways:

(a) Prepare primary tabulations in a form to fit the tariff classification and supplementary tabulations in a classification designed to meet the needs of economic analysis;

(b) Prepare primary tabulations in a classification designed to meet the needs of economic analysis and supplementary tabulations in a form to fit the tariff classification.

Neither of these methods completely meets both needs. From an economic analysis point of view the second method is preferable.

Problem of obtaining accurate commodity information. The primary objective of commodity classification is to get a consistent summary of millions of international trade transactions. To achieve this objective a good workmanlike classification is of course needed. The classes called for must be mutually exclusive, all inclusive, and clearly defined. For example, classes of " Crude minerals " and " Mineral fuels " are not mutually exclusive and leave the classification of coal uncertain, an incentive to inconsistent classification. Similarly, classes of " Household furniture " and " Office furniture " are not all inclusive and leave the classification of professional, public building, and other kinds of furniture uncertain. A class labeled " Tobacco " is not clearly defined as to whether only unmanufactured tobacco or both manufactured and unmanufactured tobacco is to be included.

Inaccuracy and inconsistency are encouraged by poorly constructed classification. But they can occur even with a well-constructed classification following trade practices. For example, shippers may warp commodity descriptions as a result of the differences between the statistical classifications and the commodity classifications used to determine ocean freight rates. In the explanation of statistics in the 1946 edition of the annual publication *Foreign Commerce and Navigation of the United States*, the Bureau of the Census of the U.S. Department of Commerce says:

Although increased accuracy of the commodity classification in the United States export statistics has been obtained, there still remains an outstanding source of error which cannot be remedied under present conditions. This error arises from the fact that the commodity classification used for export statistics is different from the classification systems in each of the ocean-freight-rate conference tariffs. This difference in the commodity classification systems results in inaccuracies in the commodity description and in the commodity code number inserted on the export declaration by the exporter.

The shipper, in presenting a number of copies of the export declaration to the Collector of Customs before the merchandise is laden on the vessel, knows that one copy will be sent to the steamship company for its use in preparing the manifest listing all cargo on board the vessel. He prepares the export declaration, therefore, in a form which will confirm the information he already has presented to the steamship company for inclusion in the ocean bill of lading when he arranged for transportation of his merchandise at a certain freight rate.

The rate structure for the various ocean-freight-rate conferences assign specific rates both in individual commodities and to certain general categories of merchandise, the commodity classifications differing among ocean-freight-rate conferences and in each case differing from the statistical classification. The difficulties inherent in this situation are obvious. A specific commodity may carry a higher ocean-freight rate than do articles included within a certain broad category in which the shipper might with reason classify his shipment. The shipper, for example, who has arranged for transportation of harmless chemicals, may describe it as a shipment of pharmaceuticals because the latter class carries a lower freight rate than does the former. Again, a shipment of knives might be described as " tools " because tools carry a lower freight rate than do knives. Similarly, it is apparently very common to describe shipments of automobile storage batteries as " automobile parts."

It is the opinion of the United States foreign trade officials that this type of error is one of the most important sources of commodity inaccuracy in the United States export statistics. A similar situation undoubtedly exists in the statistics of other countries. An analogous warping of descriptions also undoubtedly occurs in the statistics of all countries as a result of the incentive to describe merchandise in a way that will secure the lowest possible payment of duty. Further inaccuracy in the commodity information arises from carelessness on the part of importers and exporters in preparing the declarations from which the statistics are compiled, inability or unwillingness to provide the full information needed for proper commodity classification, etc.

Many of these inaccuracies in the statistics arising from improper and inaccurate commodity descriptions can be reduced by providing a detailed coding manual of the individually-named products which would be included in each commodity class. In recognition of this fact the United Nations Statistical Office and the Inter American Statistical Institute are jointly preparing a coding manual for the SITC. The manual will list tens of thousands of names of individual merchandise items covered by the SITC. Many of these will be alternative names for the same thing: " plumbago " for " graphite," " signal oil " or " water-white oil " for " kerosene," etc. Other product names will be the common names of articles which should be included in categories such as SITC 013-09 " Meat extracts and preparations of meat, N.E.S." or SITC 048-09 " Cereal preparations for food, N.E.S." Further refinements of this coding manual will be its assembly in the form both of lists of commodities to be included within each numbered SITC class and of a separate listing of these products in alphabetical arrangement. When prepared in English, Spanish, and French, the two arrangements should be even more useful for international use.

TECHNICAL PROBLEMS

Levels of classification. There remain to be discussed several technical aspects of commodity classification. First of all, most classification systems provide more than one level of classification detail. The SITC, described above, has four levels of classification detail, that is, sections, divisions, groups, and items. The League of Nations Minimum List also has four levels, that is, sections, chapters, primary items, and subitems. Almost all countries having a detailed foreign trade commodity classification tabulate the statistics at a summary level; the most common is the provision for a grouping of commodities into from 5 to 20, 30, or more major sections similar to the 10 major sections of the SITC.

In addition to two levels of classification (the major sections and the full detail), most countries have one or two intermediate levels of grouping used for certain trade statistics tabulations. In the United States export commodity classification, for example, there are two intermediate levels at about 100 and at about 1200 between the major grouping of 11 and the detail of 2900 items. One of the uses of these 100 and 1200 intermediate groupings is in presenting the export statistics in country-by-commodity arrangement where full commodity detail is neither necessary nor desirable.

It can be concluded that, for all-round usefulness of a commodity classification, provision should be made for some three or four levels of commodity detail. Since classifications are set up in terms of classes, subclasses, sub-subclasses and items, this sort of grouping of commodities into levels of detail can be arranged relatively easily.

System of numeric notation. An aspect of commodity classification related to the problem of the levels of classification is that of the numbering system used to identify the individual classified items. With a manual system of compiling trade statistics a system of number identification would not be indispensable if the commodity classification were a relatively simple one. In this case, the classifications would always be identified by their word description. Costa Rica and Nicaragua, for instance, do not use numeric notations. Even there, however, a system of numeric or symbolic notations would have obvious advantages in ease and brevity of reference. With the mechanical punch-card equipment almost universally used by countries to compile their trade statistics, a number-identification system becomes a necessity. Because of the characteristics of the mechanical equipment, the numbering system can best be constructed within the 10-digit arabic system.

In developing a numeric-notations system for mechanical tabulating, it becomes convenient to reserve each digit of the identification number as an indication of the level of classification. The description of the SITC provided above made it clear that the first digit of the code indicates each of the 10 major sections and the first and second digits taken together indicate the 50 divisions. In the complete 5-digit SITC code number, the third digit indicates the 150 groups and the fourth and fifth digits indicate the 570 items. For example, in the SITC list, the designation of item 841–12 (Gloves and mittens of all materials except rubber gloves) indicates this item belongs to Section 8, Miscellaneous Manufactured Articles. Within this section it belongs to Division 84, Clothing. Within this division it belongs to Group 841, Clothing, except Fur Clothing; and it is item No. 12 in group 841.

With a code number system of this type, mechanical sorting and tabulating of punch cards is facilitated when it is desired to prepare tabulations at different levels of commodity detail. If a tabulation by

SITC division is needed, the sorting and tabulating of the cards can be carried out on only the first 2 digits of the 5-digit code, and the tabulated results will be an accurate compilation of statistical information in terms of the 50 SITC divisions. If 3 digits are used, the tabulation will be an accurate compilation in terms of the 150 SITC groups.

There is one difficulty in following completely a system where each digit or two in the code number indicates a level of classification detail; namely, that the system increases the number of digits in the code number. This is explained by the fact that in a decimal system of totally significant numeric notations all available 10 subdivisions of the higher class very seldom are used. In this system, numbers show the degree of detail in classification. Beginning with the first digit (to identify the major class) the farther to the right we move, the more detailed classification we recognize. Since not all subdivisions are used, we observe that the more detailed the classification the more wasteful the use of digits becomes. Examination of one system of significant numeric notations shows that in the second position out of the available 100 numbers only 78 are used (loss 22 per cent), that in the third position out of the possible 1000 numbers, only 700 are used (loss 30 per cent), and in the fourth position the loss is 68 per cent. In the SITC there are 570 items, so that a 3-digit non-significant number would be sufficient for identification of each item. The use of the totally significant notations increases the number of digits in the SITC code number to 5. If the classification covered, say, 6000 items instead of 570 (as the commodity classifications of some countries do) it might be necessary under a system of significant notations, where each digit or two indicates a level of classification detail, to have code numbers of 8 or 9 or even more digits instead of the minimum of 4 digits which would be needed for 6000 non-significant code numbers.

The objection to the long number is obvious. It would lose the advantage of brevity, would be difficult to remember (the average person can probably remember only a 6- or 7-digit number with reasonable accuracy) and would lead to transpositions and other errors. In addition mechanical processing costs of punching (perforating) and sorting cards would be increased. To avoid this difficulty a code number of fewer digits could be used to identify each item and an alternative mechanical procedure used to tabulate at intermediate levels of classification detail. Under this alternative procedure a supplementary code for the intermediate levels of classification detail would be mechanically punched into the cards at slight cost when needed on the basis of the code identification of the most detailed classifications. This supplementary "short" code would have all the characteristics of the 1- or 2-digit identification of intermediate detail in the "long" code. The extra cost of the mechanical punching of the supplementary code would be more than compensated by the advantage of shortening the primary code number from, say, 8 or 9 digits to 4, 5, or 6.

The actual design of a code number system for commodity classifications must work out an optimum solution to these conflicting factors of convenience and cost. The optimum system will usually make some use of individual digits in the code number to indicate major or intermediate levels of classification detail but, to avoid too many digits in the code number, will avoid an exhaustive attempt to have each digit or group of digits indicate a level of classification detail. If it were not for the practical and cost difficulties of a code number with a large number of digits, it would· be scientifically logical to have an elaborate numbering system indicating levels of classification detail.

From one point of view the limitation in this regard is similar to that limiting the elaborateness of the commodity classification itself. It would be very desirable in many ways to set up a commodity classification for international trade statistics analogous to the scientific classifications in the physical sciences. Practical and cost considerations limit the desirability of such classification. They result instead in a classification designed to show significantly the actual volume of trade in particular commodities, rather than one designed to classify all commodities whether or not they move in international trade in appreciable volume. Similarly, practical and cost limitations limit the advisability of an elaborate system of numeric notations.

Frequency of change of commodity classifications. One aspect of commodity classification in international trade statistics where there are no firm principles to be followed is that of the frequency with which classifications should be changed. Technological and trade changes provide a strong incentive for frequent changes in the commodity classifications. The need for comparability of the statistics from year to year provide a strong incentive for keeping changes at the minimum. Some countries have solved this conflict of incentives by making changes very infrequently; others have adopted a policy of frequent changes. As in many other problems the best solution is probably some halfway house. For example, it would appear to be generally acceptable for commodity classifications in trade statistics to change somewhat more slowly than the rapid rate of technological change might appear to warrant. At the same time the trade statistics commodity classifications cannot be too far out of date.

Important assistance in minimizing the inconveniences of commodity classification changes to the user is provided by those countries which each year tabulate commodity information on a comparable basis for a series of preceding years, generally five. The user is thereby spared the labor of reconstructing for prior years commodity information comparable to that in the latest year, a project which may be quite difficult if there have been commodity classification changes during the years covered.

One technique which facilitates the comparison of year-to-year commodity information is the practice of maintaining the same commodity code number over the years if there is no appreciable change in the content of the item, but of changing the code number whenever the content is appreciably changed (by, say, more than 5 or 10 per cent), by a split-up of an item involved or by combining or reshuffling commodity items. The user of the statistics may then rely on code number changes as an indication of changes in the coverage of the classification, and is spared the trouble of continuously scrutinizing the description of each commodity item to see whether the name and therefore presumably the content have been changed, and whether a change in name signals a change in classification or is merely the result of editorial refinement of the description.

CONCLUSION

In millions of business transactions in international trade, with the great number of kinds and limitless number of varieties of commodities involved, the classification serves (or should serve) as a powerful instrument for better, more economical, and more effective collection, presentation, and analysis of commodity information. However, classification alone will not meet all requirements and satisfy all needs for better trade statistics. Something else should be added, including such factors as standardization of terminology, development and improvement of standards for the reporting of commodity information on shipping declarations and other commercial papers, and more diligent cooperation of countries with the United Nations in its efforts to achieve complete and accurate reporting by countries of commodity information on their external trade.

The problem of classification is highly technical and more difficult than it might appear to the casual observer. This difficulty is intensified by the fact that agreement in this field depends to a high degree on a desire and willingness to cooperate and to resolve conflicting needs into a mutually acceptable classification.

CHAPTER 5

Valuation

J. EDWARD ELY
Bureau of the Census

NICHOLAS M. PETRUZZELLI
*Office of International Trade,
U.S. Department of Commerce*

INTRODUCTION

The fact that government activities, including the collection of Customs duties and foreign exchange and other controls, are a major influence on the form and content of international trade statistics is well illustrated by valuation definitions and valuation practices. The value figures shown in most countries' trade statistics are often affected by national considerations which are unrelated to the need for statistical information on external trade. Thus, although the basic value definitions which might be used in compiling the statistics may be readily classified, extra-statistical considerations have led to the development of many peculiar definitions. Furthermore the value information shown in the statistics within the prescribed definitions is frequently affected to a considerable degree by the existence of these extra-statistical factors.

Despite the substantial influence of these factors, an orderly presentation of the valuation picture requires that valuation concepts and definitions for statistical purposes be described first, thereby leaving for later discussion and illustration the problem of extra-statistical influences.

STATISTICAL CONCEPTS AND DEFINITIONS

Statistical uses of value figures. The usefulness of value information is an obvious characteristic of international trade statistics. Since comprehensive merchandise trade figures were first compiled, value figures have been taken as an over-all measure of the amount of trade. In fact the inauguration and development of the compiling of comprehensive trade statistics among the countries of the world can with reason be attributed to the interest of governments in the value balance of their merchandise trade.

This interest in the over-all merchandise value balance has been superseded during the past thirty years or so by the broader interest in the whole balance of payments. With merchandise trade representing something in the neighborhood of 80 per cent of the total world balance of payments transactions, the increased interest in balance of payments information has given an increased importance to the value figures in the merchandise trade account.

Value information in the trade statistics is not limited to balance of payments purposes and to use as an over-all measure of the trade. Another use of value figures is in analysing the relationship between external trade and the domestic economy. Value figures have also long been important as a unit of measure of exports of commodities for which there is no other common denominator except perhaps shipping or net weight, which has obvious limitations. There is no physical unit of quantity, for example, which will permit the satisfactory summarization of information on broad groups of commodities such as chemicals, pharmaceuticals, raw materials, manufactured products, etc. (nor for that matter on many narrowly defined items such as " household glassware "). The use of value figures for broad summarization has long been common. Since this results in distortions during periods of price change, it has had to be supplemented by index number analysis as described in Chapter 10.

From the point of view of commodity analysis of international trade, value figures also provide an approximation to changes in the trend of trade in finer commodity detail than that shown in the commodity classification, even where a reasonably satisfactory unit of quantity exists. If a country's statistics merely show the number and value of imports of passenger automobiles, a rough measure of changes in their size and character can be obtained by noting the change in the average value.

The value figures in the international trade statistics of individual countries have also historically provided important information of price changes in individual commodities where the figures on imports or exports of particular products segregate items which are reasonably homogeneous and where information on the net weight or other unit of the item is provided so that unit prices can be computed. Historically, import and export statistics for items such as molasses, sulphur, coffee, tin, etc., have been a principal source of unit price information. With the development of separately compiled price information, the usefulness of international trade statistics in providing measures of commodity price changes has been decreased. However, this use of the information cannot be entirely overlooked.

Basic definitions for statistical purposes. On the basis of this brief description it is apparent that different statistical uses of the information may sometimes be better served by different definitions of value. For example, the user interested in relating trade to the domestic economy might be better served by a trade valuation approximating domestic prices. From the point of view of balance of payments the ideal definition of value for transactions settled in foreign exchange would be along the following lines:

In the case of exports, the declared value would be the national currency equivalent, at the rate of exchange appropriate to the transaction, of the gain to the exporting country of foreign exchange or of the decrease in its foreign obligations, resulting from the transaction.

In the case of imports, the declared value would be the national currency equivalent, at the rate of exchange appropriate to the transaction, of the loss to the importing country of foreign exchange or of the increase in its foreign obligations resulting from the transaction. (*Source:* Various United Nations papers, including specifically E/CN. 3/126, 14 March, 1951).

Even here the definition may need refinement to provide for separate reporting of value components to be included in the merchandise accounts and in the transportation accounts. This could probably be accomplished by specifying that the foreign exchange gain or loss should be reported separately for the merchandise valued at a specified point in the process of sale (f.o.b. or c.i.f. for example) with any foreign exchange gain or loss properly chargeable to the transportation account reported separately.

At any rate no country uses such a foreign exchange " gain or loss " definition in compiling its import and export statistics. There are instead essentially four working definitions which countries use in compiling their trade statistics. These call for the merchandise to be valued at specified points in the process of sale. Two of the points are in the exporting country (f.o.b. or market value in the exporting country) and two are in the importing country (c.i.f. or market value in the importing country):

1. *F.O.B. value in exporting country.* Imports or exports may be valued at the f.o.b. (free on board carrier) value in the exporting country. There are certain variations in this value which generally, however, can still be classified as f.o.b.-type valuations. The f.o.b. value may be defined as f.o.b. carrier at the principal market in the foreign country; or at the place in the foreign country at which the goods were first shipped for export, even though either of these places may be an interior point rather than a border point of exportation. The value, instead of being f.o.b. the exporting carrier, may alternatively be defined as f.a.s. (free alongside ship) exporting carrier. All these variations from the usual f.o.b. value definition may be still taken as essentially of an f.o.b. type.

2. *Market value in exporting country.* The export or import valuation may be based on the market price in the exporting country, a value which may be different from an f.o.b. value. The market price, if the market is the point of export, does, of course, omit the cost of loading the goods on the carrier and other added costs of export sale. The market value may differ from the f.o.b. value substantially in those cases in which goods may be sold below cost as a dumping operation, either governmental or cartel. If the market is at an interior point, the defined market value may either exclude or include the cost of transport to the point of exportation.

3. *C.I.F. in importing country.* A third point at which imports or exports may be valued is on a c.i.f. (cost, insurance, and freight) basis on the carrier at the point of import. This definition is similar to the f.o.b. type in (1) above, except that the insurance and freight charges (for carriage, ocean, or other), are included where the goods move from the exporting to the importing country by vessel or air. In the instance of direct shipments between two contiguous countries where the value is defined at point of import or export, the f.o.b. and c.i.f. type of values may, of course, be identical.

4. *Market value in importing country.* The fourth basis of valuation is at the market price in the importing country. Although valuation on this basis will often be very similar to c.i.f., differing perhaps only by the amount of unlading and related costs, there are instances where the market price in the importing country may differ substantially from c.i.f. This may occur, for example, if c.i.f. excludes import duties (the usual practice). It will also occur if the shipment is made at a lower than normal price because of government or cartel dumping (assuming the c.i.f. value is ascertainable in such cases). Differences between market price in the importing country and the c.i.f. price will also occur where there may be a heavy local demand for the product so that the local market price is higher than the c.i.f. price. The market price may, however, be lower than the c.i.f. if the product is receiving a government subsidy in connection with rationing.

Value definitions used for exports. Almost all the countries of the world use an "*f.o.b. exporting country*" definition in valuing exports. As far as is known all countries, except Canada, the United States, Finland (in part), and Ethiopia, value their exports on an f.o.b. point of exportation basis.   Canada values exports at the f.o.b. value of the goods at internal points where they were originally consigned for export (thereby omitting inland freight to the Canadian frontier) or the exporting point on goods consigned for export at an interior point (see Chapter 15).   The United States uses an f.a.s. value definition.   Finland values exports of timber f.a.s. but other exports f.o.b.   In Ethiopia the Customs returns for exports do not include the cost of transportation from interior Custom Houses where the goods were valued to the border.   The predominant choice of an f.o.b.-type definition for export valuation has obvious advantages.   The domestic exporter will generally know the f.o.b. value whether or not he actually sold the goods on the basis of the c.i.f. cost in the foreign country.   The f.o.b.-type valuation is furthermore an appropriate value definition from the point of view of relating export trade statistics to the domestic economy and for use in making up the international balance of payments statement.

The number of countries currently using *market price in the exporting country* as a basis for valuing exports is relatively small.   The use of this basis is generally for an official price list rather than for the definition under which the exporter declares the value of his shipment.

As far as known no country values its exports on the basis of the *c.i.f. value* in the *importing country*.

As described in more detail below under consignment sales and intra-company transfers, some countries value exports on the basis of the *market price in the importing country*.   This generally occurs where a country has no domestic market (or a very small one) for the particular products it is exporting and where the domestic exporter, which may be a subsidiary of a foreign firm, does not know how much the goods will be finally sold for or how much it costs to produce the goods and move them to point of export.   In such instances the country may value its exports on the basis of the market value of the goods in the foreign countries to which they are shipped.   In some countries, of which Australia is an example, the value may be translated back to the equivalent of an f.o.b. exporting country value by deducting the amount of ocean freight and insurance, either accurately or by rough estimates.   If this adjustment is made, the basis for the valuation is, of course, an f.o.b. exporting country definition.

Value definitions used for imports.   An " *f.o.b. exporting country* " type of valuation is used rather infrequently for imports.   Of the 94 countries in the January-June 1951 quarterly issue of *Direction of International Trade* (UN-IMF-IB) only 15 are stated to value imports on an f.o.b. basis.   Of these Canada, the United States, and the Union of South Africa use as their basic import value definition roughly either " f.o.b. exporting country " or " market price in exporting country." Duties are assessed on the basis of whichever of the two values is higher.

Not many countries use the *market price in the exporting country* in valuing their imports. As noted above, this type of valuation definition is used by Canada, the Union of South Africa, and the United States as an alternative to valuation " f.o.b. exporting country."

C.i.f. in the importing country is the basis of most countries' import values. It has the advantage that ad valorem duties are assessed on the basis of a value more nearly comparable to domestic value than an f.o.b. or foreign market type of valuation. The c.i.f. cost essentially measures the price at which goods come into competition with domestic products.

Valuation on the basis of a *market price in the importing country* is a type of value definition used by some countries. This method has the advantage of more accurately valuing imports on the same basis as domestic products than a c.i.f. figure. Because there is an area of interpretation as to what the domestic market price is, the use of the market price in the importing country allows greater flexibility of government control of the duties assessed on imports at an ad valorem rate. Since the use of a value definition based on the market price in the importing country almost inevitably requires Customs determination of the value, the use of this value definition can shade readily into the " official " valuations as described below.

Desirable value definitions for statistical use. From the point of view of maximum comparability of the statistics of trading partners an f.o.b. value definition would appear to be best for both imports and exports. For balance of payments purposes f.o.b. value for exports and imports would provide a good working definition approximating for all practical purposes the gain to the exporting country and the loss to the importing country resulting from foreign trade transactions, excluding shipping, insurance, and other services. F.O.B. definitions for exports and imports would exclude ocean freight, insurance, and other service costs from the merchandise accounts and treat these items as separate accounts where they more logically belong from a balance of payments point of view. Universal f.o.b. values for both exports and imports would result in both the importing and exporting country measuring the value of the transaction at the same point, thereby leading to increased comparability in the statistics of the importing and exporting countries.

An f.o.b. value definition for imports would, however, not be as valuable as a c.i.f. definition for comparing imports with the domestic economy.

The use of trade statistics to measure the effect of trade on domestic industry, agriculture, and commerce (either for one country or for a number of countries on a comparable basis) would probably best be served by a c.i.f. import value. Although this might be a valid statistical reason for choosing c.i.f. rather than f.o.b. value for imports the predominant choice of c.i.f. value historically was probably made for duty collection purposes rather than to meet statistical needs. An ad valorem duty based on c.i.f. value more precisely penalizes foreign products in relation to the price of domestic goods than a similar duty based on f.o.b. value. Under an f.o.b. definition the price of domestic goods would be related to prices in foreign markets no matter how far distant.

Because both c.i.f. and f.o.b. values for imports may be useful for certain statistical purposes, there might be good reason for data to be made available on both bases—not necessarily in full commodity and country detail for both value definitions but at least in summary commodity and country groupings for the value definition not used in the primary detailed tabulations. Such supplementary value figures could probably be estimated with reasonable accuracy by the use of conversion factors derived from available information on ocean freight and insurance rates. These conversion factors could be constructed either for conversion from f.o.b. to c.i.f. or vice versa. Some countries have already developed such conversion factors.

NON-STATISTICAL FACTORS

Introduction. A prime obstacle to obtaining value figures most useful for economic analysis is the existence of government activities affecting both the value definitions and the value figures reported in the statistics. The most important of these government activities are the collection of Customs duties on imports and exports, control of foreign exchange, subsidization of exports and imports, and government trade. Because the effect of these non-statistical factors depends to a large extent on particular circumstances, a substantial part of the discussion in this section of the chapter is given over to illustrations of the operations of these factors in individual countries.

Customs duties. Most countries impose Customs duties on imports and many impose duties of one sort or another on exports. While a specific rate of duty (a specified amount of duty for each physical unit of weight, volume, etc.) has obvious advantages in administration, it also has obvious weaknesses during periods of price changes. Duties are therefore frequently (an increasing frequency since World War II) related directly to the value of the merchandise by means of ad valorem rates calling for a certain percentage of the value of the goods to be paid as duty. In addition tariffs sometimes provide that the rate of duty at either specific or ad valorem rates is to be higher for merchandise falling in higher value brackets. Since the government wishes to maximize its revenues, or at least to prevent evasion of duties through undervaluation, and since the trader wishes to keep his duty payments at a minimum, the valuation placed on an item of trade assumes major fiscal importance and statistical significance is sometimes quite lost sight of. Since, in addition, international trade is carried out by traders who are subject to the laws of each others' countries only to a limited extent, and since the value of an article is frequently a difficult thing to determine, there is obviously a wide area for undervaluation by traders, or indeed, overvaluation by government.

Official valuation. Governments have attempted to solve the difficulty by many devices, including that of arbitrarily assigning export or import values on the basis of pre-determined price lists, generally where Customs collectors cannot be relied upon to police the valuations. Under this procedure the valuation is determined without reference to cost, invoice, or other value information pertaining to the individual transaction. Changes in the official values [1] in the pre-determined price lists may in fact actually represent changes in rates of duty rather than changes in the market or other price for the product. The valuation assigned to a particular shipment then becomes an administrative tool for duty collection purposes, and statistical needs are given little or no attention.

Illustrations of official valuation of exports. *Peru* is an illustration of a country which values a large part (about 25 per cent by value) of its exports on the basis of official values. For exports of metallic and non-metallic minerals, wool, cocoa, cattle hides, gums and balata rubber, crude petroleum and gasoline, the value is on the basis of market prices abroad. These products represent a substantial part of the total exports from Peru. The valuation is based on prices in the United States and British markets; it includes not only the value of the products in the form exported but in many cases the cost of refinement abroad. In setting these official values, the Peruvian authorities adjust the values assigned to such exports in order to maximize the amount of revenue to be derived from export duties. This, of course, tends to add another element of overvaluation. Exports of cotton, sugar, and flax (about 50 per cent of total exports by value) are valued on the basis of domestic market prices. Since the price quotations are frequently at an interior Peruvian point the prices exclude the cost of transportation to the point of exportation. There is an additional difficulty

---

[1] For consistency, throughout this chapter the use of pre-determined price lists is referred to as " official valuation " (and the lists themselves are referred to as " official values ") even though in some cases it would perhaps have been more appropriate to have referred to the procedure as " arbitrary " or " tariff " or " proclaimed " valuation.

in that the price quotations refer to average prices for several grades in the case of cotton, for example, and these average quotations are applied to each grade. For other products exported from Peru the value is derived in the following manner: (1) dutiable items are assigned official values based on the average f.o.b. declared values for previous years; (2) non-dutiable merchandise is assigned the actual f.o.b. values declared by exporters on the export documents.

Mexico up to 1941 valued minerals and metals for tax purposes as though they were already refined or processed for industrial use, on the basis of monthly arithmetic averages of daily price quotations for similar products in the New York market and in other important markets of the United States and United Kingdom. In general this resulted in a substantial overvaluation of exports of metals and minerals in the Mexican export statistics since the values shown in the export statistics included, in addition to the value of the product as exported, the later cost of refining, transportation, insurance, handling charges, foreign import duty, etc.

Since 1941 the value of Mexican exports of metals and minerals has been determined by applying to the metallurgical content of the exported products a calculated value based on the foreign market value, but with the following deducted: cost of refinement, cost incurred in processing, freight, insurance, commission, and other expenses of sale. The objective is to have the valuation on the basis of f.o.b. values at the Mexican point of exportation.

The change in the method of valuation in 1941 to bring the export values more nearly to an f.o.b. basis provided an opportunity to determine the approximate extent of the overvaluation which had existed in 1940 and previous years. Despite the fact that the volume and probably the composition of exports of minerals and metals did not change much between 1940 and 1941 (the total weight was 368,000 metric tons in 1940 and 400,000 in 1941) and despite the fact that foreign market prices also showed relatively unimportant changes between the two years, the value of exports of metals and minerals in the Mexican export statistics dropped from 641 million pesos in 1940, when the valuation was based completely on foreign market prices of refined metals, to 367 million pesos in 1941, when the valuation more nearly approximated the Mexican f.o.b. price. While there was a change in the market rate of exchange for the peso between 1940 and 1941 the statistics were compiled on the basis of an arbitrary rate of exchange which remained practically unchanged from 1940 to 1941. The decrease from 641 to 367 million pesos was therefore largely a reflection of the change in method of valuation. It might also be noted that this overvaluation in Mexican export figures prior to 1941 had a very substantial effect on the accuracy of the over-all Mexican export statistics since Mexican exports consist primarily of exports of these products.

Portugal is another example of a country employing official valuation of export products. Prior to 1942, Portugal's system for valuing exports rested primarily on an official schedule of commodity appraisals incorporated in a decree law dated May 26, 1928. This schedule was the last of a series originally devised to serve the dual purpose of determining the dutiable value of exports and exchange requisitions against them. Export appraisals were undertaken without strict regard for market prices. Because Portuguese export statistics for years prior to 1942 were in large part derived from official values, they may have failed to reflect the true commercial values of exported goods.

At the beginning of 1942, a more realistic valuation procedure was instituted. The schedule of pre-determined export values was retained for goods subject to ad valorem duty for which it was apparently primarily intended. The ad valorem exports are estimated to be about one-third of the total value of exports. The official values were revised upward to bring them into line with prevailing market prices, and subsequent periodic revisions have since been made to maintain a closer relationship between official values and actual selling prices. Exports dutiable at specific rates and non-dutiable exports are valued, under the new procedure, on the basis of merchant's declarations.

Venezuela's exports of crude petroleum (representing well over 90 per cent of total exports, since 1925) are assigned a nominal value of 30 bolivars per metric ton in official statistics, although the world market value (mainly United States prices at Gulf ports) varied from one-half to two-thirds of that amount in the years from 1925 through 1944 and most of 1945. At the end of 1945 when United States prices of crude petroleum started to rise and in subsequent years when they attained nearly double their pre-war levels, the same official valuation continued to be used in Venezuela. Thus, in 1945 and thereafter, petroleum exports as recorded in the trade statistics were undervalued. According to careful estimates by the Venezuelan Government, the overvaluation of petroleum exports in the pre-war and war years 1938 through 1944 averaged 302 millions of bolivars per year, and in the post-war period the undervaluation has reached as much as 300 million bolivars per year.

The bolivar values of other exports and certain other agricultural products (except coffee and cacao, for which the valuation practice is described below under subsidized exports) are determined on the basis of official Customs valuations which are by law supposed to be revised every 15 days in accordance with the prices prevailing in the individual ports for the products involved. In reality, however, the valuation of these exports is probably inaccurate owing to the practice in Customs offices of setting arbitrary values which appear to be seldom revised regardless of qualities, current internal prices, and real export values of the products involved.

Illustrations of official valuation of imports. *Iraq* provides an example of an import value based on the domestic market price officially determined by Customs. This applies to many imports dutiable at ad valorem rates where the items are valued by the Customs authority on the basis of wholesale domestic cash prices less Customs duties. Such imports tend to be overvalued due to the fact that prices in Iraq have been higher than prices in Egypt, India, the United States, the United Kingdom, and other countries that are important suppliers of goods to Iraq. Internal prices in Iraq assigned to imported merchandise are, therefore, higher than the invoice prices of these goods. The overvaluation of total imports into Iraq in 1948, for example, was estimated at $3,643,120 (United States dollars) in a total import trade reported at the equivalent of $145,781,220. Moreover, individual commodities in Iraq's import trade are overvalued in varying percentages depending upon differences in their respective prices within the country as compared with their prices in the countries of origin and world markets generally.

Canada also has an official valuation procedure for some commodities under certain circumstances. Importers' declarations are generally used as a basis for valuation of imports, but an exception to this general rule is the use of official values for fruits and vegetables, livestock, meats, sugar, eggs, poultry, and other agricultural products to compensate for seasonal low-price conditions. They are usually canceled within a period of 9 months or less. Such values are used, however, when the potential volume of imports of the commodities affected is greatest, namely when the Minister of National Revenue finds conditions which prejudicially or injuriously affect the interests of Canadian producers or manufacturers. Official values have been used also for raw materials and manufactured products, including bituminous coal, lime ferromanganese, brass and copper products, cotton and artificial silk fabrics, and various articles of clothing. Although these values when used have affected only a minor part of the total of imports, the amount of deviation from declared values introduced into the import statistics for these commodities was substantial in some periods.

Belgium uses import values on a c.i.f. basis, but these values must not be less than the normal wholesale prices of similar goods on the Belgium market at the time of importation less duty at the minimum tariff rate. Since the determination of domestic market value may be difficult for products not widely traded on the domestic market this provision may on occasion bring in an element of official valuation.

United Kingdom and the *United States*. Even in these nations, where import values are not officially determined, there may be an element of official valuation. The value as determined by Customs may contain such an element to the extent that the United Kingdom values imports subject to ad valorem duties at open market values, and the United States values certain products at the United States price of the same or similar items, and to the extent that the imported articles do not have a well-organized domestic market.

Uruguay provides an illustration of the substantial effect official valuations may have on import statistics over the years. Neither the detailed nor the aggregate figures in pesos, the national monetary unit, shown in the official Customs returns of Uruguay for the past century and currently, have borne any real relationship to the c.i.f. landed cost. The valuations represent official valuations fixed for the purpose of assessing ad valorem duties. The tariff while being ad valorem in form actually is, therefore, essentially specific in incidence.

A comparison of real c.i.f. values as estimated by the General Statistical Officer of Uruguay, and official values totals for the same years as shown in the trade returns, reveals that the official values totals were 40 per cent lower than the real c.i.f. values during the 1937–1940 period; 62 per cent lower in the war years 1941–1945; and as much as 70 per cent lower in the post-war years 1946–1948. A study made by the General Statistical Office of Uruguay a number of years ago comparing estimated real c.i.f. values of import totals by countries with corresponding official values indicated that official import valuations were understated for most countries. However, for a few countries the official import value totals were above the estimated c.i.f. figures.

It should be noted that Uruguayan import figures in terms of United States dollars have been compiled and published by the Foreign Exchange Control Authorities since 1942. The value is taken from " clearance permits authorized " (despachos authorizados). Although these import figures are adequate for general purposes such as for balance of trade and payments analysis, they are not sufficiently detailed commodity-wise for other purposes.

Decrease in use of official values. Though many countries used official values in their early statistics, the use of this method of valuing imports or exports either for statistical or duty collection purposes has been declining over the years. The United Kingdom abandoned official values for exports in 1801, and for imports in 1871 (Chapter 14). The United States abandoned a type of official value for exports in 1821 (Chapter 13). A number of countries which have changed from official values to declared values are listed herewith together with the date of change:

Countries Changing from Official to Declared Values
(with Date of Change)

Austria, imports and exports, 1925.

Argentina, imports, 1941.

Belgium, imports and exports, 1918.

Bolivia, imports, 1919, exports, 1907.

Chile, imports, 1917.

Czechoslovakia, imports and exports, 1923.

Denmark, imports and exports, 1919.

Ecuador, exports, 1916.

Finland, imports and exports, 1919.

France, imports, 1921, exports, 1927.

Germany, imports, 1921, exports, 1911.

Greece, imports and exports, 1926.

Honduras, exports, 1919.

Hungary, imports and exports, 1925.

Italy, imports and exports, 1921.

Netherlands, imports and exports, 1919.

Norway, imports and exports, 1922.

Paraguay, exports, 1939.

Peru, imports, 1922

Spain, imports and exports, 1931.

Sweden, imports and exports, 1914.

Switzerland, imports and exports, 1917.

Source: Introduction of official annual trade reports of the countries mentioned: *cf.* League of Nations, *Memorandum on International Trade and Balances of Payments 1912–1926*, Volume II (Geneva, 1928), notes for each country mentioned, *viz.*, Chile, p. 171; Netherlands, pp. 533–534; Finland, p. 322; Belgium, pp. 92–93; Bolivia, p. 108; Denmark, p. 249; Germany, p. 359; Greece, p. 377; Italy, p. 453; Czechoslovakia, p. 234; Austria, p. 79; Hungary, p. 418; and France, pp. 336–337. Also, League of Nations, *International Trade Statistics 1938* (Geneva, 1939), for Spain, p. 100. For Paraguay, unpublished data, U.S. Department of Commerce.

Despite this evidence of a decrease in the use of official values it should be noted that the tendency for countries to base their import and export duties on ad valorem rates acts to add an element of official valuation.

Indirect effect of Customs duties. Even where arbitrary valuation is not used, the value figures shown in the trade statistics are frequently subject to the duty collection influence to some degree, either in terms of the value definition used or in terms of the procedure followed to arrive at a value figure for individual shipments. A value definition may be set up to meet the needs of ad valorem duty collection. Nevertheless it may be applied to items free of duty or dutiable at specific rates, even though it may be difficult to administer and therefore inappropriate for items not subject to ad valorem rates. In the United States and the United Kingdom for example, the import value definitions have been largely set up for ad valorem duty collection purposes but are applied to free and specific rate commodities which represent the bulk of the trade (85 per cent in the United Kingdom and 90 per cent in the United States).

The United Kingdom import value definition is " open market value." The United States definition provides a whole series of rather complicated alternatives of which the most important is foreign market value (price offered for sale for consumption in country of export) or export value (price offered for sale for export to United States), whichever is higher. If neither of these can be determined, the United States market price (minus duties and ocean freight and insurance) is to be used. Provision is made for valuation on the basis of cost of production if none of the above values can be determined. For certain items, including coal-tar finished and intermediate products, knit gloves, and clams, the import value is the American selling price of similar competitive items produced in the United States. In the case of the United States the application of a very complicated value definition designed for goods dutiable at ad valorem rates to free and specific rate items tends to valuations not conforming to the definitions. Because collectors of Customs are preoccupied with determining values of the 10 per cent of imports subject to ad valorem rates of duty for which they have a fiscal responsibility to see that proper amount of duty is collected, there is little or no review of the value declared by the importer for the 90 per cent of imports free of duty or dutiable at specific rates. A pre-war study of some 12,000 import shipments showed 60 per cent different from the value definition called for.

The existence of export and import duties and taxes may also indirectly cause difficulties in the valuation shown in the trade statistics. Import duties paid by a national to his own government should quite properly be excluded from the import value. Most countries follow this practice by defining import value as c.i.f. excluding import duties. Export duties create a somewhat more difficult problem. If the export value is defined as f.o.b. including export duties, the value will approximate the amount paid by the foreign purchaser. Some countries, however, define the export value as f.o.b. *excluding* export duties. For example, the 1950 *Supplement* to the United Nations *Monthly Bulletin of Statistics*, in describing the statistics of each of the countries of the world, states under the description of the following countries' statistics that export duties are excluded from the export value by definition: Colombia, Dominican Republic, Iceland, Portugal and Tunisia.

There may also be some difficulties where countries use an import value definition based on f.o.b. or market value in the supplying country and the supplying country has an export duty. If the importing country omits the amount of this export duty from its import value the value is less useful from a balance of payments point of view since the export duty would in fact normally be part of the price paid by the importing country.

Subsidized exports and imports. Valuation problems similar to those for Customs duties and taxes may arise in connection with subsidized exports and imports. An example of the effect of an export subsidy is the current United States subsidy to United States exporters for exports of a number of agricultural products, including wheat, wheat flour, raisins, prunes, apples, oranges, pears, etc. The practice in the United States export statistics is to exclude the amount of the subsidy payment from the value shown on the export statistics. Some difficulty has been experienced in making certain that exporters do exclude the subsidy in reporting an export value figure; values including the subsidy have in some cases been reported by exporters and included in the United States export statistics.

It would appear preferable to have the export value include only the amount paid by the foreign importers. That part of the value paid to the exporter by his own government as a subsidy for the export of the product is not paid for by the foreign importer and should therefore not be included in the value figures.

Some countries have nevertheless included the amount of subsidies in their export figures. For example, during the period 1934–1941 Venezuela provided direct subsidies to its exporters of coffee, cacao, and a varying number of other agricultural products to compensate for the substantial appreciation in the value of the Venezuelan bolivar which took place from 1932 to 1934. Without such subsidies the Venezuelan exporters of these products would have had a substantially lower return in bolivars from their sales abroad. In 1941 the system of direct subsidies was abandoned. Instead, exporters of these products were given a preferential rate of exchange under which they received a larger number of bolivars for foreign sales than they would have in the free market. A government decree of 1948 announced that preferential rates of exchange were to be in effect for coffee and cacao (the agricultural products still receiving a preferential rate at that time) only when world prices for these products were below certain levels. As a result of this decree and the incidence of higher cacao and coffee prices since 1948, preferential exchange rates for these products have been largely eliminated. During the whole period of direct and indirect subsidy the values shown in the export statistics included the subsidy even though the actual transactions were made at values excluding the subsidy. Other countries have apparently also had their statistics affected in a similar fashion.

In contrast to export subsidies it would appear preferable for the amount of import subsidies to be included in the import value figures since the total amount paid the foreign supplier for the imports includes the amount paid as a subsidy to the importer. As noted in Chapter 17, France excluded subsidies paid to its importers from the value shown in its import statistics during the period 1946–1949, but subsequently revised the figures to include the amount of the subsidy.

Foreign exchange and other controls. An additional important non-statistical influence on valuation arises from foreign exchange and other governmental controls. An exporter in a country having exchange control will have an incentive to undervalue his exports in order to limit the amount of foreign exchange which must be turned over to the exchange control authorities as a result of an export transaction. The exchange control and Customs authorities will, of course, attempt to prevent such under-valuation, but the existence of the controls may adversely affect the statistical accuracy of the value figures. Similarly exchange control may lead to overvaluation to allow an importer to build up his private foreign exchange resources. For example, if country A licenses the expenditure of foreign exchange only for imports of goods it considers essential, an importer in A wishing to avoid this control may arrange with his foreign supplier in, say, country B to overvalue a shipment of an " essential " item from B to A. The excess foreign exchange granted to the importer in A by his government may then be held in country B for use in paying for the imports of " non-essential " goods (or for the purchase of " non-essential " services such as travel) for which the government of country A would not grant a license to spend foreign exchange. The importer may indeed use this excess foreign exchange to increase improperly the quantity of imports of " essential " items over the amount he is permitted to import; his intent being to sell the excess in a " black market," that is, outside the price-controlled market where the licensed part of the import may have to be sold.

Official valuations have obvious limitations as an instrument to prevent over- or undervaluations designed to avoid exchange controls. A more effective device is to require the presentation of invoices and other documents in support of the valuation and to compare prices for individual transactions with prices in the domestic market and in foreign countries. Price information in foreign countries may be obtained through national consuls stationed abroad. One instrument which countries have used for many years to prevent undervaluation of imports, and which can be adapted to preventing overvaluation designed to avoid exchange controls, is to require that importers present a " consulated " or " consular " invoice as part of the import requirements. This is a form prescribed by the importing country to be filled out by the foreign supplier and presented for certification to the consul of the importing country stationed in the exporting country. The consul reviews the statements on the form and certifies that the value and other information shown is correct to the best of his knowledge. If the consul is familiar with prices in the exporting country he can effectively prevent either undervaluation designed to avoid the payment of full ad valorem duties in the importing country or overvaluation designed to avoid any existing exchange control restrictions in the manner described above. Since exchange controls are relatively new, methods for preventing evasion are perhaps not as well developed as those for Customs duties.

It should be pointed out that the effect of exchange control on the values shown in the statistics is not limited to the statistics of the country imposing the duties or enforcing the exchange control. Somewhat the same thing is true of Customs duties. In both cases the statistics of the partner country may also be affected since, to preserve consistency, the exporter or importer in the partner country may also under- or overvalue the goods at time of export or import to match the valuation claimed by the person he is trading with in the other country. An exporter to a country having exchange control or imposing an ad valorem import duty may, as part of the procedure for obtaining a consulated invoice, have to present to the consul of the importing country stationed in the exporting country a copy of the export declarations he files at time of export. The exporter runs no particular risk of prosecution for under- or overvaluation on his own export document if no export duty is involved and the document is used only for statistical purposes, or if used for export control purposes the under- or overvaluation does not violate the export control requirements.

Exchange control may also result in the use of arbitrary exchange rates in valuing a country's foreign trade, a situation which is discussed in Chapter 6, " Exchange Conversion."

Government exports and imports. Shipments moving in international trade under special government arrangements such as Lend-Lease, Reverse Lend-Lease, British Empire Mutual Aid, UNRRA, Mutual Defense Assistance Program, reparations and restitutions, etc., have presented certain problems in valuation. In the country originating such shipments the problem of valuation must frequently be solved by using an estimated value figure. In the United States, for example, where a number of these special program shipments have originated, it has not been possible for government agencies administering these special programs to derive a completely accurate figure equivalent to the f.a.s. export value used in the statistics. An individual shipment of a particular product may not be separately recorded by the government agency making the shipment, and the cost of the particular item, therefore, cannot be determined. In such cases an average price for all units of, let us say, wheat purchased by the government agencies during preceding months, is computed and applied to the number of units of wheat in a particular export shipment. Such a valuation process is, of course, only approximate since the wheat in that particular shipment may not have been purchased at the average price. An added difficulty in the United States has been that such estimated figures do not include the cost of moving the products from an interior point, where it may have been purchased, to seaboard. It has therefore sometimes been necessary in compiling United States export statistics to estimate the cost of moving special government program exports to seaboard by arbitrarily adding from 5 to 20 per cent to the value of the product to cover this cost. Even greater problems of valuations may arise in regard to reparations and restitution movements where the products may be used equipment difficult to value.

The country importing products under these special programs may face equal if not greater difficulties in deriving an estimated value figure for the transactions.

Imports under governmental purchase arrangements whether by international arrangements or not may also cause difficulties in the value figures since such purchases are frequently made outside normal commercial channels. It may therefore be difficult for the importing government agency to provide a value figure in accordance with the statistical value definition.

OTHER VALUATION PROBLEMS

Errors due to value definitions not conforming to sales practices. Where a duty is not collected and where the data are reported solely for statistical purposes, a value figure declared by the trader in accordance with a prescribed definition is generally shown in the statistics. In this case the value is not greatly influenced by non-statistical factors. However, as indicated earlier, the exporter may under- or overvalue even here in order to be consistent with the foreign importer's attempt to undervalue to avoid duty payments or overvalue to avoid exchange control restrictions. Except for this, the value should be subject only to inadvertencies in reporting or to tendencies on the part of exporters to report a more readily available figure rather than one conforming with the definition, particularly a complicated definition set up primarily for ad valorem duty collection purposes. Even if the definition is relatively simple the trader may still report an inaccurate but more readily available figure. For example, there is a tendency for United States exporters to report value f.o.b. factory interior point rather than f.a.s. point of export (see Chapter 13). Other countries undoubtedly face similar difficulties in attaining accurate conformance to required definitions. The most effective way to minimize errors of this type is to design valuation definitions and practices which most closely approximate normal sales practices.

Consignment sales.   In countries that supply raw materials, where there may be no ad valorem export duty and therefore no incentive for incorrect valuation, there may still be a source of inaccuracy where products are exported on consignment and therefore not actually sold until reaching an overseas point of consumption.   For many exports of raw materials from countries in Latin America, Asia, and Africa as well as Australia, Canada, etc., the exporter may declare the value on the basis of an intelligent guess as to the actual amount he will eventually receive for the shipment.   When prices rise his guess is likely to be too low;   too high if prices fall.   Often the error may be substantial.

In some of the British West Africa Colonies (as described in Chapter 16) the problem of valuation for consignment sales is complicated because these sales are handled by government marketing boards which have valued exports on a domestic cost basis.   A value based on realization value would be more analogous to a commercial value and more accurate from a balance of payments point of view.

There have been attempts to overcome this type of valuation difficulty in the export statistics.   Australia, for example, appears to have had reasonable success with valuing goods shipped on consignment at an Australian f.o.b. equivalent of the current prices being offered for similar goods of Australian origin in the principal markets in the country to which the goods are dispatched for sale.   There is no correction at a later date for differences between this value and the actual selling price of the goods valued on this basis.   The Union of South Africa follows a similar practice in valuing exports of metal and minerals for which there is no local market.   In this case the value in the statistics is the current price being realized overseas, minus freight, insurance, and other charges.

Other countries, such as Canada and Malaya, have attempted to overcome the difficulty by correcting the first-released valuation figures at a later date after the goods have actually been sold and the value determined.

It would seem desirable for countries having a substantial amount of exports made on consignment to provide for later revision of the first-reported estimated value figures if the statistics are to achieve maximum accuracy and usefulness.   The usefulness of a dual reporting system might however not be worth the rather substantial cost of the extra compilation and revision work (see Chapter 2 for difficulties in making revisions).   In actual practice it can be assumed that in countries where raw materials are exported on consignment in substantial volume the merchandise export statistics are primarily used to provide information on the quantities of the products exported.   An alternative to the correction procedure would then be to recognize that the values shown in the merchandise statistics are approximations and to use figures on sales realization from other sources in any analysis of the country's balance of payments. The merchandise trade figures could then remain uncorrected.

Intra-company shipments. Imports or exports which are really intra-company transfers of commodities present somewhat the same difficulties as consignment sales since there is again not a commercial transaction at the time of export. Intra-company transfers, however, present a greater difficulty since a commercial transaction may not take place even after export.

Although the company involved in an intra-company transfer may be quite willing to make a reasonable effort to provide value information, it may not be in a position without making many (perhaps unrealistic) assumptions to derive a value figure reasonably analogous to the value which would have been reported if the transaction had been a commercial transfer between companies.

In general, intra-company transactions are more frequent and important in the trade figures of countries supplying raw materials where large foreign firms are engaged in extracting the raw materials. As illustrations of this type of activity, the following are reasonably representative: petroleum and gold in Venezuela; petroleum, gold, and platinum in Colombia; copper and gold in Peru; iodine, iron, and nitrate in Chile; bananas in a number of Central American countries.

A common method to value exports of this type is to use a foreign market value either adjusted back to an f.o.b. equivalent or without adjustment. In more developed countries including those receiving raw materials under intra-company transfers, the balance of payments statistics may present figures on the intra-company transfer of foreign exchange as a substitute for the merchandise trade figures which may show a value figure based on market value for the commodity shipments.

Exports and imports by parcel post. Valuation problems in regard to imports and exports by parcel post centre about the difficulty of recording and compiling value figures for large numbers of small shipments. In the United States, for example, the number of parcel post shipments is approximately as large as the number of non-parcel post shipments.

As described in Chapter 3, some countries exclude parcel post shipments completely except for dutiable imports or exports. Other countries also include a relatively small number of high-value parcel post shipments in the regular commodity statistics, thereby keeping the compiling work at the minimum and the total value included at the maximum. Some countries include all parcel post shipments but provide no commodity detail except for dutiable shipments. In such cases the value of the non-dutiable parcel post shipments is estimated in total by multiplying a count of the packages by an estimated average value per package. A similar method of estimating may be employed to obtain a value figure for the low-value parcel post shipments where only high-value parcels are included in the commodity statistics.

Improvement and repair trade. There is an inconsistency among countries in the valuation of goods imported for repair or improvement. Some countries include in the trade figures only the added value at time of export; others include the full value at time of both import and export. Similar differences in practice exist in the statistics of the country exporting the goods to another for repair or improvement. The United Nations in its draft of definitions for international trade statistics referred to previously recommends that the value of a broken article shipped for repair be based on its value in good condition less the probable cost of transport and repair. The cost of transport and repair would probably be known, but there might well be practical difficulties in determining the value, in good condition, of a partly used piece of machinery with an unknown amount of depreciation and obsolescence. If the machinery had been sold the sales price would have been the value but it might be an undue burden to require a determination of the value of the item in good condition merely because it is being sent abroad for repair.

Articles sent abroad for improvement (such as wool for cleaning) are usually new or recently traded in so that no great difficulty would be experienced in reporting value before or after improvement.

CONCLUSION

The following conclusions appear warranted on the basis of this survey of the definitions and practices followed by countries in valuing exports and imports in their trade statistics.

In the first place there is a wide diversity among countries in valuation definitions used and in methods of obtaining value information. Furthermore, even within individual countries different types of exports and imports may be valued under different procedures.

It may also be concluded that the definitions and practices followed in arriving at the values shown in the statistics are greatly influenced by duty collection and other control procedures. Complicated valuation definitions and practices in the import and export statistics frequently result from the complicated nature of the value definition required by law or regulations to be followed in the collection of duties or the administration of other controls. The use of official values has declined over the years, but they are still used in a number of countries.

It is finally apparent that there are many obstacles in the way of achieving uniformity among the nations of the world in valuation definitions and practices. Even if a common set of definitions were agreed upon (probably along the lines of a balance of payments definition) there would be substantial duty, control, and practical obstacles in each country to the adopting of a common definition and practice in its primary tabulations. It would appear that most countries could, as an alternative, more readily provide supplemental value information in terms of a common set of definitions.

CHAPTER 6

Exchange Conversion

EARL HICKS
International Monetary Fund

INTRODUCTION

International trade consists in the purchase of goods produced and priced in one currency system and their sale in another currency system. To make such a transaction either the buyer or the seller must make a conversion of a value expressed in a foreign currency to a value expressed in his own currency in order to determine whether the transaction is worthwhile. To make national statistics of foreign trade, the Customs or statistics authorities of a country must make conversions into national currency of all transactions reported in foreign currency and must either accept without consideration, or examine and correct, the conversions that have been made in the documents submitted by importers and exporters. Finally, to make world totals and other internationally comparable trade statistics, an international compiler must convert aggregates reported by each country in its national currency into a single currency. Conversions are therefore inherent in all trade statistics, and the accuracy and usefulness of any compilation of trade statistics depend in large part on the reasonableness of the systems of conversion all along the line.

The conversion problem is usually thought of as one that arises in making international compilations of trade data in a common currency. This question, which is an important part of the larger question in Chapter 12 of making international comparisons of trade statistics, is discussed here.

But the primary purpose of this chapter is to point out that the compilation of national trade statistics in national currency is dependent upon the conversion into national currency of many values expressed originally in foreign currencies, to explain the nature of the problem that thereby arises, and to describe the procedures for conversion used by countries in the compilation of national trade statistics.

CONVERSION PROBLEMS

Nature of the problems. If all currencies were freely convertible into any other currency, if governments made no attempt to use the exchange system as a source of taxation or as an instrument of economic policy, and if economic changes took place so nearly uniformly in all countries that neither the exchange rate nor the relationship of domestic to foreign prices changed during the period of the statistics, there would be no serious problems in national or international statistics arising from conversions. During the entire period after World War II, however, one major currency and a number of others have been inconvertible, the exchanges have been widely used as taxation and economic policy instruments, and both relative prices and exchange rates between major currencies have changed greatly. The post-war trade statistics of all countries are consequently subject to errors arising from the difficulty of knowing the true equivalent of one currency in terms of another.

What trade statistics should consider one currency to be worth in terms of another depends in the first instance upon the purpose for which they are to be used. Trade statistics must provide important parts of two pictures and, when any of the problems mentioned above exist, there is no single answer to the conversion question. On the one hand, trade statistics are important parts of most countries' national-income, money-flows, and price statistics. If they are to have a correct relationship to these aggregates, the value of exports must be the sum in domestic currency that was received by the domestic factors that produced it; the value of imports must be the sum in domestic currency that was spent upon them by consumers and investors (exclusive, of course, of domestic distribution costs); and the average prices they reflect must be those received by the factors or paid by the purchasers. On the other hand, trade statistics are for almost all countries the most important part of its balance of payments with the rest of the world and important parts of the data on world production, distribution, and consumption of world trade commodities. If they are to be a correct measure of the sources and uses of foreign exchange and if they are to have a correct relationship to the payments statistics of the rest of the world and to the commodity statistics of countries exporting and importing similar commodities, the value of exports must be the national currency equivalent of the foreign exchange they earned; the value of imports must be the national currency equivalent of the foreign exchange they cost; and the prices they reflect must be the national currency equivalent of their foreign exchange prices.

When the currencies of some of the important trading countries of the world are inconvertible, when the country whose trade statistics are under examination employs multiple currencies, or when the exchange rates of important trading countries of the world have changed, an aggregate of a country's exports or imports that provides the proper part to one of these pictures will not provide the proper part for the other; and unless the conversion procedures of the country's Customs authorities have been carefully thought out, its statistics will not provide a correct part to either picture.

For the purpose of describing the conversion problems that various exchange systems create we may first divide all exchange systems into two classes: single currency systems and multiple currency systems. Secondly, the single currency systems may be further divided into convertible and inconvertible systems. In single currency systems in which exchange is convertible in either direction for all current transactions (at a single rate, officially determined and maintained over considerable periods, or a so-called fluctuating rate that varies from day to day either in response to market forces or in response to a combination of market forces and the purchases and sales of the monetary authorities), it is clear that there are no important conversion problems aside from those that arise from changes in the single rate by devaluation or depreciation or by the accumulation of day-to-day changes. If, however, a country's currency is not convertible for all current transactions at the single rate, a discount market may develop in one or more countries abroad in which the currency is bought and sold at " broken cross rates." This raises the first class of conversion problems. Multiple currency systems are almost necessarily inconvertible systems, but they raise additional and different conversion problems that are discussed below as the second set of conversion problems. Either single currency systems in which exchange is not convertible for all current transactions or multiple currency systems necessitate laws or regulations, and these may or may not be effectively enforced. When they are not effectively enforced or when certain types of transactions are exempted from the regulations, another class of conversion problems arises through the existence within the exchange markets of a country of an additional rate at which some trade transactions are conducted. These rates, which may be called " free rates " if they are lawful or " black market rates " if they are unlawful, are discussed as the third class of conversion problems. Finally, all rates of every system are subject to changes;

and the fourth class of conversion problem involves the interpretation of trade data between periods separated by change in one or more exchange rates.

Broken cross rates. When some currencies are inconvertible, the cross rates between the inconvertible currencies themselves and between each of the inconvertible currencies and the convertible ones, may be broken in some parts of the world. Cross rates are the exchange rates between any two currencies derived from the rates for each of these currencies in terms of a third currency. If in New York sterling is worth $2.80 and the Swiss franc is worth $0.24, then the Swiss franc cross rate for sterling in New York is £1 = 11⅔ Swiss francs. The cross rates are orderly in New York if £1 = 11⅔ Swiss francs is the exchange rate for sterling in Switzerland and for Swiss francs in London; the cross rates are broken if that is not so. When the cross rates are broken, the value of imports and exports in countries permitting transactions at broken cross rates may represent the sums in national currency that importers paid for the import (or for the exchange to buy the import) and that exporters received for the export (or for the exchange obtained for the export). Or they may represent the national currency equivalent, at the official rate, of the foreign currencies spent for imports and received from exports. If the break in the cross rates applies equally to the official rate and to such " free " or other rates at which all or any part of trade transactions are actually conducted, the two answers will be the same and properly related to national statistics of income, money flows, and prices. But there will be in this case no means by which they can be combined properly with the statistics of other countries into international tables in which expenditures or receipts of any currency are equated at cross rates equal to those used in the statistics of countries that keep the cross rates at par or that have broken cross rates at different levels.

If, on the contrary, the break in the cross rates is confined to the " free " rate while the official rate is kept at par with all currencies, the trade statistics of the country may either fit into international compilations but be improperly related to other domestic statistics, or fit into domestic statistics and be improperly related to international statistics. With which they fit will depend upon whether the national statistics are made by converting foreign currency sums at the free rate or at the official rate. To the extent that the conversions for different transactions are inconsistent, or that transactions reported in national currency are inconsistent with the method by which customs converts into national currency sums reported in foreign currency, the data will not fit properly into either picture. Broken cross rates mean that there is no universal relationship between the value of currencies, and consequently aggregates of sums originally expressed in various currencies must at some point add as equalities things that are not equal or as inequalities things that are equal.

The importance of this problem to post-war trade statistics is sufficiently indicated by the fact that the sterling area, whose currencies have been subject to broken cross rates in many parts of the world, accounts for more than one-quarter of the world's exports.

Multiple currencies. The second source of conversion problems lies in multiple currency systems. Multiple currency systems are devices that, for any of a number of purposes, set the value of national currency in terms of foreign currencies at different points for different types of international transactions. The multiple rates may, for example, provide more favorable rates for imports of so-called essential goods than for other imports, more favorable rates for imports of goods deemed to be important to development, or more favorable rates for imports from countries whose currencies are inconvertible and held in excess supply to the monetary authorities of the multiple currency country. Multiple rates may also provide more favorable rates for the exports of new industries or those deemed incapable of competing internationally without such a benefit, or for exports to countries whose currency is especially wanted by the monetary authorities of the multiple currency country. For multiple currency countries, aggregates of trade transactions expressed in foreign currencies cannot be accurately translated into national currency equivalents properly related to other national statistics, and aggregates expressed in national currency cannot be accurately translated into equivalents in a foreign currency.

Most of the countries that use multiple currency systems have chosen to make their national statistics measure, insofar as possible, the foreign exchange proceeds and expenditures of trade, rather than the national currency receipts and payments of their exporters and importers. In these cases they are either compiled and published in terms of dollars or of an artificial unit representing a fixed fraction or multiple of a dollar, or they are compiled and published in units labeled as national currency units but representing conversions at a single rate instead of at the multiple rates that in fact governed the transactions. They are ordinarily suitable, therefore, to the study of problems involving foreign exchange receipts and payments and the comparison of export and import prices with world prices.

It follows that, in the compilation of trade statistics expressed in dollars or in any other currency ordinarily used for international comparisons, the multiple currency problem is not serious. In the statistics of other countries there is ordinarily no special problem arising from trade transactions with multiple currency countries. Most multiple currency countries will not accept their own currencies in payment for exports, and both export and import contracts with them are ordinarily made in the currency of the partner to the transaction or in the currency of a third country. Hence, exports to and imports from multiple currency countries are ordinarily reported in the documents submitted to the partner countries in the partner's currency or in a non-multiple third currency. Both the statistics of multiple currency countries and those of their trading partners are in most cases then produced in such a way that world trade aggregates and the comparison of trade statistics between countries are not very seriously in error owing to the use of multiple currency practices.

However, when the usefulness of national trade statistics in the study of economic events within multiple currency countries is considered, the problem of multiple currencies is by no means minor. The statistics of multiple currency countries, if made comparable in terms of foreign exchange values to the statistics of other countries, cannot have a correct relationship to the statistics of domestic incomes, money flows, or prices. Countries using multiple currency systems tend, on the whole, to be ones for which fluctuations in the volume and value of exports tend to be relatively large, for which increases or decreases in the volume and value of trade have relatively greater domestic effects than in other countries, and, lastly, for which fewer and less accurate statistics on other aspects of the national economy are available. For all these reasons the loss of true national currency trade statistics through the use of multiple currency systems is specially regrettable. Without trade statistics correctly valued at domestic prices, much of the basis for the determination of comparative costs and of the best utilization of resources disappears.

The trade of countries employing multiple rates in 1952 amounted to less than 15 per cent of the world's total trade. But the use of the national trade statistics of the multiple currency countries for the study of problems that must be approached in terms of national currency figures is lost through the use of multiple currencies. The quantitative importance of the problem is therefore better indicated by the number of multiple currency countries—about 20—than by their importance in world trade.

Free and black market rates. Free rates restricted to specified exports or imports and curb or black market rates used by those who circumvent regulations, are similar to multiple currencies in the problems they create for trade statistics. During the post-war period such rates have existed in several countries whose trade is important in the world aggregate and in which national trade statistics are compiled in national currency. The currencies of some of the countries having free and black market rates are also used in the declaration of values to the Customs authorities of their partner countries. The correct value of the exports and imports of countries having free and black market rates and the correct value of other countries' transactions with them are therefore subject to conversion errors.

Changes in exchange rates.   Probably the most important conversion problems in trade statistics are those that arise from changes in exchange rates, and especially from more or less simultaneous exchange rate adjustments by several countries that have a large trade with each other.   The exchange rate changes of September 1949 involved the currencies of countries whose trade amounted to half the world total, and almost two-thirds of the trade of the devaluing countries was with each other.   The magnitude of the change *vis-à-vis* non-devaluing countries was about 30 per cent for most of the devaluers.   The meaning of trade statistics for the post-war period is importantly affected by these devaluations, by the unequal development of economic events in different countries that in part produced them, and by the economic adjustments that they entailed.

Changes in exchange rates introduce into conversions, and hence into trade statistics, problems of timing.   The change is not likely to occur at the end of the trade statistics accounting period.   Moreover, contracts for purchases and sales, billing dates, and other parts of the procedure of exporting and importing will usually precede by an appreciable and unknown period, and by different periods for each transaction and for the exporting and importing country in the transaction, the dates of shipment or receipt or such other dates as are used in the compilation of the statistics.

More important, however, is the fact that the change raises problems in the meaning of the data.   The interpretation of a value time series requires that price relationships remain reasonably stable and that the amount and direction of changes be more or less known.   But it is the object of a devaluation to change the relation of domestic to foreign prices.   Ordinarily it is hoped by those who make the decision that the national currency prices of the export and domestic products of the devaluing country will remain roughly as they are, that the change in the relation of domestic prices to import prices will be more or less equal to the change in the exchange rate in order to curtail imports, and that the change in the prices of other countries' domestic or competitive goods when measured in the national currency of the devaluing country will also be more or less equal to the change in the exchange rate in order to stimulate the devaluing country's exports.   But to the extent that the devaluation of any currency brings about a rise in domestic prices or a fall in foreign prices, the interpretation of all countries' trade data over the hiatus of the devaluation is difficult whether the data are expressed in national currency or in foreign currency.

The devaluations of September 1949 made the interpretation of trade data especially difficult since on the average almost two-thirds of the trade of the devaluing countries was with each other.   Hence the devaluations not only changed the relation of domestic and export prices to import prices, but changed price relationships among the import commodities. For most of the devaluing countries the value of exports measured in dollars fell sharply in the first months after the devaluation; measured in their national currencies, exports increased appreciably; and measured in the weighted average of the currencies of their customer countries (a rough measure of the import purchasing power of exports), some rose and some fell.

CONVERSION PRACTICES IN THE COMPILATION OF NATIONAL STATISTICS

Introduction. To describe the practices used by countries in the compilation of national statistics, the classification of currency systems into single currency systems and multiple currency systems is again useful. All single currency countries whose currency is convertible and those whose currency, although not convertible, is bought or sold on the home market at only the official rate, constitute one class of countries. All multiple currency countries, and those which in effect have more than one rate by permitting some transactions with inconvertible currency countries to take place at disparate cross rates, constitute a second class of countries.

Single currency countries. Most of the countries of the world have single currencies maintained at a fixed parity over a considerable period and with cross rates conforming to the generally recognized parities of all countries.   Most such countries prescribe rules for the conversion of foreign currency values into national currency either for the use of the trader in making a declaration in national currency or for the use of the Customs authorities in converting declarations received in foreign currencies.   In some cases the rules are the source of minor errors in trade statistics, since, in the interests of simpler administration, of limiting requests for information to items that traders can best be expected to know and whose accuracy the authorities can most readily ascertain, or of protecting the procedures for the collection of Customs duties, the rules sometimes have the effect of specifying that the conversion rate used shall be one that is not appropriate to the transaction. (See, for example, the discussion of Mexico's valuation of metal exports in Chapter 5.) On the whole, however, the errors arising from the rules are of little importance to their statistics, for in the absence of broken cross rates, multiple currencies, and other exchange rate anomalies it is possible and rational to aggregate exports and imports by making such conversions as are necessary at official rates.

This means, of course, that countries with inconvertible currencies that are bought and sold in some foreign markets at a discount nevertheless value all currencies for which conversions are necessary at the official rate. It is possible under some circumstances for importers in, say, the United States to acquire inconvertible currencies at a discount and use them to buy imports from the country in question. But such transactions are very minor exceptions and not the rule. If the exporting country should know the facts and value the export in its national statistics at less than the official rate, this action would involve calling a unit of its currency less than a unit of its currency, and it would involve saying that identical export commodities sold in the same market at the same time represented different amounts of national currency. Similar difficulties would be involved in attempting, in the compilation of international tables in terms of dollars, to single out such transactions and convert them at the discounted rate. The problem of such transactions is both better and more easily solved by recognizing that amounts of such currencies bought at a discount were at the same time sold at a discount and that the loss of foreign exchange involved is more rationally attributed to the transaction giving rise to the sale than to the import purchased by the buyer. Indeed, the loss of foreign exchange through the capital transaction that would probably have been the origin of the sale of the currency at a discount can just as readily be a loss to any foreign holder of capital in the country in question as to a domestic holder.

For the single currency countries the procedures followed in the conversion of trade documents submitted in foreign currencies can be summarized as follows:

Currency of declaration. Most such countries accept declarations in either national currency or the currency of purchase or sale and specify the procedures the trader should use in converting declarations from foreign currency to national currency. Currency of declaration procedures are more commonly specified for imports than for exports since exports are normally reported in national currency and often the national currency value would be the only one known to the exporter. In these cases rules for the compilation of national export statistics in national currency would not be needed and the problem of conversion would arise only in combining the country's data into international tables in a common currency. Some single currency countries, such as Costa Rica and Honduras, require that both import and export declarations be made in dollars and specify the dollar/foreign currency rate that shall be used. Some, on the other hand, may require that all import and export declarations be made in national currency and provide no instructions on conversion. (For example, see description of the United Kingdom practice in Chapter 14.)

Time to which rates used refer. The time to which conversion rates apply (as used by Customs or by traders on instruction from Customs) varies from that ruling at the time license is granted for the import or export (Sweden) to that ruling at the time of import or export clearance of the goods through the national Customs (most Continental European countries). Although the exact reference time is not of great importance except when there are substantial changes in exchange rates, it is significant that most countries use a rate referring to a time substantially later than that in effect at the time the transaction (and the price) was arranged.

Buying and selling rates. Most countries specify either the buying, selling, or mid-point rate for all declarations. Again, although differences between buying and selling rates are not ordinarily of great importance, it is significant that very few countries specify the use of either the buying or selling rate so as to make the rate used for each transaction as nearly as possible appropriate to the transaction.

Multiple currency countries. For multiple currency countries the problems are more difficult and in some cases the procedures are not known. Inasmuch as multiple currency countries do not accept their own currencies in payment for exports almost all transactions would be effected in foreign currencies and require conversion for reporting and statistical purposes. Hence difficulties arising from the inappropriateness of rules would tend to be more numerous than in single currency countries and, since multiple currency systems are by nature complicated, their difficulties would tend to be more serious. Moreover, since multiple currency systems have by definition more rates, any one rate tends to change more frequently than the rates of single currency countries, thereby introducing further sources of difficulty.

The procedures, as far as known, of some multiple currency countries can best be described country by country:

Chile. Trade data are published in terms of the " gold peso," an artificial unit representing a fixed fraction of the United States dollar. Imports are required to be declared in foreign currency and are converted into gold pesos at the fixed relationship between the gold peso and the United States dollar and the parity relationships between foreign currencies and the dollar. Such minor exports as are declared in pesos are converted from paper pesos to dollars at the paper peso/dollar " market rate " and then to gold pesos. What is meant by the " market rate " is not known.

Colombia. Trade data are published in national currency. The procedures for exports are unknown. Imports are required to be declared in foreign currency and are converted to national currency at the official rate of the preceding month. Import statistics can therefore be converted into dollars, but they cannot be properly related to domestic statistics.

Indonesia. Trade data are published in national currency. Trade values, both exports and imports, are reported to Customs in foreign currencies and converted to national currency, by Customs, at the official rate.

Iran. Data are reported in national currency. Exports are reported in national currency on the basis of wholesale prices in local markets. Imports are required to be declared in foreign currencies and are converted into national currency at the official rate ruling at time shipping documents were negotiated. Hence, export data provide statistics comparable to domestic statistics and import data provide statistics comparable to international statistics.

Italy (1946–1947 when multiple rates were employed). Data reported in foreign currencies were converted by Customs to United States dollars on the basis of the foreign currency/United States dollar rate of exchange and then to lira on the basis of the " average " lira/dollar rate. The " average " rate was the average between the official rate and the free rate.

Peru (when multiple rates were in effect). Data were published in national currency. Export and import data were intended to represent the national currency equivalent of foreign exchange received or paid, with foreign currency declarations converted at rates applicable to the transaction. Conversion to United States dollars can only be approximated by applying data on the values of trade effected at the various rates.

Thailand. Data are published in national currency. Exports of rice and tin are required to be declared in foreign currency and are converted to national currency at the official rate. All other exports are declared in national currency. Imports are required to be declared in foreign currency and are converted into national currency at the official rate if Customs believes the declared values are reliable. Otherwise, values obtained from local wholesale prices are substituted. Conversion to United States dollars can only be approximated by using data on the exports of rice, tin, and all other commodities.

Uruguay. Data are published in United States dollars. All exports and imports are required to be reported in foreign currencies. These are converted by Customs into United States dollars at official cross rates. There is no basis for the calculation of trade statistics that would be comparable to national statistics.

Venezuela. Data are published in national currency. Exports, in exporters' declarations, are expressed in national currency in accordance with nominal values issued monthly for specific goods by Customs. Imports are required to be declared in foreign currency. These are converted by Customs at the official rate for the month preceding that in which the goods arrive.

CONVERSION PROCEDURES IN INTERNATIONAL COMPARISONS

Basic trade data are reported in most countries in terms of several currencies and are converted by their Customs or statistics authorities into data in national currency. A considerable part of the basic data becomes available to countries expressed in dollars. It follows that if all the original data were expressed in dollars or in other currencies at proper cross rates the correct reconversion of these data into international tables expressed in dollars requires that the conversion made by the national Customs or statistics authorities be reversed. This is the basic principle that the International Monetary Fund has attempted to follow in making trade conversion factors for its own use and for the use of the United Nations. A table of these conversion factors is published each month in the joint Fund, International Bank, United Nations publication *Direction of International Trade*.

Briefly the International Monetary Fund's procedures can be summarized as follows:

1. For countries with single and relatively fixed buying and selling rates of exchange with a spread of 2 per cent or less between the buying and selling rates, the following conversion factors are used:

    a The par value—for all Fund members for whom par values have been agreed upon.

    b The legal rate—for Fund members not having an agreed par value and for non-member countries, if a legal or official basic rate is in effect.

    c The midpoint between the official buying and selling rates—used if the conversion factor cannot be determined under either a or b.

2. For countries employing a single fluctuating rate of exchange. In all such cases an attempt is made to determine what the Customs Department procedure is in the original compilation of trade data. Usually one of two procedures is followed by Customs, and the Fund's procedure would accordingly be:

    a Application of a constant factor corresponding to that employed by the Customs Department.

    b Application of a factor determined monthly on the basis of the rate of exchange prevailing during the month.

3. For countries employing *multiple* rates of exchange:

    a If it is known that Customs officials compile trade data on the basis of a selected rate (either one of the existing exchange rates or a rate determined solely for trade conversion purposes), the equivalent of this factor is used.

  b If it is known that Customs officials use more than one rate in compiling trade statistics, the average rate used is either obtained from the countries concerned, or is calculated, within the limits of practicality, by weighting each rate by the portion of trade taking place at that rate.

  c In a few cases it is not known whether Customs officials follow method a or b. In these cases correspondence on the question is continuing and the present factors must be considered to be tentative.

4. Dates of applicability of changes. In the event of a change in a fixed rate or a change in a multiple currency system the old factors are applied to the data for the entire month in which the change occurred or, if the change occurs very late in a month, to the whole of the succeeding month, except in the instances in which information from the Customs officials indicates that a different procedure should be followed. In the case of fluctuating rates, the changes from month to month are not likely to be large enough to make it worthwhile to recognize the lag between the current rate and the trade to which it refers.

CONCLUSION

Exchange conversion is inherent in trade statistics and adds appreciably to the difficulty of constructing useful national and international trade statistics and to the possibility of using them to provide the information they should be able to give. For single currency countries these problems are not very serious. For multiple currency countries and countries in which important cross rates are broken they are sufficiently serious to deprive all those who need the data—including the government of the multiple currency country—of reliable information on either or both the foreign exchange and domestic income aspects of foreign trade. When the value of the unit of account is different for different purposes no one can know the true amount of any aggregate.

CHAPTER 7

Country Classification

U.S. Tariff Commission

INTRODUCTION

One of the most common criticisms of foreign trade statistics is that the data published by a given exporting country for its shipments to a given importing country often differ materially from the data given by the importing country for its trade with the exporting country. The disparities are sometimes very great. To the layman they seem inexplicable and cause distrust of foreign trade statistics generally. These disparities relate both to the total value of trade in all commodities and to the quantity and value of the trade in many individual commodities.

There are several causes for these disparities between the statistics of exporting and of importing countries. The most important are:

a Differences between the countries with respect to which of the three basic methods (described below) they adopt for showing the " provenance " of imports (to use a convenient technical term) and the destination of exports.[1] Discussion of this subject occupies the greater part of the present chapter.

b Differences in the detailed definitions used in connection with a given method, even if both countries apply the same basic method.

c Differences in methods of valuation (Chapter 5) and exchange conversion (Chapter 6).

---

[1] The French word *provenance*, which has come to be rather commonly used by economists and statisticians in English-speaking countries, may be conveniently used as a general term with respect to imports, whichever of the three basic methods for reporting imports is used. It is broader than such words as " source " or " origin." Similarly the term *destination*, not qualified by any adjective, may be conveniently used as regards exports, whichever of the three methods of reporting is employed.

d Differences as regards the coverage of the statistics (Chapter 3) and the definition of certain individual commodities (Chapter 4).

e Inability (sometimes unwillingness) of importers, and still more of exporters, to furnish accurate information; it is usually more difficult to furnish correct data as to destination of exports than as to provenance of imports.

The factors mentioned under *a* and *e* above tend to cause special difficulty with respect to statistics of the trade with land-locked countries such as Switzerland, Czechoslovakia, Bolivia, and Rhodesia, the larger part of the trade of which necessarily moves through neighboring countries. Exporters of goods which may ultimately go to a land-locked country often do not know the final destination, and report as the destination some intermediate country from which they are later reshipped. Importers are much more likely to know the true source of the goods they bring in. The difficulty arising from this cause is almost as serious with respect to countries which are not strictly land-locked, such as Poland, but which in fact conduct a great part of their trade through other countries.

A striking illustration of this difficulty as to trade with land-locked countries is furnished by the statistics of the United States and Switzerland. During the 1930 decade the imports from the United States reported in the Swiss statistics were usually several times greater than the exports to Switzerland reported in United States statistics. Many goods shipped from the United States which ultimately reached Switzerland were credited in United States statistics as exported to Germany, the Netherlands, Belgium, France, or Italy. The disparities were more marked in pre-war than in post-war years.

The differences in definitions referred to in point *b* above may be most conveniently discussed in connection with the subsequent discussion of the three basic methods of reporting provenance and destination. The general subjects of methods of valuation of imports and exports referred to under *c* and the coverage of the statistics and the classification of commodities (point *d* above) are mentioned here only because differences in these respects contribute to the disparities between the trade statistics of exporting and of importing countries. In particular, discrepancies between the statistics of pairs of countries may be due to differences in the handling of in-transit shipments as described in Chapter 3.

The disparities between trade statistics of exporting and importing countries should not lead to the conclusion that statistics of total exports or total imports of individual countries, either as to all commodities or as to individual articles, are equally unreliable. The apparent trustworthiness of the grand totals for the several countries is indicated (not, of course, demonstrated) by the data as to total world trade compiled by the

League of Nations (*The Network of World Trade*, Geneva, 1942). In 1928, for example, imports into all countries were reported as $35·5 thousand million and exports from all countries as $32·6 thousand million, a difference of about 9 per cent. In 1938, the corresponding figures were $24·6 thousand million for imports and $21·9 thousand million for exports, a difference of about 12 per cent. The excess of imports over exports is largely explained by the fact that many if not most countries include in the value of imports transportation and insurance charges to ports of importation, but do not (as would be very difficult to do) include in export values transportation and insurance charges to ports of destination.

Statistics as to the provenance of imports and the destination of exports are needed for a number of important purposes. They are essential to any broad grasp of world economics. More specifically, such data are one of the major bases for knowledge of economic geography—of the areas where goods are produced and where they are consumed and of the movements from surplus to deficit areas. Consideration of the problems of international balances of payments, which have become of major importance in national and international policy, requires a broad knowledge of the value of the goods which each country receives from, and sends to, each other country. Moreover, as more fully set forth in a subsequent section, the trade policies of each country—as to such matters as tariffs, preferences, and the imposition and allocation of quantitative restrictions on trade—are necessarily based largely on the statistics of trade according to provenance and destination.

Because of the recognized importance of trade statistics from these points of view, nearly all countries of the world have long maintained elaborate trade statistics. These statistics, however, leave much to be desired as to accuracy, in some cases as to fullness, and often as to promptness of publication. Although other aspects of trade statistics also need much improvement, the greatest need is perhaps in the field of provenance of imports and destination of exports.

Whatever method of reporting provenance and destination is employed, the technical difficulties of obtaining satisfactory data are serious. The basic documents used by the government agencies compiling the statistics are declarations by the importers and the exporters. Often the forms used do not even call for some of the information needed for satisfactory trade statistics. Still more often the person filling out these forms (who frequently is not the actual importer or exporter but his agent or his clerk, sometimes a mere office boy) fails to exercise adequate care. Occasionally the facts are deliberately misrepresented. These basic declarations often are, and certainly more generally ought to be, supported by more detailed documents such as commercial invoices, invoices certified by consular offices, bills of lading, etc. Apart from the burden on the government authorities in thorough examination of such supplementary documents, the interested parties sometimes object to furnishing them or furnish them in inadequate or incorrect form.

The principal trading countries of the world are fully aware of the importance of accurate statistics as to provenance and destination of trade. They are constantly making efforts to improve their trade statistics. They often make detailed studies of particular cases where the statistics on their face do not appear to show the true movements of trade. The United States has been very active in this direction; its special inquiries have resulted in much valuable information and in material clarification of the problems involved in the attempt to show provenance of imports and destination of exports. Its data of trade by countries have been much more trustworthy since than before the war.

International efforts to improve trade statistics as regards provenance and destination have also been important. At the conference leading to the International Convention Relating to Economic Statistics (Geneva, 1928) this subject was extensively discussed, and important provisions regarding it were included in the International Convention which resulted. The Committee of Statistical Experts set up under the League of Nations to aid in carrying out the provisions of that Convention gave several years of study to methods of reporting provenance and destination of trade. The Statistical Commission of the United Nations has begun work in this field.

METHODS OF REPORTING PROVENANCE AND DESTINATION OF TRADE

Three basic methods. Notwithstanding general recognition of the importance of lessening the disparities between the statistics of exporting and of importing countries, no uniformity has been achieved among the countries with regard to the basic methods of reporting provenance and destination of trade. Some changes which tend toward greater uniformity have indeed been made by a number of countries. It is improbable, however, that all the countries will in any foreseeable future time agree to a single method of reporting.

There are three basic methods of reporting provenance and destination; the first two are both widely used, whereas only a few countries use the third method. In brief terms (hereafter set forth in more detail) these methods are:

1. *The production-consumption method.* Under this, imports are

credited to the country of primary origin or production, and exports are credited to the country of ultimate consumption.

2. *The consignment method.* Under this, imports are customarily credited to the country from which last directly consigned and exports to the country to which first directly consigned.

3. *The purchase-sale method.* Under this, imports and exports are credited to the country with which the financial transaction of purchase or sale occurred.

All three of these methods have advantages. All three involve practical difficulties. The International Conference on Economic Statistics (Geneva, 1928) recognized the merits of all three. It stated that it would be advantageous if each country could use all three methods at the same time, but it added that this would be very expensive and that it could hardly be expected that any country would employ all three or that any considerable number would employ more than one method. The Conference refrained from expressing an opinion as to which was the best method. It pointed out that many of the countries were so wedded to their own particular system that they would be unlikely to change it even if considerable international pressure were brought to bear.

As a matter of fact, a good many countries have since the Geneva Conference shifted from the consignment method to the production-consumption method of reporting. This, however, has not been due to any international expression of preference for the latter method, but rather to the needs of internal policy in individual countries. At present, the number of countries which use the production-consumption method is much larger than the number which use the consignment method. The United Kingdom is the most important trading country now using the consignment method; that fact is probably in part attributable to the position of the United Kingdom as a great entrepôt market which reships (directly or indirectly) a large fraction of its imports to third countries.

The International Conference on Economic Statistics provided for an experiment to determine the relative results, in the statistics of the trade of a given country, obtained by applying each of the three methods for reporting provenance and destination of trade. This experiment was conducted by the Committee of Statistical Experts, which published the results in 1933. It requested each signatory country (the United States was not a signatory) to report, as to each of a number of major articles, imports and exports according to each of the three methods. A considerable number of representative countries carried out the experiment with a fair degree of care and completeness. Though the outcome was not altogether conclusive, the experiment seemed to indicate that less disparity between the statistics of exporting and of importing countries arises when the method of consignment is used by both than when the method of production-consumption is used by both, or than when the two use different methods. This is what might be expected. It should be borne in mind, however, that the minimizing of disparities between its own statistics and those of the countries with which it trades is by no means the only motive leading a country to give preference to one method of reporting provenance and destination as compared with another. This point will be better understood by considering the purposes, and the merits and demerits, of the several methods, as is done in the following sections.

Production-consumption method. The definition laid down in the International Convention Relating to Economic Statistics as to the method of reporting trade according to " country of origin or production and country of consumption " are as follows:

The expression " country of origin or production " shall mean, in the case of natural products, the country where the goods were produced, and, in the case of manufactured products, the country where they were transformed into the condition in which they were introduced into the country of import, it being understood that repacking, sorting, and blending do not constitute transformation.

The expression " country of consumption " shall mean the country in which the goods will be put to the use for which they were produced, or in which they will undergo a process of transformation, repair, or supplementary treatment, it being understood that repacking, sorting, and blending do not constitute transformation or supplementary treatment.

These definitions are substantially those set forth by the United States Department of Commerce in its instructions to exporters and importers.

It is evident that the conception of country of origin or production is usually definite enough in the case of natural products, but may often not be so in the case of manufactured products. Differences of opinion may exist not merely among individuals in the same country but among the statistical authorities of different countries as to the extent to which an article must be processed in a country in order to make it a product of that country. However, for most countries this difficulty is not one of major importance in affecting the accuracy of trade statistics. Concerning this complex problem much has been written in official publications, both of an international and of a national character, as well as in unofficial publications.

Of the three methods of reporting statistics of provenance and destination of trade, the production-consumption method is on its face the most logical. To most persons in fact it appeals as being the only appropriate method for meeting the various goals mentioned above. It furnishes the broadest picture of world economic geography. It is on the whole the method best adapted to an understanding of international balances of payment—though it needs much supplementation by other sources of information. Still more important is the fact that the system of production-consumption reporting for imports and exports has great advantages from the standpoint of the determination and administration of commercial policy.

For this latter purpose each country needs to know as accurately as possible the ultimate sources of its imports; statistics as to destination of its exports are considerably less essential from this point of view, though of no little importance. For example, in negotiating a treaty or agreement as to tariff rates, the country needs to know what part of its imports of each commodity considered for a possible concession come from the partner country in the negotiations, as compared with the imports from other countries. The United States, for example, in negotiating for reductions in its tariff lays great emphasis on the " principal-supplier rule," seeking ordinarily to grant a concession (which under United States practice will be generalized to all countries) only if the partner country is the principal source of imports, or at least a major source. Again, where, as is the widespread practice in the British Commonwealth of Nations, there are preferential rates of duty, it is obviously essential that the importing country should know what goods actually originate in the countries entitled to preferred treatment. Moreover, in the many cases in which countries impose quantitative restrictions on imports and allocate the permissible totals among different sources of supply, it is essential that the reports as to the imports from each supplying country shall be as accurate as possible. Certain international agreements as to allocation of commodities in short supply, or as to limitation of exports of strategic articles to certain countries, also require accurate data regarding trade by countries of provenance and destination.

Broadly speaking, during the pre-war decade, and during the period since the end of World War II, most nations have increasingly adopted policies and practices as to control of imports which cannot be satisfactorily decided upon, or satisfactorily administered, without reliable statistics as to the ultimate sources of imports. It is chiefly for this reason that a considerable number of countries which formerly employed the consignment method for reporting trade statistics have shifted to the production-consumption method.

The technical difficulties involved in ascertaining the true country of origin or production of imports, even of natural products, are in certain cases serious. Imports, however, present much less grave problems than those which arise in determining the country of consumption of exports. Importers can usually, though by no means always, ascertain fairly accurately the true primary origin of the goods they import, even if they have passed through other countries en route. Exporters often simply do not know the final destination of the goods they ship (in some cases there is also unwillingness to disclose the facts). Sometimes an export is to a free port, from which the goods are expected to go ultimately either to the country in which the port is situated or to other countries. Sometimes goods are shipped " for orders " en route. Sometimes the destination is changed before the goods are landed.

The Committee of Statistical Experts of the League of Nations, considering all these conditions, reached the conclusion that in countries using the production-consumption method of reporting trade statistics there is little possibility of material improvement in the accuracy of the returns as to exports. On the other hand, it believed that the returns on imports could be materially improved, and that greater use should be made of them.

The Committee of Statistical Experts accordingly undertook to obtain from each importing country—including not only those which already used the method of reporting imports according to country of origin or production but also those using the consignment method and those using the purchase-sale method—special reports as to the actual primary origin of their imports of a selected list of major commodities. It was expected that countries already using the origin-or-production method as to imports would exercise special care in reporting on these selected articles. Most of the commodities in this list were foodstuffs and raw or semi-manufactured materials, but a few were finished articles. The Committee believed that by combining imports of these items as reported by all the countries, according to countries of origin, it would be possible to determine with a large measure of accuracy the final destinations of the exports of these articles from each of the producing countries—information often not obtainable otherwise.

For several years before the outbreak of World War II put an end to the activities of the League of Nations, the Secretariat of the League published the statistics for this list of articles compiled in the manner described. The results were reasonably satisfactory, and the statistics proved of much utility. The system has not yet been reestablished (1952).

Since it is more difficult to show correctly country of consumption of exports than country of origin or production of imports, the statistics of two countries, both of which use the production-consumption method, often conflict both as to total values of trade between them and as to trade in individual commodities. The reported exports from country A to country B may be materially out of line with the reported imports of country B from country A. It is because of these unavoidable discrepancies that the Committee of Statistical Experts of the League of Nations sought to make data regarding imports the basic material for general analysis of world trade in major individual commodities.

Method of consignment. In the International Convention Relating to Economic Statistics the definitions of the country of consignment for the purpose of trade statistics are set forth as follows:

The expression " country of consignment or provenance " shall mean the country from which the goods were originally despatched to the country of import, with or without breaking bulk in the course of transport, but without any commercial transaction in the intermediate countries (if any).

The expression " country of consignment or destination " shall mean the country to which the goods were actually despatched, with or without breaking bulk in the course of transport, but without any commercial transaction in the intermediate countries (if any).

The Committee of Statistical Experts of the League of Nations, in analyzing the results of the experiment regarding methods of reporting provenance and destination of trade to which attention has already been called, stated that objection had been made to the above definitions of consignment because of the apparent conflict between the phrase " originally despatched " in the first paragraph and the phrase " actually despatched " in the second paragraph. The Committee also noted that the use of the phrase " originally despatched " in the first paragraph tended to cause confusion as to the difference between the method of consignment and the method of production-consumption, which calls, in the case of imports, for the " country of origin or production." These defects in the definitions, if they are defects, have not been remedied by any subsequent international action. Presumably each country using the consignment method has continued substantially to follow its own previous practice in defining both the country from which imports are consigned and the country to which exports are consigned. Presumably also the intent of the countries using this system is ordinarily to show for imports the country from which they were last despatched and for exports the country to which they are first despatched. This does not mean, of course, that imports should be, or are, credited to the last country from which they have physically departed, or exports credited to the first country which they will reach physically. Movements in both directions may be on through bills of lading and may pass through another country, or two or more other countries, en route.

The method of reporting trade statistics according to country of consignment has the great advantage of simplicity. Importers and exporters alike are usually able to furnish the information with little difficulty, and this information can be relied upon fairly well, especially if their declarations are supported by invoices or bills of lading. Such statistics present a picture of the immediate, as distinguished from the ultimate, trade relations between different countries. Information on this basis is of particular interest to merchants and distributors of the goods entering into international trade, and to transport companies. As already stated, the United Kingdom uses this system perhaps chiefly by reason of its complex trade relations as an entrepôt; some of the other countries which use it also have an important entrepôt trade.

Obviously, however, as regards most of the major goals of statistics of provenance and destination the consignment method of reporting is not as satisfactory as the production-consumption method.

Purchase-sale method. The International Convention Relating to Economic Statistics defines country of purchase as the country in which the seller of the goods " carries on his business " (usually the country in which he resides), and conversely defines the country of sale. These definitions are clear enough, except in the rather numerous cases where transactions are conducted by agents rather than by principals. The Customs authorities in the few countries employing this system express the belief that it yields particularly useful results from the point of view of balances of payments, but the correctness of that opinion is contested both by some of their own citizens and by experts in other countries. The purchase-sale system does not, of course, attempt to reflect the actual physical movement of goods, but merely the financial relations involved. Although, when not unduly complicated by agency relationships, the system is satisfactory enough with regard to direct transactions of purchase or sale, the many transactions of a triangular or multiangular character cannot be satisfactorily described or analyzed by this method—or for that matter by any other single method of reporting provenance and destination.

DEFINITIONS OF COUNTRIES AND GROUPING OF COUNTRIES

In order that the statistics of different countries regarding provenance of imports and destination of exports may be comparable, it is important that the several reporting countries should define the countries with which they trade in a standardized manner. For most countries definitions of boundaries are simple enough, although complications inevitably arise when boundaries are changed as the result of war or other causes. In some cases, however, it is difficult to determine precisely what areas should be included with a given country. For instance, is Puerto Rico a part of the United States or not? Are the Channel Islands a part of the United Kingdom or not? Is Algeria a part of France or not? It is better in such instances to present more rather than less detail than is needed.

The Committee of Statistical Experts of the League of Nations, carrying out a provision of the International Convention Relating to Economic Statistics, prepared and published a list of countries for trade statistics, including a grouping by continents. For the most part this list is rather generally utilized in actual trade statistics, although a country often presents the data with a more detailed breakdown of countries than is required by the standard list.

In recognition that this League of Nations list of countries has become out of date, the United Nations Statistical Office proposed in 1951 a somewhat different approach to the problem of achieving comparability of definition of countries in trade statistics. It proposed that each government use as the definition of each of its trade partners the Customs area of that partner as defined by the partner. The definition of a country's Customs area would be determined not by an international organization but by the individual country itself, which might, of course, change the definition from time to time. The international organization would then merely become a clearing office for the country definitions rather than a promulgator of definitions.

In line with this objective, the United Nations Statistical Office has prepared a draft description of the Customs areas of the world based on official information available to it in February 1951 (E/CN.3/127— 7 March, 1951). It is apparent from this document that the operation of this proposed procedure would not be altogether simple. For example, difficulty would probably be experienced with United States naval bases in a number of areas of the world—Cuba, Jamaica, Philippines, etc. The document itself points out a number of cases where the Customs area is not coterminous with the area of political control; for example, the Channel Islands are not part of the Customs area but are a part of the political area of the United Kingdom; although the volume of trade of most of such areas is relatively unimportant, it would seem necessary that guidance be provided regarding them.

One difficulty experienced in adopting any standard international definition of countries lies in the reluctance of some countries to accept a definition of the Customs area of another country which may not reflect their own belief as to what are, or should be, the political boundaries of the country. An illustration is the current practice of the United States of providing for separate country classification of its trade with Estonia, Latvia, and Lithuania, three areas which, in the United Nations Statistical Office draft description of Customs areas, are included within the Union of Soviet Socialist Republics. The United States recognizes each of these areas as a country separate from the USSR, and each maintains a legation in the United States.

In the statistics of any country regarding the total value of its imports and exports, it is important to show all individual countries (each being properly defined), and also to group them in some logical manner. Countries should obviously be grouped by continents.[2] It is advantageous also to divide the continents, or at least some of them, into great economic regions.[3]

The British countries very naturally distinguish between their trade with Commonwealth countries and their trade with non-British countries. Other countries with important colonial possessions or affiliated empire countries also tend to distinguish between the trade with them and the trade with third countries. (See Chapter 9 for discussion of the grouping of countries into currency areas for balance of payments purposes.)

Quite different is the question how countries, or groups of countries, should be shown in the statistics of the trade in individual commodities. Though with modern methods of machine tabulation by cards it is possible, at relatively low cost, to group countries as regards each commodity in any way desired, the expense of publishing the results in this fashion may make it hardly worth while to add the trade statistics for individual commodities by continents or subcontinents, except for a limited number of commodities where the trade is widely distributed geographically. It may be noted that for most articles the sources of imports are relatively few in number, whereas for many export articles the countries of destination are numerous.

Where individual commodities are shown in trade statistics according to country of provenance of imports or country of destination of exports, the order in which the countries are listed must be to some extent dependent on the actual facts of importation and exportation, as well as upon the costs of compiling and publishing the data. Listing according to magnitude is undesirable. In some cases alphabetical listing of the countries is satisfactory enough. In other cases it is preferable to arrange the names of the individual countries according to continents, even if combined totals of trade by continents are not shown. There can be no objection to saving costs of tabulation, and more particularly costs of printing, by grouping minor figures under the heading " all other countries."[4] The

---

[2] The position of the Soviet Union, which is situated both in Europe and Asia, is a special one; since the greater part of the population and industry are in Europe, the Soviet Union is usually classified in trade statistics as a European country. A similar but much less important problem arises regarding Turkey, which is usually classified as an Asiatic country.

[3] It is particularly important in the case of North America to distinguish, a northern North America substantially Canada, b the United States, and c southern North America. The trade of Canada and the United States is radically different from that of southern North America, which more closely resembles the trade of South America.

[4] It sometimes happens that where a very small quantity of imports or of exports is credited to a given country, this is the result of an out-and-out error in classification.

question which figures are minor obviously depends not on their absolute magnitude but on the proportion which they constitute of the total imports or exports of the given commodity.

CONCLUSION

In the reported statistics of trade between two countries the statistics of the one country as to its exports to the other often differ materially from the statistics of the other country regarding its imports. Various causes contribute to these disparities, one of the most important being differences between the two countries as to the basic methods of geographic assignment of trade. There are three principal methods: *a* the production-consumption method; *b* the consignment method; and *c* the purchase-sale method. The first method, that of reporting imports according to the original country of production and exports according to the ultimate country of consumption, has become increasingly prevalent, but many countries still report trade according to the country of consignment, and some according to the country where the financial transaction takes place. It is easier for importers to determine the original source of the goods they bring in than for exporters to determine the final destination of the goods they send out. Some progress has been made in eliminating disparities in trade statistics, but it is improbable that they will be by any means completely eliminated.

The disparity in trade statistics as between pairs of countries should not cast undue doubt on the accuracy of the statistics of the total trade of the several countries, either as to all commodities combined or as to individual commodities.

CHAPTER 8

Publication and Use of National Statistics

PATRICK J. LOFTUS
United Nations Statistical Office

INTRODUCTION

National publications must serve many purposes. They must present summary information for the general user and detailed data for the specialist and for those interested in trade in particular commodities and with particular countries. They must be useful alike to the administrator and to the businessman or economist. They must throw light on the features of the external trade of the country which are most relevant to domestic problems, and they must also be of use to those in other countries and in international organizations who have broader and different interests.

Most countries publish a monthly account in more or less summary form, together with a more detailed annual account, of their external trade. Some combine the two objects, with some success, in one series of monthly publications in which the December issue serves as an annual statement. A few countries (*e.g.*, Burma) also issue daily lists of important consignments. There is considerable variety in the form of publications and this chapter will attempt to describe the main variants and their uses.

A list of the regular trade publications of countries which now issue statistics of their external trade is given in the Appendix to this volume.

It may not be completely exhaustive, even of publications which are both current and regular; it comprises only primary sources available in the Statistical Office of the United Nations in 1952. Practically all the publications listed can be readily obtained from the issuing country, and they are generally available in national statistical offices and in the more important libraries.

AGGREGATE STATISTICS

Aggregate tables. In the national publications, the highest level of summarization is contained in the aggregate tables. These show, for each category of trade (*e.g.*, imports, exports, re-exports), the value of the transactions during the current period as compared with that of previous periods. Table 1 contains the United Kingdom aggregate figures as

Table 1

United Kingdom: Aggregate Monthly Table
(In thousands of pounds. Source table shows value in pounds without rounding)

Month	Imports			Exports, United Kingdom Goods		
	1948	1949	1950	1948	1949	1950
January	161,901	186,983	201,168	119,559	159,232	175,910
February	148,110	161,978	181,657	112,927	140,732	155,756
March	178,077	189,766	221,293	120,985	159,964	184,397
April	185,057	187,709	211,375	126,434	137,406	149,877
May	175,800	195,684	228,724	129,966	151,429	182,569
June	177,170	202,636	238,571	134,163	143,265	175,843
July	185,634	186,953	225,231	146,015	141,844	182,258
August	173,357	200,792	215,199	130,945	137,141	189,452
September	169,485	181,650	193,916	131,411	142,019	171,406
October	174,650	199,099	223,003	140,259	156,066	202,189
November	181,602	201,051	234,927	147,133	160,395	211,839
December	178,006	196,015	239,290	145,783	153,849	188,886
Corrected total for year	2,078,040	2,274,138	*2,602,945	1,582,867	1,786,083	*2,170,085

Month	Exports, Imported Merchandise			Total Exports		
	1948	1949	1950	1948	1949	1950
January	5,362	5,090	5,771	124,921	164,322	181,681
February	3,875	4,349	5,273	116,802	145,082	161,030
March	6,102	5,898	6,742	127,088	165,862	191,139
April	5,264	5,535	5,810	131,698	142,941	155,687
May	5,602	5,585	5,806	135,569	157,015	188,375
June	4,685	4,254	6,192	138,849	147,519	182,036
July	6,450	4,112	6,152	152,465	145,957	188,411
August	4,049	4,194	7,450	134,994	141,336	196,902
September	5,125	3,537	9,125	136,536	145,556	180,531
October	5,348	5,238	9,368	145,607	161,304	211,557
November	5,134	5,938	10,266	152,268	166,334	222,105
December	6,356	4,692	7,256	152,140	158,542	196,142
Corrected total for year	63,627	58,049	*84,962	1,646,495	1,844,133	*2,255,048

The monthly totals are revised when full information as to dutiable imports is available, and corrections are made in the total for each year on the completion of the " Annual Statement of Trade."
Source: Accounts Relating to Trade and Navigation of the United Kingdom, December 1950.
* Uncorrected figures.

published in its account for December 1950. It will be seen that comparable data are given for earlier months back to January 1948. The chief use of these data is to provide information on the relation between total imports and total exports. In the case of the United Kingdom it is necessary to subtract exports of imported merchandise from imports in order to obtain aggregate " imports retained in the United Kingdom." The balance of merchandise trade is obtained by subtracting total exports from total imports. Fluctuations in these aggregates are, of course, indicative of general business conditions.

Readers who are interested in the aggregates for a number of countries at the same time will find it convenient to obtain them from the United Nations *Monthly Bulletin of Statistics*, which shows these figures for all countries which publish them. Table 2 shows a portion of the foreign trade table from the United Nations *Monthly Bulletin*, giving data for certain countries as reported by those countries. In other United Nations publications, the data are further summarized, for easy reference, into figures expressed in millions of United States dollars with one or two decimal places.

Aggregates by countries. The second common feature of the national publications is the table of aggregates of trade with each partner country. These tables show the value of imports according to the countries from which they originated (or were consigned or purchased, as the case may be) and the value of exports to each country to which they were destined (or consigned or sold, as the case may be). Reference should be made to Chapters 5, 6, and 7 concerning the practices of the different countries in the matter of valuation and methods of attributing trade to partner countries. These tables show the multilateral nature of international trade, indicating how surpluses in the transactions with some partners are offset by deficits with other partners. Tables 3 and 4 show summarized data of this kind published by France and Switzerland. In both tables the countries of origin and destination are arranged in an order based on continental divisions; France publishes subtotals for continents, whereas Switzerland does not. Another contrast is that the French data cover the portion of the year up to the month of publication (*i.e.*, January–July 1950), whereas the Swiss data cover only the month of publication (*i.e.*, October 1950).

More important, however, than these differences of presentation are the less obvious differences in content. In Chapter 7, reference is made to the fact that the Customs area of a country may differ from the political area usually covered by the country name. Thus the United States Customs area includes Alaska, Puerto Rico, and Hawaii, which are not states of the Union. United States trade statistics, therefore, include the

Table 2

External Trade: Value of Imports and Exports (Millions)

Monthly averages or calendar months

Year and Month	Turkey Turquie		Union of South Africa Afrique du Sud.		United Kingdom Royaume-Uni		
	Imports Special	Exports Special	Imports General	Exports General	Imports General	Exports	
						General	Re-exports
	£ (T)		£ (S.A.)		£		
1937. . .	9·5	11·5	8·61	3·54	85·7	49·7	6·2
1938. . .	12·5	12·1	7·97	2·71	76·6	44·4	5·1
1939. . .	9·9	10·6	7·61	2·84	73·8	40·5	3·8
1945. . .	10·5	18·2	9·37	6·46	92·0	37·2	4·2
1946. . .	18·7	36·0	17·87	7·95	108·4	80·5	4·2
1947. . .	57·1	52·0	24·98	8·60	149·5	99·8	4·9
1948. . .	64·2	45·9	29·46	11·40	173·2	137·2	5·3
1949. . .	67·7	57·8	26·27	13·07	189·6	153·7	4·8
1950. . .	66·7	61·5	25·61	20·69	216·9	187·9	7·1
1949							
January. .	66·0	58·4	31·77	12·96	187·0	164·3	5·1
February .	55·8	40·5	26·55	13·33	162·0	145·0	4·3
March . .	60·8	76·6	27·32	12·24	189·8	165·9	5·9
April . .	64·5	57·9	27·54	9·43	187·7	142·9	5·5
May . .	56·8	60·4	26·51	9·46	195·7	157·0	5·6
June . .	75·0	38·3	35·00	11·77	202·6	147·6	4·3
July . .	65·5	30·2	35·25	10·90	187·0	145·9	4·1
August . .	66·2	32·3	24·23	10·19	200·8	141·3	4·2
September .	78·6	36·9	19·47	13·14	181·7	145·5	3·5
October. .	61·7	70·3	22·34	15·53	199·1	161·3	5·2
November .	90·3	89·7	19·91	16·31	201·1	166·3	5·9
December .	71·6	102·5	19·34	21·59	196·0	158·5	4·7
1950							
January. .	50·9	74·3	24·17	16·63	201·5	181·7	5·8
February .	46·8	53·1	14·63	16·19	182·1	161·1	5·3
March . .	56·4	41·8	18·92	18·53	221·6	191·1	6·7
April · . .	51·2	45·5	18·74	13·11	211·5	155·7	5·8
May . .	76·5	47·4	22·54	14·14	228·7	188·4	5·8
June . .	78·1	36·9	29·42	14·33	238·6	182·0	6·2
July . .	66·5	26·2	30·01	21·28	223·9	188·5	6·2
August .	82·3	41·3	29·15	20·34	215·2	197·0	7·5
September .	65·8	60·6	26·88	26·83	193·9	180·5	9·1
October. .	75·9	80·1	30·66	27·37	223·0	211·6	9·4
November .	78·5	112·1	33·77	31·79	234·9	222·1	10·3
December .	70·9	118·2	28·49	27·74	239·3	196·2	7·3

Source: United Nations *Monthly Bulletin of Statistics,* July 1951.

Table 3

Trade of France, by Countries (January–July 1950)

Country	Imports	Exports		Imports	Exports
	Thousand francs			Thousand francs	
EUROPE	194,054,338	252,695,839	ASIA . . (detailed by countries).	70,814,600	17,052,613
Western Germany . .	40,691,772	38,662,137			
Soviet Zone of Germany .	27,355	16,761			
Austria	1,764,701	2,743,997			
Bulgaria	100,903	34,068	AFRICA . (detailed by countries).	31,249,340	16,543,455
Denmark	5,227,443	11,140,453			
Spain	7,970,262	6,351,967			
Finland	4,222,868	4,102,942			
Great Britain . . .	22,909,579	52,932,252	AMERICA . (detailed by countries).	135,519,524	58,993,592
Greece	1,521,283	2,542,837			
Hungary	590,616	689,652			
Ireland	87,278	952,946			
Iceland	28,995	49,074			
Italy	21,275,030	15,772,263			
Norway	3,362,984	9,647,243	OCEANIA . (detailed by countries).	29,841,449	6,136,475
Netherlands . . .	14,981,147	21,417,269			
Poland	2,768,221	4,147,426			
Portugal	1,583,970	2,701,567			
Roumania . . .	9,677	113,825			
Sweden	9,269,781	12,940,317	Total Foreign Countries.	461,479,251	*352,753,903
Switzerland . . .	16,612 261	22,589,978			
Czechoslovakia . .	3,157,502	2,805,160			
Turkey	2,673,812	3,294,045			
Belgium-Luxembourg. .	30,359,157	34,655,338	Total French Countries (detailed by countries).	160,530,678	207,664,726
USSR	926,463	562,531			
Yugoslavia . . .	1,330,885	1,325,658			
Other countries of Europe:					
Cyprus, Gibraltar, Malta.	579,372	365,054	Grand total.	622,009,929	*560,418,629
Others	21,021	138,079			

* Includes ships' stores, 1,331,929 francs.
Source: Statistique Mensuelle du Commerce extérieur de la France.

trade *of* these territories and exclude United States trade *with* them.   The
Geneva Convention, on the other hand, specifies that, in the trade statistics
of its signatories, the term United States should relate to the United States
excluding Alaska and Hawaii.   In the same way, the trade statistics of
France have included the territory of the Saar since April 1948, but in the
trade statistics of Switzerland the Saar is shown as a separate territory.
In Table 4, Switzerland has shown the Saar figure immediately after the
figure for France and it is necessary to add the two figures together to
obtain data relating to the present Customs area of France which can be
compared with the data published by France herself.[1]

The information contained in the table of aggregates by countries has
important uses in economic analysis.   It also forms the basis of bilateral
trade agreements and multilateral payments arrangements.   The continued reduction in the size of the areas within which free convertibility

[1] This matter of uniformity in the specification of Customs areas is being studied by
the United Nations.   The Statistical Commission is expected (1952) to make recommendations designed to improve international comparability in this respect.

Table 4

Trade of Switzerland, by Countries (October 1950)

Country	Imports	Exports
	Francs	Francs
Germany	54,827,550	40,545,351
Austria	6,161,210	8,329,954
France	57,108,691	33,150,860
Saar	4,604,060	247,736
Italy.	28,361,638	64,731,788
Trieste	16,913	463,337
Belgium-Luxembourg . .	26,556,737	29,359,799
Netherlands	13,721,194	9,464,364
Great Britain	35,100,254	11,857,922
Eire	554,351	641,040
Gibraltar, Malta, Cyprus . .	9,428	51,892
Spain	2,962,754	4,406,297
Portugal	3,717,265	3,517,939
Denmark . . . : .	6,553,653	4,423,985
Iceland	28,350	23,981
Norway	1,984,068	1,833,588
Sweden	7,541,646	5,867,234
Finland	1,818,685	1,005,081
Poland	3,170,623	3,250,457
Czechoslovakia	7,483,039	9,324,877
Hungary	3,516,010	3,614,735
Yugoslavia	1,567,809	5,455,780
Greece	1,084,295	592,094
Albania	———	8,987
United States	66,725,990	62,617,638
Other countries * . . .	147,863,714	109,246,171
Total	483,039,927	413,032,887

* This heading covers 86 countries which are separately specified in the source.
Source: Statistique Mensuelle du Commerce extérieur de la Suisse.

of currencies exists has led a number of countries to compile their trade data according to currency areas in addition to the compilations according to political or geographic areas. Thus France presents, in its monthly trade bulletin, an interesting time series of the value of its total exports and imports distinguishing exports to, and imports from, (1) the dollar area; (2) the sterling area; (3) the rest of the world. This kind of information on the direction of trade is of growing importance for analysis of international trade. Users with interests extending beyond individual countries will find very useful data in the international publications, which present these figures for a large number of countries in more comparable form than the national publications.[2]

Aggregates by categories of commodities. The types of aggregate tables described above are published each month by practically every country whose international trade is of any importance. The smaller countries publish these data less frequently and less regularly. Of the large countries which do not publish even these aggregate data, the most notable are the USSR and certain countries of Eastern Europe. Argentina, which suspended publication early in 1948, resumed publication in 1950. In addition to the kinds of aggregate tables mentioned, many countries publish tables of their imports and exports classified into large categories of commodities such as Food, Raw Materials, Manufactures, etc. These tables are extremely useful for the information they provide concerning the structure of trade of the different countries. For certain kinds of users, they present the data in a form which otherwise requires much tedious addition of detailed items. A good example of this kind of presentation is contained in the United Kingdom trade returns, which show data for the following summary categories:

1. Food, drink and tobacco, subdivided into nine important groups;
2. Raw materials and articles mainly unmanufactured, subdivided into 14 important groups;
3. Articles wholly or mainly manufactured, subdivided into 21 important groups.

Further information on the kinds of summary presentation recommended by international bodies (such as the Brussels List, Minimum List, etc.) and used by certain countries are considered in Chapter 12. *See also* Chapter 4.

DETAILED STATISTICS

Alternative classifications. To business interests and trade analysts, the most important information in the trade publications is that given in the detailed tables. This information is of great importance also for government purposes, particularly in trade negotiations and tariff making. The purpose of the detailed tables is to enable users of the data to ascertain the quantity and value of imports (or exports) of each commodity coming from, or despatched to, each country of origin (or destination). This

[2] See Statistical Office of United Nations, *Statistical Papers*, Series D, " Summary of World Trade Statistics "; and Series T, " Direction of International Trade " (Joint Publication).

information may be presented in two different ways since two systems of classification are involved. One way is to classify the transactions according to the basic commodity classification and then to cross-classify in order to distinguish the countries of origin, or destination, for each of the commodity items (commodity-by-country tables). The second way is to classify the transactions according to the country classification and then to cross-classify in order to distinguish the commodities making up the trade with each country (country-by-commodity tables). Both systems are in general use. The first meets the convenience of those whose chief interest lies in the commodity analysis of the data; the second facilitates the work of those whose interest lies in the country analysis of the data. The two systems are equally acceptable to the user who is seeking only data of trade in a single commodity with a single country. The two systems involve the same number of cells and present substantially the same problems to the compiler.

Monthly and annual tabulations. It will be realized that, for countries whose trade is large and diversified, the amount of work involved in tabulating and publishing completely detailed tables of the kinds described above is too great to be undertaken on a monthly basis. Each country has therefore had to make decisions, in accordance with its particular needs and circumstances, as to how much data it can publish on a regular, systematic basis. The choice has, to a large extent, lain between publishing up-to-date information in limited detail or very late information in complete detail. Most countries have therefore relegated the complete details of their trade to an annual publication while presenting summary and semi-detailed information in a monthly publication. The decisions as to the amount of data that should be published monthly, and as to the methods of presentation, have varied greatly from country to country. The result is that the monthly trade publications show a great variety of forms, whereas the annual publications show a striking uniformity among the different countries. Let us consider the trade publications of Norway, which is a good example of a country which limits, fairly severely, the amount of detail it publishes monthly.

Illustrations: *Norway.* The monthly publication of Norway consists of approximately 40 pages.[3] The first few pages present the aggregates together with index-numbers of volume and price, for each month of the current year, compared with the months of the 2 preceding years. Then come 2 pages of tables setting out the value of imports and exports according to the 48 chapters of the League of Nations Minimum List for the current month and the expired portion of the current year. Then come the main tables consisting of the following:

[3] *Bulletin Mensuel du Commerce extérieur*, October 1950, Oslo.

1. Quantity and value of principal commodities [4] imported and exported in the current month and in the expired portion of the current year: 19 pages.
2. Value of imports and exports (same periods)—aggregates by countries of origin and destination: 3 pages.
3. Value of imports and exports (same periods) subdivided into the 48 chapters of the Minimum List and cross-classified by countries of origin and destination: 13 pages.
4. Quantity and value of principal articles exported (same periods) distinguishing the countries of destination: 7 pages. This table covers approximately 35 commodities or commodity groups important in the export trade of Norway.

Norway excludes from her monthly publication all detailed commodity-by-country data, except for a list of some 35 commodities or commodity groups of exports for which she provides country details. Table 5 shows

Table 5

Monthly Data: Norwegian Exports of Canned Fish, October and January–October 1950

(Quantity in tons; value in 1000 kroner)

Country	October		January—October	
	Quantity	Value	Quantity	Value
Total	2,848	10,292	30,652	110,920
Belgium, Luxembourg .	66	250	526	1,915
Ireland	69	194	387	1,368
Greece	20	64	374	1,215
United Kingdom . .	149	493	8,495	28,572
Sweden	33	238	140	1,203
Czechoslovakia . . .	—	—	60	179
West Germany . . .	68	241	498	1,823
East Germany . . .	—	—	32	107
Austria	58	167	488	1,396
Other Europe . .	78	392	436	2,005
Egypt	302	735	558	1,365
United States . . .	878	3,479	9,801	38,845
Canada	109	488	595	2,815
Australia	515	1,722	4,875	16,573
New Zealand . . .	186	732	1,247	4,645
Other countries . . .	317	1,097	2,140	6,894

Source: Bulletin Mensuel du Commerce extérieur, October 1950, Oslo.

[4] The commodities are detailed according to the items of the Minimum List with additional subitems where necessary to distinguish certain large classes of exports such as the different kinds of fish.

Norway's exports of canned fish in the period January–October 1950 as extracted from the *Bulletin Mensuel* for October 1950.

The corresponding data for the year 1948, as published in the "Annual Trade" volume, covered almost 5 pages because the group "Canned fish" was detailed by countries for each of the following components:

0473	Roe.
0475	Smoked small herring in oil.
0476	Smoked brisling in oil.
0477	Smoked small herring in tomato.
0478	Smoked brisling in tomato.
0479	Smoked small herring, other.
0480	Unsmoked small herring in oil.
0482	Unsmoked small herring in tomato.
0484	Unsmoked small herring, other.
0485	Unsmoked brisling, other.
0486	Smoked spring herring or large herring (kippers) in oil.
0487	Smoked spring herring or large herring (kippers) in tomato.
0488	Smoked spring herring or large herring (kippers), other.
0491	Unsmoked spring herring or large herring, other.
0492	Other canned herring.
0493	Other soft roe.
0494	Mackerel.
0495	Other canned fish.
0496	Fish balls, puddings, cakes, etc.

Table 6 shows the beginning of this table of detailed data on Norwegian exports of canned fish in 1948.

A comparison of Tables 5 and 6 illustrates the high degree of summarization that is carried out for the purpose of reducing the size of the monthly publication. That this kind of summarization is necessary to reduce the volume of work involved each month, in a country the size of Norway, can be seen from examination of the annual publication for 1948. This document runs to 480 pages. In addition to the usual aggregate tables and certain summary tables, it contains the following main detailed tables:

1. Quantity and value of imports of each commodity distinguishing the countries of origin (imports of commodities-by-countries): 182 pages.
2. Quantity and value of exports of each commodity distinguishing the countries of destination (exports by commodities-by-countries): 84 pages.
3. Quantity and value of:
   a Imports from each country distinguishing the principal commodi-

Table 6

Annual Data: Norwegian Exports of Canned Fish, Year 1948

Commodity and Country	Weight (kilograms)	Price per kilogram (kroner)	Value (kroner)
Fish and fish products			
In airtight containers, *total*. .	33,855,003		120,118,690
Roe	831,740	1·88	1,560,043
Belgium, Luxembourg .	2,581		5,350
Denmark	13,834		26,163
Netherlands . . .	3,613		6,374
United Kingdom . .	728,533		1,369,898
Canada	2,160		4,057
United States . . .	40,825		75,632
Netherlands Antilles . .	35,295		63,504
Falkland Islands. . .	2,760		5,533
Smoked small herring in oil .	11,203,418	3·77	42,283,702
Denmark	6,612		22,736
France	11,560		41,480
(etc.)			

Source: Norges Handel, 1948, Oslo, 1950.

ties and groups of commodities (imports by countries-by-commodities).

b Exports to each country distinguishing the principal commodities and groups of commodities (exports by countries-by-commodities): 102 pages.

It will be seen from this discussion that Norway's monthly publication contains only a fraction of the information that could be provided, whereas the annual publication contains a great volume of detail presented according to two systems of classification, *viz.*, trade by commodities-by-countries and trade by countries-by-commodities. The general pattern of Norway's annual trade volume is followed by so many other countries that it can be regarded as a fairly standard annual trade volume. The monthly trade publication, on the other hand, may be taken as an example of the publications of those countries which restrict fairly severely the amount of data they publish.

United Kingdom. The extensive monthly information published by the United Kingdom is described in Chapter 14. It has a counterpart in a number of other large trading nations such as France, Netherlands, Belgium, and Germany, where the monthly publications are also extensive but incomplete to varying degrees.

United States. The publications of the United States are an example of maximum information on an up-to-date basis. As the United States accounted for 21 per cent of the world's exports and 12 per cent of the imports in 1949, the United States trade returns are of great value, not only for analysis of United States trade but also for the up-to-date information they provide concerning the trade of other countries with the United States. The monthly trade returns of the United States are spread over a number of separate publications which together cover all the kinds of tables that are discussed above for Norway and in Chapter 14 for the United Kingdom. Like the United Kingdom, the United States publishes its annual trade volume very late—the issue which appeared in 1950 contained data for the year 1946.[5] This United States volume contained the same kind of tables as Volume I, II, and III of the United Kingdom *Annual Statement of Trade*, but without the data for previous years which the United Kingdom publishes. The United States publishes in even-numbered years only a volume similar to the United Kingdom Volume IV —trade by countries-by-commodities. The United States volume presents figures in this form for both the even-numbered year and the preceding year.

It will be seen, however, from the following description of the United States current monthly, quarterly, and annual publications that these present in advance almost all the information shown later in the annual volumes. The current publications do, however, suffer from a number of defects in comparison with the annual volume. The figures are preliminary and do not reflect later corrections; the commodity and country descriptions are abbreviated, sometimes disturbingly so; the publications containing data on trade by countries-by-commodities show substantially less commodity detail than that presented in the annual volume, etc. The following publications contain the main current data on United States trade:

1. *Summary of Foreign Commerce* (quarterly).[6]
   Gives data on the quantity and value of each item imported and exported in the cumulative quarters of the year, with certain additional summary tables for months and quarters.

2. *Exports of Domestic and Foreign Merchandise* (monthly, Report FT 410).
   Gives data for current month on the quantity and value of exports and re-exports (separately) of each item, distinguishing the principal countries of destination.

[5] *Foreign Commerce and Navigation of the United States*, Calendar Year 1946, Washington, 1950.
[6] Also a Monthly Summary, until 1951 when publication was suspended.

3. *Exports of Domestic and Foreign Merchandise* (monthly, Report FT 420).
   Gives data for the current month on the value of exports to each country of destination, distinguishing under each country, the value of each subgroup of commodities exported to it.

4. *Imports of Merchandise for Consumption* (monthly, Report FT 110).
   Gives data for the current month on the quantity and value of imports for consumption of each item, distinguishing the principal countries of origin.

5. *Imports of Merchandise for Consumption* (monthly, Report FT 120).
   Gives data for the current month on the value of imports for consumption from each country of origin, distinguishing under each country, the value of each subgroup of commodities imported from it.

All these publications except the first—*Summary of Foreign Commerce* (quarterly)—contain data for the current month only. This disadvantage is offset, however, by the publication once a year, about March, of special issues of *Reports* FT 110, 120, 410, and 420, which aggregate the data of the 12 separate monthly issues to provide data for the whole year. Thus data for the whole year in great detail (both commodity-by-country and country-by-commodity tables) are available within approximately 3 months of the end of the year. These annual issues of the monthly foreign trade reports are not described as the " annual publication," since that term is better reserved for *Foreign Commerce and Navigation of the United States*, referred to above. The rapidity of publication which the United States achieves in its detailed monthly data reflects in large part the advanced techniques of the Foreign Trade Division of the Bureau of the Census. From the great mass of machine cards containing the detailed transactions in the current month, the Division produces, mechanically, a pack of summary cards containing the data for the monthly publications. The tabulation of these summary cards is done in such a way that the machine sheets are ready for printing by means of offset reproduction. At the end of each year, the packs of summary cards for each of the 12 months are put together and summarized mechanically to obtain a pack of cards for the year. Without such devices it would be impossible to maintain this rapidity of publication. However, this use of machine sheets to prepare copy for offset reproduction does result in abbreviated commodity and country descriptions in the current publications, a fact which was noted earlier.

The system has, for certain users of the data, one disadvantage which is found also in the publications of many countries. To obtain detailed

Table 7

Annual Data: United States Exports of Domestic Merchandise by Commodity-by-Country of Destination, 1945

Cutlery, Iron, and Steel

Razors, Safety, except Electric			Safety Razor Blades			Scissors, Shears, Snips, N.E.S.		
B No. 611200.	*Dozen*	*Dollars*	B No. 611300	*Hundreds*	*Dollars*	B No. 611400	*Dozen*	*Dollars*
Total .	330,348	536,318	*Total* .	3,435,754	3,672,056	*Total* .	138,074	655,561
Greenland .	13	130	Greenland .	105	174	Greenland .	66	702
Iceland .	575	1,562	Iceland .	3,992	6,556	Iceland .	425	3,120
Canada .	6,326	7,621	Canada .	95,518	71,184	Canada .	54,268	194,538
Newfoundland Labrador.	637	1,527	Newfoundland Labrador.	3,537	2,707	Newfoundland Labrador.	506	2,043
Mexico .	17,001	34,916	Mexico .	74,904	130,921	Miquelon St. Pierre.	7	25
Guatemala .	2,191	4,903	Guatemala .	11,368	15,333	Mexico .	4,337	23,579
British Honduras.	148	373	British Honduras.	1,583	1,478	Guatemala .	1,234	4,207
El Salvador .	1,071	2,671	El Salvador .	13,402	12,768	British Honduras.	64	662
Honduras .	1,052	2,364	Honduras .	7,364	9,423	El Salvador.	296	1,514
Nicaragua . (etc.)	1,032	1,432	Nicaragua .	4,141	4,803	Honduras .	958	5,187
Nigeria .	117	267	Liberia .	435	591	Gold Coast.	91	916
British West Africa, N.E.S.	336	475	Belgian Congo.	222,738	133,597	Nigeria .	44	475
Port Gnea Angola.	24	31	East Italian Africa.	1,600	1,518	British West Africa, N.E.S.	7	66
Liberia .	482	1,273	French Somaliland.	80	55	Liberia .	1,169	4,529
Belgian Congo	10,117	16,797	British East Africa.	3,612	4,713	Belgian Congo.	2,702	11,926
Mozambique .	1,569	2,374	Mozambique	4,092	4,513	British East Africa.	304	977
Madagascar .	1,091	1,267	Madagascar.	12,160	10,644	Mozambique	45	973
Union of South Africa.	21,602	29,573	Union of South Africa.	171,214	172,352	Union of South Africa.	11,504	83,277
Northern Rhodesia.	29	75	Northern Rhodesia.	800	400	Northern Rhodesia.	12	50
Southern Rhodesia.	3,551	4,019	Southern Rhodesia.	13,251	8,980	Southern Rhodesia.	362	4,962

Source: *Foreign Commerce and Navigation of the United States*, calendar year, 1945.

Table 8

Quarterly Data: United States Exports of Domestic Merchandise, by Commodity, January–December 1949

Commodity Description and Code	Net Quantity	Value (dollars)
Cutlery	——	9,567,678
Razors, safety (611200) . . doz.	110,680	558,532
Safety razor blades (611300) . 100	2,697,364	2,969,693
Scissors, shears, and snips (611400) . doz.	151,265	966,111

Source: *Summary of Foreign Commerce*, January–December 1949.

Table 9

Monthly Data: United States Exports of Domestic Merchandise, Commodity-by-Country, 1949

(Data are described as monthly since they are extracted from the annual issue of the monthly *Report* FT 410)

Commodity and Country of Destination	Net Quantity	Value (dollars)
Safety Razors, excluding electric	(dozens)	
Canada	7,293	81,388
Mexico	8,956	43,481
Guatemala	439	3,589
(etc.)		
Egypt	2,513	1,968
Liberia	289	1,269
Union of South Africa	5,079	39,332
Total	110,680	558,532
Safety Razor Blades	(hundreds)	
Canada	30,950	13,615
Mexico	246,214	254,190
Guatemala	18,778	30,797
(etc.)		
Belgian Congo	91,416	27,037
Ethiopia	100	122
Mozambique	13,349	4,626
Union of South Africa	91,998	170,374
Total	2,697,364	2,969,693
Scissors, Shears, and Snips	(dozens)	
Canada	49,798	397,056
Mexico	8,215	31,145
Guatemala	1,076	6,039
(etc.)		
Belgian Congo	7,336	12,379
British East Africa	200	3,312
Union of South Africa	2,239	20,767
Total	151,265	966,111

Source: Report FT 410, *United States Exports of Domestic and Foreign Merchandise,* calendar year, 1949.

commodity-by-country or country-by-commodity data for a period of less than a year (*e.g.*, 6 months) it is necessary for the user to add up data from each of the monthly publications. Certain operations of this kind are, however, done by the Foreign Trade Division on request, subject to payment of the additional costs involved.

Table 7 sets out data on United States exports of certain kinds of cutlery as extracted from the annual volume for 1945. Table 8 shows the same data for the year 1949 as presented in the fourth *quarterly* issue of the *Summary of Foreign Commerce*. These two tables may be compared with Table 9, which shows similar data from the special yearly issue (1949) of the monthly *Report* FT 410.

AVAILABILITY OF THE STATISTICS

Time lags in publication. Serious difficulties are presented to the users of the detailed statistics by the time lags in publication, which are sometimes so great that the data have ceased to be of use to a majority of the users by the time they appear. This is certainly so for the annual publications which appear more than 2 years after the end of the year to which the data relate. Yet in spite of the great need that exists for the detailed annual data there are very few countries which succeed in publishing them within 12 months of the end of the trade year. This problem is receiving attention in a number of countries, and the tendency has been for countries to expand the details given in their monthly publications and to dispense with the expensive and time-consuming annual publication. The Belgo-Luxembourg Economic Union sets a good example in this respect. The monthly bulletin of external trade of Belgo-Luxembourg published by the National Institute of Statistics, Brussels, contains not only the usual summary tables but also tables of commodities detailed by countries of origin and destination. In addition tables are provided of the trade with each country subdivided by commodity groups. Where the user requires analysis of a commodity group in the trade of Belgium with a given country, he can usually supplement the information contained in the country tables with information available in the commodity-by-country tables. Belgo-Luxembourg has in this way arranged to meet many of the needs which can, in other countries, only be met by the annual publication. It did not, at least up to 1952, publish an annual volume.

Monthly trade returns are published by most important trading countries within 2 months of the end of the month to which the data relate. The best performances in this respect are by the United Kingdom (see Chapter 14) and by Switzerland, whose monthly trade returns are available within 3 weeks of the end of the month. The monthly returns of the United

Kingdom showing cumulative data and figures for the current period are compared with those of similar periods in the 2 preceding years. Switzerland, however, achieves rapid publication by confining the return to data for a single month, *i.e.*, no cumulative data are provided. The result is that to obtain commodity-by-country detail for longer periods, such as for 12 months or for the expired portion of the year, the user is faced with the exacting task of adding details from 2 to 12 separate publications. Speed of publication can only be achieved by some loss of detail and therefore of usefulness. For example, the task of tracing commodity exports from Hong Kong to China for periods longer than a month is complicated by the fact that the Hong Kong monthly return gives no cumulative data, and subdivides China into three separate areas. It may be doubted whether speed of publication is, in this case, worth the loss in usefulness that is involved.

Availability of unpublished details. Though 2 months appears to be the normal time lag in the publication of reasonably detailed monthly trade accounts, 2 years is the typical lag for annual accounts in final form (preliminary detailed data is sometimes released within a few months). It is therefore necessary for the user to investigate, through the authority responsible for the statistics, what details can be obtained in addition to those published in the monthly account. In many countries the extraction of such additional information on special request has been routinized and constitutes a very useful supplement to the monthly publication. These special extractions have a further usefulness in that they indicate to the compiling authority some of the weaknesses in the publication and enable it to initiate improvements.

Generally, if a user requires greater detail than is given in a publication (either monthly or annual), he can usually obtain it on payment of a fee necessary to cover the cost of extracting the data from the basic records, provided always that the detail is there distinguished (see Chapter 2). For example, in many of the items of the United Kingdom monthly account, the details are given for the most important countries; all other countries are lumped together as " other British " or " other foreign " countries. Data on the components of these residual groups of countries can usually be provided by the Customs and Excise Department for a very small fee. Again, the *Annual Statement of Trade of the United Kingdom* contains many more items than are contained in the monthly account and provides country detail for each of these items. The content of the annual volumes gives the upper limit of the commodity detail that can be obtained from the Customs statistical office. Where less detail is shown in the monthly account this is due either to economies in the monthly machine tabulations or to savings on printing costs. In either case a special request may be made to the Customs statistical office for details supplementary to those contained in the monthly publication. The same is true of most other countries.

Censorship. The great majority of countries publish their trade statistics in varying detail, as we have seen. From time to time, however, political or military considerations lead countries to suspend publication of certain information. During World War II, for example, practically all countries of the British Commonwealth suppressed their detailed trade publications. They published only such summary information as would not expose the nature and direction of their international trade. Similarly, the United States has omitted from its trade tables, as from May 1949, detailed commodity and country information on a selected list of commodities of military importance, and has included these commodities under five omnibus items which are designated as " special categories " and which were introduced into the trade tables in June 1949. Exports in these special categories amounted to $229 million in 1949 out of a total of exports of domestic merchandise amounting to $11,885 million. The informative value of the United States trade returns is not seriously impaired by this suppression.

Much more damaging to international knowledge is the kind of suppression practised by the USSR and certain countries of eastern Europe which publish no details whatever concerning their international trade. The Russian suppression of this information dates from before World War II. In the absence of data from these countries, it is necessary for the research worker to comb the trade publications of other countries which have trade relations with the USSR and east European countries. In *Statistical Papers*, Series T, issued by the Statistical Office of the United Nations jointly with the International Monetary Fund and International Bank, data on the direction of the trade of USSR, Rumania, Poland, Bulgaria, Czechoslovakia, Hungary, and Argentina are given. These data, being derived from the trade returns of other countries, are clearly incomplete. It is to be hoped that the international relations of these countries will improve sufficiently to enable them to resume publication of this information, which is of such value for economic progress.

USE OF THE STATISTICS

General. Reference has already been made in passing to many of the uses of international trade statistics. It remains to summarize and to extend the list of uses, and to give some simple illustrations. Records of foreign trade are needed both in the formulation and in the administration of public policies in many fields. The information contained in the data is a guide in the determination of policy, where the same records serve as a check on operational performance. This is particularly true of commercial policy in its various aspects, *e.g.*, trade agreements, tariff policy, international commodity schemes. During times of war and of international stress, policy in this field may include direct control by a country over its imports and exports; the records of foreign trade are then quite indispensable. In addition there are from time to time special policies or projects which depend for their development and operation on detailed trade statistics. Two post-war examples are the various programs of relief shipments and the European Recovery Program (Marshall Aid) of the United States. All this is quite apart from the purely administrative uses of trade records, *e.g.*, in Customs administration or port development.

Next, all those concerned in their commercial activities with international trading—whether as producers or merchants, as importers or exporters—have special interest in the statistics. The trader will need to compare his own foreign business with the general volume of trade, to estimate the size of the market and his own competitive position, and to seek out new opportunities for trade, in other commodities or in other territories. For such purposes he cannot proceed without full and up-to-date information on international trade; this is illustrated below.

Finally, there are the manifold requirements of economic analysis. Some of the more important of these are discussed in later chapters. There is the analysis of the structure of world trade—the development of trade in particular commodities and between particular regions—which is considered in Chapter 12. There is the problem of import and export prices, and of the terms of trade, to which reference is made in Chapter 10. There is the question of the place of merchandise trade in the more comprehensive balance of payments of a country, as raised in Chapter 9. Finally, and perhaps more important than anything else, there is the relation of foreign trade to the domestic economy, as elaborated in Chapter 11.

Uses of the detailed tables. The importance of external markets to producers and sellers of commodities has created a great demand for the kind of information given in the detailed tables. A producer who can add to his domestic demand a part of the foreign demand is usually in a position to secure substantial economies in production. By extending the market for his products, he can usually reduce his average cost per unit of output. There have even been periods of such severe competition for foreign markets that producers have been willing to sell their goods abroad at prices below average cost per unit. Provided they could obtain prices higher than their marginal costs, they would make a profit.

Extension of this practice, of course, leads to the phenomenon known as "dumping." The detailed tables of the trade statistics are the main source of information in the search for markets. Any event which serves to dislocate established directions of commodity trade tends to increase the demand for this information. Thus, a country's access to its normal markets may be denied as a result of balance of payments deficits or surpluses, or as a result of political considerations such as the abrogation of a trade agreement, or, in extreme cases, as a result of war. Traders in countries which have access to these markets can make use of the trade statistics of the country which is thus cut off, to ascertain the size and nature of the market in which they may substitute their products or obtain their supplies. The size of the market, as revealed by the trade statistics, can also be a guide for price policy.

Let us place ourselves in the position of a United States manufacturer of safety razor blades who is seeking to extend his sales outside the domestic market. He will consult the United States Export Reports FT 410 and find the quantity and the value of United States exports of these blades, by countries, in recent years. As the list of countries given is very long, we shall not reproduce the data, but confine ourselves to only a very small part of the published statistics. Our manufacturer finds that there is a large market for United States safety razor blades in certain countries, on the basis of the statistics in Table 10.

Table 10

United States Exports of Safety Razor Blades

(Number of blades in thousands)

Country	1948		1949		1950	
	Number	Dollars	Number	Dollars	Number	Dollars
Total . . .	254,833	2,565,972	269,736	2,969,693	248,410	2,864,629
Belgium . .	1,155	13,569	6,830	133,436	3,986	71,718
Switzerland . .	6,839	60,928	1,090	14,197	1,343	18,948
Italy . . .	6,027	63,416	11,386	147,641	27,164	344,616
India . . .	38,195	290,519	—			
Hong Kong . .	1,026	5,921	7,809	42,898	4,406	42,448
(etc.)						

The manufacturer notes that total exports of blades have varied only slightly; exports to Belgium have increased (from 1948 to 1949 by almost 6 times in quantity and by almost 9 times in value); exports to Switzerland have decreased very substantially; exports to Italy have increased substantially; those to Hong Kong have varied. On the other hand,

India, which took approximately 15 per cent of the total number of blades exported by the United States in 1948, took none in 1949 or 1950. It is clear from these figures that the large (and possibly expanding) market in Belgium is worth further study. We may, therefore, consult the Belgian trade returns for further information about the market. In the *Monthly Bulletin of External Trade*, published by the National Institute of Statistics, Brussels, we find the data shown in Table 11.

Table 11

Imports into Belgo-Luxembourg of Safety Razor Blades

Kind—and Country from which Imported	1948		1949		1950 (January—July only)	
	Kilograms	1000 francs	Kilograms	1000 francs	Kilograms	1000 francs
Finished and Unfinished:						
Total . . .	16,000	11,182	57,000	39,973		
Switzerland . . .	4,000	2,479	3,000	1,968		
Sweden . . .	not specified	not specified	14,000	3,224		
United Kingdom . .	not specified	not specified	31,000	27,787		
Unfinished:						
Total . . .					8,000	1,032
Sweden . . .					6,000	708
Finished:						
Total . . .					25,000	16,754
United Kingdom . .					9,000	4,219
United States . .					7,000	8,701

The fact that Belgium does not record any imports or blades from the United States in 1949 draws attention to certain factors of importance to the users of this kind of data. It will be clear from earlier chapters that this apparent abnormality can arise because the blades were exported from the United States late in 1949 and did not reach Belgium until 1950; or because the Belgium trade returns are insufficiently detailed to reveal these transactions; or, finally, because the blades were reconsigned to another country either before or after they reached Belgium but without crossing the Customs frontier. If we examine the 12 monthly issues of *Report* FT 410 of the United States, we find that in each of the months January to October 1949 there were no exports of blades to Belgium, but that the consignments were concentrated in the months of November and December. It is probable, therefore, that these exports from the United States did not appear in the Belgian trade returns until the beginning of 1950. It will be noted that the Belgium trade returns for January–July 1950 show imports from the United States to the value of 8·7 million francs, which is equivalent to $174,000 as compared with the United States export figure of $133,000 in 1949, though only $72,000 in 1950. It appears, therefore, that the market for United States razor blades in Belgium is of recent development. The manufacturer may therefore find it profitable to appoint an agent in Belgium who can investigate the market somewhat further and undertake the marketing of the razor blades.

The manufacturer can repeat this process by consulting the trade returns of the other countries, given in the United States export statistics, for information about other markets. He will have noted that exports from the United States to Hong Kong increased in 1949. The average value of blades exported was under 0.6 cents per blade in both 1948 and 1949, and still under 1 cent in 1950. There is, therefore, a market in that area for low-priced blades. In the case of United States exports to India, he may conclude that the disappearance of India from the United States export statistics in 1949 and 1950 is probably due to payment difficulties resulting from the suspension of convertibility between sterling and the dollar in 1949. He may therefore consider the possibility of investing in the production of razor blades in India itself, although for this he will require much more information than is available from the trade returns.

This analysis clearly does not exhaust all the aspects of the problem that might be examined. According to the purposes of the research, it might be necessary to consider, for example, whether the changes in the direction of the trade are due to temporary currency difficulties, or to a temporary availability of dollars which is unlikely to recur. Again, the substitution of United States blades may be due to a temporary supply difficulty in the countries which normally fill this market. Facts such as these lie behind the data which are contained in the trade accounts and which constitute the basis of the investigations. Intelligent use of the import returns for the kind of purpose here discussed must, of course, be supplemented by knowledge of the import programs, quotas, and tariff system of the countries involved.

In the above example, the use of foreign trade data for market analysis has been drastically simplified for purposes of illustration. It would, of course, be necessary for the analyst to investigate the data carefully, having reference to valuation, exchange conversion, country classification, and other problems as described in Chapters 3, 4, 5, 6, and 7.

Accuracy and use of statistics. The accuracy that a given user will require of the data in trade publications depends on the use he is making of the data. Clearly accuracy has no meaning except in relation to purpose. Thus, for general economic analysis, it is seldom necessary to extract trade data in units or less than 1,000,000 dollars or pounds. The United Nations Joint Publication (*Statistical Papers*, Series T, " Direction of International Trade ") sets out the aggregates-by-country figures in units of $1 million with one decimal place. The practice seems adequate for this purpose. For trade of a country by commodities it is seldom necessary to extract the data in greater accuracy than in thousands in physical units and thousands of units of national currency. When it comes to the derivation of price data, much greater accuracy is necessary and the full units available for both quantities and values must be used. Users of trade publications can save themselves much labour by deciding in advance the degree of accuracy they require and thereafter extracting from the publications no more than the appropriate number of digits.

PART II

Important Derived Uses
of the Statistics

CHAPTER 9

Merchandise Trade in the Balance of Payments

WALTER R. GARDNER

International Monetary Fund

INTRODUCTION

The foreign trade of a country constitutes only one segment—albeit a major segment—of its international transactions. The full story of the country's international transactions is shown in its balance of payments. Two major problems arise in fitting the merchandise item into the rest of the balance of payments. One is to differentiate merchandise trade from other transactions which may bear a close resemblance to it. The other is to account for the means of payment, since the merchandise item itself must be consistent from the standpoint of coverage, valuation, and timing with this payments accounting.

The balance of payments is a complete statement of economic transactions between residents of the reporting country and foreigners. Whatever is not classified as merchandise must be embodied in some other item, and whatever is included in merchandise is thereby removed from other categories. At least two items are always affected by the definition

155

Figure *A*. MASTER TABLE FORM FROM INTERNATIONAL

TABLE I. BALANCE OF

A. CURRENT TRANSACTIONS

Reporting Country ....   Period Covered ....

Currency .... Unit ....   Exchange Rate: U.S. $ .... per.................

Item	Credit (Receipts)	Debit (Payments)	Net Credit or Debit (-)
1. Merchandise (1.1 plus 1.2)			
1.1 Exports and imports (both f.o.b.)			
1.2 Other			
2 Nonmonetary gold movement (net)			
3. Foreign travel			
4. Transportation (4.1 plus 4.2)			
4.1 Gross freight.......................			
4.2 Other			
5. Insurance			
6. Investment income (6.1 through 6.3)			
6.1 Direct investment			
6.2 Other interest			
6.3 Other equity			
7. Government, not included elsewhere (7.1 plus 7.2)........			
7.1 Military expenditures, and surplus property			
7.2 Other			
8. Miscellaneous.........................			
Total goods and services (1 through 8)..............			
9. Donations (9.1 through 9.4)			
9.1 Personal and institutional remittances			
9.2 Other private transfers			
9.3 Reparations			
9.4 Official grants			
10. Total current transactions (1 through 9)			
ERRORS AND OMISSIONS (16 minus 10)			

adopted for one. If an intelligible picture is to be presented of the inter-national economic position of a country, all the inter-related elements of its balance of payments must be based on some common set of principles. This is what the International Monetary Fund, which coordinates the statistics in this field, has undertaken to do in its *Balance of Payments Manual*, on the basis of which most countries of the world report their international transactions, and in its *Balance of Payments Yearbook*, which presents them to the public.[1] Table I from the *Manual* (see Figure *A*) is

---

[1] The *Manual* is a volume of 111 pages, which outlines the principles underlying the balance of payments and presents tables with detailed instructions for preparing both

MONETARY FUND *BALANCE OF PAYMENTS MANUAL*

PAYMENTS SUMMARY

B. MOVEMENT OF CAPITAL AND MONETARY GOLD

Period Covered ....

Exchange Rate: U.S. $.................... per....................

Item	Net Movement Increasing (+) or Decreasing (-)		
	Assets	Liabilities	Net Assets
PRIVATE (excluding banking institutions)			
11. Long-term capital (11.1 through 11.6)			
11.1 Direct investment.			
11.2 Portfolio securities: bonds.			
11.3 Portfolio securities: shares			
11.4 Amortization			
11.5 Other contractual repayments			
11.6 Other			
12. Short-term capital (12.1 plus 12.2).			
12.1 Currency, deposits, Government obligations			
12.2 Other			
OFFICIAL AND BANKING INSTITUTIONS			
13. Long-term capital (13.1 through 13.6)			
13.1 Official loans			
13.2 Bank loans			
13.3 Portfolio securities			
13.4 Amortization			
13.5 Other contractual repayments			
13.6 Other			
14. Short-term capital (14.1 through 14.4).			
14.1 Payments and clearing agreements			
14.2 Liabilities to IMF and IBRD			
14.3 Other liabilities to official and banking institutions . . .			
14.4 Other			
15. Monetary gold.			
16. Total movement of capital and monetary gold (11 through 15).			

global and regional reports. The *Yearbook* is an annual publication of about 400 pages in which the data for 50 to 60 countries are presented with explanatory text. Accurate and intelligible balance of payments statistics are essential to the Fund's work as an operating organization in the field of foreign exchange. It obtains balance of payments reports from its 51 members and from a number of cooperating non-member countries. Through its training program it has prepared technicians of more than 20 countries to use the sources and methodology required for producing modern balance of payments statements; and new groups are being taken on for training each year. Hence the principles adopted by the Fund and implemented in its working statistics provide the basis for the exposition in this chapter.

The Fund was organized in 1946. It is an inter-governmental body designed to maintain orderly exchange rates and to achieve as much freedom as possible in inter-national payments with a view to encouraging world trade. It has resources in gold and member currencies equivalent to more than $7 billion.

the master table in which the data from subsidiary tables are brought together to give the story as a whole.

The information in Table I is presented in what might be called the standard form. In its analytic work the Fund has employed a different form that focuses on the compensatory official financing involved. This form reveals the extent to which the monetary authorities have supplied financing to compensate for a lack of balance in merchandise and other transactions that are undertaken for their own sake rather than to offset a tendency toward surplus or deficit in the balance of these transactions as a whole. The deficit (or surplus) so indicated is of the greatest significance in analyzing a country's foreign exchange problem. The "dollar shortage" for example, has been reflected in the heavy compensatory financing of the United States surplus and the deficits of the outside world. The deficits are not merely trade deficits. They are the net result of trade, services, ordinary donations, private capital movements, official investment, and other transactions undertaken for their own sake. All of these must be rolled together in assessing a country's payments problem. But foreign trade is usually the largest single element. For the purposes of this chapter it will be easier to develop its relations to the other items in terms of the standard table, which is uniform for all countries, than in terms of the less familiar and more flexible compensatory financing form.[2]

FOREIGN TRADE VERSUS SERVICES

In the master table form (Table 1, Figure A), the first item is merchandise trade. Consideration of the extent to which this item may differ from the ordinary Customs House figures of a country will be left to a later section of this chapter. It will be helpful at the outset to explore a series of cases in which the distinction between merchandise and other items of the balance of payments of the country may not be immediately apparent.

Gold. Questions of this character are raised emphatically by the second item in the table—non-monetary gold. The movement of non-monetary gold is really part of the foreign trade of a country. On the export side it represents the sale of current gold production, gold scrap recovered from industrial uses, or gold drawn from mine inventories or private hoards.[3]

---

[2] Examples of the compensatory financing form as applied to the United States and Danish data are given in the last section of this chapter.

[3] It could be questioned whether movements in private hoards should not be compared to shifts in private foreign exchange balances rather than to commodity flows. Even though the gold is privately hoarded in the form of bullion, it may be held for the ultimate purpose of monetary use abroad. For statistical reasons, however, it is convenient to include private hoarding with industrial consumption of gold since the available statistics are ordinarily computed for the combined item and separation into the two components may be impossible. Industrial consumption is clearly a commodity use of gold; and even hoards may take the form of simple ornaments and goldware resembling other forms of domestic wealth which also are a store of value. Further-

On the import side it represents gold absorbed into industrial use, mine inventories, or private hoards. (It cannot, of course, go back into the ground.) These are movements of gold as a commodity, similar to those of other commodities in international trade.

Gold is peculiar, however, in the way it affects international monetary reserves. Sales of ordinary merchandise increase those reserves only if the sale is to foreigners. Domestic sales of newly mined gold, however, to the Central Bank or Treasury of the producing country effect the same additions to the country's international reserves as if the gold has been exported and sold abroad. Foreign exchange or its equivalent is created in the hands of the monetary authorities by either process. Hence newly mined gold is regarded as an export of the country whether sold abroad or directly to the local monetary authorities. Similarly gold consumed at home is treated as an import even when it is purchased from the domestic monetary authorities since it reduces their international reserves in the same way as a purchase abroad. It has precisely the same effect as a commodity import.

Implicit in this treatment is the view that the change in monetary gold holdings—*i.e.*, in the central gold reserves of the country—is the proper measure of the monetary gold movement (item 15). Indeed, the estimate of the non-monetary gold movement (item 2) is derived by taking the difference between net gold transactions with foreigners and the change in monetary gold holdings of the country. Insofar as these two movements differ from one another, the explanation lies in the non-monetary movement of gold. For example, if a country has a net gold export with no change in its central gold reserves, it must be because new production or gold drawn from other private sources is being shipped abroad.

While this method produces correct figures for the global trade of a country with the world, it does not yield statistics that can be confidently classified by countries. This is obvious when, for example, gold production is sold to the Central Bank without any international transactions. In such a case it is impossible to attribute either the non-monetary or the monetary movement involved to a particular foreign country. The same difficulty may exist even when gold is sold abroad. In this case the country to which the gold is sent can be identified, but it may be impossible to say whether the movement is monetary or non-monetary. Gold production may be sold to the domestic central bank, which in turn may sell it abroad within the reporting period. Basically the sale reflects gold production and it would show as such in the global figures; but there is

---

more, pure gold may be hoarded more for domestic use than as a form of foreign exchange. Hence the Fund has included private hoards with non-monetary gold; but the case for this procedure is not conclusive.

nothing directly to distinguish the sale abroad from a use of the bank's regular gold reserves—in fact the local Central Bank may continue to hold the bars it acquired from the domestic mines and sell other bars abroad. Hence there is no general principle on which the distinction between monetary and non-monetary gold can be applied, country by country. Where, however, domestic transactions between the public and the Central Bank or Treasury are negligible, a regional allocation can be made on the basis of direct dealings with foreigners. Fortunately this condition is often realized in practice. Other types of cases in which such an allocation can be made are discussed on page 23 of the Fund's third *Balance of Payments Yearbook*, 1949–50.

Because of these peculiarities of the two gold items and their close interrelations, non-monetary gold must be kept separate from ordinary merchandise transactions even though it represents a commodity movement. Where, however, can the line be drawn between gold proper and merchandise that employs gold as a raw material? This line has been drawn at a point where the gold embodied in a product constitutes 80 per cent of its value. At that point or above, the gold content is regarded as virtually the equivalent of bullion. Plate, sheet, wire, and other partly worked products in which the value of the gold is 80 per cent or more of the total value are recorded in gold transactions rather than in merchandise trade. Unrefined gold, including gold mixed with other metals (*e.g.*, copper bars) and the recoverable gold content of scrap and sweepings, gold concentrates, and ores, are also included in gold transactions. This broad definition of gold was adopted in the Fund's *Manual* because many gold-producing countries export their production in an unrefined form and many gold-consuming countries import their requirements in a partly worked form. At the Regional Conference of Statisticians in Rangoon in 1951, however, where Fund representatives conducted a series of meetings on balance of payments methodology, the conclusion was reached that less precision in the definition would be advisable. It was agreed that gold plate, sheet, and wire should always be grouped with gold bullion, but it was considered that other gold articles in which the bullion content was high might be closer to genuine goldware than to bullion. It was recommended that the decision as to whether they were in fact bullion masquerading as goldware—possibly for the purpose of evading trade regulations—should be left to the authorities of the countries concerned.

Travel. Although the essential similarity of the non-monetary gold movement to merchandise transactions is evident, the merchandise aspects of foreign travel may be less apparent. Item 3 raises some borderline questions, however. Travelers abroad purchase goods, a portion of which they consume on the spot and the rest of which they bring home. The travelers are considered to be residents of their home countries. Strictly speaking, therefore, these goods are merchandise imports; but they are not included in the merchandise item since to do so would involve major reporting difficulties and they appear, in any case, to be more closely associated with travel psychology than with the business considerations that ordinarily govern merchandise imports.

Transportation. International transportation (item 4) should be clearly distinguishable from merchandise; but because of the widely employed c.i.f. method of valuing imports it may be necessary to leave international freight improperly recorded as a merchandise import and to employ the transportation item to offset such freight as is paid by residents to resident shipping companies. This is a case in which a wrong content for one item (merchandise) requires a dovetailing wrong content for another item (transportation) in order to offset domestic transactions and also avoid double counting of international freight. The Fund tries to minimize such cases by adjusting c.i.f. values to f.o.b. wherever possible. The problem is more fully discussed later in this chapter in the section on valuation. Since transportation services are continuously being embodied in the value of merchandise, the question as to where domestic transportation (properly part of the merchandise export) ends, and international transportation (set up as a separate balance of payments item) begins, is closely involved with the valuation procedure.

Aside from this basic difficulty, there are some ordinary borderline questions in the transportation item. Ships' supplies purchased in foreign ports might well be regarded as merchandise imports, but they are so intimately bound up with the transportation process that they are included in item 4, as are also repairs that stop short of changing the character of a ship or plane. Repairs that go so far as to involve conversions or reconversions are included in merchandise transactions because they result in a new product.

Government transactions. Item 5 (Insurance) raises no problems from the standpoint of merchandise transactions other than the c.i.f. difficulty discussed in connection with the transportation account, and item 6 (Investment income) involves no transactions that might be considered merchandise.[4] Government transactions in item 7, however, require careful interpretation. Insofar as the government buys or sells goods

[4] Branches or subsidiaries in the reporting country may ship goods to their parent companies abroad, and use the sales proceeds to transfer investment income. Similarly parent companies may ship equipment to their branches or subsidiaries and charge them directly to the investment account. The goods involved in these transactions, however, are conceptually quite separate from the investment income or capital movements with which they are associated; and, in the balance of payments statement, they are entered directly in the merchandise account.

abroad in the ordinary course of business, the goods are included with other merchandise transactions in item 1, but it does not seem reasonable to treat in this fashion liquidation of the great supplies of surplus property abroad with which various governments were left at the end of the war. The supplies were not drawn from current production or ordinary stock in trade. Their liquidation was of a quite abnormal character, and hence all such sales have been included in government transactions rather than as ordinary merchandise exports. For the importing countries the transactions bear a different aspect, however. The importing country had to decide whether to buy new products or surplus property of a similar type at lower prices. Surplus property in the form of merchandise (blankets, medical supplies, ships, etc.) is an alternative to other merchandise imports and serves much the same purpose. It has been included in the merchandise import item. Acquisition, however, of foreign surplus property other than merchandise (*e.g.*, air bases and other fixed military installations) is recorded in government transactions in item 7. Like the travel item, item 7 also includes purchases of supplies abroad for the foreign operations of embassies, military forces, or other government agencies. Members of these organizations (like travelers) are considered to be residents of their home countries. When the supplies, however, are purchased outside the country in which they are consumed, they are recorded as an import of the home country. In this case they must cross a border, and the exporting country must include them in its own exports, thus implying an import at the other end. The only important operations of this character are those connected with armed forces abroad.

Miscellaneous. Item 8 (Miscellaneous) covers miscellaneous service transactions such as workers' earnings, private pensions, management and brokerage fees, film rentals, patent royalties, communications, advertisements, and subscriptions to the press. It appears to call for little comment in connection with the merchandise item, although it might be noted in passing that profits and losses on merchandise transactions abroad are recorded in item 1.2 rather than in item 8. In the text section below on coverage, the possibility of including them in item 8 is considered.

PAYMENTS MECHANISM

This concludes the discussion of the service items, many of which raise borderline questions as to whether or not a portion of their content is merchandise. The other major problem, as was noted at the beginning of this chapter, is that of accounting for the means of payment with which the merchandise item must be consistent. This aspect will be considered only briefly here because most of the questions that it raises are treated in a subsequent section on the coverage, valuation, and timing of the merchandise item itself.   It can be stated broadly, however, that, apart from barter which is a rare phenomenon in modern economies, goods are either given away or paid for with money or financial claims.   If they are given away, a donation occurs, which is recorded in item 9 (Donations).   The goods that are given are entered as a credit in item 1 along with merchandise for which payment is made.   The amount of the gift is simultaneously recorded as a debit in item 9, thus keeping the accounts in balance.   A donation is not necessarily a voluntary gift.   Migrants' remittances to their relatives abroad, institutional charity, and governmental grants are, of course, voluntary;   but reparations may equally involve a transfer of goods without a quid pro quo.   In this case the donation is forced.   There may also be automatic donations such as occur when a migrant moves from one country to another, thereby transferring his property from the former to the latter.   No quid pro quo is involved in this case—merely an automatic donation.   If the migrant brings goods with him they should be entered in item 1 and the corresponding donation (migrants' transfer) in item 9 unless, in view of their minor character and the omission of such imports from national income accounting, the two items are canceled against one another and omitted.   Ordinarily, only the cash and other capital assets and liabilities of the migrant are of sufficient importance to merit recording in the balance of payments of a country.

While donations as a whole have been of great importance in the post-war world because of the increased tempo of private gifts and even more because of Marshall Plan aid, military assistance, and other forms of governmental grants, most merchandise transactions still involve a financial payment.   This means that most merchandise transactions affect the capital account in a country's balance of payments.   The payments need not be immediately in cash.   Goods may be sold on credit, i.e., a claim to cash in the future.   Or they may have been prepaid, i.e., the cash may have been transferred before the goods were finished so that the final sale merely liquidates a debt to the importer.   Whatever the immediate means of payment, the transaction is recorded in the appropriate item in the capital account.   Shifts of cash will be in item 12.1 or 14, and creation or liquidation of commercial credits in item 12.2.   A different possibility is that a parent concern may ship supplies or equipment to a branch abroad and charge it against its investment in the branch.   The financial side of the transaction will be entered in item 11.1.   Or imports may be charged directly against long-term credits (e.g., Export-Import Bank loans), in which case the financial entry would be in item 13.1. Not only is there a variety of possibilities on the immediate accounting, but also there is constantly going on an interchange among the capital items themselves with gold, loans, and securities being converted into deposits, and vice versa.   The net result of all these capital transactions, together with donations, must dovetail with the shifts of goods and services.

This means that goods should be entered in item 1 as of the time owner-ship changes, and either a gift or a corresponding capital transaction is recorded.   As we have seen, the corresponding capital transaction may be a cash payment, a credit, or a liquidation of debt; but the moment at which it occurs determines the moment for entering the goods in the account.   Similarly, the value at which the goods are entered should be the exact equivalent of the donation or capital transaction involved. These are matters that will be discussed more fully later, but one further observation may be made at this point.   It is evident that an exchange record which merely records money transfers through the banking system cannot yield accurate entries for the merchandise item.   Goods may be donated; and, even where payment is required, the immediate payment for the goods may not be in money.   When payment in money is finally made, it may include interest on a credit which should not be recorded in merchandise at all.   The donations-capital account with which the mer-chandise item should agree is the complete account—not merely a record of money transfers.[5]

RELATION OF THE MERCHANDISE ITEM TO CUSTOMS RECORDS

The interrelations of the merchandise item with the rest of the balance of payments have perhaps now been sufficiently discussed to suggest the framework within which it rests.   It is time to turn to the make-up of the item itself.   Customs House figures are the main source of foreign trade data.   They must be modified, however, in adapting the item to balance of payments use.[6]   The adjustments are for coverage, valuation, and timing.

Coverage.   Since the balance of payments is intended to cover all merchandise transactions, both commercial and non-commercial, adjust-ments for coverage must frequently be made to incorporate merchandise transactions not recorded in the trade statistics.   These adjustments vary from country to country depending on the practice of the Customs

---

[5] For discussion of the possibilities of an adjusted exchange record, however, see the section on exchange-control statistics below.

[6] Since Customs data as a rule conform more closely than unadjusted exchange control records to balance of payments requirements, the *Manual* takes the Customs data as a starting point.   A number of countries, however, base their balance of payments figures on exchange control records of merchandise transactions (see the section on exchange control statistics below).   In either case the data must be modified to conform with the Fund's *Balance of Payments Manual*.

authorities. Where trade statistics refer only to special trade, provision is made for their conversion to a general trade basis.[7] Examples of other merchandise transactions which are frequently not included in trade statistics are: parcel post; shipments of less than a stated minimum value; fish and other marine products caught by domestic vessels and sold directly in foreign ports; ships and aircraft exported or imported under their own power; non-commercial exports and imports such as grants and reparations in kind; migrants' household goods and personal effects; and shipments to branches and subsidiaries. In some countries where direct foreign investment creates a sort of foreign enclave there is an even more serious omission. The trade connected with the investment of foreign oil companies in Iraq, for example, is not recorded in the Customs House statistics. The oil interests occupy areas that are largely independent of the rest of the economy and for the most part export their production directly through their own pipelines. Because of their special situation Iraq treats them as residents of the country of the parent (*e.g.*, the United Kingdom). The Fund's *Manual*, however, treats branches and subsidiaries as separate entities and residents of the countries in which they operate. In the case of the oil company branches and subsidiaries in Iraq, all their transactions outside that country (including trade, transfers of income abroad to their parent companies, capital movements, etc.) should enter the balance of payments as genuine international transactions. In order to implement these principles and record the full merchandise trade of Iraq, it is necessary to add the exports and imports of the oil companies to those reported by the Customs House. In 1948, when exports reported by the Customs House amounted to less than 8 million dinars, the adjustment for exports of the oil companies involved an addition of more than 11 million dinars. The adjustment for oil company imports (mainly capital equipment) was less striking, but it amounted to a quarter of the total reported by the Customs House. In neighboring Iran, although exports and imports by the oil companies have been recorded by the Customs authorities and published alongside the other trade statistics, they have not been included in the foreign trade totals.

For a number of countries silver bullion, demonetized silver coins, and newly minted coins not yet in circulation may also have to be added to the trade returns. Such silver, like non-monetary gold, is merchandise rather than money. This is perhaps least readily apparent in the case of newly

---

[7] " Special " trade includes only exports of domestic produce and imports for domestic consumption (including withdrawals from bonded warehouses). Re-exports and entries into bonded warehouses are excluded. " General " trade includes re-exports as well as exports of domestic produce and all imports whether for consumption or re-export. For further discussion see Chapter 3.

minted coins. Such coins, however, do not begin to function as money until they go into circulation. Before that time no payments are effected by their international shipment. Rather they are sent to the government for which they have been minted as goods that have been processed; and the government (assuming that it has supplied the silver for minting) pays only for the processing. Once put into circulation, however, they function as money at face value.

A more difficult, though less obvious, question might be raised concerning the classification of silver bullion moving into and out of central bank reserves as merchandise rather than money. Such bullion may be money for the purpose of computing the central bank's reserve requirements against its domestic note issue; but it does not function as an international money. It does not have the official monetary market that gold commands by reason of its role as a legal standard of value the world over. Gold moves among Central Banks and Treasuries at parity prices, whereas silver bullion must be sold like other commodities on markets governed by a changing demand and supply. Rarely, if ever, is it transferred from one country to another at its fixed coinage value. Once out of the country which grants it a fixed status in its domestic monetary system, silver bullion becomes merely a commodity which takes its chances on world markets at prices that bear no resemblance to its legal value at home. Nor can a foreigner realize that legal value even if he ships it back to the country of its origin.

Silver coins in monetary use, however, must be treated as similar to banknotes. It is money of the issuing country at face value; and any foreigner who holds it has valid foreign exchange on that country. International movements in it are entered in the capital accounts of the balance of payments rather than in the merchandise item.

In addition to these adjustments for reported items, allowance must be made for smuggled goods and contraband where these are known to be significant. Comparison of trade statistics with those of the partner countries from which the smuggled goods are believed to have come is one rough means of ascertaining the extent of smuggling. Primarily on the basis of this method the Chinese authorities estimated that smuggling and undervaluation amounted to about 20 per cent of both exports and imports in 1947. The 1948 underrecording of exports was estimated to be as high as 40 to 50 per cent, but the adjustment to imports was reduced to 15 per cent. (See Chapter 3 on coverage for additional discussion of smuggling, and Chapter 5 on valuation for additional discussion of undervaluation.)

In its uniform schedule the Fund includes in the merchandise category some transactions that are on the borderline between goods and services.

These include the supply of electric power and gas, which are regarded as physical products, and conversions and reconversions of ships and aircraft since these radical transformations really create new carriers.

Deductions, as well as additions, must be made in order to eliminate from recorded trade those items that do not involve an international transaction and items that belong elsewhere in the balance of payments schedule.   Deductions of the first type include shipments to armed forces and diplomatic missions, and returned imports and exports.   Diplomatic representatives and members of armed forces stationed abroad are considered residents of their own country, and shipments to them from their home country are therefore not regarded as international transactions. Returned imports are treated as negative imports rather than as exports (where they are recorded in the Customs figures), and are deducted from both imports and exports (as recorded by Customs) in order to avoid overstatement of these totals.   Similar treatment is given to returned exports, *i.e.*, they are deducted as negative exports.   Any items which are covered elsewhere in the schedule must also be deducted if they have found their way into the Customs House figures.   Among such possibilities are bunker fuel and ships' stores (included with transportation), sales and purchases by tourists (included with tourists' expenditures), and, in particular, gold transactions.   Films or other commodities exported and imported on a rental basis are obviously not merchandise transactions since there is no change in their ownership.   If they have been recorded in the Customs House figures they must be removed.   The rentals concerned are included with miscellaneous services (item 8).

In addition to these adjustments for coverage of merchandise shipments that cross the reporting country's border, some provision must be made for transactions between residents and foreigners in merchandise abroad. A British merchant, for example, may buy goods in Australia and sell them to the United States.   Such goods are purchased by a British resident and sold to foreigners; yet it is a question whether they should be entered in the British merchandise item at all.   The goods at no point enter the British economy; only the profit on the transaction is retained by a British resident.   This could be entered in miscellaneous services. It would still be necessary to show the full cost of the goods in a purchase-sale adjustment (or in multilateral settlements) because this amount is paid to Australia by the British merchant and received by him from the United States.   The two sides of the transaction may be of particular importance because sterling is paid to Australia and dollars are received from the United States, thus affecting the foreign exchange position of the United Kingdom.   In its *Manual* the Fund handles the foreign exchange impact of such a transaction directly by recording the entire amount of merchandise transactions abroad in the merchandise item of the reporting country; but, as noted, this treatment is not essential.

Valuation. The first problem of valuation concerns the point at which the goods are valued. Many countries value both exports and imports at their own Customs frontiers (*i.e.*, exports are valued f.o.b.[8] and imports c.i.f.[9]); others value both exports and imports at the frontier of the exporting country (*i.e.*, both exports and imports are valued f.o.b.). Various other alternatives exist such as the f.a.s. basis [10] employed for exports from Argentina, Finland, and the United States, or valuations at some interior point of sale or purchase. In order to achieve uniformity of valuation, the Fund schedule provides for the recording of both exports and imports on an f.o.b. basis at the frontier of the exporting country. Subsequent costs of transfer are treated in the transportation and insurance accounts as being paid directly by the importing country. Where the payment is in fact indirect, this method may lead to the exclusion of certain transactions between residents and foreigners. For example, the exporter may pay freight and insurance costs to foreign ships and insurance companies, and subsequently be reimbursed by the foreign importer. Such freight and insurance payments are not shown in the balance of payments of the exporting country since in effect the exporter acts merely as an agent for the foreign importer who ultimately pays the freight and insurance. If imports are recorded on a c.i.f. basis in the trade statistics, freight and insurance must be deducted from imports to arrive at the f.o.b. value.

An alternative procedure would have been to value exports f.o.b. and imports c.i.f., but this solution was rejected for a number of reasons. In the first place, transportation and insurance represent distinct international services which it is desirable to record separately in the balance of payments. These services may be rendered by nationals of countries other than that of which the exporter is a national. If goods go from country *A* to country *B*, they may be shipped in vessels of country *C* and insured in country *D*. In a regional classification of the balance of payments, therefore, it is essential to distinguish between the goods and the transportation and insurance services. A further reason is that the inclusion of freight and insurance with imports involves the overstatement of international transactions to the extent that these services are provided by residents of the reporting country. An offset to this overstatement may

---

[8] F.O.B. (free on board) includes cost of the merchandise and all charges incident to placing the goods on board a carrier at the exporting country's border.

[9] C.I.F. (cost, insurance, freight) includes cost of the merchandise, and insurance and freight charges to the border of the importing country, whether paid to foreigners or residents.

[10] F.A.S. (free alongside ship) includes all items listed in footnote 8 except loading charges.

be made by including credit entries for services rendered by residents in the transportation and insurance items. This, however, means that the totals for goods and services rendered (credits) and goods and services received (debits) are both overstated by this amount. In cases where transportation and insurance of imports by nationals is negligible, imports may be entered on a c.i.f. basis in the global balance of payments without undue error. Difficulties are experienced, however, in the regional balance of payments if goods from one region are transported or insured by residents of another region.

Other discrepancies in valuation arise when the values of exports or imports recorded in trade returns differ from the amounts actually paid or payable. In some instances certain elements, such as export duties, may be omitted, and in other instances Customs procedure may require the use of some specified foreign or domestic price other than that at which the transaction was in fact carried out. Or there may be cases, notably those involving transactions between a parent company and its branches and subsidiaries, where the price quoted may be quite nominal and should be replaced by market prices representing as nearly as possible the value of the goods at the frontier of the exporting country. In the case of banana exports from subsidiaries of United States companies in Central America to the United States, the market value is assumed to be the wholesale price in the United States less estimated freight and insurance charges. The Guatemalan balance of payments, for example, shows an adjustment for undervaluation of banana exports amounting in 1948 to over twice the original valuation. In cases where no payments have been made (*e.g.*, reparations in kind), the valuation of these goods in the trade returns may have to be adjusted to a uniform basis. Where goods are exported on consignment it is not possible to record the transaction value at the time the goods are shipped, and an adjustment must subsequently be made to correct the value originally assigned.

A special problem of valuation arises when a country has a system of multiple exchange rates. In these circumstances it is necessary to express all transactions in terms of a fixed international monetary unit such as United States dollars or the country's own gold currency unit. Since the trade statistics are normally expressed in terms of local currency, the recorded values must be converted into figures expressed in a fixed monetary unit. This calculation necessitates the classification of exports and imports into as many groups as there are effective exchange rates. Where any portion of the export proceeds is sold on a free market, giving rise to the phenomenon of broken cross rates, trade must also be classified in accordance with the currencies in which the transactions have been conducted. If the rates fluctuate, weighted averages may be used, preferably on a monthly or quarterly basis. The difficulties involved in the preparation of a balance of payments for a country with multiple exchange rates may be illustrated by the case of Thailand. In converting trade figures from domestic currency values to United States dollars, different rates were used according to whether transactions occurred at the official or the free market rate and, in the latter case, according to whether they were made in dollars or sterling.[11]

Timing. The balance of payments seeks to record economic transactions at the time they occur. For merchandise trade the international transaction occurs when ownership passes from a resident to a foreigner, or vice versa. As was pointed out earlier, this is the moment when a financial claim arises, although the claim need not be settled in cash immediately. This moment does not necessarily coincide with the time at which the merchandise crosses the frontier of the country concerned. In the majority of cases, however, no substantial error is involved in assuming that the transaction occurs when the merchandise is recorded in the trade statistics, that is, when the goods cross the frontier.

Adjustments for the timing of merchandise transactions are made in the balance of payments only when a substantial interval occurs between the change in ownership and the physical transfer of the goods. The procedure is to record changes in foreign-owned stocks in the country and changes in stocks abroad owned by residents. Canadian wheat, for example, may be shipped to the United States for storage. In this case the increase in Canadian wheat stocks in the United States (entered as a negative credit in the Canadian balance of payments) cancels out a corresponding amount of wheat exports recorded by the Canadian Customs. Canada does not receive a net merchandise credit on the operation in its balance of payments until the wheat held in the United States is sold. A different illustration was provided during World War II when the British Government purchased the total wool clip of the Dominions, a considerable part being held in the Dominions until the post-war period. The wool sales to the British were immediately entered as merchandise credits in the balance of payments of the Dominions. The later shipments of wool out of the Dominions, although recorded as exports in their Customs statistics, were offset by the decrease in British-owned stocks.

The adjustments for coverage, valuation, and timing in the Fund's schedule are worked out in detail in Tables II, II(a), II(b), and II(c), which are reproduced here (see Figure *B*) from the *Balance of Payments Manual*.

---

[11] Valuation problems are discussed in detail in Chapters 5 and 6. At its fifth session in May 1951, the United Nations Statistical Commission adopted a resolution recommending that a study be made of valuation practices and that a report be made to its next session regarding the desirability of modification and expansion of the provisions of the 1928 International Convention Relating to Economic Statistics.

Figure *B*. TABLE FORMS FROM INTERNATIONAL MONETARY
FUND *BALANCE OF PAYMENTS MANUAL*

TABLE II.   MERCHANDISE TRANSACTIONS

Reporting Country ....

Currency .... Unit ....

Period Covered ....

Exchange Rate: U.S. $.................. per..................

Item	Credit (Receipts from Exports or Sales)	Debit (Payments for Imports or Purchases)
EXPORTS AND IMPORTS		
1. "General" trade (1.1 plus 1.2).................................		
1.1 "Special" trade		
1.2 Other		
2. Merchandise adjustments (2.1 plus 2.2)		
2.1 For coverage (Table II(a), items 5.1 and 5.2)		
2.2 For valuation (Table II(b), items 5 and 10)		
3. Freight on imports (3.1 plus 3.2) ....,.....................		
3.1 Paid to residents		
3.2 Paid to foreigners		
4. Insurance on imports (4.1 plus 4.2)		
4.1 Paid to residents		
4.2 Paid to foreigners		
5. Total adjusted f.o.b. values (Transfer to Table I, item 1.1)*.............		
6. Total adjusted imports at c.i.f. values (Transfer to Table I, item 1.1 only if item 5, debit, is not available) †....................		
OTHER SALES AND PURCHASES		
7. Merchandise transactions abroad (Table II(c), item 3) ....·.		
8. Adjustment for changes in stocks (Table II(c), item 6)		
9. Total (7 plus 8) (Transfer to Table I, item 1.2)		

Notes by author; not on form:
   * For exports, which are on an f.o.b. basis, this item will be the sum of items 1 and 2.
   For imports: (*a*) If import entries in items 1 and 2 are on an f.o.b. basis, item 5
         will be equal to the sum of items 1 and 2.
        (*b*) If import entries in items 1 and 2 are on a c.i.f. basis, item 5 will
         be obtained by deducting the total of items 3 and 4 from the total
         of items 1 and 2.
   † If import entries in items 1 and 2 are on an f.o.b. basis, item 6 will be obtained by
adding items 1, 2, 3, and 4.   If import entries in items 1 and 2 are on a c.i.f. basis,
item 6 will be obtained by adding items 1 and 2.

Table II starts with the trade statistics as published and provides for the
various adjustments necessary to insure uniformity.   Where the trade
statistics refer only to special trade, provision is made for their conversion
to a general trade basis, and where imports are recorded on a c.i.f. basis
provision is made to convert them to an f.o.b. basis.   Further adjustments for coverage and valuation are provided for in Table II(a) and
II(b), respectively, and the totals are transferred to Table II.   Timing

Figure *B* (*Continued*)

TABLE II(a).   MERCHANDISE TRANSACTIONS:
ADJUSTMENTS FOR COVERAGE

Reporting Country ....   Period Covered ....

Currency .... Unit ....   Exchange Rate: U.S. $................... per...............

Item	If Included in Table II, Item 1, Enter X	If Not Included in Table II, Item 1, Enter Amount
ADDITIONS TO EXPORTS		
1.1 Silver (other than current coin)		
1.2 Parcel post.		
1.3 Shipments of less than stated minimum value.		
1.4 Fish and other marine products		
1.5 Ships and aircraft		
1.6 Conversions and reconversions of foreign ships and aircraft		
1.7 Noncommercial exports (1.7.1 through 1.7.3)		
1.7.1 Grants in kind.		
1.7.2 Reparations in kind		
1.7.3 Other		
1.8 Electric power and gas		
1.9 Other merchandise not included in Table II, item 1 (describe)		
_____		
_____		
1.10 Total (1.1 through 1.9)		
ADDITIONS TO IMPORTS		
2.1 Silver (other than current coin)		
2.2 Parcel post.		
2.3 Shipments of less than stated minimum value.		
2.4 Ships and aircraft		
2.5 Conversions and reconversions of domestic ships and aircraft abroad		
2.6 Noncommercial imports (2.6.1 through 2.6.3).		
2.6.1 Grants in kind.		
2.6.2 Reparations in kind		
2.6.3 Other		
2.7 Electric power and gas		
2.8 Other merchandise not included in Table II, item 1 (describe)		
_____		
_____		
2.9 Total (2.1 through 2.8)		

adjustments are provided for in Table II(c) along with merchandise
transactions abroad, which were discussed in the section on coverage.   It
was there noted that the Fund's *Manual* includes such transactions on a

Figure *B* (*Continued*)

TABLE II(a) contd.   MERCHANDISE TRANSACTIONS: ADJUSTMENTS FOR COVERAGE

Reporting Country ....   Period Covered ....

Currency ...., Unit ....   Exchange Rate: U.S. $.................... per....................

Item	If Not Included in Table II, Item 1, Enter X	If Included in Table II, Item 1, Enter Amount
DEDUCTIONS FROM EXPORTS		
3.1 Shipments to armed forces and diplomatic missions stationed abroad		
3.2 Sales to foreigners of bunker fuel and ships' stores		
3.3 Gold: coin, bullion, partly worked, and unrefined		
3.4 Exposed films exported on a rental basis		
3.5 Returned imports....................................		
3.6 Returned exports....................................		
3.7 Other (describe)		
....		
3.8 Total (3.1 through 3.7)		
DEDUCTIONS FROM IMPORTS		
4.1 Shipments to foreign armed forces and diplomatic missions stationed in your country		
4.2 Purchases abroad of bunker fuel and ships' stores		
4.3 Gold: coin, bullion, partly worked, and unrefined		
4.4 Exposed films imported on a rental basis		
4.5 Returned imports....................................		
4.6 Returned exports....................................		
4.7 Other (describe)...................................		
....		
4.8 Total (4.1 through 4.7)		

	Amount
TOTAL ADJUSTMENTS	
5.1 Exports (1.10 minus 3.8) (Transfer to Table II, item 2.1)	
5.2 Imports (2.9 minus 4.8) (Transfer to Table II, item 2.1)	

gross basis in order to make them classifiable by countries; but an alternative, and perhaps preferable, method of achieving the same end was suggested.

Figure *B* (*Continued*)

TABLE II(b). MERCHANDISE TRANSACTIONS: VALUATION ADJUSTMENTS

Reporting Country .... Period Covered ....

Currency .... Unit .... Exchange Rate: U.S. $.................. per..................

Item	If Valuation in Table II, Item 1, Is Correct, Enter X	If Correction Is Needed, Enter Amount (+) or (−)
ADJUSTMENT OF EXPORTS		
1. Internal freight and insurance charges		
2. Export duties		
3. Revaluation of commercial exports resulting from (3.1 through 3.3)		
3.1 Direct investment		
3.2 Consignment trade		
3.3 Other causes.......................................		
4. Revaluation of noncommercial exports (4.1 through 4.3)		
4.1 Grants in kind......................................		
4.2 Reparations in kind		
4.3 Other		
5. Total (1 through 4) (Transfer to Table II, item 2.2)		
ADJUSTMENT OF IMPORTS		
6. Internal freight and insurance charges		
7. Import duties		
8. Revaluation of commercial imports resulting from (8.1 through 8.4)		
8.1 Direct investment		
8.2 Consignment trade		
8.3 Subsidies and price control		
8.4 Other causes		
9. Revaluation of noncommercial imports (9.1 through 9.3)		
9.1 Grants in kind......................................		
9.2 Reparations in kind		
9.3 Other		
10. Total (6 through 9) (Transfer to Table II, item 2.2)		

PROBLEMS OF REGIONAL CLASSIFICATION

Reference has already been made to some of the problems arising in a regional classification of the balance of payments. The *Balance of Payments Manual* contains a comprehensive appendix dealing with the classification of international transactions by geographic areas.

The global balance of payments may be subdivided either by countries or by currencies. Both types of classification have their advantages. A classification by countries throws light on the relations of a country's economy to individual foreign countries and areas. When the same system of compilation is followed by a great number of countries, it becomes possible to construct consolidated balances of payments for and

Figure *B (Continued)*

TABLE II(c).   OTHER TRANSACTIONS IN MERCHANDISE

Reporting Country ....   Period Covered ....

Currency .... Unit ....   Exchange Rate: U.S. $.................. per..................

Item	Credit (Receipts)	Debit (Payments)
MERCHANDISE TRANSACTIONS ABROAD		
1. Proceeds of sales; cost of goods sold		
2. Freight and insurance adjustment		
3. Adjusted proceeds and costs (1 minus 2) (Transfer to Table II, item 7)		
ADJUSTMENT FOR CHANGES IN STOCKS		
4. Changes in stocks of domestically-owned goods held abroad (4.1 plus 4.2)		
4.1 Originating in exports from your country (increase (-) or decrease (+)).		
4.2 Of foreign origin (increase (+) or decrease (-)).		
5. Changes in stocks of foreign-owned goods held in your country (5.1 plus 5.2)		
5.1 Originating in exports from your country (increase (+) or decrease (-)).		
5.2 Of foreign origin (increase (-) or decrease (+)).		
6. Total changes in stocks (4 plus 5) (Transfer to Table II, item 8)		

between groups of countries that can advantageously be studied as aggregates. A currency classification, on the other hand, is useful for analysis of the financing problems arising from balance of payments deficits (or surpluses) in respect of hard and soft currencies. Even if all currencies were convertible at par, a currency classification would contribute to an understanding of the mechanism of multilateral payments. The ideal solution would be a balance of payments cross-classified by both countries and currencies. Such a classification, however, would be too complicated to be statistically feasible on a uniform basis.

As the nearest approach to the " ideal solution," the Fund has combined with a basic geographic classification the most significant distinctions regarding currency. A multilateral settlement item has been included in the regional table in order to show the extent to which transactions between two countries have been settled in the currency of a third country, *e.g.*, dollars or sterling. If the United Kingdom uses dollars to pay some Latin American country, the fact that its dollar balances have been reduced by a transaction with Latin America (rather than by a transaction with the United States itself) will be disclosed by the multilateral settlement item. Although the item will not disclose whether the occasion for the dollar payment was a merchandise import from Latin America or a service or capital transaction, it will show the region in which the dollars were in fact spent. Such a classification lends itself to analysis of foreign exchange problems from the standpoint both of hard and soft currency transactions and of the fundamental geographic relationships.

A number of considerations prompted this major emphasis on the geographic analysis. Trade statistics and certain other basic data are classified by countries rather than by currencies. Furthermore, a currency classification is of little value for the analysis of the balance of payments of countries settling virtually all international transactions in their own currency or in a single foreign currency, such as United States dollars. Even when a country conducts transactions in a number of different currencies there is no assurance that the proportion in which different currencies are used will not vary considerably from time to time even though the pattern of trade may not change. Basically the flow of international transactions tends to reflect the diverse distribution of natural resources, labor and management skills, and accumulated savings in the different regions of the world. These are the persistent governing factors that create the structure of the international balance of payments. Foreign exchange problems grow out of the divergences from this fundamental structure that are brought about by wars, depressions, inflationary expansion, or other major dislocating influences. They are the monetary reflection of the regional dislocation. Since the fundamental nature of the problem is regional, the geographic classification is the most permanently meaningful, important though the shifting currency compartments may be in shaping current developments. The Fund has endeavored to show the essentials of the currency problems in terms of the regional pattern.

In order to show the world pattern of trade and other international transactions some broad groupings are required. The Fund employs a table with the following regional headings:

United States.
Canada.
United Kingdom.
Rest of sterling area:
  In Europe.
  In Far East.
  Elsewhere.

Continental Europe:
  OEEC countries.
  Eastern Europe.
Middle East.
Far East.
Latin America.
Rest of world.

Although it is believed that these groupings will serve a wide range of purposes, they have been selected primarily with a view to analyzing balance of payments problems. The United States is at the center of such a picture. The post-war dollar shortage has been very largely a matter of transactions with that country. Canada, also separately shown, has to a varying extent formed part of the hard currency area in the Western

Hemisphere. Individual hard currency countries scattered elsewhere in the world cannot be separately shown in this summary table; but they are few in number and far less important than the United States and Canada.

The sterling area is shown with the United Kingdom differentiated from the rest of it. Because it cuts across normal geographic groupings, provision has been made for dividing the rest of the sterling area into the portions in Europe, in the Far East, and elsewhere. This permits Europe and the Far East to be completed as regional wholes.

Continental Europe itself is divided into the OEEC countries and Eastern Europe. By combining the OEEC countries of Continental Europe with the United Kingdom and the rest of the sterling area in Europe, data can be shown for the entire group of countries participating in the European Recovery Program and composing the European Payments Union. For the remainder of the world, the Middle East, the Far East, the Latin America are shown separately. These are the great raw material areas, which have special balance of payments possibilities as well as problems.[12]

It is evident that the dozen categories in this table provide considerable scope for analysis. They are sufficiently flexible to permit combinations for different purposes, not only for the balance of payments analysis for which they were created. Statistics on this basis have only begun to be reported to the Fund; but as more comprehensive data becomes available over a series of years the network of world trade can be effectively studied in its relation to the network of international transactions as a whole.

There is, however, an inherent difficulty in allocating merchandise geographically. It revolves around the question of whether the goods should be allocated to the selling or purchasing country or to the country of ultimate origin or destination. Should tea, for example, sold to a British merchant and resold to Denmark be allocated to India or the United Kingdom in the Danish records? On strict balance of payments principles the allocation would have to be the United Kingdom since a merchandise transaction has been defined as a transfer of ownership of goods between a resident and a foreigner. From the broader standpoint of economic analysis, however, it would appear to be more enlightening to allocate the tea to India. To preserve consistency, India in its reports should allocate the tea to Denmark rather than to the United Kingdom. Unfortunately such consistency is difficult to preserve in actual reporting. In many cases the ultimate destination is unknown at the time of the

---

[12] Examples of 1949 regional data are given in the last section of this chapter, where the necessary adjustments to the merchandise item are shown for Norway and a full regional balance of payments is presented for Denmark.

transfer of ownership. Furthermore, even if perfection could be achieved in this respect, the origin-destination method would apply only to goods that had kept their form virtually unchanged. A slight amount of processing (affecting the value perhaps by only 2 or 3 per cent) would immediately make the processing country the country of origin. There appears to be no way to deal adequately with this inherent difficulty in the origin-destination method short of breaking commodities apart into their separate value-added components and allocating each component to its appropriate country.

Despite the shortcomings of the origin-destination approach as it is applied in practice, the Fund considers the statistics prepared on that basis to be the most significant for economic analysis. It has, therefore, provided for entering them in the regional classification of the balance of payments. Since trade entries in the balance of payments, however, must conform with the payments mechanism, it is necessary to adjust the origin-destination figures to a purchase-sale basis. This is done by an adjustment item that leaves both sets of figures in the regional table. The solution is similar to that under which both regional and currency classifications are provided in the same table by introducing a multilateral settlements item as the bridge between them.

EXCHANGE-CONTROL STATISTICS

If the Customs returns do not supply the necessary data, purchase-sales statistics (as well as multilateral settlements) may have to be derived from the record of foreign exchange transactions. The majority of countries in the world today have such a record because, in one form or another, they are operating an exchange-control system. In the section on the payments mechanism attention was drawn to the fact that an exchange record which merely records money transfers through the domestic banking system cannot yield accurate entries for the merchandise item. Important blocs of transactions may involve no money transfer of this type: e.g., goods financed by inter-governmental grants, barter trade, shipments of goods between parent companies and their branches or subsidiaries abroad, imports financed by foreign loans or by drafts on foreign balances that are used for a variety of purposes (not confined to merchandise) and are replenished by exports and other transactions so that only the relatively small net transfers from time to time involve a money flow through the domestic banking system. In the post-war world omissions of this character may be on a large scale. Even the merchandise transactions that are fully recorded in the money flows may be valued on a basis that includes interest, freight, and insurance on the operation; and they may be recorded at periods that precede or follow by several months the dates when the goods were actually sold. This is a formidable list of obstacles to the use of a simple exchange record as an alternative to the Customs figures.

For adequate administration of an exchange control, however, it is usually necessary to have a more complete and logical statement of international transactions than is provided by a simple record of money flows through the domestic banking system. This basic record is supplemented by other required information. If the supplemental information is adequate and the classifications of the basic exchange record are sufficiently detailed from the balance of payments standpoint, the exchange record so amplified will supply merchandise data that are superior to those of the Customs record. Merchandise transactions that give rise to financial claims will be covered more extensively than in the Customs record; the valuation will be more accurate because it will exactly match the financial claim created; and the timing will be superior because the amplified record will note the day when the financial claim was created or discharged by a merchandise transaction and will permit the entry to be timed accordingly. A modern exchange record of this type, however, is something that can rarely be achieved completely; and in practice much of the supplemental data must be drawn from the Customs record itself. Only by working to improve both the exchange and Customs records simultaneously can the merchandise data required for consistent economic analysis be developed.

FOREIGN TRADE IN THE NATIONAL ACCOUNTS

The treatment of exports and imports in the domestic setting is discussed in Chapter 11, but one aspect is appropriately considered here. Merchandise, donations, and capital movements are all components of the balance of payments. Sometimes, in translating foreign trade statistics from the balance of payments to the national accounts, the trade statistics are seriously distorted by an arbitrary treatment of donations.

Donations are neither merchandise nor capital. Commodities given to foreigners, e.g., through UNRRA, are entered in the balance of payments as merchandise exports—not donations. Similarly, cash given to foreigners is entered initially as an increase (credit) in balances due to foreigners; and then, if the foreigners spend it for goods, the cash credit is canceled and a merchandise credit takes its place. Neither the shifts in short-term liabilities nor the merchandise exports are entered as donations as such. What is entered in donations is the gift involved. The debit entry on account of the gift indicates that the merchandise export (or increased cash liability) gives rise to no *quid pro quo*. It does not mean that the merchandise export is in any sense unreal. It is quite as real as any other export; but it is matched by a gift rather than by the acquisition of another commodity or service or by a capital transaction.

When the international accounts of a country are worked into the statement of its gross national product and expenditure, considerable violence will be done to this balance of payments picture if the existence of international donations is not recognized. Failure to recognize them makes it necessary also to deny the foreign trade with which they are coupled. One major country, for example, adopts the fiction that goods donated to foreign countries are really consumed at home by its own residents; they are deducted from merchandise exports as recorded in the balance of payments. Similarly it considers any merchandise gifts from foreigners as not received at all, and hence deducts them from merchandise imports. If the gift is in cash, rather than in kind, a different and equally fictional treatment is applied; a cash gift *to* foreigners is treated as an import of goods and services *from* foreigners. The fiction is that no gift at all is made and hence the money must have been used by the reporting country to purchase goods and services abroad for itself. Imports which never occurred are therefore imputed to the country's balance of payments. By the same process, exports which never occurred are added to total exports of goods and services of the reporting country when cash gifts are made by foreigners.

In view of the great magnitude of post-war donations in the form of inter-governmental grants (e.g. UNRRA, Marshall Aid, military assistance), this fictional treatment of foreign trade may seriously misrepresent its impact on the national economy. But there is nothing inherently necessary in the fictional approach. The major balance of payments categories of (1) goods and services, (2) donations, and (3) capital movements can be utilized directly to give an accurate statement of the international component of the national product. This component is either the net export of goods and services or, in reverse, the net of donations and capital movements combined; both give the same figure. The report prepared in August, 1952, by a Committee of National Income Experts appointed by the Secretary General of the United Nations embodies this approach. While it subdivides the International Monetary Fund's category of services into what it regards as (1) services proper and (2) net factor income payments, the division does not alter the basic consistency of the experts' concept of the national accounts with the Fund's concept of the balance of payments. It is to be hoped that this realistic approach, which records merchandise transactions as they in fact occurred, will be generally accepted in national income work.

ILLUSTRATIVE REPORTS TO THE INTERNATIONAL MONETARY FUND

Merchandise entries; United States, 1950, and Finland, 1949. Table 1 shows the derivation of the merchandise entries in the United States balance of payments for 1950 and illustrates the diversity of the adjustments required in employing trade returns for balance of payments purposes. The references in parentheses to items 1.1 and 1.2 are to the items so numbered in Table I (Balance of Payments Summary).

Table 1

	Exports	Imports
	(in millions of dollars)	
Exports and imports as recorded, f.a.s.	10,272	8,845
Adjustments for coverage		
Additions		
Silver.	6	106
Parcel post	72	—
Goods in kind	289	—
Reparations in kind	—	10
Electric power and gas	2	6
Military procurement of goods consumed outside country of origin	—	177
Non-military procurement	—	6
Deductions		
Films on rental basis	—11	—
Surplus property exports	—25	—25
Trade with Panama Canal Zone	—23	—3
Migrants' household effects	—	—
Other	—	—1
Adjustments for valuation		
Revaluation resulting from		
Direct investment (bananas)	—	95
Grants in kind	—	—
Other	—5	—
Adjusted total (item 1.1)	10,577	9,216
Other sales and purchases		
Merchandise transactions abroad	53	54
Adjustment for changes in stocks	—	—
United States-owned goods abroad	11	6
Foreign-owned goods in United States	—	7
Total (item 1.2)	64	67

Although the adjustments for most other countries are less numerous, they are frequently of greater quantitative importance.   Table 2 illustrates the importance of these adjustments in the case of Finland in 1949.

Table 2

	Exports	Imports
	(million markkas)	
Exports (f.o.b.) and imports (c.i.f.) as recorded . . .	65,610	66,280
Adjustments for coverage		
Additions		
Loading charges for some goods	120	—
Reparations to USSR	12,230	—
Smuggling	—	230
Gifts in kind	—	630
Electricity	—	10
Deductions		
Gold transactions	−100	−20
Adjustments for valuation		
Revaluation of imports under documentary credits*. .	—	2,350
Adjustments for timing		
On goods shipped under Armistice agreement with USSR†.	−620	—
Adjusted total (item 1.1)	77,240	69,480

* Imports under documentary credits have been converted into domestic currency in the trade statistics at the exchange rates prevailing when the credits were opened. This adjustment is necessary to correct the undervaluation of imports under documentary credits opened prior to devaluation, but utilized subsequently.

† According to the Armistice Agreement with USSR, Finland was obligated to transfer to the USSR goods equivalent in value to former German claims on Finland. This debt was fixed in 1946 at 5988 million markkas and a special account was opened with the Bank of Finland and credited with that amount.   The adjustment shown here is made in order to show the merchandise transfers as of the time when this account was debited for deliveries.   In 1949 recorded exports amounted to 1150 million markkas, but the special account was debited for 530 million markkas only.

Merchandise imports by regions; Norway, 1949.   The adaptation of trade statistics for use in a regional balance of payments is illustrated in Table 3 showing the derivation of the merchandise import entries in the Norwegian statement for 1949.

Table 3

	Trade Returns (Special Trade Imports c.i.f.)	Adjustments			Adjusted Total
		For Coverage	To f.o.b. Basis	To Purchase –Sale basis	
		(In millions of Norwegian kroner)			
United States . .	589	1	−57	62	595
Canada . . .	88	—	−7	−15	66
United States . .	1073	46	−101	337	1355
Rest of sterling area					
In Europe . .	4	—	—	2	6
In Far East . .	57	—	−2	−33	22
Elsewhere . .	141	—	−4	−100	37
Continental Europe					
OEEC countries . .	1886	6	−123	78	1847
Eastern Europe . .	306	—	−26	−6	274
Middle East . . .	123	—	−2	−106	15
Far East . . .	90	—	−2	−47	41
Latin America . .	333	—	−17.	−140	176
Rest of world. . .	126	10	−9	−32	95
Total . . .	4816	63	−350	—	4529

Compensatory financing ; United States, 1947–1950. Table 4, which summarizes the United States balance of payments in the post-war period, has been selected to illustrate the compensatory financing form used by the Fund in analyzing foreign exchange problems. It shows the extent of the United States surplus for which compensatory financing was supplied (1) by foreign countries using their gold and dollar reserves, or (2) by grants and loans from the United States and international institutions. A major part of this surplus took the form of net exports of merchandise. Movements of services, private donations, private capital, special official financing, and errors and omissions were substantial, but to a considerable extent offsetting, in the years before 1950. A full discussion of the compensatory financing concept is given in the Fund's *Balance of Payments Yearbook* for 1938, 1946, and 1947 (pp. 4–24) and for 1949–1950 (pp. 19–23).

Compensatory financing by regions; Denmark, 1949. The financing form is also used in presenting regional balance of payments statements. A country may have surpluses with some areas and deficits with others. If its surpluses are with soft currency areas and its deficits with hard currency areas, an exchange problem may arise even though it has an over-all balance. The 1949 regional data for Denmark are given in Table 5.

Table 4

INTERNATIONAL TRANSACTIONS OF THE UNITED STATES
(In millions of United States dollars.   No sign indicates credit ; minus sign (—) indicates debit.)

	1947	1948	1949	1950
A. GOODS AND SERVICES				
Exports, f.a.s.	15,127	13,077	12,298	10,641
Imports, f.a.s.	−6,072	−7,787	−7,105	−9,283
Trade balance	9,055	5,290	5,193	1,358
Foreign travel	−206	−292	−325	−350
Transportation	1,027	657	521	128
Investment income	1,191	1,515	1,346	1,600
Government, not included elsewhere	470	−269	−374	−427
Other services*	209	199	140	190
Total	11,746	7,100	6,501	2,499
B. PRIVATE DONATIONS AND CAPITAL MOVEMENTS				
Donations	−662	−649	−513	−480
United States private capital:				
Direct investment	−1,123	−1,265	−1,329	−1,145
Other long-term	−56	−178	59	−437
Short-term	−46	69	61	−276
Foreign private capital	−60	−36	145	763
Total	−1,947	−2,059	−1,577	−1,575
C. SPECIAL OFFICIAL FINANCING				
Lend-lease settlements, etc.	254	161	19	25
Repayments of United States Government loans	278	296	198	323
Short-term procurement credits, etc..	16	93	−171	−81
United States Government project grants	−310	−247	−314	−807
United States Government project loans	−75	−65	−103	−164
IRO, ICEF, and United Nations (Palestine refugee) donations	−33	−116	−103	−57
IBRD project loans	−5	−15	−54	−64
Total	125	107	−528	−825
D. NET ERRORS AND OMISSIONS	980	1,046	936	156
E. SURPLUS (*A* THROUGH *D*)	10,904	6,194	5,332	255
F. COMPENSATORY OFFICIAL FINANCING				
United States Government				
Grants extended	−1,263	−3,897	−4,816	−3,190
Credits: Long-term	−4,020	−1,205	−586	−251
Short-term	−24	−141	116	108
International institutions				
UNRRA	−543	—	—	—
IBRD loans	−295	−178	−7	—
IMF advances	−462	−203	−99	21
Foreign governments and banks				
Use of dollar assets (−)†	−1,450	960	224	1,314
Net sales (−) of gold to United States‡	−2,847	−1,530	−164	1,743
Total	−10,904	−6,194	−5,332	−255

* Including non-monetary gold movement.
† Including, in 1947, 1948, and 1949, private balances which are not available separately.
‡ Includes purchases from or sales to private industry in the United States and international institutions other than the IMF and IBRD.

Table 5

REGIONAL CLASSIFICATION OF THE INTERNATIONAL TRANSACTIONS OF DENMARK, 1949

(In millions of Danish kroner.   No sign indicates credit;   minus sign (—) indicates debit.)

	United States	Canada	United Kingdom	Rest of Sterling Area — In Europe	Rest of Sterling Area — In Far East	Rest of Sterling Area — Elsewhere	Continental Europe* — OEEC Countries	Continental Europe* — Eastern	Middle East†	Far East†	Latin America†	Rest of World‡	Unallocated	Total
A. GOODS AND SERVICES														
Exports, f.o.b.	118	10	1564	39	32	19	1310	353	41	25	53	80	—	3644
Imports, f.o.b. §	−577	−13	−1257	−6	−29	−40	−1235	−471	−17	−37	−110	−80	—	−3872
Trade balance	−459	−3	307	33	3	−21	75	−118	24	−12	−57	—	—	−228
Foreign travel	−45	—	3	3	—	15	−56	—	14	6	24	8	−6	−50
Transportation	−46	3	26	3	36	—	−23	−10	—	11	5	3	—	−51
Investment income	3	—	−19	5	—	—	−29	2	—	—	1	1	−6	−75
Other	—	—	−1	—	—	—	24	—	—	—	—	—	−5	30
Total	−547	−3	316	44	39	−6	−9	−126	38	5	−27	12	−11	−272
B. OTHER NON-COMPENSATORY TRANSACTIONS														
Private capital movements	−26	−3	−37	−5	5	−5	−45	24	−4	−11	−1	—	−3	−111
Amortization	−19	—	−6	—	—	—	−20	30	—	—	—	—	—	−15
Other	−4	—	−9	—	—	—	2	—	—	—	—	−2	—	−13
Total	−49	−3	−52	−5	5	−5	−63	54	−4	−11	−1	−2	−3	−139
C. ERRORS AND OMISSIONS	−18	10	30	−29	−45	12	7	23	−27	6	5	−27	30	−23
D. SURPLUS OR DEFICIT (—) (A through C)	−614	7	294	10	−1	1	−65	−49	7	—	−23	−17	16	−434
E. COMPENSATORY OFFICIAL FINANCING														
Multilateral settlements	25	−7	−104	−10	—	—	95	51	−7	—	12	−38	−17	—
Other	—	—	—	—	—	—	—	—	—	—	—	—	—	—
ECA grant	434	—	—	—	—	—	—	—	—	—	—	—	—	434
ECA loan	66	—	—	—	—	—	—	—	—	—	—	—	—	66
Drawing rights (net)	—	—	—	—	—	—	79	—	—	—	—	36	—	79
Other loans	—	—	—	—	—	—	—	—	—	—	—	9	—	36
Payments and clearing agreements	—	—	−179	−1	1	−1	−93	−4	—	—	21	8	1	−247
Other short-term	89	—	−11	1	—	—	16	2	—	—	−10	2	—	64
Monetary gold	—	—	—	—	—	—	—	—	—	—	—	—	—	2
Total	614	−7	−294	−10	1	−1	65	49	−7	—	23	17	−16	434

* Excluding Spain, which is included with "Rest of world."
† Excluding sterling area and overseas possessions of the United States.
‡ International institutions (IMF and IBRD) and areas not listed elsewhere.
§ Including non-monetary gold movement.

CHAPTER 10

Index Numbers of Volume and Price

R. G. D. ALLEN
London School of Economics

GENERAL CONSIDERATIONS

Nature of the problem. For any country, the recorded aggregates of imports or exports are in terms of values at current prices. If the aggregates are used over a period of years, then they show only the combined effect of changes in the volume (or quantum) of trade and of changes in prices. One of the essential problems in analysing such data is to separate out the effect of the two factors—to determine how much of the change in value is due to changing prices and how much arises because of changes in volume of trade. This is the problem considered in the present chapter.

The trade aggregates may be defined in various ways, *e.g.*, special or general trade (see Chapter 3), and they may be shown in major groups of commodities according to various classifications (see Chapter 4). These differences are of little relevance to the present problem, which is to split changes in any given aggregate into volume and price components, whatever the aggregate may be. Usually, the split is to be made separately for imports and for exports (and for re-exports if distinguished), and for each of the major commodity groups of imports and of exports, according to the particular classification adopted.

Trade aggregates comprise a heterogeneous group of commodities for which there is no significant quantity measure common to all. It may be convenient, for some particular purposes, to combine all commodities into an aggregate in terms of "shipping tonnage," or some similar measure. This does not, however, solve the general problem of defining the volume change, since a ton of wheat is not to be taken as of equal standing as a ton of machinery, except (perhaps) for purposes of arranging shipping. The problem is essentially one of index numbers. It is only through the construction of index numbers, on lines to be indicated, that it is possible to get any measure of changes in volume of imports or exports.

One solution of the problem. Consider the data in Table 1 on exports of motor cars from the United Kingdom, as given in the publications of the British Board of Trade.

Table 1

Engine capacity	1948			1950		
	Number (000)	Value (£000)	Price (£ per car)	Number (000)	Value at 1950 prices (£000)	Value at 1948 prices (£000)
	1	2	3	4	5	6
Not over 1000 c.c. . . .	15·9	3,527	222	28·8	7,210	6,394
Over 1000 and not over 1600 c.c.	127·5	33,138	260	166·1	47,896	43,186
Over 1600 and not over 2200 c.c.	24·4	9,789	401	47·9	19,181	19,208
Over 2200 c.c. . . .	7·8	4,624	593	31·6	16,873	18,739
Total	175·6	51,078		274·4	91,160	87,527

To simplify the problem, suppose that only four types of car are exported, one type in each of the four ranges of engine capacity, and that each type is sold at a uniform price. The prices in 1948 are shown in column 3, obtained by dividing the value of column 2 by the numbers of column 1.

The aggregate of exports of motor cars is not homogeneous since it is composed of four types of cars in varying proportions. It is, therefore, not appropriate to take the total number of cars exported to measure changes in the volume (or quantum) of exports. In fact, the increase in numbers, by 56 per cent from 175,600 in 1948 to 274,400 in 1950, understates the growth in exports by volume, since relatively more large cars were exported in 1950 than in 1948. The question is: what measure can be given to the increase in exports by volume?

Write the change in value of exports in percentage form:

$$V = \frac{91{,}160}{51{,}078}100 = 178$$

i.e., an increase of 78 per cent from 1948 to 1950. This arises partly because more cars were exported in 1950 and partly because prices were higher. The influence of rising prices needs to be eliminated. One way to do this is shown in column 6 of the table, which is the product of columns 3 and 4. The total of column 6 represents what the 1950 exports would have cost if the prices had remained unchanged (as in 1948). It is to be contrasted with the total of column 5, which is the actual cost of the 1950 exports (at 1950 prices). The totals of columns 2 and 6 show that the value of exports increased from £51,078,000 in 1948 to £87,527,000 in 1950 at a *fixed* set of prices, those of 1948. The ratio of these two totals is a measure of the change in exports by volume; no price changes are involved. The index of volume is

$$Q = \frac{1950 \text{ exports at 1948 prices}}{1948 \text{ exports at 1948 prices}}100 = \frac{87{,}527}{51{,}078}100 = 171$$

This index is called base-weighted since the fixed prices used are those of the first or base year 1948.

A corresponding measure of the increase in export prices can be derived from the condition that volume and price measures multiply to (and hence account for) the change in value of exports, *i.e.*, it is P where

$$V = P \times Q$$

i.e., $1 \cdot 78 = P \times 1 \cdot 71$ (omitting the 100 in V and Q)

i.e., $P = \dfrac{1 \cdot 78}{1 \cdot 71}100 = 104$ (putting back the 100)

It is easily seen that

$$P = \frac{1950 \text{ exports at 1950 prices}}{1950 \text{ exports at 1948 prices}}100 = \frac{91{,}160}{87{,}527}100 = 104$$

Since the comparison of the two sets of prices is by means of the quantities exported in the second or current year 1950, this price index is called current-weighted. It is obtained most easily by division of the volume index (already obtained) into the value change. The result is:

$$V = P \times Q$$
$$1 \cdot 78 = 1 \cdot 04 \times 1 \cdot 71$$

The conclusion is that the value of exports of motor cars increased by 78 per cent from 1948 to 1950, an increase of 71 per cent in volume combined with an increase of 4 per cent in price.

The method is standard, adopted by many countries in their compilations of index numbers of volume and price. It can be readily extended to cover wider groups or the total of exports or imports. For the aggregate of all British exports in the years 1938 and 1947, the method gives the following totals: [1]

	Value of Exports in	At Prices of	£ (millions)
(1)	1938	1938	471
(2)	1947	1947	1138
(3)	1947	1938	524

Here (1) and (2) are recorded values; only (3) is the result of a special compilation, a cross-valuation of 1947 exports, item by item in quantity, at prices of 1938. The following index numbers are for 1947 with 1938 = 100:

$$\text{Value} \quad V = \frac{(2)}{(1)}100 = \frac{1138}{471}100 = 241\cdot6$$

$$\text{Volume} \quad Q = \frac{(3)}{(1)}100 = \frac{524}{471}100 = 111\cdot2$$

$$\text{Price} \quad P = \frac{(2)}{(3)}100 = \frac{1138}{524}100 = 217\cdot2$$

and
$$2\cdot416 = 2\cdot172 \times 1\cdot112$$

An increase of 142 per cent in value of exports from 1938 to 1947 is composed of an increase of 117 per cent in price and of 11 per cent in volume.

Quantities and prices. In the example of motor cars, quantities were numbers of cars and prices were in units of pounds per car. The definition of quantities and prices for the various " commodities " in trade aggregates, however, needs some examination. The quantity can generally be measured in alternative units, *e.g.*, numbers of motor cars, or weight in short tons, or volume in " shipping tons " as crated for export. If the commodity is homogeneous, this will not matter since there will be a definite and fixed relation between the units. If the commodity varies in type or quality over time, and particularly if the " commodity " is in practice a group of rather different items varying in composition, then the unit of quantity does matter. For example, of 175,600 cars exported from the United Kingdom in 1948, about $4\frac{1}{2}$ per cent were of the largest type; $11\frac{1}{2}$ per cent of the 274,400 cars exported in 1950 were of this type. If the cars were recorded by weight, the proportion of the largest cars would be higher each year and (more important) the measure of the change from 1948 to 1950 would be different.

[1] See Table 3, p. 195.

There is a corresponding element of arbitrariness about the price per unit when the "commodity" varies in content. It follows that the "prices" to be used in an index number of price changes can be variously interpreted. On the one hand, a price can mean *unit value, i.e.,* total recorded value of a commodity group divided by the total quantity in certain selected units. On the other hand, it can mean a *price quotation* for a commodity of certain definite specification and on a definite market on which imported or exported commodities are handled. Unit value reflects not only changes in price quotations, but also changes in the make-up of the commodity group in question, *e.g.,* motor cars of various types. By restricting the scope of the group, *e.g.,* by taking only motor cars of the same engine rating in one group, the difference between unit value and price quotations can be reduced, but never eliminated completely. In practice, any commodity group includes some variations in type or quality, and the value recorded in trade aggregates will not be derived from any single price quotation.

For example, in Table 1, above, the four entries in column 3 are taken as price quotations, on the simplifying assumption. For the aggregate of cars exported in 1948, however, only a unit value can be obtained, *i.e.,* 175,600 cars costing £51,078,000, giving £291 per car on the average. This unit value of £291 per car depends on the composition of the exports by type of car. Therefore, if 274,400 cars had been exported as in 1950 but at the same 1948 prices, then their cost would have been £87,527,000, as shown in column 6 of the table. This gives a unit value of £319 per car exported, though all the separate price quotations are exactly as before. Further, in practice, even the four "prices" of column 3 are unit values, since each of the four types of cars is itself heterogeneous to a greater or lesser extent.

As a practical matter, index numbers must be derived from trade aggregates as recorded. Prices are then to be taken and interpreted as unit values. This will be assumed to be the case in the present chapter. It can be noticed, however, that some countries use price quotations instead of unit values in some of the computations; but this is seldom done in more than a small section of the whole, and it does not generally alter the basic nature of the computation built up from unit values.

The practice in the compilation of the index numbers has been largely determined by the fact that it is the volume or quantum index which is of prime interest, the corresponding price index being derived to match, *i.e.,* as an index of unit values. Many countries, however, are feeling the need for a separate index of import or export prices in the sense of price quotations as made to or by importers and exporters. Such index numbers are probably treated best in relation to, or as part of, general index numbers of wholesale prices based on price quotations on various markets.

TYPES OF INDEX NUMBERS

Introduction. A simple solution of the problem of defining volume and price index numbers has been given. The problem was put in its simplest form, and the many complications met in practice were ignored. Moreover, it is easily seen that the solution offered is not unique; it is only one of many possible solutions. The remainder of this chapter is concerned with the complications and it is necessarily somewhat technical in character.

An algebraic notation is now introduced to facilitate the exposition. If a country exports only one commodity of unchanging quality, let q units be exported at a price p in any period. Then the value of exports is

$$V = p \times q$$

Let subscripts o and n denote any two periods compared, so that

$$V_o = p_o q_o \qquad \text{and} \qquad V_n = p_n q_n$$

i.e.,
$$\frac{V_n}{V_o} = \frac{p_n}{p_o} \times \frac{q_n}{q_o}$$

and the value change V_n/V_o is split into a price component p_n/p_o and a volume component q_n/q_o. But as soon as more than one commodity enters into exports, such a split ceases to be unique. If Σ denotes summation over all commodities, with p and q applying to a typical commodity, then

$$V_o = \Sigma p_o q_o \qquad \text{and} \qquad V_n = \Sigma p_n q_n$$

i.e.,
$$\frac{V_n}{V_o} = \frac{\Sigma p_n q_n}{\Sigma p_o q_o}$$

It is no longer possible to split the value change in any simple way, *e.g.*,

$$\frac{V_n}{V_o} \text{ is } not \text{ equal to } \Sigma\frac{p_n}{p_o} \times \Sigma\frac{q_n}{q_o}$$

nor to any other simple components representing price and volume changes separately. Any split of V_n/V_o must be more complicated and, moreover, it can be made in alternative ways. One way is to introduce the " cross-valuation " $\Sigma p_n q_o$, representing the exports of the first period (o) valued at the prices of the second period (n). The price component is then the ratio of this cross-valuation to V_o, a ratio which measures price changes by means of fixed quantities q_o of exports. The volume component is the ratio of V_n to the cross-valuation, a measure of quantity changes by means of fixed prices p_n of exports. A second way is to introduce the cross-valuation $\Sigma p_o q_n$, i.e., the exports of the second period valued at the prices of the first period. A second pair of components, one for price and the other for volume, is then obtained; it is this pair which has already been derived in the simple example of exports of motor cars.

In algebraic terms:

$$\frac{V_n}{V_o} = \frac{\Sigma p_n q_o}{\Sigma p_o q_o} \times \frac{\Sigma p_n q_n}{\Sigma p_n q_o} = \frac{\Sigma p_n q_n}{\Sigma p_o q_n} \times \frac{\Sigma p_o q_n}{\Sigma p_o q_o}$$

where the first term of each pair is the price, and the second the volume, component. These are two of many different possible splits. The whole problem arises because of the heterogeneous aggregate (here $V = \Sigma pq$), and the practical question is to decide what *type* of index numbers to employ in any particular case.

This formulation of the problem also throws light on another point. Though very simple, it is often forgotten in practice and much misunderstanding may result. The figure to be split is the change in value from one period to another, and value is the *product* of price and quantity. It follows naturally that the value change to be analysed is in *ratio* form V_n/V_o and not a difference $V_n - V_o$, i.e., a percentage increase, not an absolute increase in money units. Further, the split sought is the *product* of two components, and not a sum; and each component, one of price change and the other of volume change, is in ratio form. In short, a percentage change in value is analysed into the product of a percentage change in price with a percentage change in volume. It is not generally meaningful to attempt to divide an absolute change in value into the sum of a change due to price movements and a change due to volume. This point is illustrated later with an actual example (p. 196).

Finally, the quantity q and the price p used here for a typical " commodity " must in practice be interpreted in terms of a group of items varying in composition. The " quantity " is selected for convenience and applied to the group " commodity " as a whole. The " price " is then the unit value for the group " commodity " and dependent on the composition of the group.

Classification of index numbers. Various types of index numbers can be used to separate volume (quantum) changes from price (unit value) changes. They can be grouped into two broad classes, fixed-base and chained index numbers, as shown algebraically in Table 2 with the notation already given. The index numbers in the table, as in all algebraic developments in this chapter, are expressed in the form of ratios; these can be multiplied by 100 to convert to the percentage form usually quoted.

In *fixed-base index numbers*, the current period (n) is compared directly with a selected and fixed base period (o). Apart from recorded values of

Table 2

Types of Index Numbers

Type	Volume Index	Price Index
A. Fixed base index numbers		
Base weights ($w_0 = p_0 q_0$)	$Q_1(o, n) = \dfrac{\Sigma p_0 q_n}{\Sigma p_0 q_0}$ $= \dfrac{\Sigma w_0(q_n/q_0)}{\Sigma w_0}$	$P_1(o, n) = \dfrac{\Sigma p_n q_0}{\Sigma p_0 q_0}$ $= \dfrac{\Sigma w_0(p_n/p_0)}{\Sigma w_0}$
Current weights ($w_n = p_n q_n$)	$Q_2(o, n) = \dfrac{\Sigma p_n q_n}{\Sigma p_n q_0}$ $= \dfrac{1}{\dfrac{\Sigma w_n(q_0/q_n)}{\Sigma w_n}}$	$P_2(o, n) = \dfrac{\Sigma p_n q_n}{\Sigma p_0 q_n}$ $= \dfrac{1}{\dfrac{\Sigma w_n(p_0/p_n)}{\Sigma w_n}}$
Cross weights (Fisher "Ideal")	$Q_3(o, n) = \sqrt{Q_1 \times Q_2}$ $= \sqrt{\dfrac{\Sigma p_0 q_n}{\Sigma p_0 q_0} \times \dfrac{\Sigma p_n q_n}{\Sigma p_n q_0}}$	$P_3(o, n) = \sqrt{P_1 \times P_2}$ $= \sqrt{\dfrac{\Sigma p_n q_0}{\Sigma p_0 q_0} \times \dfrac{\Sigma p_n q_n}{\Sigma p_0 q_n}}$
B. Chained index numbers		
Moving anterior weights	$Q_1(n-1, n) = \dfrac{\Sigma p_{n-1} q_n}{\Sigma p_{n-1} q_{n-1}}$	$P_1(n-1, n) = \dfrac{\Sigma p_n q_{n-1}}{\Sigma p_{n-1} q_{n-1}}$
Moving current weights	$Q_2(n-1, n) = \dfrac{\Sigma p_n q_n}{\Sigma p_n q_{n-1}}$	$P_2(n-1, n) = \dfrac{\Sigma p_n q_n}{\Sigma p_{n-1} q_n}$
Moving cross weights	$Q_3(n-1, n) = \sqrt{Q_1 \times Q_2}$ $= \sqrt{\dfrac{\Sigma p_{n-1} q_n}{\Sigma p_{n-1} q_{n-1}} \times \dfrac{\Sigma p_n q_n}{\Sigma p_n q_{n-1}}}$	$P_3(n-1, n) = \sqrt{P_1 \times P_2}$ $= \sqrt{\dfrac{\Sigma p_n q_{n-1}}{\Sigma p_{n-1} q_{n-1}} \times \dfrac{\Sigma p_n q_n}{\Sigma p_{n-1} q_n}}$

Each of these index numbers can be chained by multiplication to give an index comparing period n with period o, e.g.,

$$Q_1(o, n) \text{ (chained)} = Q_1(o, 1) \times Q_1(1, 2) \times \ldots \times Q_1(n-1, n).$$

trade, the index numbers shown require only the construction of the cross-valuations already mentioned, i.e.,

Current quantities valued at base prices $\Sigma p_o q_n$

Base quantities valued at current prices $\Sigma p_n q_o$

The ratios between these and the recorded values, $\Sigma p_o q_o$ and $\Sigma p_n q_n$, provide two index numbers of volume and two of price. Of those for volume, Q_1 compares quantities, q_n with q_o, by valuing at fixed prices, those of the base period p_o, and so is base-weighted. Q_2 makes the same comparison with the aid of current prices p_n, and is current-weighted. As shown in Table 2, each can be written as a weighted average of quantity relatives. Q_1 averages q_n/q_o with weights taken as base-period values, $w_o = p_o q_o$ for each commodity. Q_2 is the reciprocal of a similar weighted average, i.e., q_o/q_n weighted with current values $w_n = p_n q_n$. The price index numbers P_1 and P_2 are similar. The geometric average of the two Q's, or of the two P's, gives the Fisher " Ideal " form of the index, a form which can be described as cross-weighted.

Exactly the same forms are used for *chained index numbers*, but the comparison is between the current period (n) and the previous period ($n - 1$). To get an index comparing with a fixed base period (o), a series of index numbers of one period compared with the previous period is linked by multiplication, from the current period back to the base period.

In practice the link between one period and the previous one can be interpreted in several ways, *e.g.*, one year with the previous year, one month with the monthly average (or the corresponding month) of the previous year.

The index numbers of volume and price can be paired off to analyse the change in value from period *o* to period *n*:

$$V(o, n) = \frac{\Sigma p_n q_n}{\Sigma p_o q_o}$$

With fixed-base index numbers, the pairings (by multiplication) are as follows:

$$V = P_1 \times Q_2 = P_2 \times Q_1 = P_3 \times Q_3$$

Since V is known from recorded trade aggregates, only one index of each pair need be calculated and the other follows by division into V. For example, suppose that the cross-valuation $\Sigma p_o q_n$ is computed (as is commonly done in practice) and that Q_1 is then obtained as the base-weighted volume index. By division into the value change, a price index is derived which can be identified as the current-weighted form, *i.e.*,

$$P_2 = \frac{V}{Q_1}$$

The same relations hold for chained index numbers. For example

$$P_2(o, n) \text{ (chained)} = P_2(o, 1) \times P_2(1, 2) \times \ldots P_2(n-1, n)$$
$$= \frac{V(o, 1)}{Q_1(o, 1)} \times \frac{V(1, 2)}{Q_1(1, 2)} \times \ldots \frac{V(n-1, n)}{Q_1(n-1, n)}$$
$$= \frac{V(o, n)}{Q_1(o, n) \text{ (chained)}}.$$

Illustrations. The construction of fixed-base index numbers is illustrated in Table 3, which relates to exports of domestic produce of the United Kingdom as derived from official data published by the British Board of Trade. In the comparison of 1935 with 1930, it is seen that the index numbers of volume lie close together, as do those of price. In this period, the general relations

$$V = P_1 \times Q_2 = P_2 \times Q_1 = P_3 \times Q_3$$

become

$$0 \cdot 746 = 0 \cdot 858 \times 0 \cdot 870 = 0 \cdot 821 \times 0 \cdot 908 = 0 \cdot 839 \times 0 \cdot 889$$

It matters little which pairing of index numbers is used, and P_3 may be taken with Q_3 in reaching a conclusion. The broad result is that the recorded reduction of 25 per cent in value of exports from 1930 to 1935 is compounded of a reduction of about 16 per cent in price and a reduction of about 11 per cent in volume. A similar conclusion is reached for the period 1935–1938. On the other hand, the comparison of 1947 with 1938

Table 3

United Kingdom Exports of Domestic Produce

Values	Comparison		
	1930/1935	1935/1938	1938/1947
	£ (millions)	£ (millions)	£ (millions)
First year, recorded value (1) . . .	571	426	471
value at second-year prices (2)	490	486	1147
Second year, value at first-year prices (3)	519	418	524
recorded value (4) . .	426	471	1138

Index numbers		1935 (1930=100)	1938 (1935=100)	1947 (1938=100)
Value	$V = \dfrac{(4)}{(1)}100$ . .	74·6	110·5	241·6
Volume	$Q_1 = \dfrac{(3)}{(1)}100$ . .	90·8	98·1	111·2
	$Q_2 = \dfrac{(4)}{(2)}100$ . .	87·0	96·9	99·2
	$Q_3 = \sqrt{Q_1 \times Q_2}$.	88·9	97·5	105·0
Price	$P_1 = \dfrac{(2)}{(1)}100$ . .	85·8	114·0	243·6
	$P_2 = \dfrac{(4)}{(3)}100$ . .	82·1	112·6	217·2
	$P_3 = \sqrt{P_1 \times P_2}$ . .	83·9	113·3	230·0

leads to a much less definite result since the pairs of index numbers are quite widely divergent:

$$2·416 = 2·436 \times 0·992 = 2·172 \times 1·112 = 2·300 \times 1·050$$

No close estimation of price and volume changes is now possible; the changes in composition of trade following World War II make it impracticable to answer accurately the question of what part of the recorded increase of 142 per cent in value of exports is due to price changes and what part due to changes in volume. In particular, even the direction of the change in volume is uncertain since Q_2 shows a slight decline and Q_1 an increase. Though P_3 and Q_3 may be used as indicators, it must be remembered that each of these is only an average within a wide range.

For each of the periods of Table 3, it is seen that $P_1 > P_2$ and $Q_1 > Q_2$, i.e., the base-weighted form is higher than the current-weighted. This is usually, but not inevitably, the case. Broadly, the relation holds whenever demand or consumption tends to fall off for commodities which have risen most in price over the period concerned, the usual state of affairs.

The construction has proceeded in terms of the product of percentage changes. When it is concluded that a fall of 16 per cent in price is combined with a fall of 11 per cent in volume to account for the recorded fall of 25 per cent in value of exports between 1930 and 1935, this simply expresses the approximate relation:

$$0 \cdot 75 = 0 \cdot 84 \times 0 \cdot 89$$

An attempt to express the same thing in actual changes (in millions of pounds) does not give anything better. For example, the price index P_2 may be used as a deflator in the period 1930–1935:

	£ (millions)		£ (millions)
1930 recorded value	. . . 571		
1935 value at 1930 prices	$\dfrac{426}{0 \cdot 821} = 519$	$\therefore$ decrease due to volume	. . 52
1935 recorded value	. . . 426	$\therefore$ decrease due to price	. . 93
		Total decrease . . 145	

A different result is obtained if another deflator is used, say P_1:

	£ (millions)		£ (millions)
1930 recorded value	. . . 571		
1935 value at 1930 prices	$\dfrac{426}{0 \cdot 858} = 497$	$\therefore$ decrease due to volume	. . 74
1935 recorded value	. . . 426	$\therefore$ decrease due to price	. . 71
		Total decrease . . 145	

This is not a good method of deflation since P_1 is base (1930) weighted and it is not appropriately divided into the current (1935) value. However, it is quite commonly attempted in practice; the difficulty is not so easily seen in computing absolute changes as in pairing off percentage changes. A further (and quite valid) result is obtained if the calculation is worked the other way around, the effect of price being estimated before that of volume. With P_1 used as an appropriate inflator, the computation proceeds:

	£ (millions)		£ (millions)
1930 recorded value	. . 571		
1930 value at 1935 prices	$571 \times 0 \cdot 858 = 490$	$\therefore$ decrease due to price	. . 81
1935 recorded value	. . 426	$\therefore$ decrease due to volume	. . 64
		Total decrease . . 145	

It is clearly less ambiguous, and more intelligible, to express the component changes directly in the form of percentage movements, and to take them as multiplicative in analysing the percentage change in value.

INDEX NUMBERS IN PRACTICE

Practices of various countries. A survey of practice in the more important countries [2] leads to the following general comments.

[2] See United Nations Paper E/CN3/107 (April 1950).

The most common practice is the direct computation of the base-weighted volume index Q_1 with the aid of the cross-valuation $\Sigma p_o q_n$. The corresponding current-weighted price index P_2 is then derived by dividing V by Q_1. This is the method adopted by the United Kingdom and by many other countries, e.g., Belgium, Czechoslovakia, France, Netherlands, and Norway. In some countries, the same pair of index numbers is computed by obtaining P_2 by direct computation and Q_1 by division of V by P_2; this is true of India (index numbers on base 1927–1928 as computed before 1949) and also of Malaya.

A few countries compute the pair of index numbers P_1 and Q_2 with the aid of the single cross-valuation $\Sigma p_n q_o$. The leading example is Canada, but other countries such as Finland also use the method. Australia computes index numbers for imports and for exports on rather different methods, and makes alternative calculations for each. The Australian price index numbers used by the United Nations Statistical Office, however, are of the form P_1, and the corresponding Q_2 form is then derived by division of V by P_1.

At least two countries, Portugal and Switzerland, compute base-weighted index numbers for both volume and prices, i.e., P_1 and Q_1, without matching a pair to give the split of the value change. However, the corresponding index numbers, Q_2 and P_2 are derivable by division into V (from recorded trade), and either pair, P_1 with Q_2 or P_2 with Q_1, can be used. The cross-weighted forms, P_3 and Q_3 also follow from the index numbers computed. Brazil can also be put in this category; she makes separate calculations, though on incomplete coverage, of P_1, P_2, Q_1 and Q_2.

There remain at least four countries using more complicated methods involving crossed weighting usually combined with some form of chaining. The leading example of the simplest form of crossed weighting is provided by the index numbers computed by Italy since 1948. The forms P_3 and Q_3, of Fisher type with fixed and current weights crossed, are used for the monthly as well as for the annual index. In the other countries, the United States, Ireland and Sweden, some form of chaining is adopted, at least for the monthly or quarterly index numbers.

In Sweden, the annual index numbers are of the Fisher forms P_3 and Q_3, taken directly back to a fixed base. The quarterly index numbers are chained to the preceding year; the price index takes the form $P_1 (n-1,n)$ where $(n-1)$ represents the average for the preceding year and n is the current quarter, whereas the volume index is derived by division into the value change.

The United States index numbers computed annually are of the form $P_3(o, n)$ (chained) with the corresponding index $Q_3 (o, n)$ (chained) obtained by division into $V(o, n)$. The basic calculation is, therefore,

$$P_3(n-1, n) = \sqrt{\frac{\Sigma p_n q_{n-1}}{\Sigma p_{n-1} q_{n-1}} \times \frac{\Sigma p_n q_n}{\Sigma p_{n-1} q_n}}$$

The compilation is done separately for each economic class of commodities, and the combined index is obtained by use of group weights, again using weights in both years $(n-1)$ and n. The monthly index numbers are chained in much the same way, but each month is related to the monthly average of the previous year, i.e., the chaining proceeds from year to year. The Irish computations are similar, except that the *monthly* price index numbers are not of crossed-weight form, but are $P_1(n-1, n)$ for imports and $P_2(n-1, n)$ for exports.

Accuracy of index numbers. It goes without saying that the first requisite of accurate index numbers is accuracy in recording of trade by value. But this is by no means all. The index numbers computed in practice involve some cross-valuation, e.g., $\Sigma p_o q_n$, the value of trade in the current period at prices of the base period, as used in Q_1 and P_2. Two very important requirements for accuracy thus arise. One is the accurate recording of quantity data, item by item through the list of commodities. The other is consistent pairing off of quantity with value data, item by item. The prices p are, in fact, unit values obtained by dividing quantity into value for each separate item; they are only accurate to the extent that the recorded quantity matches exactly the recorded value. It is not sufficient, for example, to aggregate quantities for only part of the shipments comprising the record of value. Moreover, the cross-valuation is a multiplication of quantities *in one period* with unit values *in another period* and so there must be consistency over time; the quantities and values in one period must refer to exactly the same item as those in the other period.

All this is seldom realized, or even closely approached, in practice. The requirement of consistency over time is particularly difficult to meet. Suppose that the item concerned consists of exports of automobiles of a particular engine rating. Inevitably, the composition of the item will change over time as different kinds of cars are exported, as new models are introduced, and as new makes are put on the export market. New commodities raise the difficulty in its most aggravated form. Some allowance can be made in many cases, e.g., by inventing a " price " for the new commodity in periods before it entered into trade. Such allowances are easier when the chained, as opposed to the fixed-base, method is employed. In the end, however, new commodities become so numerous, or include such major innovations (e.g., television receivers), that the whole method of cross-valuation breaks down.   This point is developed below when runs of index numbers are considered.

Another defect in practice is that it is generally impossible to run through the whole list of commodities, item by item, obtaining quantity data to match values in all cases.   These are nearly always items so mixed in content that no meaningful quantity can be recorded, *e.g.*, the familiar " all other " item at the end of a category in a commodity classification. Methods of allowing for this difficulty are examined in the following paragraphs.

It remains true, however, that the prime requirement is for quantity and value data in the basic records which are as accurate in themselves, and as comparable over time, as can be achieved.   No allowances for defects, no manipulation of data, can do more than help to cover up deficiencies.

Adjustments for incomplete coverage. It is generally impossible in practice to include all individual commodities entering into trade in the compilation of an index of volume or price which involves a cross-valuation of quantities in one period at prices of another.   The individual items are often thousands in number and, even so, include some mixed, miscellaneous, or " all other " groupings.   Information on quantities is lacking for many items in the trade records, particularly for those of a miscellaneous kind.   Such items cannot be included in a cross-valuation and so do not appear directly in the compilation of index numbers. Typically some 75 per cent of all trade by value is given in sufficient quantity detail to be used directly in the compilations, though proportions as low as 50 per cent and as high as 95 per cent or more are found for some countries.   The question is what adjustment, if any, should be made in the final index to allow for incomplete coverage in commodity detail. This is considered at some length in a technical paper issued by the Statistical Office of the United Nations.[3]

The common practice among individual countries is to make such an adjustment and to do so by assuming that the *price changes* for the items not covered are the same as those for items which are included directly in the computation.   Some of these countries make the adjustment only in the total index for imports or exports, *i.e.*, the price changes in all items not included are assumed to be the same as the price change shown by the aggregate of all items covered by the computation.   Finland and Ireland are two countries adopting this method.   The nature of the adjustment can be seen from the following algebraic analysis.[4]

[3] " Indexes of Quantum in International Trade," *Statistical Papers*, Series M, 3 (30 August, 1949).
[4] For a further account, including numerical examples, see the United Nations Statistical Office Paper cited.

Suppose that the pair of index numbers calculated is

$$Q_1 = \frac{\Sigma p_o q_n}{\Sigma p_o q_o} \quad \text{combined with} \quad P_2 = \frac{\Sigma p_n q_n}{\Sigma p_o q_n}$$

so that the computation depends on the single cross-valuation $\Sigma p_o q_n$. Here Σ extends over *all* items in the total trade aggregate. In practice, the computation uses only a selection of items, and Σ' is written for the sum over these selected items. Then the cross valuation, and the two corresponding recorded values, for the selected items are

$$\Sigma' p_o q_n \qquad \Sigma' p_o q_o \quad \text{and} \quad \Sigma' p_n q_n$$

The index numbers formed from the partial coverage are

$$Q_1' = \frac{\Sigma' p_o q_n}{\Sigma' p_o q_o} \quad \text{and} \quad P_2' = \frac{\Sigma' p_n q_n}{\Sigma' p_o q_n}$$

The assumption is that the prices of items not covered all move in the same way as P_2', obtained from covered items. So, on this assumption

$$P_2 = P_2' = \frac{\Sigma' p_n q_n}{\Sigma' p_o q_n} \quad \text{and} \quad Q_1 = \frac{V}{P_2} = \frac{V}{P_2'} = \frac{V}{V'} \times \frac{V'}{P_2'}$$

i.e.,

$$Q_1 = \frac{V}{V'} Q_1'$$

where

$$V' = \frac{\Sigma' p_n q_n}{\Sigma' p_o q_o} \quad \text{which in general differs from} \quad V = \frac{\Sigma p_n q_n}{\Sigma p_o q_o}$$

Hence, the volume index derived by this method Q_1 differs for the unadjusted volume index Q_1' on the partial coverage, to the extent that the recorded value change in total differs from the recorded value change in the items covered.

Other countries, including most of those with very detailed trade returns, adopt the same method, but applied to each major commodity class separately. Here the assumption is that the price changes in items not covered within each separate class are the same as the price change shown by the items included in the calculation for the class. The adjustment is exactly as shown above, but, since it is made for each class, the adjustment is different for one class than it is for another and the total index is obtained by aggregating the separately adjusted class index numbers. This method is followed by the United States, the United Kingdom, Canada, Netherlands, and Sweden, amongst others. The method, or something similar, is necesary if index numbers for separate classes are published in addition to a total index for the whole trade aggregate. It can be noticed that Belgium adopts the method in computing class index numbers, but the total index is obtained by the broader method of assuming price changes in items not covered to be the same as all other items in the total aggregate.

An alternative method is to assume that *quantity changes* for the items not covered are the same as those for the items included in the calculation. The practical method is similar but the adjustment now affects the price index rather than the volume index. For example, if Q_1 and P_2 are the index numbers used, then with the notation above

$$Q_1 = Q_1' \quad \text{and} \quad P_2 = \frac{V}{V'}P_2'$$

This method is adopted by a few countries, *e.g.*, Spain, Dominican Republic, and (for special indexes with moving weights) Portugal. The index numbers computed by France before 1948 were adjusted by a method akin to this, since miscellaneous items within each major class were assumed to be a fixed proportion by quantity of the major class as a whole.

Finally, some countries make no adjustment for incomplete coverage. France (in the index numbers computed for 1948 and later years) and Italy are the leading examples. In this case, the index numbers cannot be taken as applying to the total aggregate of imports or exports, but only to that part of the aggregate used directly in the compilation of the index numbers.

The coverage of commodities directly included in the compilation of index numbers varies considerably from one country to another, and varies as between the aggregate of imports and of exports for one country. The coverage (by value) for imports varies between 55 per cent for Finland, 68 for Sweden, 72 per cent for Canada, 75 per cent for the United States on the one hand, and 94 per cent for Italy, 95 per cent for United Kingdom on the other (data for 1947 or 1948). There is generally less variation in the coverage for exports as between various countries. It is interesting to note, however, that the export coverage is lower than that for imports in many countries, particularly when manufactured goods predominate in exports and food and raw materials in imports. For example, the coverage in United Kingdom trade is about 75 per cent for exports as against 95 per cent for imports, whereas the United States coverage is 50 per cent for exports as compared with 75 per cent for imports. The adjustment for incomplete coverage is generally to be taken as a closer approximation where the direct coverage is larger.

A few countries claim to be able to include all items directly in their compilations of the index numbers. Czechoslovakia and Germany (Bizone) achieve this by grouping commodities in convenient categories and converting all quantities in a given category to a common unit such as the metric ton or cubic metre. Denmark obtains the same result by filling in the gaps where unit values cannot be derived from the trade returns (*e.g.*, because of lack of quantity data). The substitute prices are obtained by taking official price quotations for similar items. This is an instance of the use of price quotations instead of unit values in the index numbers of the " prices " of imports and exports.

An interesting experiment in an attempt to derive a " price " index closer to the concept of price quotations than to that of unit values is provided by some special index numbers calculated by the United Kingdom. A limited number of specific commodity items is selected (120 for imports, 150 for exports), including only items which are fairly homogeneous in quality and content. The unit values of the items, as derived from trade records and used in the index numbers, are approximations to price quotations at import or export. Further, to avoid changes in quality or composition which take place in the longer run, the index numbers are computed for the 12 months of each year with base and weights taken as the average of the previous year. This is a variant of the form $P_1 (n - 1, n)$ with moving anterior weights. The difficulty here is that a close approximation (though never a very close approximation) to price quotations can only be achieved at the expense of a low coverage of total trade. It remains true that a good price index for imports and exports, in the sense of price quotations for specific qualities rather than unit values, is only to be obtained by getting actual price quotations from the markets for imported commodities or for goods destined for export. It is probable that this can be done best as part of the compilation of index numbers of wholesale prices.

INDEX NUMBERS OVER A PERIOD OF YEARS

Runs of index numbers. So far the development has been concerned with comparisons between two periods only, *i.e.*, with index numbers which compare the " current " period n with a " base " period o. In practice, of course, the index numbers are compiled and published for a run of periods; months, quarters, and years. There are now some additional problems to be considered.

If the index selected is of the fixed-base type, then a particular period (denoted by the subscript o) is chosen as the base to relate to all other periods in the run of the index.[5] It remains, however, to choose the

[5] For the base, there is a choice between one particular year and a group of years. For example, Switzerland selects 1938 as the base of the volume index but the average of 1929–1938 as the base of the price index. There is usually little to choose between the two methods. There is possibly some advantage in taking an average of years as the base of a price index, since the weights involve the base quantities imported or exported and these may vary somewhat erratically from one year to another, with greater stability over a run of years.

period which is written as 100 in the run, *i.e.*, the *comparison base* as opposed to the fixed base of the index. It is desirable, and usually the practice, to select the fixed base as the comparison base. But it is possible to have a comparison base different from the fixed base and, as long as this is clearly indicated, no confusion need arise in practice. Several countries find this procedure convenient. Switzerland, for example, computes a base-weighted price index P_1 in which the fixed (weights) base is the average of 1929–1938, whereas the comparison base is the single year 1938.

Some care is needed in handling index numbers for which the fixed base and the comparison base are different. Suppose that the index is a base-weighted volume index of type Q_1 with period o as base. The run of the index, with period o also as a comparison base, is then

$$Q_1(o, 1) = \frac{\Sigma p_o q_1}{\Sigma p_o q_o}; \quad Q_1(o, 2) = \frac{\Sigma p_o q_2}{\Sigma p_o q_o}; \ldots Q_1(o, n) = \frac{\Sigma p_o q_n}{\Sigma p_o q_o}$$

If period 1 is now selected as a comparison base, then the new run is obtained by dividing through by $Q_1(o, 1)$:

$$Q_1'(1, 2) = \frac{Q_1(o, 2)}{Q_1(o, 1)}; \ldots Q_1'(1, n) = \frac{Q_1(o, n)}{Q_1(o, 1)}$$

The index $Q_1'(1, n)$ can be written in aggregate or in weighted average form as follows:

$$Q_1'(1, n) = \frac{\Sigma p_o q_n}{\Sigma p_o q_1} = \frac{\Sigma w_1(q_n/q_1)}{\Sigma w_1} \quad \text{where} \quad w_1 = p_o q_1$$

Notice that the weights w_1 are *not* the original weights $w_o = p_o q_o$ (the values of trade in the fixed base period), *nor* the corresponding values of trade in the comparison base period $p_1 q_1$. They are

$$w_1 = p_o q_1 = p_o q_o(q_1/q_o)$$

i.e., the original weights $p_o q_o$ modified by multiplication by the quantity change q_1/q_o from the fixed base to the comparison base.

If the index selected is of the chained form, then there are alternative ways of presenting a run of the index. The run may be shown in the form in which it is derived, as a series of separate links, each comparing the current period with the previous one. Alternatively, the links may be chained together so that, in the current period, the index is shown chained back to some convenient and fixed comparison base, *e.g.*,

$$Q_1(o, n) \text{ (chained)} = Q_1(o, 1) \times Q_1(1, 2) \times \ldots Q_1(n - 1, n)$$

The choice of comparison base here is nothing to do with the form of the index; it is largely a matter of convenience.

Long-run comparisons. Whatever form is selected for the index, there is always the risk that it will develop a bias in the course of time. In any case, the index must be expected to become less reliable as a measure of volume or price changes as the run becomes longer. It follows that the index must be examined at intervals with a view to revision, *e.g.*, by re-weighting and by re-basing.

With a fixed-base system, the need for revision is obvious when the base becomes so remote that the comparison is uncertain. A general test is provided by a compilation and comparison of the base-weighted and current-weighted forms, Q_1 and Q_2 in the case of volume index numbers. When Q_1 and Q_2 begin to diverge significantly, then there is need to consider the re-weighting. Most countries using fixed-base index numbers do, in fact, re-weight them at fairly regular and frequent intervals, perhaps every 5 or 10 years. For example, by 1951 most countries were either using a post-war year (often 1948) as base or considering a change to such a year from a pre-war base.

When the base of the index is changed at intervals in this way there is a series of quite separate runs of index numbers, each run being valid only for the limited interval for which it is compiled. Comparisons over longer intervals of time can only be achieved by splicing together the separate runs. For example, suppose that a volume index is always of the base-weighted form Q_1 but that the base is changed every 5 years with consequent re-weighting. Then, for a long-run comparison of year n with year o, the separate index numbers may be spliced by direct multiplication:

$$Q_1(o, n) = Q_1(o, 5) \times Q_1(5, 10) \times Q_1(10, 15) \times Q_1(15, n)$$

where $15 < n < 20$ in this instance. Since there are several forms of a fixed-base index, it is clear that the splicing can be done in several ways; it is certainly not a unique process. As between period 5 and 10, for example, the link can be provided by $Q_1(5, 10)$ or by $Q_2(5, 10)$, and these will differ; or it may be given better by the crossed form $Q_3(5, 10)$. The difficulty is that, if there is any bias in one of the links, then it remains, and may indeed be amplified, in the chain needed for a long-run comparison. The very fact that the base of the index needs to be changed after a time implies that comparisons over even longer intervals are suspect, no matter what devices are adopted to chain together the separate runs of index numbers. By their nature, index numbers can seldom be used for more than very rough comparisons over long intervals.

A chained-index system does not appear, at first sight, to be subject to the same limitations. The chaining can be continued indefinitely and there is no reason to expect that the successive links get more inaccurate with the passing of time. There is, however, still the need to consider revision—and to place wide margins of error on long-run comparisons.

A comparison of the Q_1 and Q_2 forms will again show this up. The two forms, taken back to period o as a comparison base, are now

$$Q_1(o, n) \text{ (chained)} = Q_1(o, 1) \times Q_1(1, 2) \times \ldots Q_1(n - 1, n)$$

$$Q_2(o, n) \text{ (chained)} = Q_2(o, 1) \times Q_2(1, 2) \times \ldots Q_2(n - 1, n)$$

Each pair of links, $Q_1(n - 1, n)$ and $Q_2(n - 1, n)$, may not be far apart in value; but the chained index numbers $Q_1(o, n)$ and $Q_2(o, n)$ can, and usually will, diverge significantly in time. Indeed, it is now clear that the chained form of index, with chaining done annually, is simply a fixed-base index with base changed every year (instead of less frequently) and spliced together into a chain of annual links.

The conclusion remains that index numbers provide only rough comparisons in the long run. This can be illustrated with the data of Table 3. There are three separate runs of index numbers for volume and price of United Kingdom exports, covering the periods 1930–1935, 1935–1938, and 1938–1947, respectively. An index for 1947 with 1930 = 100 can be computed by linking together the three runs, with various results. For example, an index of the volume of exports can be obtained by linking base-weighted forms Q_1, by linking current-weighted forms Q_2, or as a compromise by linking cross-weighted forms Q_3:

Index numbers 1947 (1930 = 100)

Q_1 form	$0.908 \times 0.981 \times 1.112 \times 100 = 99$
Q_2 form	$0.870 \times 0.969 \times 0.992 \times 100 = 84$
Q_3 form	$0.889 \times 0.975 \times 1.050 \times 100 = 91$

The results diverge considerably, and the weak link is clearly the last (1938–1947), covering World War II with its consequent dislocation of trade.

Illustrations. Figure A illustrates the method of long-run comparison of trade by means of index numbers of volume. The basic data are the values of British domestic exports and retained imports as recorded in the period 1901–1950 (British Isles up to March 1923 and subsequently United Kingdom, excluding the Republic of Ireland). For each series, index numbers of volume are constructed, partly from some very detailed calculations by W. Schlote [6] and partly from official compilations. There are two main runs for each index, spliced together in 1930. The first is Schlote's run of index numbers for 1901–1930, based on 1913, and calculated without break in base-weighted form. The second is derived from British Board of Trade index numbers from 1930–1950 and reduced to 1930 as 100.

---

[6] *Entwicklung und Strukterwandlungen des englischen Aussenhandels* (Gustav Fischer, Jena, 1938); English translation by Chaloner and Henderson, *British Overseas Trade* (Blackwell, Oxford, 1952).

Figure *A*.   BRITISH EXPORTS AND IMPORTS, 1901–1950

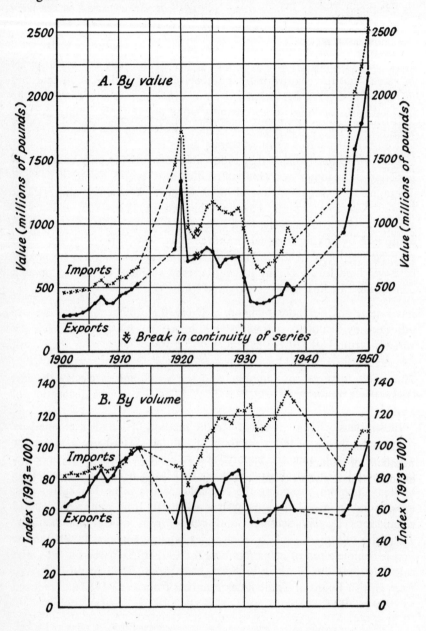

The second run is an example of the chaining of separate index numbers as examined above. The British Board of Trade has used successively 1930, 1935, 1938, and 1947 as the base of the official index numbers. The link between one series and the next is constructed from the cross-weighted form Q_3; there are three such links: from 1930 to 1935, from 1935 to 1938, from 1938 to 1947. Interpolation within the links is by the official base-weighted form Q_1, and extrapolation after 1947 is made similarly.

It is clear that comparisons of volume of trade over a period as long as 50 years can only be of the roughest kind, indicating orders of magnitude rather than accurate measures of changes. The composition of British imports, and still more of British exports, was completely different in 1950 from what it was in 1900, so that a change in " volume " from 1900 to 1950 can have no very precise meaning. The approximate nature of the compilations, involving so many links forged from different index numbers, only serves to emphasize what is, in any case, quite obvious.

There is one further complication to note, of a kind often met in practice. In 1923 there is a break in the original series of values of trade, due to the change in area resulting from the exclusion of the Republic of Ireland. From March 1923, all trade figures are higher in value than they would have been on the pre-1923 basis.[7] The index numbers of volume are adjusted, by Schlote, to allow for this break. The assumption that the *variation* from year to year in volume of trade is the same for the British Isles as for the United Kingdom is then made to permit the United Kingdom index numbers for 1930–1950 (1930 = 100) to be grafted on to the earlier index numbers adjusted to relate to the British Isles up to 1930.

TERMS OF TRADE

Definitions. Suppose that adequate compilations are made of index numbers of volume and price (unit value), both for imports and for exports over a given period. Comparing a current year (n) with a base year (o), denote the volume index numbers for imports and exports by Q_i and Q_e, respectively, and the corresponding price index numbers by P_i and P_e. The volume of imports in percentage of the volume of exports, for year n, relative to year o, defines the gross (barter) terms of trade:

$$G = \frac{Q_i}{Q_e} \times 100$$

This is in index number form with year o as 100. It measures the real gain from trade, comparing imports actually received with exports actually

---

[7] This is because United Kingdom exports to the Republic of Ireland exceed Ireland's exports to the rest of the world (outside the British Isles), and similarly for imports.

despatched.   Changes over time in the index G then show variations in the real gains from trade actually realized.   A rising value of G shows that more imports are purchased for a given volume of exports.   This may be because import prices have fallen or because of other factors in the balance of payments, such as increased use of " invisible " receipts.   To isolate the price effect from the others, define the price of exports in percentage of the price of imports, for year n in relation to year o, as the net (barter) terms of trade:

$$T = \frac{P_e}{P_i} \times 100$$

again in index number form with year o as 100. T measures the real cost of imports in terms of exports.   Changes in T represent the varying volume of imports which could be obtained, on the basis of price relations only, in return for a given volume of exports.   A rising value of T shows that imports are becoming relatively cheaper than exports and the terms of trade are said to move in the favourable direction.   Notice that

$$\frac{G}{T} = \frac{Q_i}{Q_e} \times \frac{P_i}{P_e} = \frac{V_i}{V_e}$$

i.e.,
$$G = \left(\frac{V_i}{V_e}\right)T$$

where V_i and V_e are index numbers of values of imports and exports (year o as 100).   Relative movements in imports and exports by quantity G and by price T are by no means independent; they combine to give the relative movements of value of imports and exports.

A rising value of T is favourable in the sense that more imports can be got from a unit of exports.   This is not the whole story, since at the same time the volume of exports may be increasing (also favourable) or decreasing (an offsetting unfavourable factor).   For example, in depression, the United Kingdom terms of trade tend to rise, since import prices fall more than export prices.   This favourable turn in the terms of trade is, in part at least, offset by a large contraction in the volume of both imports and exports.   More imports *could* be obtained provided that the volume of exports could be maintained; in fact, exports fall off and, to a less extent, imports also.   An index which reflects changes in the volume of trade as well as the terms of trade can be defined as the volume of imports obtainable from the income earned from exports.   Denote the index by I, the income terms of trade.[8]   Therefore by definition,

$$I \times P_i = \text{Income from exports} = Q_e \times P_e$$

[8] Introduced by Dorrance, " The Income Terms of Trade," *Review of Economic Studies*, 1948–1949.

Then $\qquad\qquad I = Q_e \times T$

i.e., the index I is the product of the volume of exports Q_e and the index of the terms of trade T, again with year o as 100. I can fall, even when the terms of trade are becoming favourable, provided that Q_e falls, as during depression.   Conversely, I can rise even where the terms of trade become unfavourable, as in the United Kingdom after 1945.

Figure *B*.   BRITISH TERMS OF TRADE, 1901–1950

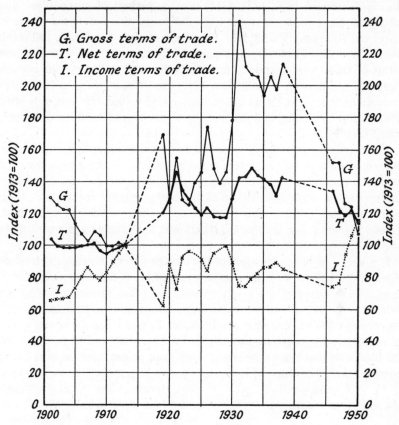

Illustrations.   Changes in the terms of trade of the United Kingdom during the period 1901–1950 are shown in Figure *B*.   The three forms *G*, *T*, and *I* as defined above are plotted on the chart; they are derived from index numbers of volume and price of domestic exports and of retained imports, expressed with 1913 = 100.   The volume index numbers are those calculated for Figure *A* and described above; the price index numbers are computed in the same way and on a comparable basis.

It has already been stressed that index numbers covering a period as long as 50 years must be very approximate. This limitation applies equally to the derived index numbers of the terms of trade shown in Figure B. The chart must not be used for more than an indication of orders of magnitude and of general directions of movement in the terms of trade. The data, however, are sufficiently good for some broad conclusions.

The net terms of trade T in the United Kingdom are more favourable during depression (e.g., 1931–1934) than in periods of prosperity. The effects of the two world wars were different; the net terms of trade improved following World War I but became less favourable following World War II. However, it is particularly relevant to notice that the terms of trade were unusually favourable in 1938 (following the depression). If comparison is made with 1929, the terms of trade in 1947–1949 were quite as favourable as in the earlier boom year. It was only after devaluation of sterling in 1949 that the terms of trade worsened as compared with 1929.

The picture is considerably modified when allowance is made for the volume of trade as well as the net terms of trade, as in the income terms of trade I. The index I falls both during the depression and during each of the two world wars, followed in each case by marked recoveries. High points for the income terms of trade occurred in 1913 and 1929, both " good " years. The level of 1913/1929 was not reached again until 1949 and was surpassed in 1950.

It is useful to have a measure of the change (improvement or deterioration) in the balance of merchandise trade which is due to a given movement in the terms of trade—as opposed to other factors affecting the balance. As with all index-number calculations this can be done in alternative ways. With base-year weighting, let V_e and V_i be the actual values of exports and imports, respectively, in the base year, and let P_e and P_i be the base-weighted index numbers of price (unit value) from the base to the current year. The value of base-year exports at prices of the current year is $V_e \times P_e$, and similarly, $V_i \times P_i$ for imports. The balance of merchandise trade, actually $(V_e - V_i)$ in the base year, would be

$$(V_e P_e - V_i P_i)$$

at current-year prices. The improvement in the balance, from the base to the current year, due to price movements alone is:

$$(V_e P_e - V_i P_i) - (V_e - V_i) = V_e(P_e - 1) - V_i(P_i - 1)$$

On the other hand, with current-year weighting, let V_e' and V_i' be actual values in the current year and P_e' and P_i' current-weighted price index numbers from the base to the current year. Then the improvement in the balance from the base to the current year is found to be:

$$V_e'\left(1 - \frac{1}{P_e'}\right) - V_i'\left(1 - \frac{1}{P_i'}\right)$$

The changes from 1947 to 1950 in the United Kingdom are:

	1947	1950
Value of domestic exports, £ (millions) . . .	1138	2170
Value of retained imports, £ (millions) . . .	1735	2518
Balance of merchandise trade, £ (millions) .	−597	−348
Price index numbers (current-weighted, 1947 = 100)		
Domestic exports	100	118
Retained imports	100	127
Terms of trade	100	93

The improvement in the balance due to price movements (in millions of pounds)

$$= 2170\left(1 - \frac{1}{1\cdot18}\right) - 2518\left(1 - \frac{1}{1\cdot27}\right) = -204$$

i.e., there is a deterioration of £204 millions. The *deficit* of merchandise trade, however, *decreased* by £249 millions (from £597 millions to £348 millions). Hence, from 1947 to 1950, there was an improvement to this extent, the net result of an improvement of £453 millions because of a higher volume of exports relative to imports, and of a deterioration of £204 millions due to adverse terms of trade.[9]

[9] An alternative measure of the effect of the terms of trade on the balance of merchandise trade is obtained by subtracting the current value of exports deflated by export prices (real exports) from the same value deflated by import prices (real imports obtainable from exports). With current-weighted index numbers, the improvement in the balance is:

$$V_e'\left(\frac{1}{P_i'} - \frac{1}{P_e'}\right)$$

equivalent to the measure given above if V_i' is put equal to V_e'. The deterioration from 1947 to 1950 is then £149 millions. See Adams and Reddaway, "The Real Product of the United Kingdom, 1946–1951", London and Cambridge Economic Service *Bulletin*, September, 1952.

CHAPTER 11

Exports and Imports in the Domestic Setting

D. H. JONES
Dominion Bureau of Statistics, Ottawa

INTRODUCTION

A thorough survey of international trade will naturally, at some stage, deal with the relation of imports and exports to the internal economy of a country. In fact it would not be untrue to state that most of the interest in external trade derives from its internal implications.

The purpose of this chapter is to indicate some of the ways in which exports and imports impinge on the internal economy, and also to examine briefly the technical equipment more commonly used in quantitative analysis of the inter-relationships of the " external " and " internal " economies. On the whole, this material is directed more to the business man and the student than to the professional economist.

An initial step in analysis is the determination of the place of imports and exports in the economy in an over-all or " aggregative " sense. Most students of economics will be familiar with the concepts of " national accounts," which give quantitative expression to the economic activity of a country during a specified time period, showing production, wages, profits, expenditures, etc., and the relations amongst these magnitudes. These data form an excellent background for a study of international trade statistics.

AGGREGATIVE RELATIONS

Net national income at factor cost. This aggregate represents the income received by or accruing to the factors of production resident in a country, net of amounts charged respecting depreciation of fixed assets. National Income is generally expressed as the sum of wages and salaries and supplements, investment income (profits, rent, interest), and income of small businesses, self-employed professionals, and farmers. National Income may be considered as conceptually equal to Net National Product, if depreciation allowances actually charged by businesses are believed to be a fair measure of real capital consumption.

Gross national product at factor cost. This aggregate is intended to measure the total " final " output of a country, including the output of goods to be used for replacing worn-out or obsolete capital equipment. Production is valued at *market prices less net indirect taxes*. The term *gross* appearing in the definition indicates only that no deductions have been made respecting the using up of fixed capital employed in the production process. This aggregate, as is the case with most aggregates appearing in the National Accounts, is net in the important sense that inter-industry sales and purchases of goods and services on current account are excluded. This is to insure that resources which move through various levels of processing are not duplicated in the final total. Gross National Product is conceptually equal to National Income *plus* depreciation allowances and similar " non-cash " expenses charged against income. It is perhaps a better measure of the real flow of goods and services than National Income (Net National Product), especially in the short run, since depreciation allowances, although intended to reflect using up of fixed capital in the production process, are more realistically viewed as appropriations of income to be used for eventual purchases of capital assets. In this latter sense, it may be thought of as the conceptual equivalent of " Gross National Income."

Gross national product at market prices. This aggregate is equal to Gross National Product at Factor Cost *plus* net indirect taxes (indirect taxes less subsidies). Indirect taxes consist chiefly of sales taxes, Customs duties, local rates, etc., which affect directly the prices of commodities or services on which they are levied. It is chiefly of interest as the counterpart of *Gross National Expenditure at Market Prices*, which shows national product as the sum of " final " expenditure by business, government, and consumers, net additions to inventories, and net lending to non-residents. The treatment of exports and imports and international transactions generally in the " Gross National Expenditure " presentation is frequently a cause of confusion, and it is advisable to examine it carefully. In the first place it should be noted that the term " national " appearing in the description refers to the *total* only. The total is equal to Gross National Product, and for reasons of symmetry is referred to as Gross National Expenditure. The main components of the scheme, Personal Expenditures, Government Expenditures, and Gross Domestic Investment (" Capital formation ") include not only expenditures on home production but also expenditures on imported goods as well. The final entry, Net Foreign Investment, approximates the concept " net balance on current international account " familiar to users of balance of payments statistics, and balances the table by simultaneously adding home production not already accounted for (*i.e.*, exports of goods and services) and subtracting the import content of all other components of the table, including the import content of exports. At the same time, it reduces the total by the (net) amount of investment income paid to non-residents, since by general agreement such payments are not considered as a part of Gross National Product or Income.

A variant of Gross National Product, which measures production *before* deduction of investment income paid to non-residents is known as " Gross Geographical Product." It is particularly useful in analyzing activity in colonies or dependencies whose productive resources are largely owned or controlled by non-residents.

In some countries, the Net Foreign Balance is split, for presentation in Gross National Expenditure, into its gross positive and negative components. These components may be referred to as Gross Exports of Goods and Services, and Gross Imports of Goods and Services. Users of these statistics should note that these components will include service and income transactions as well as merchandise transactions. Table 1 illustrates the relations amongst the most common aggregates.

Table 1

Most Common Aggregates, Country *A*

(Figures are hypothetical)

Item	Value	Item	Value
Wages, salaries, etc.	50	Expenditure on goods and services	
Investment income . .	15	By persons . . .	60
Income of small business, farmers, professionals, etc. . .	25	By governments . . .	20
Net national income at factor cost	90	Gross home investment	
Depreciation, etc. . . .	20	Additions to fixed assets .	20
Gross national product at factor cost	110	Additions to inventories.	10
Net indirect taxes . . .	10	Net foreign investment . .	10
Gross national product at market prices	120	Gross national expenditure at market prices . . .	120
Plus net payments of interest and dividends to non-residents .	10		
Gross geographical product at market prices . . .	130		

Imports. A question[1] of general interest in connection with imports is: " What proportion of income is spent on imported goods ? "

The correct answer to this question cannot be obtained directly from Table 1. The denominator of the required fraction or proportion will be Gross National Product at Factor Cost (considered as the equivalent of Gross National Income). The numerator will be *imports less the import content of exports.* Gross National Income is chosen as the benchmark for the comparison since it includes income set aside for capital replacements (some of the imports will be capital goods for replacement purposes), and excludes indirect taxes (which would artificially inflate the denominator of the fraction relative to the numerator, as the import figure used will most certainly not include Customs duties levied by the importing country).

The import content of goods exported should be deducted from imports in deriving the numerator of the comparative fraction, since it does not represent a use of the country's income but is rather a charge against production. We are referring here not only to what are generally called re-exports but also to the import content of goods manufactured domestically and exported. The import content of exports is not ordinarily available from official sources, and the independent research worker interested in this problem may have to rely on approximations based on general knowledge of the country's trade structure. In a highly indus-

---

[1] The question, " What proportion of a country's product is imported ? " is not, strictly speaking, a meaningful one, since imports are by definition not a part of the national product.

trialized country the import content of home consumption and exports may be quite similar.   If so, it can be determined by comparing imports with gross national product (at factor cost).   In other cases, where exports consist chiefly of relatively unprocessed items, the whole of imports may be considered to enter into home consumption.   It is also possible that the major portion of imports will represent materials for processing and subsequent export, and can scarcely be said to enter into the domestic economy at all.

Exports.   Two questions which we will wish to examine are:

1. What proportion of a country's income is derived from exports?
2. What proportion of a country's production is exported?

The answer to question 1 will depend on our definition of " income." If we use the concept of income before depreciation, then we should express net exports, *i.e.*, exports *less* import content of goods exported, as a proportion of Gross National Income (Product) at Factor Cost.

The same ratio will provide the answer to question 2, if production is defined as inclusive of production for replacement of capital goods used up in the production process.

If it is desired to use Net National Income (Product) as the denominator for either comparison, then it will be necessary to deduct from net exports the " depreciation content," *i.e.*, the element of receipts from exports which is necessary to provide for replacement of fixed capital used up in producing goods for export.   The depreciation content will not necessarily be the same for exports as for home produced goods used domestically.

Census gross and net values of production.   The aggregates used in National Accounts are not the only series available for use in assessing the relative importance of exports to the economy.   In fact, it is probably more common to find the Gross Value of Production and Net Value of Production as defined for industrial census surveys used in this connection, especially where the field of interest is narrowed to a particular group of commodities, for example, " manufactured products."   The Gross Value of Production should be avoided in comparisons of this type, since it contains a large element of duplication (double counting).   The Net Value of Production or " Value Added " is very similar in concept to the Gross National Product at Factor Cost, and may be employed in exactly the same way.   Its peculiar advantage lies in the fact that it can generally be subdivided into fairly fine industry divisions and is more clearly a measure of tangible commodity production than Gross National Product. The latter measure includes a substantial element of " service " production of a purely domestic nature.

Export subsidies and indirect taxes. In analyzing the relation of imports, exports, production, and income, it may be necessary to pay some attention to the influence of indirect taxes and subsidies, both on exports and imports and on the aggregates with which they are compared. Gross National Product (Income) at Factor Cost excludes indirect taxes and includes subsidies. If export subsidies exist, they should be added back to nominal export values before comparisons are made with production, otherwise the importance of exports may be understated. Indirect taxes on exports are uncommon, for obvious reasons. Where they exist they should properly be excluded from nominal export values. Admittedly such devices may affect the amount of foreign exchange derived from export transactions; however, these devices do not appear to be related to the measurement of real resources channeled to non-residents.

Customs duties on imports, and import subsidies if such exist, will not in general affect recorded import values; and since they do not directly affect foreign exchange requirements, they are not relevant to the structural relationship under discussion in this section.

PRESENTATION FOR NATIONAL ACCOUNTS

Treatment of export and import data in national accounts. The adjustments of trade figures for balance of payments purposes are described in Chapter 9. The National Accounts include entries for external trade and the data for them are generally derived from the balance of payments accounts and not from external trade statistics directly. The adjustments of recorded trade figures are thus taken over into the National Accounts; some variations do occur, however, and care is needed in assessing the significance of external trade in the National Accounts.

As already noted, international transactions appear in the aggregate of expenditure which make up Gross National Expenditure ($=$ Gross National Product). To current expenditures by persons and government and gross domestic investment expenditure is added an item which can be described as " net balance (credit or debit) on international account for goods and services." The relevant net balance is that arising in current transactions in goods and services together with investment income received or paid on international account; it takes receipts from exports of merchandise, from exports of services (all the so-called " invisibles " including government expenditures) and from investment income from abroad, and subtracts the corresponding payments. The net balance is the total of items 1 through 8 shown in Figure A of Chapter 9.

Difficulties and misunderstandings may arise in the treatment of " unilateral " transactions or " donations." These can be private or on government account and they are of two types: gifts or grants in kind, and gifts or grants in money or other capital forms. With the first type, the gift or grant takes the form of an export of merchandise or services (or an import if the gift or grant is received), and it finds its place in the net balance for goods and services and hence in Gross National Expenditure. It should not appear elsewhere in Gross National Expenditure, *i.e.*, in personal or government expenditure. The other type of gift or grant does not enter into the net balance appearing in Gross National Expenditure.

Balance of payments accounting is on the double-entry system. Consequently a gift or grant in kind appears in the balance of payments, not only as an export or import of goods or services, but also under the heading " donations " (see item 9 of Figure *A* of Chapter 9). The item " donations " of the balance of payments is not included in the net balance for goods and services which appears in Gross National Expenditure. What does appear in Gross National Expenditure is simply a surplus (or deficit) of exports over imports, with no deduction or adjustment for donations. The exports are real, whether they are paid for or whether they are gifts.[2]

Another difficulty is that the National Accounts apply to nationals of the country as a political area, whereas the balance of payments often apply to a currency area which may not be quite the same as the political area. For example, in the years 1940–1948 before the entry of Newfoundland into the Canadian Federation, the Canadian National Accounts included none of the transactions of Newfoundland residents, but the Canadian statistics of the balance of payments covered such transactions (since Newfoundland was in the Canadian currency area). An adjustment is needed to make the trade and other figures in the balance of payments relate to Canada only.

Sector analysis. In a number of countries, conventional statements of national income and expenditure are supplemented by a more detailed set of accounts which show the important transactions of each of the four major sectors of the economy, *i.e.*, Business, Government, Persons, and Non-Residents. These accounts are interrelated in such a way that it is possible to trace transactions from one account to another. All economic transactions will be two-sided; generally there will be a purchaser and a seller, or a donor and donee, or a payer and a receiver. The accounts referred to are constructed with the aid of familiar techniques of double accounting; each entry in a given account will be matched by a

---

[2] When the net balance for goods and services comes to be interpreted in the complete balance of payments in terms of net foreign investment, then it is the net result of capital movements and donations. An export surplus can be reduced by gifts or grants to foreign individuals or governments to give foreign investment proper. It is only here, in the capital account, that the fact that exports are not " paid for " but given away becomes relevant.

corresponding entry in another account (or, in some cases, by an entry of opposite sign in the same account).

The Transactions with Non-Residents account for a country is obtained by a rearrangement of the conventional balance of payments (adjusted in a manner described earlier), in the following way:

1. The viewpoint is reversed. In a conventional balance of payments statement, transactions are viewed from the standpoint of the country itself. Thus, imports are payments, and exports are receipts. The Non-Residents account, however, is constructed from the viewpoint of all non-residents who have transactions with the country. Consequently, Receipts of Non-Residents will include " imports " of the

Table 2

Transactions of Non-Residents with United States, United Kingdom, and Canada, 1948

(NA means information not available)

Item	Payments	Receipts	Net Payments (+) Receipts (−)
United States	(million dollars)		
Factor incomes* . . .	NA	NA	+988
Commodities and services			
Business	12,280	8464	+3816
Government	566	2328	−1762
Persons	62	1203	−1141
Net capital movement . .			−1901
United Kingdom	(million pounds)		
Factor incomes* . . .	162	122	+40
Commodities and services			
Business	2029	1938	+91
Government	——	154	−154
Persons	——	97	−97
Net capital movement . .			+120
Canada	(million dollars)		
Factor incomes* . . .	70	325	−255
Commodities and services			
Business	3974	3151	+823
Government	——	——	——
Persons	——	169	−169
Net capital movement . .			−399

* Wages, salaries, interest, dividends, remitted branch profits.
Sources: United States: *Survey of Current Business* (July 1949).
    United Kingdom: *National Income White Paper* (Cmd. 7649).
    Canada: *National Accounts*, Preliminary 1949, and unpublished information.

country in question and Payments by Non-Residents will include " exports " of the country in question.

2. A basic distinction is made between goods and services transactions and income transactions. Investment income and other factor incomes such as wages and rents appearing in international transactions are given separate treatment.

3. Receipts and Payments are usually classified by sectors, distinguishing between receipts and payments by *Business*, *Government*, and *Persons*.

On the whole, this treatment is, to say the least, confusing, and even experts have been driven to the point of frenzy attempting to interpret the Non-Residents Account.

Table 2 (p. 219) shows the Non-Residents Account relating to three particular countries for the year 1948.

Although these totals may not seem to have great merit as they stand, they become meaningful when related to the other accounts. Each entry in the Non-Residents account will have a counterpart somewhere else in the system. Two of the entries in the Business Account, which shows the cost elements and disposition of the output of private business, will be purchases from non-residents (a cost element), and sales to non-residents (a disposition of product). As an example, take Table 3, the Business

Table 3

Business Operating Account, Canada, 1948
(In millions of dollars)

Revenue	
Sales to residents	
Business (Capital account)	3,309
Government	869
Persons	9,747
Sales to non-residents	3,974
Adjustment*	− 107
Total	17,792
Expenditure	
Factor costs	11,625
Net indirect taxes	1,767
Depreciation allowances, etc.	1,141
Purchases from non-residents	3,151
Adjustment*	+ 108
Total	17,792

* Statistical discrepancy.
Source: National Accounts, 1941–1948, and unpublished revisions.

Accounts for Canada in the year 1948. The items " Sales to non-residents " and " Purchases from non-residents " are those appearing in the Non-Residents Account shown in Table 2.

For a comprehensive analysis of the Non-Residents Account of the United States, reference should be made to " International Transactions in the National Income Accounts," by W. S. Salant, appearing in the November 1951 issue of the *Review of Economics and Statistics*.

External trade and business. The importance of *foreign markets* and *foreign supply sources* to domestic industry is the *sine qua non* of foreign trade economics and needs no special treatment here. However, it might be desirable to emphasize one aspect of those inter-business transactions which cross international boundaries, which may require special treatment by the analyst; *i.e.*, international shipments of unfinished products, for processing, between parent companies and foreign subsidiaries. Valuation of such shipments is generally required for customs purposes (unless the goods move " in bond ") on the basis of what a fair " selling price " might have been. This may, and frequently does, result in extremely arbitrary valuations of such items in recorded trade data.

In the Gross National Expenditure table, it should be noted that the entry " Gross Domestic Investment on Capital Formation " will include the value of imported capital goods, chiefly in the form of machinery and equipment and construction materials. Considerable information on the structure of the export trade may be obtained in some countries from results of the censuses of production and distribution. Censuses of distribution generally treat the transactions of export and import merchants, brokers, and agents as the transactions of distinct kinds of business and tabulate relevant information separately. It is also the practice in some countries (for example, the United Kingdom) to request, in connection with surveys of production, an analysis of sales or shipments by manufacturers, in order to show separately direct export sales. In Canada, information on the destination of sales of manufacturers, and also wholesalers, is obtained at decennial intervals. Export sales by wholesalers and independent agents will be considerably less in most cases than total exports since a substantial proportion of export sales are made directly by producers.

External trade and government. Possibly one of the most significant aspects of international trade today is the extent to which it is directly or indirectly controlled or affected by national governments. The activities of governments which affect import and export trade are numerous and varied, and range from the most indirect control through manipulation of the exchange rate, through various types of duties, restrictions, quotas, licensing policies, embargoes, etc., to direct dealing in certain commodities (for example, wheat) by means of government departments or agents. In addition, a good deal of the financing of exports may be borne by government.

The usefulness of external trade statistics to governments is some indication of the importance which is attached to external trade in most countries. Statistics of merchandise exports and imports are invariably the first to be collected. As is commonly known, this interest dates from the mercantilist period, when the acquisition of gold through an export surplus was considered to be one of the prime requirements for the economic well-being of a nation.

Interest is now focused on the use of foreign trade as an instrument of foreign policy. Motives range from sincere moral concern for the plight of underdeveloped countries and the need for reconstruction and rehabilitation of countries whose economics were crippled by the war, through varying degrees of enlightened self-interest and considerations of mutual security, to out-and-out economic warfare. Marshall Plan aid, now handled by the Organization for European Economic Cooperation, and the economic and military aid furnished to Turkey, Greece, and other countries by the United States, have involved amounts of goods and money which are almost inconceivable in pre-1939 standards. Technical aid under the United States Point Four program and the Colombo Plan are less imposing in the quantitative sense but perhaps even more imposing from a moral point of view, since they are less directly related to the present (1952) East–West power struggle. The extremes in economic warfare are illustrated by the numerous and ever-increasing barriers to East–West trade in forms ranging from actual prohibition of trade in certain commodities to various ingenious devices depending on arbitrary interference with means of international commerce and discriminatory use of tax and licensing authority.

External trade and individuals (persons). The freedom of the private individual to import and export varies from country to country. In general tourists or business travelers are permitted to purchase and import goods, duty free, up to specified amounts. This results in a not inconsiderable movement of such goods as radios, chinaware, textiles, and so on, especially between countries with common frontiers. Parcel post shipments comprise the other major component of direct imports or exports by individuals as such; shipments of relief goods, food, clothing, etc., by charitable organizations acting on behalf of individuals may also be mentioned here. Personal property (*e.g.*, clothing, automobiles) accompanying persons crossing international boundaries is generally considered as " temporary trade " only, although in some countries, automobiles in such temporary transit may be subject to Customs duty. The Personal Expenditure component of Gross National Expenditure includes expenditure abroad by residents. Conversely, it excludes expenditures in the designated country by non-residents. The reverse statement is true for Gross National Product (Expenditure) since the expenditures of non-residents represent a direct use of national product, and residents' expenditures abroad do not. The adjusting entry is implicit in the Net Foreign Investment component of Gross National Expenditure.

EXPORTS AND IMPORTS AND PRODUCTION

Indices of production. So far we have been dealing with comparisons of imports and exports with production and similar aggregates in terms of money units, and we have confined our attention mainly to relations within a particular year. For many purposes we will wish to examine the actual volume of trade (in terms of unchanging prices) in its relation to the actual volume of production, giving particular attention to the relative movements of these aggregates over a period of years. In such cases it will be convenient to make use of indices of " real production " or " physical volume of production " and corresponding indices of volume of imports and exports.

Indices of real production may be obtained basically in two ways:

a By summing weighted indexes of real output in various sections of the economy;

b By eliminating the influence of price changes from the Gross National Product.

It is difficult to make direct measurements of real output in some sections of the economy (*e.g.*, government), consequently indices of type *a* above are generally confined to production in industries such as mining, manu-facturing, construction and power, where indications of real output are easier to come by (examples, " tons " or " yards " made, hours worked, etc.) Thus, indices of type *a* may be expected to measure only output of commodities. As a measure of total output they are found wanting if an appreciable part of a country's output consists of services, especially services whose output cannot be expected to rise or fall proportionately with commodity output.

Since we are here dealing chiefly with exports and imports of commo-dities, type *a* indices may be considered very useful for comparative purposes. Their chief disadvantages are that they generally do not include production of non-manufactured agricultural products (a serious qualifica-tion for certain countries), and that they may include certain types of production not traded internationally on a large scale (*e.g.*, " con-struction ").

Indices of the volume (" quantum ") of imports and exports are available for a number of countries. These series are constructed from information contained in trade returns as described in Chapter 10. A peculiar difficulty involved in comparisons of the industrial production index and the volume of exports index for a country is related to the weighting problem. The general practice, in compiling indices of industrial production, is to assign weights to its component relatives which are proportionate to the value added in production during a specified base period. Indices of the real volume of exports, on the other hand, are weighted in accordance with the gross value of exports in a base period. The possibility that exports may contain a high import content has been noted previously in another connection. For comparison with production, then, the import content of exports should be eliminated from the weights used for the export volume index, so that the various types of commodities exported may be assigned a relative importance proportionate to the value added in the exporting country, rather than their total value. Thus, most available indexes of exports, although useful for certain purposes, are not entirely suitable as measures of the changes in the amount of home production exported.

Domestic disappearance. Here we deal with the use of detailed import-export-production statistics in combination to yield estimates of " domestic disappearance " of commodities.

Domestic disappearance equals production plus imports minus exports. A number of qualifications and refinements to this basic formula may be noted:

1. *Inventory adjustment.* A portion of the goods available for domestic consumption may in fact be stored, *i.e.*, held over to a subsequent period. We may wish to refine our estimates of domestic disappearance by adjusting for changes in stocks held at various levels. As a minimum, production may be adjusted for changes in factory stocks, to give shipments.

2. *Comparability.* If our comparisons are made in terms of physical units, *i.e.*, tons, or barrels, or bushels, we need not worry about incomparabilities due to pricing. However, if comparisons are made in terms of values, then the data should be examined to see that production, imports, and exports are valued at uniform prices. The main difficulty in comparing foreign trade values with the value of production is that the value of production often includes a certain amount of duplication. A secondary problem is that exports are normally valued f.o.b., whereas production values are usually, though not always, valued at point of production.

3. *Lags and leads.* There will frequently be a lag between the time a good is shipped for export and the time it is actually exported. This type of discrepancy will be more serious if we are dealing with monthly or quarterly data than if we are dealing with annual data.

4. *Units.* When comparisons are being made in physical terms, it may be necessary to use conversion tables. For instance, exports of a given commodity may be reported in long tons, imports in short tons, and production in pounds.

5. *Classification and content.* It may be difficult to obtain series which absolutely correspond in definition. For instance, a production series might refer to electric domestic washing machines (complete), and the corresponding import and export series might include also " parts thereof." Customs statistical classifications were devised more for administrative than economic purposes, and one of the greatest problems encountered in comparison of the type under discussion will be the incomparability of production and trade statistical classifications. The difficulties become more pronounced if we are dealing with an extended period of time, since there will be numerous changes causing grouping, splitting, and reclassification of items. In some countries, it has been found necessary or desirable to obtain data on exports and imports directly from producers or consumers for comparison with production statistics. Although data on exports and imports obtained directly from producers or consumers solve the problem of commodity classification differences, users of such statistics must be aware that the figures have been derived from a different source than those in the trade statistics. For example, the export figures obtained from producers are on an export sale basis; they may include goods which will not, in fact, be exported at a later date, or may exclude goods which will be exported. There is of course normally a time lag between the sales for export recorded in the production statistics and the exports recorded in the trade returns. The basis of valuation may also be different.

6. *Miscellaneous.* A number of the adjustments necessary to convert aggregate import and export statistics to a basis suitable for inclusion in the balance of payments may apply with equal validity to data on individual commodities. For instance, the Customs " warehousing " adjustment, or " overvaluation " and " undervaluation " corrections may be appropriate in computing " domestic disappearance."

Statistical sources for integrated trade and production data. If comparable data on external trade and production for a specific commodity are required, it will generally be more convenient and accurate to obtain these from a single source.

A number of agencies, both public and private, in the United States, perform a valuable service by combining statistics of production, imports, and exports of various commodities to yield figures on domestic disappearance. In some cases, the series are refined to take into account changes in stocks at various levels. Although the work is naturally concentrated on United States statistics, in many cases data for other important producing countries are assembled on a comparable basis. In the field of agriculture and food products, the U.S. Department of Agriculture publishes production and consumption figures for a large number of important commodities. The data are published in several forms, principally, the annual publication *Agricultural Statistics*; a release entitled " Consumption of Food in the United States 1909–1948 " and, in summary form, in the *Statistical Abstract of the United States* (Bureau of the Census), the *Survey of Current Business* (U.S. Department of Commerce) and the " Statistical Supplement " to the *Survey of Current Business*.

Estimates of consumption of various metals and minerals are prepared by the U.S. Bureau of Mines (*Minerals Yearbook*) and by the American Bureau of Metal Statistics (*Yearbook*). Two other agencies operating in a wider field may also be noted. The Commodity Research Bureau prepares annually the *Commodity Yearbook*, which summarizes United States and world production, consumption, and trade data for a list of important staple commodities. The U.S. Tariff Commission publishes a series of analytical reports on specific commodities (" Summaries of Tariff Information ") which include, as well as analytical data on sources of supply and markets (present and potential), on tariff rates, etc., tables showing production, imports and exports, and percentages of production exported and imported.

In the United Kingdom the wartime shortages and the post-war trade crisis resulted in the development of a number of consumption series based largely on a combination of production, import, and export data. Important consumer articles, such as furniture and utensils, are treated this way, as well as more basic commodities. Frequently production series are split into two parts: production for consumption, and production for export. " Production for export " in a given period will not generally correspond exactly to actual exports, as noted previously. Assuming comparable definitions for a commodity, actual exports may come from stocks of wholesalers or other intermediaries, and may include second-hand articles; and production for export might be in fact diverted to domestic consumption. Conversely, some production destined for the home market may in fact be exported.

In Canada, the Dominion Bureau of Statistics prepares estimates of the domestic consumption of meats and other food products, from data on production, imports, and exports. These studies are published regularly in the *Canada Yearbook*, in the chapter dealing with domestic trade.

EXPORTS AND IMPORTS AND PRICES

Import and export prices. Exports and imports may be analyzed in terms of their price components and price effects. The principal topics to be considered are:

1. The structural relation of import and export prices to domestic prices: statistically speaking, the weight given to prices of exported and imported goods in calculating aggregate price indexes, such as the general wholesale price index and the " cost-of-living " index.

2. The dynamic relations amongst import and export prices and domestic prices, *e.g.*, the extent to which domestic prices are influenced indirectly by import and export prices.

3. The relation of import prices to export prices, *i.e.*, the " Barter Terms of Trade."

General wholesale price index. Many countries compile a form of " general wholesale price index." The significance of such indexes has frequently been questioned, since it is rather difficult to define exactly what is being measured. However, there is no question that the series which make up the aggregate are extremely useful in themselves, whether or not the final aggregate is itself useful. The final aggregate is, however, the most frequently quoted index, and it will be of interest to examine its components in such a way as to point up the importance of export and import prices in the structure.

A wholesale price index is a weighted average of a large number of individual price series or " price relatives." The weight used for a given price relative is generally the value marketed in a base period, such as 1937, or the average yearly value marketed in a period, such as 1935–1939. In some cases, weights may be reduced to allow for " duplication." Thus, it would not be strictly logical to apply full marketing weights to prices of each of wheat, flour, and bread when a substantial portion of the wheat was used to make flour, and a substantial portion of the flour was used to make bread. Here the weights assigned at each stage may be made proportional to the value added at each stage rather than to the gross value marketed.

In Table 4 is shown a method of arriving at the theoretical import and export content of a wholesale price index for a country. Statistics are those for Canada. The actual weights shown in section *B* of the table are those used by the Dominion Bureau of Statistics in compiling the official index; they are remarkably close to the theoretical weights.

Table 4

Weights for an Index of Wholesale Prices for Canada

(in millions of dollars)

	1935–1939 Average	1946	1947	1948
A. Theoretical weights				
Gross national product at market prices .	**4994**	**11,936**	**13,591**	**15,471**
Add: Net interest and dividends paid to abroad	232	242	275	255
Merchandise imports . . .	655	1822	2535	2598
Deduct: Government services . .	−411	−1052	−894	−917
Personal services . . .	−1026	−1879	−2066	−2251
Income in kind . . .	−470	−719	−760	−870
Services to non-residents . .	−286	−806	−862	−920
Equals: **Gross commodity product plus merchandise imports***	**3688**	**9544**	**11,819**	**13,366**
Distributed as follows:				
Merchandise imports	655	1822	2535	2598
per cent	*17·8*	*19·1*	*21·4*	*19·4*
Duty on imports	87	209	301	224
Per cent	*2·4*	*2·2*	*2·6*	*1·7*
Merchandise exports and re-exports .	1074	2489	2822	3149
Per cent	*29·1*	*26·1*	*23·9*	*23·6*
Residual†	1872	5024	6161	7395
Per cent	*50·7*	*52·6*	*52·1*	*55·3*
B. Actual weights (1935–1939 basis)	Per Cent			
Imports and duty	20·1	——	——	——
Exports	27·6	——	——	——
Domestic consumption of home-produced goods	52·3	——	— · —	——

* Excluding " non-market " commodities, *i.e.*, " income in kind."
† Equal to domestic consumption of home-produced commodities *minus* import content of goods exported, *plus* mark-up on imports.
Sources: National Accounts Publications 1946–1947, 1938–1947, 1941–1948, Preliminary 1949, and unpublished data from the records of the National Income Section and the Labour and Prices Division, Dominion Bureau of Statistics.

From the earlier analysis in this chapter, it is apparent that there is a flaw in the theoretical weighting system due to the *import content of goods exported.* The over-all weight assigned to *imports* in this calculation is exaggerated; correspondingly the weight assigned to Domestic Production for Home Use is understated. It is difficult for the estimator to correct for this factor in practical work since it will not usually be possible to classify prices into the three mutually exclusive groups required by theory, *i.e.*, " imports for domestic consumption," " domestic production for domestic consumption," and " exports."

There is another flaw in the theoretical calculation which will affect the calculation in the opposite way to that mentioned previously and will therefore to some extent tend to offset or correct it. It arises from the fact that the mark-up included in the wholesale price of goods imported has been left with the residual. If, as is frequently the case, mark-ups are calculated as a fixed percentage of invoice cost plus duty, for purposes of price analysis it would seem desirable to include the domestic mark-up on imports as a part of the " import content."

Index of retail prices, or " Cost of Living." The cost-of-living index is more familiar to most people than the wholesale price index. Its import content is of special significance since World War II for many countries dependent for certain essentials on imports experience difficulties in financing these imports; and questions as to the effect of this or that action on the domestic " cost of living " are common. The import content of the cost-of-living index is particularly significant when the question of a currency revaluation is being considered. The probable effect of devaluation on the cost of living requires initially an estimate of the import content of the index, *i.e.*, the proportion of imported goods contained in the weights, so that faced with, say, a general rise in import prices it is possible to calculate accurately the effect of this increase on the cost of living.[3]

One approach to the problem would be to calculate the import content of " Personal Expenditure on Consumer Goods and Services " as used in the National Accounts. If cost-of-living indexes were constructed in such a way that the weights assigned to individual price relatives were proportionate to the total domestic disappearance of commodities, this would show the " importance " of import prices in the index. However, cost-of-living indexes are generally representative of prices paid by certain specified groups only, *e.g.*, medium-income or low-income family groups. Consequently relatively more weight will be assigned to necessities than to luxuries and semi-luxuries. For an accurate analysis, therefore, it is necessary to examine the actual weights of the index, and determine, item by item, the import content. If, as is frequently so, the distributor's mark-up is determined as a percentage of cost plus duty, it would seem desirable to include the mark-up on the import and duty content of the weights as part of the " import content," in addition to the basic imports.

Relation of export and import prices to domestic prices. If price is viewed as " cost price," in real terms, it is apparent that the whole foundation of international trade lies in the fact that it is more economical, in terms of use of material and human resources, to produce certain commodities in one country than in another. This is a natural consequence of the uneven distribution of world resources and the principle of the " division of

---

[3] As an example of this technique, see Allen: " Prices and Devaluation," *Bulletin of the London and Cambridge Economic Service* (November 1949).

labour." It will be to the common advantage of countries to specialize in their production and to obtain goods which they need but cannot produce efficiently, in exchange.

If price is viewed as " competitive price," it is also apparent that both import and export prices will affect domestic prices and that there will be many interactions amongst the three. The strength of the influence will depend largely on the extent to which the commodity in question is both imported and domestically produced or exported and domestically consumed. Thus, high prices for beef in the United States will cause, initially, a diversion of beef from the Canadian domestic market to the export market with a consequent shortage followed by rising prices, if there are no Canadian restrictions on exports of beef. Low prices on goods imported into Canada from the United States, if not offset by duties and transportation costs, naturally tend to force down internal prices for competing goods. It should also be noted that import prices will have their effect on export prices depending on the relative import content of exports.

Terms of trade. Indices of import and export prices, or unit values, are prepared in a number of countries (see Chapter 10). The relative movements of import and export prices indicate changes in the net barter terms of trade. It is of considerable interest to know of changes in the number of units of imports which can be purchased with a given quantity of exports. If we form an index number with export prices as its numerator and import prices as its denominator, the changes in the ratio will indicate changes in the net barter terms of trade. An increase in the index number will indicate a relative improvement in the net barter terms of trade since a larger quantity of imports can be purchased with a given volume of exports relative to the base period.

Although the theory of the terms of trade seem clear, actual measurement presents some difficulties. The selection of a base for comparison is a very difficult problem, much more so than if we were selecting a base for an ordinary price index. The base period for the terms of trade index should be a year in which most countries were experiencing average trading positions, so that their terms of trade, in an absolute sense, were neither excessively favorable nor unfavorable. This condition, if met, allows interpretation of subsequent movements in the index as being towards or away from a situation which, although not necessarily the most desirable from the viewpoint of the country concerned, is certainly the most desirable from the standpoint of international trade stability.

Unfavorable movements in the terms of trade experienced by many countries in the period after World War II have been an inevitable consequence of the dislocation in trade and production caused by the war and the subsequent scarcity of hard currencies. It is true that what one country loses in this sense, another country or countries must gain. However, a situation where some countries have a continuing favored position on the international market and others must continue to obtain needed materials on unfavorable terms is considerably less beneficial to the world as a whole than the ideal balanced situation where no country could be said to have an extreme advantage over another in this sense.

Changes in the barter terms of trade have a peculiar significance in connection with the measurement of the relative importance of exports to the economy. Some comments have already been made about aggregate relations between exports and Gross National Product or Expenditure. If relevant data are available, such comparisons may be made in terms of so-called constant dollar series, using data which have been deflated, that is, corrected for price changes. In preparing deflated series, the question arises as to what price should be used to deflate exports. From one point of view, the appropriate deflator would be a composite price index in which each export price is assigned a weight proportionate to the volume of the commodity currently exported. Most countries publishing national accounts series in constant dollar terms use this technique. From another point of view, however, it appears that, since the ultimate purpose of exports is to obtain imports in exchange, the appropriate deflator for exports should be a composite index reflecting existing import prices. If the purpose of analyzing income and trade data in the particular connotation is to draw conclusions regarding the relative welfare of the economy to other countries, or with respect to the situation in earlier years, then this latter approach seems justified.

CORRELATION AND OTHER ANALYTICAL DEVICES

Introduction. So far we have dealt mainly with static or structural relations between exports and imports, and national income or product; that is, we have examined relations within a specified time period of a year. It would be necessary to digress too far into the theory of econometrics to attempt a thorough examination of the dynamics of external trade in its relation to the internal economy. However, it is of general interest to review briefly the nature of econometric studies and their usefulness.

Imports and the propensity to import. Examination of import and national income data for a country over a period of years will generally lead to the conclusion that there is a relationship between the two series; that is, they tend to increase at the same time and decrease at the same time. In technical terminology, there is a correlation between the two series. Further examination would indicate whether the relationship between the series was of a linear nature, or whether a more complex mathematical function was necessary to describe it. Once the relation had been given mathematical expression, the observed data could be used to determine the constants of the postulated mathematical relationship, and the " observed " data compared with the " theoretical " to determine the goodness of fit. The constants of the regression equation will show the " marginal propensity to import " for the country, *i.e.*, the increase or decrease in imports to be expected from a given increase or decrease in income. If the relationship between income and imports is linear, the propensity to import will be constant at various levels of income. If the relationship is not linear, then the propensity to import will appear to change from one income level to another, *i.e.*, the expected change in imports from a given change in income will depend not only on the value of the change in income but also on the absolute level of income at the time.

Determinants of imports. A country will wish to import goods which it (collectively) desires but which are not obtainable at home in sufficient quantities to satisfy demand, or which may be obtained more cheaply abroad. Its actual ability to import will be restricted, in the first instance, by the extent and direction of its export trade. The *extent* of its export trade will depend on the country's own productive capacity and its efficiency in producing, with minimum use of material and human resources, goods desired internationally. The *direction* of its export trade becomes important if multilateral settlements are difficult or impossible, as is often the case today, since in the last analysis the country must pay for its imports in acceptable currencies, or else arrange for a complex and relatively clumsy system of barter exchanges. In considering a country's capacity to import, we must naturally take into account, as well as receipts from merchandise exports, receipts from freight and shipping and similar invisible items, net receipts of interest and dividends, migrant remittances, and branch plant earnings which are important sources of foreign exchange in some countries.

Ability to import is, then, tied to ability to export in the general case. In specific cases the connection may be even more explicit where, for instance, by mutual agreement, countries restrict their imports of certain classes of goods to levels commensurate with their exports of other classes of goods. In other cases, a general world scarcity of certain commodities may lead to an international allocation scheme supported jointly by producing and consuming nations.

The ability of a country to borrow abroad through private or official channels will also have a short-run influence on its capacity to import but may be neglected as a long-run factor. A country may also receive goods in the form of donations and various types of economic and military aid in cash or in kind. Unilateral transactions of this type are similar to international loans. However, they differ in several important respects, since they are frequently not repayable, in an economic sense at least; they do not bear interest; and they may consist of specific goods only, or if in cash, may have restrictions as to where and how the money may be spent. In this sense, they are analogous to the so-called " tied loan."

To the extent that exports have a substantial import content, it may also be said that exports are a determinate of imports. If we consider imports as imports for home consumption only, however, then the only effect of exports is felt through the intermediate variable " income," except in the special case where, by mutual agreement amongst countries, imports of certain classes of scarce goods are made to depend on the meeting of certain export goals.

The relative concentration of income in a country will also have some effect on the level of imports, since the propensity to import will generally be different for high-income individuals than for low-income individuals.

Another set of restrictions on a country's capacity to import are those imposed by political considerations. Security may require that a country attempt to become independent of supplies from foreign countries at the cost of a reduction in the standard of living. It may also be necessary or desirable to protect domestic industries from severe foreign competition by artificial restraints on imports of certain classes of goods, for example, heavy Customs duties, quotas, etc. Finally, mention may be made of secondary economic factors such as the availability and cost of transportation facilities which may further impose restrictions on imports.

All these factors may operate on the various types of goods imported or desired, and the analyst must take this into account by examining imports in detail as well as in the aggregate.

Analytical techniques. No set rules can be given for analyzing the influence of exchange shortages, political, military, or general economic and geographical factors on imports; the problem is one of general research and involves the assembly and correlation of data from many sources, both private and official. However, the influence of income on imports is subject to more intensive quantitative analysis than is the case for the other restricting factors, and it is possible to make a number of observations about the technique of this analysis.

1. *Deflation.* Original data may be adjusted for price changes, so that the adjusted data will follow movements in the physical volume of imports and real income.

2. *Mathematical relationships.* It will be found frequently that one equation is insufficient to describe the relationship between imports and income. There may be " breaks," caused by depressions, wars, currency

inflations, or other profound economic dislocations, and the series may have to be decomposed into a number of time periods each with its own connecting equation. If the import and income series are plotted against one another on a piece of graph paper, it will usually be apparent when such breaks occur.

3. *Serial correlation.* Coefficients of correlation calculated from time series are always subject to serious qualification, since elementary correlation theory assumes the independence of successive pairs of observations. Time series such as income and imports generally follow a cyclical pattern. Even a casual examination of the data will show that high values of, say, income, are generally preceded and followed by high values rather than by low values, and vice versa. Furthermore, a positive rate of change in the series will be more likely to be followed by, and preceded by, a positive rate of change than by a negative rate of change. Techniques have been devised for taking this serial correlation into account.

4. *Introduction of lags.* Imports may not respond instantaneously to changes in income; it may take weeks or months for the effect of a change in income to appear in imports. Determination of the average lag may be very difficult, since it generally requires monthly or quarterly statistics. These will generally be available for imports, but not for income. The introduction of a simple lag into connecting relations is not difficult; instead of correlating imports in period t with income in period t, we correlate imports in period t with income in period $t - 1$, where 1 is the assumed lag.

5. *Refinements in the "formula."* The income series may be refined through the introduction of sums of lagged variables. Instead of assuming that imports are a function of current income, we may assume that income of previous years also has a measurable influence. This refinement is based on the well-known fact that spending patterns do not respond quickly to changes in income; people tend to cling to their old spending habits for a while, at the same time either accumulating or reducing their cash balance depending on whether the income changes are positive or negative. To account for this factor, we may introduce incomes of previous years into the calculation, and the nature of our connecting equation will be changed from the former

$$I = F(Y, a, b, c \ldots)$$

where I stands for imports, Y for income, and $a, b, \ldots$ for the equation constants, to

$$I = F(Y, \overline{Y}, a, b, c \ldots)$$

where $\overline{Y}$ is the cumulative sum of incomes over a number of past years.

6. *Categorization of imports and income.* It will generally be necessary

to pay attention to the detail of imports and income as well as their aggregates. Different classes of imports will naturally respond differently to changes in income; in fact imports are sometimes ranked according to their sensitivity in this respect. More attention may also be paid to the components of income. An initial subdivision of the income item would be by type of recipient, distinguishing between government income and private income, and, in the case of private income, between income received by individuals and undistributed income of corporations, etc. Each group of income receivers will have different spending and import propensities, and it will be necessary to examine the type of goods they purchase and the factors which influence them to spend, or refrain from spending, their income. A further analysis may require a classification of individuals' income according to size groups, that is, showing the amount of income accruing to individuals with high, medium and low incomes, since these groups will normally have different spending and importing propensities. A shift in their relative proportions could alter the average propensity to import without any apparent change in their total income.

Exports and the multiplier. Export analysis will proceed along similar lines to import analysis except, of course, that exports are best regarded as an exogenous variable in the calculations. A country's exports are largely dependent on decisions made in other countries; however, these decisions may be influenced to some extent by the exporting country through appropriate advertising techniques, " deals," export subsidies, etc. Even political pressure may be used in an effort to increase exports to weaker countries. In other cases, a country may be in a position such that the demand for some of its products in foreign markets is greater than the immediate supply. If, for one reason or another, it is not possible or desirable to allow rising prices to equate supply and demand, such a country may take steps to divert resources from home use to production for export. Examples may also be found where a condition of receiving aid or donations is that the donee country undertakes to increase its exports, resulting in so-called " forced exports."

Exports are one of a number of factors whose combined level determines the income of a country. Consumer Expenditure, Government Expenditure and Home Investment are other components. It is not easy to say which of these are the operative variables. However, let us suppose that Government Expenditure, Home Investment, and Exports are " exogenous " variables, and that the National Income and Consumer Expenditure are the operative variables. We will ignore the influence of government transfer payments in altering the marginal propensity to consume. Each of these exogenous variables will contribute to national income in two ways; (a) directly, and (b) indirectly, through the operation of the multiplier. A given outlay on, say, government expenditure, will initially result in income to the primary recipients. The recipients will spend part of their earning (or all of their earnings, if they are very poor). This in turn will create demands for other goods, which will in turn provide more incomes, which will in turn result in more expenditures, and so on. The process eventually comes to a halt, since at each stage some income is not spent.

Now, it is apparent that, in a sense, a dollar spent by non-residents, resulting in exports, is as good as one spent by the government, resulting in public works.[4] The difference in importance of the various types of spending lies in (a) their relative regularity and (b) their local impact. It is the irregular expenditure which create fluctuations in the national income. Of course, fluctuations in exports will affect (initially) the incomes of a different group of people than will fluctuations in government expenditure—it depends on the relative willingness of these recipient groups to spend the money. The local impact must also be considered in relation to the relative mobility of resources between various industries and locations. That is to say, in considering the probable effect of a shift in spending which affects a specific industry or locality, account must be taken of the ability of the sector concerned to expand or contract in response to this stimulus. The ability of a country to produce more fruit, for instance, cannot be increased overnight, nor can the country suddenly switch in production from one type of fruit to another. On the other hand, a manufacturing plant cannot be converted into an automobile garage without a considerable loss of capital, but it can switch in production from one type of product to another, often with relatively little dislocation.

In assessing the importance of exports to the national economy we should then keep in mind the following factors:

1. The role of other factors in generating income;
2. The similarities and differences of the various types of expenditure with respect to their influence on income of particular industries or localities.

The comments above on the technique of analyzing import-income relations will be applicable to export-income analysis providing it is remembered that imports have (with certain qualifications) a dependent relation to income, whereas exports are an exogenous variable (again with some qualifications). Furthermore, the value of exports is an explicit

---

[4] Except for the fact that the non-resident transaction provides foreign exchange, and the government transaction does not.

component of Gross National Expenditure; to avoid the pitfall of so-called "spurious correlation," it is necessary to eliminate from the dependent variable (income) its *structural* export content. In the same way multiple correlation between, say, exports, investment, and government expenditure on the one hand, and national income on the other hand, should not be attempted without first removing from the national income its structural components—exports, investment, and government expenditure, otherwise the regression equation will be partly an identity and the correlation coefficient will be unrealistically high. In using multiple correlation analysis on economic time series such as those under discussion it is also wise to pay some attention to the relations between the so-called independent variables, which may not in fact be independent. If this is so, then conventional multiple correlation techniques are not sufficient and use must be made of more refined analysis.[5]

Concentration of exports and imports. The relative concentration of a country's trade obviously has considerable economic and political significance. In assessing the concentration, or dependence, of a country's foreign trade on certain markets, two variables must be considered. The first of these is the number of markets in which a country trades. The greater the number of markets with which trade is conducted the less will be the concentration of trade on each, other considerations being equal. The other factor is the distribution of trade amongst these markets; the more nearly equal are the shares of various markets in a country's trade the less will trade be concentrated on individual markets.

Dr. Hirschman[6] has designed an index which measures the concentration of trade with respect to both the number of markets and the distribution of trade amongst these markets. If P_1 represents the percentage share of the first market in a country's trade and a total of n markets accounts for all trade, then the index may be written

$$I = \sqrt{P_1^2 + P_2^2 + \ldots P_n^2} \quad \text{or} \quad I = \sqrt{\Sigma P^2}$$

The index equals the square root of the sum of the squares of the percentage shares of all markets in trade and may vary between limits of 0 and 100 per cent, in theory. The lower limit denotes minimum possible concentration and the upper limit maximum concentration.

The index can be used for two purposes: it can measure the change in market concentration of single country's trade from year to year, and it can also be used to compare the relative market concentration of the trade

[5] For an example of the technique of applying multiple correlation analysis to economic time series, see Stone, " Analysis of Market Demand," (*Journal of the Royal Statistical Society*, 1945).

[6] A. O. Hirschman, *National Power and the Structure of Foreign Trade*, University of California Press, Berkeley and Los Angeles, 1945, pages 157–162.

of different countries.   A similar index could be computed to measure the concentration of a country's trade in individual commodities.

SUMMARY

The interrelations between the internal and external economy of a country are very numerous, and the treatment afforded them in the present chapter is by no means exhaustive.   A thorough treatment of the subject would have to incorporate much material presented in textbooks on the economics of international trade.   The present chapter gives relatively scant attention to subjects which ordinarily form the bulk of such texts, or which are readily available from other sources, and an attempt has been made instead to emphasize those subjects which are less fully treated elsewhere.

CHAPTER 12

International Comparisons and Standardization

WILLIAM R. LEONARD
United Nations Statistical Office

INTRODUCTION

The task of preparing reasonably comparable tables of external trade statistics is beset by almost all the difficulties discussed in the other chapters of this book. Moreover, the variations in national practices are most clearly exposed in the preparation of comparable statistics, since the export of a commodity from one country is clearly an import into another country, and the two sides of the transaction should balance, as double-entry bookkeeping is supposed to balance. But to what country is the export to be attributed: the one from which the ship, plane, or railway wagon left, or the one in which the product was mined, grown, or fabricated? To what country is it going? Will it be transhipped across several national frontiers before it reaches the person by whom it is to be consumed? Or suppose that the commodity is stored somewhere en route, or that it is packaged or slightly modified before it is shipped further; in such cases what country should be credited as the exporter? If all these answers can be detected and consistently recorded in the trade statistics, what kind or class of commodity is it among all the hundreds of thousands of commodities? An exporting country might classify ginned cotton as an agricultural product, and the importing country might consider it a semi-manufactured good. Obviously if this shipment is differently classified by the exporting country and by the importing country the double-entry nature of the system becomes sadly distorted.

National practices in the valuation of exports or imports simply add to the other difficulties. The factors of transport expense, insurance, and other costs must be taken into account because at the moment of import the product has gained a certain amount in value, but at the moment of export this added value has not been acquired. Apart from this, which can be taken account of satisfactorily without too great error, how is the product to be valued? Does it have the value shown on the invoice; does it have a sort of standard value fixed from time to time by the Customs administration; or is the value a " fair price " in a competitive market? This kind of question, particularly important in these days of trade agreements, subsidies, exchange controls, and shipments on government account, seriously affects the comparability of trade statistics.

When it is considered that there are many millions of transactions each year, and some 150 to 200 separate Customs administrations, it is quite clear that complete consistency and uniformity of treatment is a long-term goal. Nevertheless, a great deal has been accomplished by international agencies and national governments since about 1920, either to reduce the degree of incomparability or to identify it so that rough adjustments may be made. It is hoped that much more will be done.

This chapter deals with the first steps in the compilation of international tables and with the current situation. It touches both upon the compilations available at different times and upon the efforts to secure agreement among different national practices concerning valuation, classification, and the like, which continue to make comparisons difficult.

CONVENTIONS ON DEFINITION AND CLASSIFICATION

Need for standardization. Before the industrial revolution, trade had consisted largely of a rather speculative and unsystematic exchange of surpluses against luxuries; its amount reflected the fortunes of the great traders—the Venetians through the 15th century, the Dutch in the 16th and 17th centuries. The discoveries of the 17th century greatly stimulated trade, but it was not until the industrial revolution that trade expanded to important proportions. It is estimated that the total trade of the United Kingdom increased five times during the 18th century; in the first 60 years of the 19th century it increased four times. In the United States trade expanded more than five times in the 70 years ending 1860, and it doubled in the decade ending in 1870. Estimated total world trade more than doubled between 1860 and 1880; by 1908 the total amounted to about £6000 million (despite a general fall in the price level of 25 per cent), compared with £1400 million in 1860.

By the latter half of the 19th century, serious attention began to be given to uniform Customs nomenclature, statistical classification, valuation, designation of countries of origin and destination, and all the other problems which made statistical comparisons difficult. The growth of trade had been so great, and it occupied so important a position in the economic life of countries, that it became necessary to know as much as possible about the nature and extent of the trade pattern. This obviously pointed to the need for comparable definitions and common classifications. These problems were initially touched upon at the first International Statistical Congress (Brussels) in 1853. There, recommendations were made to achieve the unification of Customs schedules for statistical purposes. Growing industrialization had meant more and more detailed categories of goods, particularly in those countries which had invoked the protective tariff.[1]

Special mention should be made at this point of a paper entitled " Comparability of Trade Statistics," by A. E. Bateman, given at the seventh session (1899) of the International Statistical Institute. He discussed the difficulties of obtaining comparable statistics in terms of the varied practices of 18 trading countries (17 European countries and the United States) respecting the methods of registering imports and exports, of valuation (declared, official, or " actual "), of classification, and of

[1] This is illustrated by figures taken from " Customs Nomenclature and Customs Classification," by Ernst Trendelenburg, a paper (C. E. I. 32) prepared for the International Economic Conference (Geneva, 1927). In 1888 the German Customs schedule included about 490 items; by 1925 the number of items has increased to 2300. The French Customs schedule in 1892 had 654 tariff headings and about 1500 subdivisions; in 1925 there were 1272 headings and more than 4300 items. The experience in Italy was the same; from 1878 to 1921 the number of items increased from 535 to 2777.

Mention should also be made of the International Union for the Publication of Customs Tariffs established by international convention at Brussels in July 1890. By this convention 38 countries agreed to establish an international bureau which was to publish, at joint expense (shares being based on the importance of external trade in each country), the *Bulletin international des Douanes* in those languages " most used for trade purposes." (For full text of convention see " Accounts and Papers," *State Papers* (United Kingdom), 1890–1891, 49th volume). The purpose of the *Bulletin* was to make information generally available about the rapidly increasing complex of Customs law and regulation.

The question of unification of definitions and practices was again taken up at the Hague session of the International Statistical Congress in 1869 and at the first (Rome, 1887) and several subsequent sessions of the International Statistical Institute. The first session of the Institute discussed problems of comparability arising out of divergent classifications and valuation practices, methods of recording countries of origin and destination and of the treatment of movements of precious metals. A committee was appointed to investigate these problems and to report at the second session.

accounting for transit trade and temporary imports.   An examination of the exhibits prepared by Bateman to illustrate the different practices, or the lack of knowledge thereon, tends to cast the most serious doubt upon the validity for purposes of international comparison of any tables that might have been prepared at that time.   For example, most of the countries employed " official " values set annually by a commission or by administrative action, and those used by one country had been established 10 years previously.[2]

Other organizations also advocated rationalization of Customs nomenclature.   The International Trade and Industrial Congress (Paris, 1889) resolved that states should adopt comparable classifications and uniform nomenclature in their tariff descriptions and official statistics.   The Congrès international de la Réglementation douanière (Paris, 1900) advocated a uniform nomenclature covering a certain number of categories to assist in the compilation of statistics.   Other trade and economic conferences (Antwerp, 1894, Mons, 1905, and Milan, 1906) made similar recommendations.[3]

Brussels Convention of 1913.   It was not until the Conférence internationale de Statistique douanière at Brussels in 1910 that decisions were made which culminated 3 years later in the signing of an international Convention respecting the compilation of international commercial statistics.[4]

The contracting states agreed to compile, in addition to their national statistics, special statistics based on a common nomenclature grouping which had been prepared as part of the Brussels Convention.   The Convention authorized the creation of the Bureau international de Statistique commerciale to be financed by contributions from contracting states according to the size of their merchandise trade.   Arrangements were also made for the publication of the *Bulletin du Bureau international de Statistique commerciale* which was to contain statistics collected according to table forms prescribed in the Brussels Convention.   As events turned out, this praiseworthy effort was initially frustrated by World War I.   It was not until 1925 that the first issue of the *Bulletin* appeared with figures for the year 1922.   Though other attempts had by then been made to publish comparable commodity statistics the stimulus given by the Brussels Convention of 1913 was sufficient to carry forward the publication

---

[2] See *Bulletin de l'Institut International de Statistique*, Tome XII, Kristiania, 1900. It is interesting to note the very considerable progress achieved by 1923, when nearly three-fourths of some 40 countries selected by the League of Nations for study had adopted systems of declared values.   (See *Memorandum on Balance of Payments and Foreign Trade Balances*, 1910–1923, Volume II, Geneva, 1924).

[3] Trendelenburg, *op. cit.*

[4] Signed by 29 countries at Brussels 31 December, 1913 at the second Conférence internationale de Statistique douanière.

of the *Bulletin* until 1937 (with figures for the year 1935).   By this time, the
work of the League of Nations in publishing more elaborate trade statistics
for more countries, the development of the League's Draft Customs
Nomenclature, and the preparation of the Minimum List of Commodities
for International Trade Statistics, all served to shift the center of gravity
from Brussels.   The impetus given to the standardization of trade
statistics was nevertheless noteworthy; as late as 1947, 17 countries were
reassembling their statistics according to the five principal groups of the
Brussels nomenclature.[5] (See Chapter 4 on commodity classification for a
description of the commodity classification structures of the Brussels and
League lists.)

The first issue of the *Bulletin* contained statistics for 15 countries.   For
the five main categories of the Brussels nomenclature it showed imports
and exports by weight (where practicable) and by value in national
currencies and in French gold francs.   The detailed tables showed the
weight and value of trade classified by the 186 titles in the Brussels list;
these figures are shown in country-by-commodity and in commodity-by-
country tables.[6]

The five main categories of the Brussels list were as follows:

I	Live animals	7	headings
II	Food and beverages	42	,,
III	Materials, raw or simply prepared . .	49	,,
IV	Manufactured articles	84	,,
V	Gold and silver, unworked, and gold and silver coin	4	,,

These 186 headings were retained unchanged for the 14 years that the
Bulletin was published.   The items were not systematically grouped
within the five main categories, and although in a few cases subdivisions
were introduced it is not evident that these were used for statistical
purposes.

A great deal of discussion had been directed to the most suitable system
of classification, efforts having been made to devise a " logical " system
which would have the permanence and inevitability apparently attaching
to classifications in natural sciences.   Some of the national classifications
appeared in alphabetical order; some recognized the " natural " divisions
of the animal, vegetable, and mineral kingdoms; and others arranged the
tariff items according to the branches of industry in which the commodities were produced (*e.g.*, agriculture, forestry, fishing).   Still others

[5] According to a special study of the classification practices of nearly 100 countries
made by the Statistical Office of the United Nations.
[6] *Bulletin du Bureau international de Statistique commerciale*, Premiere année, 1922.

combined the systems, giving the main categories of animal, vegetable, mineral, and manufactured products, the last subdivided according to branches of industry. It is interesting that the Brussels list avoided many of the logical and conceptual difficulties which tend to plague the compilers of classifications. For the most part, the 186 headings were simply described as commodities (although it is evident that most headings had to contain mixtures of single commodities); comparatively little attention was given to the component material, to concepts of end use, or to similar criteria. An alphabetical list of about 2200 entries was included in each issue of the *Bulletin;* this list must have been of great assistance to countries in the preparation of comparable statistics. The list, entitled " Lexicon of Goods," was published in French, English, German, and Dutch.

Further development of standards. Shortly before events made it possible for the Bureau international de Statistique commerciale to publish trade statistics, the subject was touched upon at the Conference on International Co-operation in Statistics (London, 1919). This conference was called by the League of Nations to discuss the state of statistical affairs of the Economic and Financial Secretariat of the League, the International Institute of Agriculture, the permanent office of the International Statistical Institute and the International Labour Office. None of the organizations, except the International Institute of Agriculture, had developed plans to publish comparable trade statistics, it being generally assumed that this responsibility would in time be assumed by the Brussels Bureau. This responsibility was further recognized at the fifteenth Session of the International Statistical Institute (Brussels, 1923). As regards nomenclature, the Institute was of the opinion that the common nomenclature laid down by the Brussels Convention " might provisionally serve as a basis for international statistics . . . ; that such improvements as may be suggested by experience should be introduced into the common nomenclature; that an index of the goods included under each item of the common nomenclature should be compiled in several languages. . . ." [7]

At the same time the Institute went further in dealing with other aspects of comparability than it had at previous sessions. It urged that it would be desirable to generalize the system of valuations based on special declarations, even though the system of official valuation might continue in force; the declared value of goods should be c.i.f. for imports and f.o.b. for exports. The Institute recommended that precise definitions be established for weights and measures (gross weight, net weight, legal net weight). In proposing that countries should give exact figures of special trade the Institute gave definitions of special imports and special exports,

---

[7] *Recommendations and Opinions concerning Economic Statistics*, League of Nations, C.L. 52 (a), 1924, II.

of nationalized goods and improvement trade.   The recommendations also covered the desirable treatment of bunker fuel, temporary imports and exports, ships' stores, gold and silver coin and bullion, fishery products, the attribution of provenance and destination, and the time periods to be covered (*i.e.*, calendar months and years).

These recommendations (and those in other fields of statistics) were formulated by the Preparatory Committee.   This committee was set up by the International Statistical Institute and the Economic Committee of the League in an effort to co-operate in the improvement of statistical methodology.   The resolutions adopted at the Brussels session in 1923 were approved by the Economic Committee of the League in February 1924.   The Committee proposed that the resolutions on trade statistics should be circulated to member states for comment.   However, it felt that proposals of the Institute for international conventions relating to the system of determining weights and measures and to the method of showing countries of provenance and destination might be reserved for further study.

International Convention of 1928.   The momentum on the improvement of comparability in trade statistics culminated in the International Conference Relating to Economic Statistics.   The Conference was authorized by the Council of the League at the Council's forty-ninth session in March 1928 and met in Geneva later that year.   Representatives of 42 states attended.   At the conclusion of the Conference, 25 signed the International Convention Relating to Economic Statistics.[8]   A Final Act was also prepared and signed, which contained supplementary recommendations including one for the preparation of a statistical classification as soon as the work on tariff nomenclature was sufficiently advanced.[9]   This work was taken up at the first meeting in 1931 of the League's Committee of Statistical Experts, also established by the Convention.   By April 1933, a draft had been prepared by E. Dana Durand, chairman of the Sub-Committee established for the purpose.

The elaboration of what was to become the Minimum List of Commodities for International Trade Statistics continued, and in 1934 the Council of the League authorized the draft to be circulated to obtain the observations of governments.   By September 1935, the Council expressed the hope that governments would see their way to publishing, at least annually,

[8] International Conference Relating to Economic Statistics, C.606(2).   M.184(2). 1928, II, League of Nations, Geneva, 1928.
[9] The Sub-Committee of Experts on the Unification of Customs Nomenclature had been established in 1927 by a decision of the Council of the League following upon a recommendation of the World Economic Conference in May 1927.   (For a full account of the history and first results of this work see *Draft Framework for a Customs Tariff Nomenclature* published by the League in 1928 as document C.346. M.103. 1928. II.) The nomenclature went through various drafts and emerged in 1931 as the *Draft Customs Nomenclature*, League document C.921.M.486.1931. II B and in final form in 1937 as C.295.M.194.1937. II. B.

supplementary statistics of their imports and exports classified in accordance with the Minimum List as drawn up by the Committee.[10]

The International Conference of 1928 also examined other aspects of trade statistics, giving particular attention to definitions.   Annex I to the Convention contains detailed definitions and recommended practices.

It was agreed that statistics of external trade should be compiled in one of two ways: (a) returns of special trade compiled alone, or together with returns of general trade; or (b) returns of imports related to aggregate imports only, with re-exports of such imported goods also shown. Methods and definitions were recommended for handling improvement and repair trade, transit trade, bunker fuel, and the other perplexing variations which had caused difficulty in the preparations of comparable tables.   It was agreed also that the system of valuation should be that of declared values, although provision was made for recognizing any national fiscal requirements for valuation.   Imports should be valued at cost plus transport and insurance, exports at the value free on board at the frontier of the exporting country, and precise definitions of units of measure should be given.   The territories for which statistics should be compiled were described and made a part of the Convention, and the Committee of Statistical Experts was instructed to draw up a minimum list of statistical territories.   This was done at the first meeting in 1931.

Special attention was given to the problem of attributing trade to the country of provenance and destination, and an experiment was initiated to judge the merits of the different systems in use.   To simplify this work, a list of 22 commodities (ultimately 26) was prepared by the Committee of Statistical Experts, although co-operating countries were free to make their own selections of commodities.   This flexibility somewhat handicapped the interpretation of results.   Seventeen countries participated in the experiment which was carried out in most of the co-operating countries between 1931 and 1933.[11]   A great deal was learned by analyzing the advantages and disadvantages of the various methods subjected to test, and it was concluded that

the accurate matching of import records with export records relating to the same goods cannot be carried out, whether the country of origin and the country of consumption employ the same method of assignment or different methods. To determine the courses of the streams of trade (in different varieties of goods) about the world is not generally feasible by the plan of associating import records and export records of the same goods.

[10] *Report to the Council of the Work of the Fifth Session*, Committee of Statistical Experts, League document C.456.M.270.1936.II.A.
[11] A full account of this work is given in the report of the Second Session of the Committee of Statistical Experts (C.672.M.322.1933.A.II.) in an annex entitled *Summary of the Reports Received from the Various Countries Regarding the Results of the Experiment in the Recording of Commodities by Countries of Provenance and Destination.*

It appears, accordingly, that a complete and accurate view of the destination of the goods exported by the various countries can only be approached by such improvement of the import records of all countries as may make it possible for the exporting country to learn from these records the destination of the exports.[12]

In view of the finding, the Committee of Statistical Experts urged, and in 1934 the Council of the League decided to recommend, that governments which did not record their imports by countries of origin should prepare a supplementary annual record of the commodities contained in a special list of basic commodities drawn up by the Committee.   The list comprised the raw materials and foodstuffs subsequently included in *International Trade in Certain Raw Materials and Foodstuffs by Countries of Origin and Destination.*

COMPILATIONS BY THE LEAGUE OF NATIONS

International Trade Statistics.   During the period that questions of definition and classification were still under extensive discussion, the League of Nations began the compilation of carefully documented statistics on external trade.   One compilation was made for use at the International Financial Conference at Brussels in 1920,[13] but it was not until 1924 that systematic tables were prepared.   These were contained in the *Memorandum on Balance of Payments and Foreign Trade Balances* first published in 1924.   Volume I included a table on the imports and exports of merchandise, bullion, and specie for 35 countries for 1913, and for the years 1919–1923, in terms of national currencies.   A similar table was given by weight.   A further table gave for 24 countries the value of trade (merchandise trade only) for 1913 and for 1919–1923 in current prices and at 1913 prices.   Innovations in the compilation of trade statistics were summary tables of trade by countries which showed for 4 years (1913, 1920–1922) the percentage distribution of the imports into 38 countries from 36 of their most important trading partners, and the percentage distribution of exports from the 38 countries to 36 trading partners.   These trade-by-country tables marked the most ambitious attempt up to that time to produce what is now known as the *matrix table*, a device which greatly simplifies the task of analyzing the changing patterns of world trade.

[12] *Ibid.*, p. 4.
[13] *International Trade*, Report No. V, League of Nations, London, 1920, gave the value of special imports and exports for 25 countries for the years 1913–1919 and for the months of 1919.   The trade of 15 countries was shown in accordance with the countries of origin and consignment for 1919 and, where available, for 1913.   For 15 countries, also, the value and weight of imports and exports were given by commodity. A useful analysis of valuation practices and detailed descriptions of the series were provided.

Volume II of the *Memorandum* contained detailed trade figures for 42 countries, together with copious analytical notes describing and comparing national methods of compiling trade statistics, so that much closer approximations to valid country-to-country comparisons might be made. The tables were arranged by countries. Table 1*a* showed for any given country the value in national currency of imports and exports of merchandise (special trade), and of bullion and specie, for the period 1910–1922. Table 1*b* showed the imports and exports of merchandise only, by months, for 1921–1922. Table II typically gave for each country the value of special merchandise imports and exports for 1912–1913 and 1919–1922 with each trading partner which accounted for more than 1 per cent of total trade. Tables III*a* (imports) and III*b* (exports) showed for the same years the value and weight of principal articles imported and exported. Individual commodities accounting for less than 1 per cent of the total were not given separately. As far as possible the items were single articles—in some cases the national items were combined—and, although not entirely comparable, the content and arrangement corresponded to the Brussels list. Table IV elaborated slightly the details about the import and export of gold and silver.

These tables continued to appear each year, with the addition of more countries and a number of conceptual refinements. In 1933 the title of the publication was changed to *International Trade Statistics*, a yearbook which appeared with figures for 1930. A further volume gave statistics for 1931 and 1932. Thereafter, annual editions appeared with figures for each year from 1933 to 1938, by which time this important statistical work had to be largely suspended because of war conditions. In 1925 the League added a fifth table to the four previously given for each country; the new table, in general, gave the value of exports and imports in terms of the five groups contained in the Brussels Convention. The 1935 edition of *International Trade Statistics*, for example, gave the Brussels grouping for 55 of the 65 countries which were treated in detail, the figures having been taken either from the Brussels *Bulletin*, where available, or from national publications. The figures for France, as they appeared in Table V of the 1935 edition are reproduced here as Figure *A*.

Matrix tables for basic commodities. A very significant development occurred in 1936 when the League published the first of four annual volumes entitled *International Trade in Certain Raw Materials and Foodstuffs by Countries of Origin and Destination.*[14] In this work, particular pains were taken to " securing, as far as possible, uniformity of definitions and methods employed in the recording of imports by countries of

---

[14] League of Nations, Geneva. Four volumes, 1935, 1936, 1937, 1938. This publication was one outcome of the experimental work conducted in 1931–1933.

Figure *A*.   Brussels Grouping of Trade Statistics

FRANCE

Table V

Imports and Exports, by Classes of the International (Brussels, 1913) Classification

Special Trade Merchandise, Bullion and Specie

Value in francs (000,000's omitted)

CLASSES	1932*		1933†	
	VALUE			
	...	%	...	%
	IMPORTS			
Live animals	371	0·7	280	0·6
Articles of food and drink	10,697	20·0	9,506	20·7
Materials, raw or partly manufactured . .	12,933	24·2	13,450	29·2
Manufactured articles	5,807	10·9	5,195	11·3
Gold and silver: specie and unmanufactured .	23,601	44·2	17,579	38·2
TOTAL	53,409	100	46,010	100
	EXPORTS			
Live animals.	34	0·2	34	0·1
Articles of food and drink	2,925	13·2	2,706	9·1
Materials, raw or partly manufactured . .	3,576	16·1	3,416	11·5
Manufactured articles	13,171	59·4	12,318	41·3
Gold and silver: specie and unmanufactured .	2,470	11·1	11,343	38·0
TOTAL	22,176	100	29,817	100

* From *Bulletin du Bureau International de Stat. Commerciale.*
† Provisional figures.
Source: Selected from Table 5, *International Trade Statistics*, 1935.

origin." These efforts resulted in a new form of matrix table which showed for each of 38 commodities (in 1938) for each of 3 years the imports of each country by countries of origin—a much more determinable quantity than could be obtained by relying upon the statistics of the exporting country because special efforts were made to record the origin of this limited number of commodities.   An illustrative table is given on page 250 as Figure *B*.

The technique employed by the League in this work overcame or avoided many of the traditional difficulties attaching to the compilation of comparable tables.   For example, there were no valuation or currency conversion problems, since the physical unit or weight was employed.

Figure *B.* League of Nations Matrix Table for Basic Commodities
Trade in Unroasted Coffee: Exports of Three Principal Producing
Countries to Countries of Europe and North America in 1938
Based on Statistics of Importing Countries.

(000 metric tons)

	Three Exporting Countries			All Countries
	Brazil	Colombia	Venezuela	
Austria	3·3	0·6	—	6·3
Belgium Luxembourg	24·2	0·6	0·1	51·6
Czechoslovakia	6·0	1·2	0·3	11·8
Denmark	14·6	0·9	3·1	34·5
Finland	20·0	0·1	0·6	26·2
France	85·3	1·8	4·4	186·2
Germany	91·8	34·2	18·9	197·4
Greece	7·6	—	—	7·6
Hungary	0·7	0·6	0·2	2·1
Italy	20·8	1·8	1·9	35·6
Netherlands	22·3	2·4	0·1	52·0
Norway	3·4	0·4	0·3	19·4
Poland	3·5	0·1	—	6·1
Portugal	2·1	—	—	6·6
Roumania	0·4	.	.	3·2
Sweden	35·3	3·1	0·6	52·7
Switzerland	9·2	1·0	—	17·3
Turkey	5·3	—	—	5·3
United Kingdom	0·5	0·1	0·1	20·4
Yugoslavia	6·5	0·1	—	7·2
Canada	2·7	3·2	—	19·2
United States	544·4	205·4	10·9	901·4
Total imports	945·5†	258·4†	41·5†	1782·5†
Total exports according to export statistics of producing countries	1026·8	253·7	..	1721·3

— = less than 50 m.t.
. = unknown.
.. = not yet available.
† some small countries omitted from stub.
Source: Selected from Table 10, *International Trade in Certain Raw Materials and Foodstuffs*, League of Nations, 1939, Geneva.

Even so, the comparison of total imports as reported by importing
countries with total exports of exporting countries revealed some discrepancies. Some of the reasons for discrepancy, as recorded in the League
publications, are:

1. Time in transport.
2. Failure of exporters and importers to classify consistently.
3. The question of whether political boundaries and affiliations are fully
   understood by both exporter and importer.

4. The use of average conversion factors.

5. The question of proper attribution when commodities are slightly processed or blended.

6. Loss or gain of weight in transport.

7. Different systems of recording the country of origin or provenance.

Nevertheless, a great many of the tables show remarkable consistency, the reward of painstaking and understanding work.

Minimum List.   The 1936 volume of *International Trade Statistics* gave statistics for 19 countries according to the newly developed Minimum List of Commodities for International Trade Statistics.   In the 1938 (and last) volume, the number of countries had increased to 25.   By the spring of 1939, 31 countries and several colonial possessions of the United Kingdom had agreed to use the Minimum List.   The publication of the five Brussels groups had been discontinued.   In the tables arranged according to the Minimum List, commodities were grouped by the 17 sections and 50 chapters which summarized the 456 items of the List.   A table showing the arrangement by sections with details by chapter for the food section, is presented on page 252 as Figure *C*.

In addition to the tables arranged by sections and chapters, a table was given for most of the 25 countries showing exports and imports in national currencies arranged according to " stage of production," and " use," together with notations permitting the aggregation of durable and non-durable goods.   Within the limits set by difficulties of definition and convertibility of national classifications into the Minimum List framework, this arrangement was intended to facilitate economic analysis of changes in the trade pattern.   These supplementary classifications of the 456 Minimum List items which were themselves cross-classified have sufficient interest to be reproduced on page 253.

Totals were given for each group 1–10 above, as well as a summary by use showing separate totals for groups 1–4, 5, 6, 7, and 8–10.   A further table gave a summary by stage of production; thus all *a*, *b*, and *c* sub-groups were separately added to give totals for crude, simply transformed, and elaborately transformed goods.   Aggregates could be made for the total of durable and non-durable goods.[15]

Trade in agricultural commodities.   During the period when the Brussels Bureau and the League of Nations were developing their trade statistics, considerable impetus was given to the compilation of comparative tables

[15] For more complete accounts of the structure and use of the Minimum List, see *International Trade Statistics*, 1938, League of Nations, Geneva, 1939; also the Minimum List of Commodities for International Trade Statistics, *Studies and Reports on Statistical Methods*, No. 2, League of Nations, Geneva, 1938, and Appendices I, II, and III to the fourth *Report of the Committee of Statistical Experts to the Council* (C.268. M.136.1935.II.A. [C.E.S. 53]).

Figure *C*. A " Minimum List " Table

Imports and Exports, by Sections and a Selected Chapter
(International Classification, Geneva, 1928–1935:
League of Nations, " Minimum List ")

CANADA

Special Trade, Merchandise, Bullion and Specie

(Value in million dollars)

SECTIONS AND CHAPTERS	IMPORTS				EXPORTS			
	1937		1938		1937		1938	
	Can. $	%	Can. $	%	Can. $	%	Can. $	%
I. FOOD . . .	106·8	13·2	101·4	15·0	328·4	29·5	261·5	28·6
1. Live animals .	—	—	—	—	16·8	1·5	8·6	0·9
2. Meat .	1·2	0·1	1·6	0·2	42·2	3·8	36·3	4·0
3. Dairy products .	0·5	—	1·8	0·3	18·2	1·6	17·0	1·9
4. Fish . . .	2·0	0·2	2·3	0·3	26·8	2·4	25·3	2·8
5. Cereals .	15·6	1·9	15·2	2·2	137·4	12·4	101·6	11·1
6. Flours .	1·4	0·2	1·3	0·2	34·8	3·1	27·7	3·0
7. Fruit. .	27·6	3·5	22·7	3·4	10·0	0·9	12·7	1·4
8. Vegetables.	7·9	1·0	7·4	1·1	9·1	0·8	9·0	1·0
9. Sugar .	20·5	2·5	20·5	3·0	1·3	0·1	2·0	0·2
10. Coffee, tea.	18·4	2·3	16·6	2·5	0·1	—	0·1	—
11. Beverages .	8·9	1·1	7·8	1·2	21·5	1·9	11·3	1·2
12. Fodder, etc.	1·4	0·2	2·0	0·3	7·3	0·7	4·4	0·5
13. Tobacco .	1·4	0·2	2·2	0·3	2·9	0·3	5·5	0·6
II. FATS .	20·2	2·5	14·4	2·1	5·2	0·5	3·1	0·3
III. CHEMICALS, etc.	41·7	5·2	38·6	5·7	30·0	2·7	24·5	2·7
IV. RUBBER .	19·2	2·4	11·0	1·6	11·5	1·0	9·6	1·1
V. WOOD .	11·3	1·4	9·3	1·4	84·0	7·6	70·1	7·7
VI. PAPER .	9·6	1·2	8·4	1·2	178·0	16·0	140·6	15·4
VII. HIDES, etc.	17·6	2·2	10·7	1·6	26·9	2·4	21·2	2·3
VIII. TEXTILES	103·3	12·8	76·8	11·3	6·7	0·6	5·3	0·6
IX. CLOTHING	16·5	2·0	15·2	2·2	16·3	1·5	15·1	1·7
X. FUEL .	101·6	12·5	95·0	14·0	8·1	0 7	7 8	0·9
XI. MINERALS	31·6	3·9	24·7	3·6	20·2	1·8	17·6	1·9
XII. JEWELLERY	4·9	0·6	3·9	0·6	131·8	11·9	98·9	10·8
XIII. METALS .	105·1	13·0	73·1	10·8	187·6	16·9	167·0	18·2
XIV. MACHINERY	150·6	18·6	126·9	18·8	53·9	4·9	51·7	5·7
XV. MISCELLANEOUS	48·7	6·0	46·5	6·9	15·4	1·4	13·7	1·5
XVI. RETURNED .	20·2	2·5	21·6	3·2	6·2	0·6	5·7	0·6
TOTAL (Merchandise).	808·9	100	677·5	100	1110·2	100	913·4	100
XVII. GOLD . . .	1·3	0·2	59·3	8·0	0·1	—	—	—
GRAND TOTAL .	810·2	...	736·8	...	1110·3	...	913·4	...

of imports and exports by the work of the International Institute of
Agriculture. The Institute was founded by international convention in
1905 by 40 states; subsequently an additional 30-odd states ratified the
convention. Among other activities, the Institute undertook to assemble
and make available international statistics on a variety of subjects of
interest in the development of national agricultural policies. Important
among these were statistics of external trade. The Institute began

	Groups	Durable or Non-durable
1 — 4.	*Material for Production*	
	1. Material for food	Non-durable
	a. crude	
	b. simply transformed	
	2. Material for agriculture	Non-durable
	a. crude	
	b. simply transformed	
	3. Material for industry	Non-durable
	a. crude	
	b. simply transformed	
	c. elaborately transformed	
	4. Material for industry	Durable
	a. crude	
	b. simply transformed	
	c. elaborately transformed	
5.	*Fats and Oils*	Non-durable
	a. crude	
	b. simply transformed	
6.	*Fuels*	Non-durable
	a. crude	
	b. simply transformed	
7.	*Capital Equipment*	Durable
	a. crude	
	b. elaborately transformed	
8 — 10.	*Consumers Goods*	
	8. Food	Non-durable
	a. crude	
	b. simply transformed	
	c. elaborately transformed	
	9. Other non-durable	Non-durable
	c. elaborately transformed	
	10. Consumers' capital	Durable
	c. elaborately transformed	
X	*Unclassifiable*	

operations in 1908; tables of trade statistics (commodity-by-country tables for 15 important agricultural products) appeared for the first time in the 1911–1912 issue of the Institute's *Yearbook*.[16]

The continuation of this work was seriously delayed by World War I. However, the first issue of the *Yearbook* after the war contained expanded tables of imports and exports, covering the years 1909–1921, for 20 important agricultural products and for 14 fertilizers and chemical products useful to agriculture.   The figures were given in terms of physical

[16] *Annuaire international de Statistique Agricole*, Rome, 1914.

units, thus avoiding problems of valuation.   The number of countries or areas for which figures were published was large.   Thus, the table on wheat showed 88 importing countries and 50 exporting countries; the table on tea gave 133 importing countries and 35 exporting countries (many of these were countries which re-exported tea after processing or packing).   The tables were accompanied by detailed notes showing the sources and definitions of the statistics printed, and altogether the tables were extremely comprehensive and usable.   Publication of the *Yearbook* continued until World War II began; subsequently it was resumed under the auspices of the Food and Agriculture Organization of the United Nations.

Position in 1939.   Thus the efforts to present trade statistics of different countries in comparable tables had reached a high and promising point by 1939.   These efforts had been made by several different international organizations over a period of nearly 50 years.   The work of the International Statistical Congresses, the International Statistical Institute, the *Bureau international de Statistique commerciale*, the International Institute of Agriculture, and the League of Nations all contributed in very substantial ways to the objectives of stimulating, expanding and directing records of the flow of international trade.   By international convention, standards had been laid down for dealing with such matters as the valuation of imports and exports, the treatment of transit goods, and the definition of statistical territories.   Also, a classification of commodities had been agreed upon and was used either as a national classification, or as a supplementary classification, by many countries.

The advent of World War II completely halted work of this kind. External trade statistics are among the most sensitive statistics in time of war; both because of the information they give about trade routes and because of the light they throw upon the economic war potential of different countries.   They became a subject of the greatest importance to belligerent countries.   The trade statistics systems of many countries were greatly strengthened and improved during World War II because of the crucial nature of the information that can be derived from a properly functioning system.   The results of these improvements—and many of them were directly concerned with matters of comparability—were obviously not open to public scrutiny and so could not be communicated to countries less directly involved in hostilities.

WORK OF THE UNITED NATIONS

Standard International Trade Classification (SITC).   It remained for the post-World War II international organizations to retrieve the ground lost, to fill in as far as possible the gaps occasioned by a statistical blackout of 7 years' duration, and to re-assess matters of definition and practice in the light of post-war economic conditions of stringent trade and currency regulations and of changes in the content and pattern of trade.

It was desirable, after such a long lapse of time, to reexamine the international standards which had been laid down in the 1928 Geneva Convention Relating to Economic Statistics and by the Committee of Statistical Experts of the League. Accordingly the United Nations Statistical Commission at its second session (September 1947) appointed a Committee on Statistical Classification to examine, among other things, the classification of commodities entering into external trade.[17] At the next session, the Commission requested that a revision of the League's Minimum List be prepared, circulated to governments for comment, and be subjected to the scrutiny of a group of experts selected for the purpose. This work proceeded; the experts' draft was examined at the 1949 session; and the items selected were found to be generally acceptable. With respect to the arrangement or classification of items, however, the Commission felt that governments should be further consulted, thus postponing the final decision until the fifth session (1950). This action was taken so that it might be possible to adapt the classification to national needs as far as practicable, thus encouraging governments to use it as the basis for national classifications. The probability that more frequent than annual compilations would be needed by international agencies led the Commission to make every effort to produce a generally acceptable classification. The revised classification was approved by the Commission at its 1950 session, and endorsed by the Economic and Social Council at its eleventh session in July-August 1950.[18]

Simultaneously, preparatory work was proceeding on a reexamination of the definitions on valuation and other practices bearing on matters of comparability, contained in the 1928 Geneva Convention Relating to Economic Statistics. This work was still in process in 1952, and recommendations on further standardization may be expected. Similar work is under way in connection with statistical techniques for the preparation of quantum and unit value indexes.

The work of applying the Standard International Trade Classification (SITC) to national statistics is now the urgent problem because, as anticipated, it will be necessary for international agencies to obtain

---

[17] *Report of the Statistical Commission*, E/577, p. 15.
[18] For a fuller account of the history of the Commission's work, and the nature of the Standard International Trade Classification, see Chapter 4, the *Report of the Statistical Commission*, Fifth Session (E/1696/Rev. 1), and *Statistical Papers*, Series M, No. 10 (second issue), in which the classification is reproduced together with an introduction referring to its use and application.

compilations of comparable trade statistics at least on a quarterly basis. The adoption of the SITC as a national classification would greatly facilitate the work of a government in preparing trade statistics by avoiding the need to make a number of recompilations of national statistics. It is obviously not required that countries adopt the SITC as their national classification, although several had done so by the middle of 1951. Many countries, at least for the time being, will find it convenient to make convertibility arrangements. By the middle of 1951 it was clear that at the end of 1951 more than 50 per cent of world trade would be expressed, either directly or indirectly, according to the SITC arrangement.

Post-war compilations. Considerable work is thus being directed toward obtaining improved comparability both in commodity classification and in definition and procedures. This work is necessarily slow, and it will be some years before results appear fully in the compilations. Many countries are greatly interested in standardization, however, because of new national and international needs for accurate, timely, and comparable trade statistics, and improvements may prove less slow in appearing than is anticipated.

During the time when the groundwork was being prepared for improved comparability, several different agencies published increasing numbers of tables of external trade statistics. Monthly figures of total imports and exports appear in national currencies in the United Nations *Monthly Bulletin of Statistics*,[19] and in United States dollars in *International Financial Statistics*[20] for a great many countries, and in the publications of the Economic Cooperation Administration and the Organization for European Economic Cooperation for those countries participating in the Marshall Plan. These publications also include quantum and unit value indexes. *International Financial Statistics* gives figures for particular commodities that are especially important to the economic condition of a country.

Annual figures of imports and exports for 130 countries for the years from 1928 are contained in the United Nations *Statistical Yearbook*.[21] Quantum and unit value indexes are given for nearly 50 countries. The first issue of the *Yearbook of International Trade Statistics* was published by the Statistical Office of the United Nations in 1951. This publication, which continues the annual series of the League of Nations discontinued in 1939, shows trade figures for a pre-war year (usually 1938) and for 1947, 1948, 1949 and (so far as then available) 1950.

Another quarterly publication, supplemented in the intervening months

---

[19] Statistical Office of the United Nations, New York.
[20] International Monetary Fund, Washington, D.C.
[21] Statistical Office of the United Nations, 1948; 1949–1950.

to bring the figures for additional countries up to the quarterly dates, is the *Direction of International Trade.*[22]

This United Nations publication gives for more than 90 countries exports for each country to each other country, and the imports of each country from each other country, in United States dollars, with several geographical subtotals. Where the trade returns of a country are not available for any period, derivative figures from the trade returns of their trading partners are tabulated, thus providing some indication of the magnitude and direction of trade. Although the figures given in the *Direction of International Trade* account for about 90 per cent of estimated world trade, complete figures do not exist now for such large areas as China, the USSR and a number of central European countries. The trade of non-reporting countries with each other, of course, is missed entirely. Nevertheless, this is the most comprehensive current publication on trade direction to appear so far. It is likely that the figures will be given in national currencies from time to time to facilitate additional uses.

Developments in 1951 and 1952. The most important post-war development from the point of view of users of foreign trade statistics was the publication, by the Statistical Office of the United Nations, of the foreign trade data of a number of countries classified according to the Standard International Trade Classification. Publication began with data for the first quarter of 1951. At the time of writing (1952) the data have been published for the first half of 1951 (*Statistical Papers*, Series D, No. 8). In this publication the trade of 14 countries is set out. The publication shows for each of the 150 groups of the SITC the value in United States dollars (and, where significant, the quantity) of imports and exports into and from each of the countries. The data for the commodity groups are analyzed, in most cases, by countries of provenance and destination. A specimen page of this publication is shown as Figure *D*. (See pp. 264–5).

The presentation of the foreign trade of these countries classified according to the standard classification has been made possible by the cooperation of the countries concerned. These countries have provided their data in this form for purposes of international comparability. Many more countries are expected to provide similar data in the future, and the usefulness of this United Nations publication will correspondingly increase. In the issue referred to above, the foreign trade of countries covering 53 per cent of world exports is presented.

Matrix tables. A number of the current publications of international agencies contain *matrix tables* showing direction of trade between geo-

[22] *Statistical Papers*, Series T. Published jointly by the Statistical Office of the United Nations, the International Monetary Fund, and the International Bank for Reconstruction and Development. It first appeared in 1949 as a publication of the Statistical Office.

graphical areas, currency areas, and for other area groupings. This type of table greatly facilitates the use of trade figures for specific analytical purpose.[23] Once the basic trade figures are obtained and recorded on work sheets or punch cards, desired groupings can be made without great difficulty. Examples of the matrix tables are given as Figures *E* and *F*. Figure *E* shows for 1949 the export trade of the world distributed by currency areas. Figure *F* shows the import trade distributed in the same way.

Figure *E*. Matrix Table—Export Trade by Currency Areas

Value of Trade of Principal Currency Areas—1949

(Based on export statistics)

Values in millions of U.S. dollars

Exports of ⟶ to ↓	Dollar Area	Non-Dollar Areas					World	Deficit
		Sterling	Latin America	W. Europe	E. Europe	Rest of world		
Dollar area . . .	7,384	1,413	886	846	117	504	11,150	—
Non-dollar areas:								
Sterling . . .	3,125	6,458	463	2,238	371	1,539	14,194	1,805
Latin America . .	921	449	279	619	35	21	2,324	—
W. Europe . . .	3,753	2,389	669	5,073	877	1,354	14,115	2,378
E. Europe . . .	117	352	44	880	—	81	1,474	30
Rest of world . .	1,617	1,328	123	2,081	44	548	5,741	1,694
World	16,917	12,389	2,464	11,737	1,444	4,047	48,998	—
Surplus	5,767	—	140	—	—	—	—	5,907
Per cent coverage . .	92	83	87	100	...	71	...	—

Source: Based on material contained in *Statistical Papers*, Series D, No. 4, Statistical Office of United Nations.

The use of trade figures in matrix form summarizes almost all the problems of comparability which arise in making international comparisons, especially if the matrix deals with a commodity or group of commodities where the classification problem is important. Apart from commodity classification, a study of the tables in Figures *E* and *F* shows a number of elements which impair direct comparability.

1. *Import or export returns.* If no problems of comparability existed the tables in Figures *E* and *F* would be exactly the same. A comparison of the two tables indicates that the figures in each cell of the import table are generally higher than those in the corresponding cell of the export table. This occurs because the figures in the import table include, with the

---

[23] See Ragnar Frisch, " Forecasting a Multilateral Balance of Payments," *American Economic Review*, September 1947, for an illustration of how trade matrixes can be used in economic analysis.

cost of the merchandise, the cost of insurance and freight as recorded in the trade returns of the importing country. These differences are far from constant, and in some instances even disappear. This is due to a number of obvious factors related to the trade reporting practices of some countries. Whether for a given purpose an analyst would elect to use export returns (f.o.b. basis) or import returns (c.i.f.) would depend upon the particular aspect of the problem in which he was interested and upon the availability of data. The trade returns of the less developed countries are

Figure *F*. Matrix Table—Import Trade by Currency Areas

Value of Trade of Principal Currency Areas—1949

(Based on import statistics)

Values in millions of U.S. dollars

Imports from→ into ↓	Dollar Area	Non-Dollar Areas					World	Deficit	Per cent coverage
		Sterling	Latin America	W. Europe	E. Europe	Rest of world			
Dollar area . .	7,284	1,906	1,044	875	·129	718	11,956	—	85
Non-dollar areas:									
Sterling . .	3,356	7,191	536	2,361	410	1,964	15,818	2,005	86
Latin America .	961	481	353	.651	38	28	2,512	—	88
W. Europe .	4,110	2,734	717	5,025	963	2,120	15,669	4,300	100
E. Europe .	129	387	48	968	—	89	1,621	33	...
Rest of world .	1,550	1,114	150	1,489	48	647	4,998	—	72
World . . .	17,390	13,813	2,848	11,369	1,588	5,566	52,574	—	...
Surplus . .	5,434	—	336	—	—	568	—	6,338	—

Source: Based on material contained in *Statistical Papers*, Series D, No. 4, Statistical Office of the United Nations.
Note: As the figures in this table have been obtained from import statistics of the various countries, *reported c.i.f.* (or adjusted to a c.i.f. basis), the figures in each cell should be higher by the amount of freight and insurance than figures in the corresponding cell of the export table. Data were not available for all countries in the various areas, and it is therefore necessary to take into account the estimated percentage coverage shown for these areas in the two tables.

typically delayed and less precise than those of the more highly developed countries; hence it may be necessary, for a given time period, to rely for import or export statistics of an underdeveloped country upon the export or import statistics of the developed countries with which they trade. Obviously the use of trade returns of the trading partner has certain limitations. It tends to confuse the f.o.b. or c.i.f. basis, or make it subject to estimation, and trade figures of underdeveloped countries with each other tend to be faulty or unavailable.

The same problem is encountered with respect to countries which do not make their trade statistics public. If this case it is necessary to use the trade returns of their trading partners, but if these are likewise not published there is no solution, however crude. Unless estimates are made, the figures must be omitted altogether. The two matrix tables illustrated clearly point up these limitations. The trade of the " rest of the world " with the " rest of the world " has the lowest percentage coverage because this group contains many underdeveloped areas and some non-reporters. On the other hand, the trade of Western Europe with Western Europe is fully reported in both the export table and the import table. Because of extensive non-reporting the trade of Eastern Europe with Eastern Europe is not given at all because for the most part these countries do not make their trade returns public.

2. *Units of measure.* If physical quantities of commodities are the subject of the matrix there is no special problem involving units of measurement. If value figures are used there are serious problems of converting values in national currencies, however they are determined, into some common unit. The problems involved in this operation are very substantial, particularly in dealing with the figures of countries with multiple exchange rates or inconvertible currencies. These problems and possible methods of dealing with them are discussed more fully in Chapter 6. In the case of time series, it would be necessary for the analyst to decide whether he wishes to tabulate figures based on current values, which would reflect price changes, or fixed values, which would tend to minimize the influence of price changes in the standard value units. The decision in this instance would depend primarily on what the study was intended to show. Before World War II, it was quite usual to convert to gold metal equivalents, but for several reasons this procedure has been discarded.

3. *Grouping of countries.* Any summary table requires somewhat arbitrary groupings, whether the groupings are of commodities or of countries. This would be particularly true if the grouping were based upon some economic concept such as currency area or degree of industrialization. Even if the grouping is strictly geographical many problems of detail will arise in the classification of countries which could conceivably be grouped with one or another agglomeration. This kind of difficulty also arises in national trade returns in the handling of country detail. One country may record the trade with a given country separately, whereas another country may include the trade of the given country in a residual group such as " Other Latin America." The practice of different countries in the reporting of residuals is very different and will account for many discrepancies, mostly of a minor character, in matrix tables.

4. *Other problems.* All other problems of comparability are still present—general vs. special trade, the treatment of special situations such as bunker fuel and fish, the question of how origin and destination are reported, and questions of transport time. Nevertheless, satisfactory

analytical use can be made of summarized figures providing the user has in mind that he must allow some latitude in his calculations for the several elements of incomparability which exist.

Regional publications. Many additional summaries and rearrangements of the basic direction figures, as well as especially prepared material for certain commodity groups, are available in other publications of the United Nations, especially in the *Economic Survey of Europe*.[24] The *Survey* includes a large number of analytical tables showing European inter-trade, and trade with certain non-European countries and groups of countries, both in terms of totals and by specified commodity groups. Other special purpose matrixes appear from time to time in the quarterly *Economic Bulletin for Europe*, also prepared by the ECE. One example is given as Figure *G*.

Figure *G*.   Special Purpose Matrix Table

Table 1

Volume of Exports of Ten European Countries and the United States by Area of Destination

Index numbers (October 1948–March 1949 = 100)

Area of origin / Area of destination	Ten European countries*				United States			
	1949		1950		1949		1950	
	April—Sept.	Fourth quarter	First quarter	Second quarter	April—Sept.	Fourth quarter	First quarter	Second quarter
Europe . .	106	126	133	139	102	91	81	81
United States .	72	120	116	122	—	—	—	—
Other countries of the Western Hemisphere .	84	114	110	111	97	91	85	101
Rest of world .	103	101	107	110	106	94	80	78
TOTAL EXPORTS	101	115	121	125	100	89	81	86

* Belgium-Luxembourg, Denmark, France, western zones of Germany, Italy, the Netherlands, Norway, Sweden, Switzerland, United Kingdom.

Other special compilations, usually on a wider geographic basis, appeared in the *World Economic Report 1948*, in *Major Economic Changes in 1949*, and in the *World Economic Report 1949–1950*.[25] An appendix table in the last-named report shows the direction of trade by 14 groups of countries, with subtotals by currency areas, for 1938, 1948, 1949, and

[24] United Nations Economic Commission for Europe, Geneva, annually from 1948.
[25] United Nations Department of Economic Affairs, New York.

the first half of 1950, in millions of United States dollars at current prices. The figures are from export returns on an f.o.b. basis. The text of the report contains several less comprehensive matrix tables designed to illuminate special problems.

The two other regional Economic Commissions of the United Nations (Latin America, and Asia and the Far East) also produce annual economic reports containing trade tables of regional interest.[26] Another regional activity is that of the Organization for European Economic Cooperation which in 1950 began the publication of the monthly *Foreign Trade Statistical Bulletin*.[27] This contains detailed figures for 16 participating countries.

Food and Agriculture Organisation (FAO). The work of the International Institute of Agriculture was taken over after World War II by the Food and Agriculture Organisation. The trade tables were expanded very considerably, and the first issue of the *Yearbook* after the war (prepared jointly with the Institute), contained figures of the imports and exports of 67 important vegetable products and 13 categories of livestock and animal products. The figures on other products important to agriculture had been dropped. In that volume statistics were given for the years 1941–1942 and 1945–1946.[28]

The detailed tables initiated by the Institute were continued by the FAO in the *Yearbook of Food and Agriculture Statistics*, 1948, Volume II, Trade and Commerce, which contained exports from and imports to a similarly large number of countries for a pre-war average period (1934–1938) and for the 3 years 1945–1947. The tables were accompanied by detailed notes on the statistical characteristics of commodities and countries. The 1950 *Yearbook* (Vol. IV, Part 2, Trade and Commerce) contains figures for 1948.

In addition to the annual publication dealing with farm products, the FAO published two specialized yearbooks dealing with fishery products and with forest products. The *Yearbook of Forest Products Statistics* was first published in 1947; to 1952 four issues had appeared. The 1949 issue contained details for 13 kinds of forest products for the years 1947 and 1948. Exports in terms of physical quantities from 80 countries and imports of 82 countries were given. The corresponding value figures, converted to United States dollars, referred to 69 countries in 1947 and 53 countries in 1948 for exports, and to 73 and 57 countries, respectively, for imports.

[26] Economic Survey of Latin America; Economic Survey of Asia and the Far East; (annual), United Nations.
[27] Organization for European Economic Cooperation, Statistical Division, rue André Pascal, Paris.
[28] *Yearbook of Agricultural Statistics*, Volume II, International Trade, Rome, 1947.

The *Yearbook of Fisheries Statistics*, also published by FAO, first appeared in 1948 and contained, as far as possible, statistics for all countries from 1930 onwards, although there were many gaps, some of which have subsequently been filled in. Imports by types of fish were given for some 60 countries, both by weight and value, and exports for somewhat fewer. The 1950 volume contains 1949 figures.

Position in 1952. The importance of comparable trade statistics promptly compiled is probably greater than ever before; almost all countries subject their external trade to a greater or lesser degree of control. For this purpose it is necessary to use established definitions and classifications, and they are the more useful to the extent that they may be internationally standardized. Substantial progress has been made in the years since the effective post-war organization of international statistical services. The Standard International Trade Classification has obtained a wide measure of agreement; valuation and related practices are steadily improving; and trade figures are becoming available with less delay. It remains true that much is to be done, but with the maintenance of the very great interest in improved comparability displayed by most national governments continued progress may be expected.[29]

[29] The great interest in comparability is evidenced by the resolutions adopted by statisticians of the American nations in January 1951, and of the European nations in September 1951, both of which groups recommended that countries be requested to investigate differences in the statistics of their mutual trade not explained by differences in definition (see Chapter 2).

EXPORTS

JAN. - JUNE 1951

* = Major irregularity in quanti
M = Unit is 1,000 times the unit
X = See introduction for informa

SITC Group Exporter Destination	Unit	Quantity	Value 1000 US $
SWEDEN	W	66	49
SWITZERLND	W	22	12
INDONESIA	W	129	71
SWEDEN TOT	W	502	187
BELG LUX	W	92	54
DENMARK	W	400	124
PORTUGAL TOT	W	21	13
686 ZINC			
U S AMER TOT	W	17041	8899
CANADA	W	2001	1364
MEXICO	W	609	324
CUBA	W	169	124
ARGENTINA	W	48	25
BRAZIL	W	1915	1123
CHILE	W	189	93
COLOMBIA	W	125	83
PERU	W	27	23
URUGUAY	W	40	27
VENEZUELA	W	50	47
UNTD KGDM	W	6899	2856
AUSTRIA	W	392	258
DENMARK	W	50	39
FRANCE	W	352	168
SWITZERLND	W	369	192
YUGOSLAVIA	W	236	91
ISRAEL	W	40	43
INDIA	W	2561	1353
JAPAN	W	782	493
PHILIPINES	W	79	69
UN SO AF	W	30	25
CANADA TOT			23513
UNTD KGDM TOT	W	1122	739
BELG LUX TOT	W	61836	32555
U S AMER	W	1679	825
CANADA	W	66	39
MEXICO	W	88	71
ARGENTINA	W	359	257
BRAZIL	W	2151	1275
CHILE	W	170	101
URUGUAY	W	114	93
UNTD KGDM	W	7335	3500
AUSTRIA	W	2550	1279
DENMARK	W	5642	3127
FINLAND	W	1645	912
FRANCE	W	10870	5079
GERMANY W	W	2532	1552
IRELAND	W	364	207
NETHERLNDS	W	7605	4077
NORWAY	W	27	16
SWEDEN	W	5585	2920
SWITZERLND	W	5066	2876
GREECE	W	154	100
ITALY	W	1181	476
PORTUGAL	W	213	91
TURKEY	W	866	525
CZECHOSLVK	W	822	391

SITC Group Exporter Destination
EGYPT
IRAN
ISRAEL
CHINA
HONG KONG
INDIA
INDOCHINA
JAPAN
MALAYA X
PAKISTAN
THAILAND
UN SO AF
BEL CONG X
S RHODESIA
DENMARK TOT
UNTD KGDM
BELG LUX
NETHERLNDS
NORWAY
FRANCE TOT
GERMANY W TOT
MEXICO
UNTD KGDM
BELG LUX
DENMARK
FINLAND
FRANCE
NETHERLNDS
NORWAY
SWEDEN
SWITZERLND
GREECE
TURKEY
INDIA
INDONESIA
NETHERLNDS TOT
U S AMER
CANADA
NETH ANTIL
ARGENTINA
CHILE
UNTD KGDM
AUSTRIA
BELG LUX
DENMARK
FINLAND
FRANCE
GERMANY W
IRELAND
SWEDEN
SWITZERLND
SPAIN
CZECHOSLVK
HONG KONG
INDIA
INDONESIA
JAPAN
THAILAND
UN SO AF
SWEDEN TOT

Quantity	Value 1000 US $	SITC Group Exporter Destination	Unit	Quantity	Value 1000 US $
374	238	PORTUGAL TOT	W	254	126
88	36				
90	54	TURKEY TOT	W	227	136
43	25	UNTD KGDM	W	80	43
1197	696	NETHERLNDS	W	147	93
647	381				
37	20	687 TIN			
1233	676				
351	230	U S AMER TOT			431
30	24	CANADA			155
180	113	MEXICO			41
36	22	CUBA			81
283	148	CHILE			44
35	22	COLOMBIA			15
		PERU			18
991	570	VENEZUELA			19
184	111				
150	55	UNTD KGDM TOT	W	5451	15456
182	126				
453	264	BELG LUX TOT	W	4724	15647
		U S AMER	W	3140	10489
2416	1180	CANADA	W	406	1371
		ARGENTINA	W	40	125
5364	2983	AUSTRIA	W	20	49
43	41	DENMARK	W	11	44
268	110	FRANCE	W	80	269
431	156	GERMANY W	W	664	2250
722	460	NETHERLNDS	W	69	93
43	35	SWITZERLND	W	19	34
294	124	ITALY	W	7	24
1296	659	SPAIN	W	30	102
28	27	USSR	W	200	700
934	572	IRAN	W	10	34
1042	602	BEL CONG X	W	14	30
32	21				
136	93	DENMARK TOT	W	244	663
29	24	PANAMA REP	W	5	11
16	16	BRAZIL	W	19	41
		UNTD KGDM	W	71	200
9039	4790	BELG LUX	W	9	35
387	140	FINLAND	W	22	60
110	47	GERMANY W	W	36	110
14	11	NETHERLNDS	W	8	22
100	71	NORWAY	W	23	71
30	11	SWEDEN	W	17	32
172	114	CZECHOSLVK	W	5	19
324	125				
4624	2616	FRANCE TOT	W	299	676
182	108				
242	181	GERMANY W TOT	W	186	400
513	209	U S AMER	W	103	193
156	110	CHILE	W	3	13
40	26	UNTD KGDM	W	8	17
567	252	AUSTRIA	W	4	14
512	276	BELG LUX	W	10	41
148	62	FRANCE	W	3	10
540	172	NETHERLNDS	W	33	70
26	19	HUNGARY	W	3	10
55	16				
110	73	NETHERLNDS TOT	W	10693	32882
120	109	U S AMER	W	6719	20191
15	13	CANADA	W	14	56
16	11	NETH ANTIL	W	10	32
19	14				

PART III

Statistics of
Individual Countries

CHAPTER 13

United States

J. Edward Ely

Bureau of the Census
U.S. Department of Commerce

HISTORICAL DEVELOPMENT

Early statistics, Act of 1820. The United States may be said to have had an adequate set of import and export statistics only since about 1821. Prior to that time no information was compiled on the amount of imports of articles which were free of duty upon importation into the United States. No value figures were compiled on imports subject to specific rates of duty, and the dollar value for imports subject to ad valorem rates of duty, although apparently accurate, was compiled only as a total with no information on how much of each commodity was imported. Existing figures on the total dollar value of imports during the years 1795 to 1801 were apparently estimated at the time by the Secretary of the Treasury, and the figures for the years 1790 to 1794, and from 1802 to 1820, were apparently estimated many years later. In the case of exports it was required by statute that the dollar value in the statistics should be that reported by the master of the vessel on which the goods left the country, but it was common practice for United States Collectors of Customs to adjust this reported value quite arbitrarily. A report of the Committee of Commerce and Manufactures, 16th Congress, 1st Session, communicated to the Senate December 20, 1819, describes the method of valuing exports as follows (at that time re-exports were probably over one-quarter of total United States exports):

Where the exports are products of the United States, or products of foreign countries which pay specific duties upon importation, the valuation is generally made by the collector (at some of the principal ports) in the following manner: The valuation furnished by the master of the vessel is entirely disregarded. The current prices of each article at the port of exportation, during the whole quarter of the year in which the goods are exported, are collected from such information as the collector may possess or procure; and from all the different prices a mean value of the article is deduced, which is the same through the whole quarter. The average value of each article, thus derived from the several market prices of the quarter, is the value assigned to the article by the collector during that quarter.

Where the exports are articles of foreign origin which pay ad valorem duties as imports, and are afterwards exported with drawback of duties, the value assigned to them as exports is the foreign cost of the articles, with an addition to that cost of twenty per centum if the goods came from beyond the Cape of Good Hope, and ten per centum if they came from any other place. This is the manner of valuing these exports at some of the principal ports. At some other ports, it appears that the valuation of these exports furnished by the master of the vessel is received, and returned to the Treasury without alteration.

Where the exports are articles of foreign origin which were free from duty upon importation, or were subject to ad valorem duties as imports, and are subsequently exported without drawback of duties, the valuation given by the master of the vessel is generally adopted by the collector, and returned to the Treasury.

By an Act approved February 1820 " to provide for obtaining accurate statements of the Foreign Commerce of the United States " provision was made for the preparation of statistical accounts of the commerce of the United States with foreign countries by the Register of the Treasury to show the kinds, quantities, and values of all articles exported to and of all articles imported from each foreign country. In regard to the export valuation problems described above, the exporter, rather than the master of the vessel, was required by the statute to report the value of the merchandise, thereby probably decreasing the need for collectors to adjust arbitrarily the values figure.

Bureau of Statistics, 1866. Although the new requirements for obtaining and compiling information on imports and exports resulted in a substantial improvement in the adequacy of the United States import and export statistics, they did not apparently assure that fully adequate statistics were produced. In his 1867 annual report, the first Director of the Bureau of Statistics, which was created by Congress in 1866 to take over the compilation of the export and import statistics, stated that the statistics being prepared when he entered on his duties " were but rarely quoted, except to be confuted by less pretentious, but obviously more correct, statistics of boards of trade, chambers of commerce, and other local organizations." (*Commerce and Navigation of the United States*, year ending June 30, 1867, page VIII.) In addition, he states that the statistics " had been discredited and assailed by private individuals and the press, and even officers of the government had not hesitated to impugn their correctness in their official reports, and to stigmatize them as worthless " (page XLIII).

Even though these comments may be discounted somewhat as the over-enthusiastic criticism by a new director, his report does point out specific errors in the statistics. For example, it is stated (page XLII *et seq*.) that the import statistics erroneously included products of American fisheries ($6·1 million), American guano ($1·6 million), products of the State of Maine (amount unknown), in-transit cargo (amount unknown), etc., and that there were other important omissions and errors in the information. It is furthermore stated that importers frequently reported a dollar value figure but no net quantity for ad valorem imports, and that in such cases the Collectors estimated the net quantities quite arbitrarily. By comparing the United States export and the Canadian import statistics it was concluded that the export statistics omitted about 50 per cent of the exports to Canada by reason of lack of authority for Collectors of Customs to obtain information on exports by railway carriage or other land vehicles. The export statistics were also described as suffering from the omission of exports by vessel where regulations for the filing of information were not being observed, by omitting exports of merchant vessels, and by other errors (page XXI *et seq*.).

Although the Director of Statistics states his confidence that the errors in the statistics were being eliminated, there is later evidence that the same sort of difficulties continued. The office of Director of Statistics was abolished in 1868, and its duties were transferred temporarily to the Special Commissioner of the Revenue. When it was reestablished in 1870 the Bureau of Statistics had a new director. By 1876 estimates of the amounts of exports omitted from the statistics varied from 1 to 5 per cent, the omissions principally reflecting the lack of full returns on exports to Canada and the practice of loading vessels after the master had filed information on the cargo with the Collector. A *Report of the Commission on the Bureau of Statistics* of the Treasury Department, made in 1877, describes the difficulties the Bureau faced in getting prompt and correct returns from the Customs Houses as follows:

The preparation of the statistical returns to the Bureau of Statistics, not being directly connected with the collection of the revenue, or necessary for that purpose, has been regarded by the collectors at many of the larger ports with more or less indifference, and a disposition has been manifested in some quarters not to give to this branch of the service that attention which its importance demands. This indifference and inattention has led to carelessness and consequent inaccuracy in the preparation of the returns.

Despite these later statements there was probably some improvement in the accuracy of the information around 1866. In July of that year monthly returns from Collectors were first obtained and were published currently through the year. Undoubtedly this new procedure substantially reduced an error in coverage which previously existed when the collectors reported only on a quarterly basis and annual statistics were the only ones published. Under this quarterly reporting system, the annual figures, as published, frequently omitted information on the last quarter of the year for many important ports if the reports from Collectors in these ports were not received in time. The publishing of monthly reports throughout the year probably assured that the annual figures were more complete.

It might be noted in this connection that the peculiar fiscal year ending September 30 which was used in the statistics from 1790 to 1843 apparently originated from the fact that, in preparing the statistics for the year 1790 for presentation to Congress in February 1791, the Secretary of the Treasury limited the statement to the period ending September 30 because there was still a " deficiency of many of the returns for the last quarter of the year 1790." Having started with this peculiar fiscal year, the practice was apparently continued in later years. From 1843 to 1918 a fiscal year ending June 30 was used, and since 1919 a calendar year ending December 31.

Following enactment of the act of March 3, 1893 providing for the obtaining of information on exports by rail, the deficiency in the export statistics by reason of the omission of many of these shipments was apparently eliminated. At present the United States export and the Canadian import statistics agree very closely. Although there is no specific statutory requirement (other than the World War II and subsequent export control acts) for the obtaining of information on exports by land vehicles other than rail, information on such exports has, as far as can be readily determined, been collected and included in the United States exports statistics by regulation since such shipments first became important.

Centralized compilation of statistics, 1915. In 1915 centralized compiling of the statistics by the use of mechanical tabulating equipment was instituted. Prior to that time the export and import statistics for each Customs District by commodity and country of origin or destination had been prepared by the individual Collectors of Customs in each Customs District. The figures were then centrally consolidated on a national basis. The procedure started in 1915 called for the import entries and export declarations filed with the collectors (and previously used by them to compile the statistics for their own Customs Districts) to be transmitted to the central compiling point (in the New York Custom House) for mechanical processing in the compilation of the import and export statistics. Although this centralized compilation was started primarily to avoid the increasing expense of compiling the statistics at each Custom House, the centralized operation undoubtedly resulted in increased accuracy in the statistics by reason of greater consistency in the classification of commodities into the statistical categories, the inclusion and exclusion of particular types of shipments from the statistics, etc. This centralized compiling of the statistics is still continued. In 1923 the responsibility for compiling the statistics was transferred from the Treasury Department to the Bureau of Foreign and Domestic Commerce of the Department of Commerce. Since 1941 the compiling of the statistics has been carried out in the Bureau of the Census of the Department of Commerce.

This brief history of the United States export and import statistics has been aimed at providing some concept of the degree of accuracy in the statistics over the years. Difficulties in the current statistics are described later in the chapter. Before ending our consideration of the earlier statistics it is appropriate to point out that much of the information presented in the earlier years was substantially less detailed than that currently compiled. An outstanding change has been in the number of commodity classifications shown in the statistics. In 1820 statistics were compiled for about 125 import commodity classifications. By 1910 the number had increased to about 600 and by 1950 to 5500. For exports of domestic merchandise the increase was from less than 100 in 1820, to about 500 in 1910, to 2700 in 1950.

USE AND APPRAISAL OF THE STATISTICS

Introduction. In general, the United States foreign trade statistics supply reasonably useful and accurate information on the United States foreign trade at a level comparable with that of other large trading nations. There are, of course, difficulties with the United States trade statistics, but that is true to a greater or lesser degree of the statistics of all nations. Some of the more important of the difficulties about which the users of the statistics should be aware are described in this section of the chapter.

Coverage. The United States presents its import and export statistics in such a way that figures on both a special and general trade basis are available. The import statistics in published form are on an import for consumption (special trade) basis, but unpublished copies of machine tabulation sheets also present the import statistics on a general import (general trade) basis.   For exports, separate statistics are published on exports of domestic merchandise and re-exports of foreign merchandise; the latter include both imported merchandise which cleared Customs and was later re-exported, and merchandise imported only into bonded Customs warehouses and later re-exported " ex-warehouse."   Although the total of domestic exports and re-exports accurately represents exports on a *general trade* basis, there is some difficulty in deriving accurate export figures on a *special trade* basis.   As described in Chapter 3, exports on a *special trade* basis should by definition include both exports of domestic merchandise and re-exports of imported goods which cleared Customs (and therefore became " nationalized " under special trade definitions).   As noted above, the published re-export figures include both these re-exports and " ex-warehouse " re-exports.   Separate " ex-warehouse " re-export figures are available in unpublished form, and these may be subtracted from the published re-export figures.   The remaining re-exports, then, represent goods which cleared Customs before re-export; these re-exports when added to exports of domestic merchandise total accurately to exports on a *special trade* basis.   Since in United States trade statistics total re-exports (both those made " ex-warehouse " and those made after clearing Customs) total only 1 or 2 per cent of all exports, the figures on exports of domestic merchandise which are readily available in published form may, for convenience, in many cases be taken as approximating exports on a *special trade* basis.   Although this is probably reasonably accurate for many purposes, there may be an important loss of accuracy for commodities free of duty, such as natural rubber and coffee, which are frequently re-exported after having cleared Customs.   In such cases, figures on exports of domestic merchandise (such figures will show no exports of natural rubber or coffee) should have added to them figures on foreign merchandise re-exported after clearing Customs, in order to arrive at an export figure on a *special trade* basis.   Since free items such as rubber and coffee will ordinarily not have been re-exported " ex-warehouse " (items free of duty would not enter Customs warehouse but would instead be entered through Customs), an export figure on a *special trade* basis may be correctly derived merely by adding figures on domestic exports and figures on total re-exports; there is no need to deduct re-exports " ex-warehouse."

The United States export and import statistics include not only the export and import trade of continental United States with foreign countries, but also the export and import trade of Alaska, Hawaii, and Puerto Rico with foreign countries.   Until 1948, information was also provided on shipments from the continental United States to each of these territories and possessions, and from these territories and possessions to continental United States, in approximately the same detail as in the import and export statistics. The net imports and exports of continental United States could then be derived using these data and other available data on the trade of the territories and possessions with foreign countries. Such derivation was frequently a burdensome operation, and the fact that information was not tabulated for continental United States alone caused inconvenience. Since April 1948 there have been no statistics compiled on shipments from continental United States to the Territories of Alaska and Hawaii and from these Territories to the continental United States. As a result it is no longer possible, even at a cost of burdensome clerical time, to obtain data on the trade of continental United States alone. Information on the trade of other United States possessions (Virgin Islands, Guam, Samoa, etc.) with foreign countries as well as with continental United States is presented separately from the regular United States import and export statistics.

Coverage—government trade. The United States statistics, in general, include all types of transactions including government trade. The export statistics do not include information on shipments out of the United States for the use of the United States Armed Forces themselves, and such materials are not included in the import statistics when returned to the United States. The United States import and export statistics do, however, include information on shipments to foreign countries made by all United States Government agencies under special programs such as Lend-Lease, UNRRA, the Marshall Plan (ECA), the Mutual Defense Assistance Program (principally North Atlantic Treaty), etc. In addition to including information on such special program shipments, a policy was followed, until approximately 1948, of presenting separate information on how much of the exports was made under each of these programs. In 1948 this practice was abandoned primarily because it was found to be impractical at time of export to identify Marshall Plan exports (which were then starting) from other exports. Many non-Marshall Plan exports were changed to Marshall Plan a number of months after export, and some exports financed under the Marshall Plan at time of export were later changed to another method of financing. Since it was, therefore, not possible currently to prepare separate tabulations on that part of the United States exports which represented ECA (Marshall Plan) shipments, the practice of showing separate information on exports under other special programs, such as the Greek-Turkish Aid Program and the Army Civilian Supply Program, was abandoned. ECA shipments were, of course, by far the most important special program shipments, and without separate identification of such shipments there was little or no reason to continue the segregation of shipments under other programs. Shipments under the Mutual Defense Assistance Program were included in the export statistics when they started in 1950, and a separate figure on the total amount of such MDAP shipments included in the total dollar value of United States exports without segregation by commodity or individual country is also published.

When comparing the United States trade statistics (particularly the United States export statistics) with the matching statistics of other countries, account must be taken of whether both sets of statistics include government and special program shipments.

Coverage—in-transit trade. In-transit shipments between one foreign country and another through the United States are handled in two different ways under Customs procedures, and this affects the coverage of the United States statistics. The two methods of handling in-transit shipments are as follows:

1. *Re-exports of imported goods.* These are goods which were declared and entered into the United States as imports for United States consumption (and were included in the import statistics), but which were later diverted to a foreign country. Actually, however, these " import " and " re-export " transactions are frequently not much different from the transactions described in (2).

2. *In-transit shipments.* These are shipments of goods declared by the shippers as moving through the United States from one foreign country to another. In general, they tend to be dutiable commodities since the in-transit procedure requires that the shipments be handled as a shipment in Customs bond through the United States. In the case of non-dutiable commodities there is little incentive for the shipper to handle the movement in Customs bond. Rather than have the commodity retained in Customs custody during an in-transit movement from one foreign country to another, it is frequently easier to handle the shipment first as an import into the United States and then as a re-export. For this reason non-dutiable commodities appear less frequently than dutiable commodities in the in-transit statistics, type 2 and more frequently in the import and re-export statistics, type 1. This distinction between import and re-export movements on the one hand, and in-transit movements on the other, carries over into the statistics. It is not a very useful distinction from the point of view of economic analysis; a limitation, it might be added, shared with the statistics of other countries. In general, the United States import and re-export statistics are undercounted (and the in-transit statistics overcounted) for dutiable commodities; and the import and re-export statistics are overcounted (and the in-transit statistics undercounted) for merchandise free of duty.

The form in which the United States in-transit statistics are presented provides another difficulty. Although the import and re-export statistics cover all re-exports and present full commodity and dollar value detail, the in-transit statistics cover only goods which enter the United States by vessel or leave by vessel. The statistics on goods entering the United States during the in-transit movements do not include goods arriving by air or land carrier, and the statistics on goods leaving the United States at the end of the in-transit movement also include only departures by vessel. Since goods may arrive by vessel and depart by land or air carrier, or arrive by land or air and depart by vessel, the inbound and outbound in-transit statistics do not cover the same in-transit movements. Therefore, they do not present a full picture of the in-transit trade. This peculiar coverage arises from the fact that the in-transit statistics are compiled solely to provide information on the contribution of in-transit trade to the vessel activity in United States ports. This limited purpose in compiling the in-transit statistics contributes further to the lack of information provided by limiting the commodity information to broad commodity groupings primarily useful for vessel cargo, rather than trade, analysis.

It is obvious from this description of the situation that care must be exercised in using the United States import, re-export, and in-transit statistics to measure the movement of goods through the United States from one foreign country to another. This is particularly important in regard to the relatively heavy movements of goods through the United States between Mexico and Canada and other countries.

Coverage—miscellaneous. Information on imports and exports of gold and silver (ore, bullion, and coins), and figures on oil and coal bunkers laden at United States ports on vessels in the foreign trade (the bunker oil figures are important in deriving figures on United States consumption of petroleum), are excluded from the merchandise statistics, but information on such transactions is compiled and presented separately. Neither the import nor the export statistics include shipments of fissionable materials. Exports of merchant vessels (both new and used) are included in the export statistics. Returned Lend-Lease vessels, the only important type of imports of merchant vessels, are included in the import statistics. Imports and exports of aircraft are included in the merchandise trade figures.

Commodity classification. As in the case of other important trading countries, the United States provides a substantial amount of commodity detail in its import and export statistics. In the United States import statistics there are approximately 5500 commodity classifications[1] which are regularly used. Much of this detail arises from the complexity of

---

[1] The most detailed form in which commodity information is presented in the statistics.

the United States Tariff Acts, but a substantial amount results from the United States Trade Agreements Program which started in 1934. Under this program agreements with other countries frequently result in United States duty reductions being made only on certain specific narrowly defined products. As a matter of policy, this segregation of a new product for trade agreement purposes results in its segregation in the import commodity classification. Primarily as a result of this process, the number of import classifications has increased from less than 4400 in 1934, when the Trade Agreements Program started, to approximately 5500 in 1950.

The fact that the import commodity classification is based on the commodity classifications in the United States Tariff Act and Trade Agreements Program results in an import commodity classification structure which in some respects is difficult to use for many commercial purposes and which is frequently obsolete in terms of modern technology, but changes are impractical within the existing tariff and trade agreement classifications.

Another factor that sometimes makes the import statistics difficult to use is that the import commodity classification reflects the results of Trade Agreements Program negotiations and the Tariff Act commodity structure. The substantial detail thereby provided for many commodities is frequently not needed by users of the statistics. Gloves, for example, are classified by length, and the users of the data may find it necessary to carry out the burdensome operation of combining the statistics for many detailed classifications in which they have no interest.

In the United States export statistics there are some 2700 commodity classifications. Much of the detail in the export classification is in manufactured articles which are important in the United States export trade. Despite the fact that the export statistics, in contrast to those on imports, are not directly related to the trade agreements negotiations, the export commodity classifications are, nevertheless, subject to frequent change. In general, the United States export commodity classifications have gone through more frequent changes than those of most other important trading nations. Although these export commodity classification changes have been desirable insofar as they have enabled the classifications to keep up with technological advances the changes do make comparisons of the statistics over a period of years more difficult than they would otherwise be.

One consideration needs mention. The more detailed the classification and the more technical the nature of the products, the greater likelihood that the export shipper or foreign freight forwarder will not have sufficient information to provide a commodity description adequate to classify the shipment properly in the classification. For example, the 1949 export classification for plastics and X-ray equipment contained many classification details on which it later developed exporters were not able to provide needed information; the classifications later had to be simplified. Similar situations may exist in other areas of the export classification and may go undiscovered, with resulting inaccuracy in the statistics. The Bureau of the Census attempts to keep users of the statistics informed of such areas of an inaccurate commodity classification in its monthly publication *Foreign Trade Statistics Notes* and in its *Explanation of Statistics*, but there are probably areas of inaccuracy of which it is not aware.

As in other countries there is, of course, a tendency for export shippers to provide a description on the export declaration which will assure the lowest possible duty payments when the goods enter through Customs in the foreign country, or which will assure that the goods may enter within the import controls of the foreign country. The fact that the foreign countries do not, in general, have access to the United States Shipper's Export Declaration tends to limit the extent of this error. The United States export statistics suffer, as do the statistics of other countries, from the tendency for exporters to provide a commodity description which will assure a low ocean freight rate. This problem is discussed in Chapter 4.

There was one development during World War II which acted to limit the influence of these factors. From the beginning of government control of exports in 1941, the commodity classification used to compile United States export statistics was also used as the commodity classification for these control purposes. This added use of the export commodity classification not only increased the number of classifications but also created a greater need for added precision. Prior to World War II, the export commodity classification had merely listed the 1600 or 1800 export classifications with no indication being given as to where the individual items entering the export trade should be classified. Starting in 1944, the export commodity classification was clarified and made more precise by listing, within the then 3500 commodity classifications, the commercial or trade names of some 50,000 individual items being exported from the United States.

Thus, whereas the prewar export commodity classifications called for a classification named " Brass and bronze plates, sheets and strips," the classification in 1944 listed a number of individual items which properly fell in this classification, such as laminated brass and bronze sheets and strips, Muntz metal, phosphorus bronze sheets and strips, etc. These added descriptions followed the terminology used in the export trade and were, in fact, the descriptions provided by exporters on Shipper's Export Declarations filed with United States Customs officials at the time goods left the United States and used to compile the export statistics. By listing the individual items included within the export classifications, the classification system itself was made more precise, and misunderstandings and misinterpretations of how individual items were to be classified correctly in the classification were substantially reduced.   This is not to say that some exporters may not still misdescribe their goods or misinterpret how they should be classified.   The added precision achieved by the listing of commodity or trade names which fall within the now-existing 2700 export commodity classifications does, however, limit the area in which misdescription or misunderstandings may occur.

Small-value shipments.   There is one point about the commodity information provided on United States exports and imports of which the user of the statistics should be aware.   As in many countries, certain small-value shipments are excluded from the statistics.   The United States export statistics, for example, exclude small-value shipments over the land borders not moving by common carrier, all parcel post shipments valued under $25, parcel post shipments of any value not shipped from one business concern to another, etc.   The United States import statistics exclude information on imports which enter the United States *via* a prescribed informal Customs procedure which may be used for imports valued under $100.   All these exclusions may result in undercounting the statistics of individual commodities which may enter or leave the United States in small lots excluded from the statistics.

In the export statistics there is another type of exclusion from the commodity information.   Under present procedures, all export shipments valued under $100 which are included in the export statistics are classified by country of destination but are not classified into the individual 2700 export commodity classifications.   In tabulations presenting information on the commodities exported from the United States, these " less than $100 shipments " are classified in one export commodity classification labeled " General merchandise valued under $100."   The adoption of this procedure in compiling the export statistics was based on the finding that, whereas between one-third and one-half of the 800,000 export shipments of individual products from the United States each month are valued at less than $100, only 1 per cent, approximately, of the dollar value of all exports are represented by these low-value shipments.

The procedure was also based on the finding that the elimination of these " under $100 shipments " from the statistics on exports of individual commodities resulted in the undercounting of only a relatively few of the commodities by more than 5 or 10 per cent.   This technique for reducing the cost of compiling the United States export statistics does, therefore, reduce the coverage of the statistics for exports of some commodities, in particular for export commodity classifications such as " Books " and " Baby chicks " where a substantial part of the total exports take place in shipments of less than $100. Users of the statistics must, therefore, take account of these exclusions when they use the statistics on commodities which may be affected to some extent by this procedure. Information on which commodities are affected may be obtained from the Bureau of the Census which compiles the statistics. It should be noted, however, that for the overwhelming majority of the classifications shown in the export statistics the " under $100 shipments " represent only a very small percentage of the dollar value of the trade. The reduction in the coverage of the statistics of these commodities is, therefore, of negligible importance.

In regard to the over-all structure of the foreign trade commodity classifications, both the 5500 import commodity classifications and the 2700 export commodity classifications are grouped into 11 major headings as follows:

Animals and animal products, edible.
Animals and animal products, inedible.
Vegetable food products and beverages.
Vegetable products, inedible, except fibers and wood.
Textile fibers and manufactures.
Wood and Paper.
Non-metallic minerals.
Metals and manufactures, except machinery and vehicles.
Machinery and vehicles.
Chemicals and related products.
Miscellaneous.

These 11 broad groupings are further subdivided into about 100 subgroups, which are approximately comparable between exports and imports. Comparability in the more detailed classifications is not as great, partly because the import and export products differ so substantially, and partly because the import classifications are so strongly influenced by tariff and trade agreement factors, as described above. In addition to these primary import and export commodity classifications which are based on classification by nature of material, function of the product, etc., retabulations of the import and export statistics are also published monthly and annually in a supplemental arrangement of the detailed classifications; namely, 10 economic classifications based on the degree to which the commodities have been processed and by whether of agricultural or nonagricultural origin (agricultural crude materials, non-agricultural crude materials, agricultural crude foodstuffs, etc.). Supplemental tabulations in terms of the Standard International Trade Classification (SITC) recommended by the United Nations are also being prepared on a quarterly and annual basis.

Valuation. The United States import statistics provide information on the dollar value of imports in terms of the definition in the Tariff Act. A description of the value definition is provided in Chapter 5, " Valuation." In addition to the effect of the complexity of the Tariff Act definition on the accuracy of the dollar value data in the import statistics as described in Chapter 5, the complexities of the Tariff Act and the resulting Customs procedures affect the accuracy of the value figures in another way. Because Customs appraisal of merchandise subject to ad valorem duties may require a considerable period of time, a final determination of the dollar value in terms of the Tariff Act definition may not be forthcoming for many months after the goods enter the United States. Since the import statistics are compiled and released on a current basis, they reflect the value reported by the importer at the time of the filing of the entry. This value is not necessarily changed to the value as finally appraised by Customs perhaps months or years later.

An important example of this type of difficulty is that which occurred in determining the dollar value of goods imported into the United States from the United Kingdom where certain goods sold to retailers were subject under the British Finance Act of 1940 to a purchase tax of from 16 2/3 per cent to 33 1/3 per cent of the value. For imports made for a number of years after that date, United States Customs included the British purchase tax in the appraised value, and this valuation was included in the United States import statistics. On the basis of appeals from importers that the British purchase tax should not be included in the value as defined in the Tariff Act, the Court of Customs and Patent Appeals decided in June 1946 that the value should not include the purchase tax. When the final decision was made, the statistics for imports of such commodities from the United Kingdom during the period October 1940 through June 1946 should have been corrected to exclude the tax. However, it was impractical to make such revisions in any of the statistics for the years 1940 through 1944 since the statistics for those years had already been published in final form. Even in the case of 1945 statistics, and in the 1946 statistics through June, where the information had been issued only in preliminary form, it was decided not to make the changes because of the difficulties involved, and because there was a certain logic in maintaining a consistent value through the period up to the date of the Customs decision. However, even under this policy some revisions were included in the statistics for periods prior to July 1946 because this type of revision in the value information originally reported could not be readily distinguished from other types of revisions.

The foreign or export value determined in accordance with these definitions is converted from the foreign currency to United States dollars on the basis of the relative value of gold in the foreign and United States coins or, if convertibility does not exist, on the basis of exchange rates certified to the United States Customs by the Federal Reserve Bank of New York. In a period of inconvertible and multiple-rate currencies there will, of course, be difficulties in determining exchange rates, and the dollar value shown in the import statistics of the United States as well as of other countries will be affected. For a further explanation of this problem see Chapter 6, " Exchange Conversion."

The United States export statistics show a dollar value which is defined as the value at time and place of export. In the case of exports by vessel this is essentially an f.a.s. (free alongside ship) value. There are difficulties in obtaining correct information on this basis. United States exporters probably quote the sales price f.o.b. United States factory at an interior point in many cases; and, although the requirement is that the value shown on the Shipper's Export Declaration should include domestic freight to dock side, there are undoubtedly some cases in which this is excluded from the valuation shown on the Shipper's Export Declaration and, therefore, excluded from the valuation shown in the export statistics. In Chapter 5 certain difficulties in the valuation of exports made under special United States Government programs are described.

Country designations. One obvious problem which the United States export statistics share with the statistics of a number of other countries arises from the definition of country of destination used in compiling the statistics (see Chapter 7, " Country Classification "). In the United States statistics an attempt is made to classify exports by country of ultimate destination. For many types of exports the country of ultimate destination of an export may not be known at the time of export. Since the statistics are compiled from information obtained from the exporter at the time the goods leave the country, the information is in practice only an approximation to the country of ultimate destination, usually the country to which the goods are being shipped. In addition, inaccuracies in the statistics may result from changes in the routing of merchandise after the goods leave the country, even though at time of export there was no intention to reroute. Even in those cases where it may be learned after export that the goods have been diverted from the originally intended country of destination, information on such diversions is not used to revise the export statistics. An example of this occurred during the period of World War II; it became known that a convoy of some 40 vessels destined for Murmansk, USSR, at the time of export was later diverted to the United Kingdom, due to submarine attack. No attempt was made to change the destination of these shipments from the USSR to the United Kingdom in the export statistics since, although it was known that this particular diversion took place, it was also apparent there were undoubtedly many other similar diversions which were unknown and for which corrections could not, therefore, be made. In addition, a large part of the cargo on these vessels probably did not remain in the United Kingdom but was reshipped to other destinations, including quite probably the USSR. Mass diversions of this sort do not exist under peacetime conditions, but there are undoubtedly many isolated cases of diversions not reflected in the statistics. In this connection, it might be noted that, to the extent that exports from the United States are under control as to destination as of 1952, there should be increased accuracy in the country of destination information in the export statistics.

In the United States import statistics, import shipments are by definition credited to the country of origin, *i.e.*, the country of growth, mining, or manufacture. Since there is no problem of diversion it should be possible to prepare the import statistics in terms of country of origin on a much more accurate basis than the preparation of export statistics in terms of country of destination. Actually, however, difficulty has been experienced in obtaining accurate information on the country of origin for some types of shipments. Many of these difficulties have arisen in the post-World War II period and to a large extent have resulted from dollar shortages and scarcities of materials. Scarce materials in many cases have moved through a number of countries before arriving in the United States, and accurate country of origin information may be difficult to obtain. In addition, it has been common practice in the post-war period for countries to impose export controls in an attempt to make certain that they get dollar exchange for the merchandise. Traders in international commodities have in a number of cases been able to avoid these restrictions and to obtain dollar exchange for themselves by importing the goods from the originating country into a third country, making the payment in the currency of the third country, and then shipping the goods into the United States and obtaining dollar exchange. This problem has acted to increase the difficulty of obtaining accurate country-of-origin information. For some commodities, it has been discovered that the United States import statistics may be substantially in error in crediting the imports to the country of origin as defined. A case in point is that where investigation showed that some 50 per cent of the imports of aluminium and lead from certain European countries were incorrectly credited by country of origin in some months of 1948.

In the case of many commodities imported into the United States, namely, most raw materials and semi-manufactured products, it is doubtful that the inaccuracy in crediting imports to country of origin is very great. Partly, this is because such commodities are low in value per unit of weight and cannot support the cost of transhipments through third countries, and partly it is because there are but few producing areas. Hence, questionable information on country of origin may be readily noted in the process of compiling the statistics and an effort made to obtain correct information.

In order to reduce the error in country classification in the import statistics, the United States in 1950 introduced a procedure which is used in some other countries for this purpose. This procedure provides that the information on country of origin as shown in the import statistics is not to be based solely on the statement of the American importer, who frequently may not really know where the goods originated, but is also to be based on a statement by the foreign supplier as to the country of origin of the merchandise. This statement by the foreign supplier appears on the commercial or consular invoice which is prepared by the foreign supplier. A copy of this is presented to United States Customs by the United States importer at the time goods enter the United States. It is believed that at least some of the difficulties in regard to obtaining accurate country-of-origin information have been eliminated by this change in procedure.

In the import and export statistics the classification of countries of origin and countries of destination provides for some 138 countries. Some of these are *de jure* countries only, and the separate classification of imports from and exports to these countries is undoubtedly substantially inaccurate. The present country classification used in compiling the import statistics shows, for example, separate classifications for Estonia, Latvia, and Lithuania, even though the *de facto* situation is that these areas are administered as part of the USSR. Classifications are provided for them as countries, however, since the United States recognizes each of them separately from the USSR and each maintains a legation in the United States. Thus, although the United States export statistics have shown since World War II few or no exports to each of these countries, it is very likely that merchandise shown as destined for the USSR was actually destined for Estonia, Latvia, or Lithuania ultimately. This contrast between the *de jure* and *de facto* situation also applies to other areas of the world. In total, these difficulties are, on the whole, probably of very little conseqence in the United States export and import statistics. The usefulness of the statistics would probably be increased only to a relatively slight degree if exports and imports were credited correctly to the *de jure* country classification.

Withholding of import and export information for security reasons. In addition to omitting all information on imports or exports of fissionable materials, a policy has been followed since May 1949 of withholding information on exports of certain commodities from the United States. Information on exports of aircraft, tanks, ordnance, and a number of other

items are grouped into certain summary commodity classifications entitled
" Special categories " in order that the amount of exports of each of the
individual items may not be revealed.   The list of commodities included
in these " Special categories " was increased in July 1950, and country of
destination information for the total exports included in the special
categories was no longer shown.   In July 1950 another type of " Special
category " was also set up, namely, one in which no country of destination
detail was shown even though full commodity information was provided.
Commodities included in this second type of special category included
" Aviation gasoline, 90 octane and over," " Truck and bus casings," etc.

To the extent that commodities are included in these " Special categories " it may be impossible to combine commodities into summary
groupings if the groups should include items hidden in the first type of
" Special category."   For example, one of the commodities included in the
first type of " Special category " is radio receiving-transmitting sets.
Although other types of radio equipment such as receiving sets are not
included in the " Special categories " and are, therefore, presented
separately in the statistics, the fact that information on exports of the
transmitting-receiving sets is concealed in a special category prevents total
figures on exports of all types of radio apparatus from being obtained.
In the same way the elimination of country of destination detail in both
the first and the second types of special categories results in the figures on
the total exports to individual countries being undercounted.   For
comparison purposes, figures on the trade with individual countries in
years prior to 1950 have been recompiled to exclude the same type of
shipment now being excluded for security reasons.   Comparisons between
periods can then be made with exports under " Special categories "
excluded from both periods.

Publications and unpublished statistics.   A description of the published
information on United States exports and imports is presented in Chapter
8.   In addition to these published tables, copies of machine tabulation
sheets are on file for public reference purposes in Washington, New York,
and in some cases in other United States cities (Philadelphia, Los Angeles,
and San Francisco).   These sheets present information in other arrangements than those on published tables.   On a monthly basis, for example,
information is available in commodity-by-country-by-Customs-District
arrangement.   For each commodity the tabulation sheet presents information on the amount imported or exported to each country, and the amount
going to or coming from each country, through each of the approximately
50 United States Customs Districts.   On an annual basis information is
available for reference purposes in the form of machine tabulation sheets
in Customs-District-by-commodity-by-country arrangement.   In addition

to these copies of machine tabulation sheets available for reference purposes, special rearrangements of the data may be prepared to fit the particular needs of an individual user if he pays the cost of the work involved.

The monthly, quarterly, and annual statistics include information on approximately all the import and export shipments made within the period. The statistics for a particular month, for example, are held open for 10 days or more after the end of each calendar month until information on about 98 per cent of the number of shipments in that calendar month are received from Collectors of Customs for inclusion in the statistics.

CHAPTER 14

United Kingdom

J. STAFFORD, J. M. MATON, AND MURIEL VENNING
Board of Trade, London

HISTORICAL DEVELOPMENT

Early history. In the United Kingdom the compilation of statistics of foreign trade dates from the establishment, in 1696, of the office of " The Inspector-General of the Imports and Exports." The only earlier records are those kept initially for revenue purposes together with some derived estimates of the total value of trade, mainly of trade with particular countries. The new office, however, was created for the specific task of compiling trade statistics and was charged with the production of " a true account of the importacions and exportacions of all commodities into and out of this Kingdom and to and from what places the same are exported or imported."

The Inspector-General's primary records, compiled from information transmitted by the Customs officers at the ports, included particulars of imports and exports from and to each country for each commodity listed, the list being based on that used for tariff purposes. The annual abstracts presented to Parliament, however, showed only trade with countries, with no commodity detail. Before 1834, the only published information on trade analysed by commodity, or by commodity and country, or by port of entry or departure, was in the various special returns compiled *ad hoc* by the Inspector-General's Office.

The annual abstracts for the period 1696–1799 are all available in print in two publications; those for the period 1696–1773 are given in Sir Charles Whitworth's *State of the Trade of Great Britain* (1776) and those for 1760–1799 in David Macpherson's *Annals of Commerce* (1805). Figures covering the period 1798–1830 are included, together with much other information on trade both by commodity and country, in Marshall's *Digest of all the Accounts relating to The Populations, Productions, Revenues, etc., of the United Kingdom*, compiled mainly from Parliamentary papers and published in 1834.

The year in which Marshall's *Digest* appeared saw the publication of the first detailed statement of trade with both a country and a commodity analysis in addition to the abstracts by countries. This was contained in the first issue of *Porter's Tables*,[1] the product of the newly-formed Statistical Department of the Board of Trade. The statistics continued to be published in the same form until 1853, when the *Annual Statement of Trade and Navigation* was first published as a separate volume.

Monthly accounts relating to trade and navigation were presented to Parliament from 1845, but, since these were compiled, as far as imports of non-dutiable goods were concerned, from landing accounts which might not be completed until some weeks or months after the end of the month, they were of somewhat limited value as monthly records. It was criticism of this and other defects in the statistics which led finally to the reform of the machinery for compiling the statistics in 1871; this involved the abolition of the Inspector-General's Office, and the setting up of the present Customs Statistical Office.

It was at this date that the modern form of both the monthly and the annual accounts was laid down. There have since been changes, the most important of which are dealt with below, in the coverage of the accounts and in the system of classification of countries and commodities. It is broadly true, however, that the figures from 1871 to date can be considered for most purposes as a continuous series, requiring only minor adjustments to preserve comparability.

Coverage and valuation before 1871. Even the most limited use of the pre-1871 statistics needs first a study of just how the figures were compiled and what they represent. The user of the Inspector-General's early statistics must be referred to Clark's *Guide to English Commercial Statistics, 1696–1782*. For the subsequent period up to 1871, reference should also be made to a paper on " The Official Trade and Navigation Statistics " read by Stephen Bourne to the Royal Statistical Society in 1872,[2] and

---

[1] *Tables of the Revenue, Population, Commerce, etc., of the United Kingdom and its Dependencies.* Annually from 1834 to 1853.
[2] *Journal of the Royal Statistical Society*, Vol. XXXV, 1872. Also reprinted in *Trade, Population and Food*, a collection of papers by Stephen Bourne.

to the introductory notes to the published trade returns for the years 1853 and 1854.[3] The two most important difficulties met with in the use of the Inspector-General's figures can, however, be briefly dealt with here.

There are important changes in the territorial coverage of the statistics between 1696 and 1871. The Inspector-General's early figures related only to the imports and exports of England and Wales. Scotland appeared as a separate country of destination until the Act of Union of 1707, although only seaborne trade was included in the figures. No record of the trade of Scotland appears to have been kept before 1755; from then until 1827 a series of ledgers was kept similar to those in use in England. Ireland was also treated as a foreign country in the statistics, and records of the trade of Ireland were separately compiled on much the same lines as those for England from 1698 until 1829.[4] From 1827 onward the annual abstracts presented to Parliament were for the whole of Great Britain and Ireland. Though Whitworth's tables, referred to above, purport to relate to the whole of Great Britain, they are in fact for the trade of England and Wales only. Those given by Macpherson show the Scottish figures in addition to those for England; in Marshall's *Digest* some of the figures are for Great Britain alone and some for the United Kingdom, *i.e.*, Great Britain and Ireland.

The other main difficulty in the use of the pre-1871 figures arises from the method of valuation. With the exception of a small part of the trade, for which merchants' own valuations were accepted, the values of imports and exports included in the accounts were arrived at by multiplying the quantities declared for each commodity by an official value per unit. Lists of official values, similar to those already in existence for tariff purposes, were drawn up for statistical purposes in 1696 in consultation with " merchants engaged in the foreign trade." It is not known to what extent the original lists were truly representative of ruling prices, but, by about 1720, any attempt to keep them in line with current prices appears to have been abandoned. In effect, official values for most items remained constant for some 150 years, and it is not possible to make the ordinary uses of the value figures in the Inspector-General's statistics.

The Convoy Act of 1798 levied new duties on trade and those on exports were mainly ad valorem. This led to a wider collection of declared values. Using values as declared by merchants for a large number of commodities, the Inspector-General made estimates of the " real marketable value " of trade in the years 1798–1800. The " real " value of imports

---

[3] *Annual Statement of Trade and Navigation of the United Kingdom*, 1853 and 1854.
[4] The figures for at least the last few years were known to be incomplete as far as trade with Great Britain was concerned.

was found to be more than 80 per cent higher than the official value, and the " real " valuation of exports over 60 per cent greater.

For exports, declared values were used for statistical purposes from 1801 onward (1805 in the case of Ireland). Official values were, however, still compiled, and most contemporary sources quoted both declared and official values. For imports and re-exports, official values were replaced in 1854 by a system of " computed real values." These were not declared values but rather an up-to-date version of the old system of official values, as is clear from the official description:

The average annual Prices fixed for the Valuations are, principally, those of the London and Liverpool markets. In each place one gentleman was specially employed to obtain prices for the Custom House. Many of the principal Merchants and Brokers were consulted, and also some of the Chambers of Commerce. The Prices used and specified in the Accounts are for the Articles *in Bond*, including all the Charges of Freight and Landing, but exclusive of the Duties. . . . The Annual Commercial Volume of the United Kingdom is no longer inferior to those of Foreign Countries as regards a complete system of Real Value; and in one respect our Valuation may be considered as superior to that of other Nations, as it is founded upon Prices varying according to the origin of the Articles imported.

These prices, revised annually as necessary, were given for each article in the *Annual Statements* themselves.

When, in 1871, the declared values basis was finally adopted for imports and re-exports, as well as for exports, there was no period of " overlap " of the new system with the old. Though there is no means of assessing the effect of the changes, contemporary users of the figures appear to have regarded the computed real values as at least equal in accuracy to those declared by importers, and the value figures are often quoted as a continuous series from 1854 onward. Even the *Annual Statement of Trade* for 1871 contains a table of the values of imports in the 5 years 1867–1871 without any reference to the changed method of valuation.

Period from 1871 to 1939. In 1871, then, the trade accounts reached essentially their present form both in aim and in method of compilation. They were based on importers' and exporters' declarations of values as well as quantities, collected by Customs Officers at the ports, and transmitted to the Customs Statistical Office for compilation.

The coverage of the statistics has been affected by only two major changes since 1871. The first, in 1899, was the inclusion of exports of new ships and boats, previously excluded altogether; in the first year of inclusion these exports were valued at £9·2 million, or $3\frac{1}{2}$ per cent of total exports. The other major change in coverage was that consequent on the creation of the Irish Free State; from 1st April, 1923, trade between the

Irish Free State (now the Republic of Ireland) and the United Kingdom (Great Britain, Northern Ireland, and the Isle of Man) was recorded as external trade both in the United Kingdom accounts and in the trade statistics of the new state. An approximate measure of the change can be derived from the statistics of 1924. The separation of the Irish Free State increased the total value of the United Kingdom exports by about 6 per cent (re-exports by about 8 per cent); the inclusion of the extensive exports to the new state, previously internal trade, was only partly offset by the exclusion of the small exports from the Irish Free State direct to the rest of the world. The similar increase in the total value of United Kingdom imports was about 3 per cent.

The other changes of importance are those of classification, particularly that of countries. The method of recording countries was completely changed during the period 1904–1913. Officially, in the years before 1904, imports were classified as received from the country in which they were placed on board ship for export direct to the United Kingdom, and exports were distributed to the country to which they were shipped direct. Thus countries without seaboards were not distinguished in the statistics. What was more important, imports or exports transhipped, say, at a European port on the voyage to or from the Far East, should have been counted as trade with the European country concerned. However, both for imports and for exports, some attempt was made to adjust the figures to allow for the more important differences between shipment and origin or destination. Thus, exports were in fact credited where possible to country of ultimate destination (so far as was known to the exporter) and imports to the " country of original shipment." From 1904 particulars were collected on country of consignment where this differed from country of shipment, and for each of the years 1904–1908 the *Annual Statements of Trade* were supplemented by additional volumes showing imports and exports classified by country of consignment. Following the report of a committee appointed to consider the most appropriate method of classification, the accounts were altered from 1909 to show " country of consignment " as the main basis of classification. Since a supplemental volume giving exports and imports on the old basis was published until 1913, the effect of the change is easily assessed.

The changes in the classification of commodities did not produce the same type of sudden discontinuity. The list of headings—the official " Import and Export Lists " under which imports and exporters are required to record their goods—have undergone continuous changes, mainly in the direction of a more detailed subdivision. At the time of the 1871 reform the commodity lists were consolidated to comprise some 400 import headings and just over 200 export entries. Annual revisions have increased the detail, and the 1951 lists contain about 2500 headings for imports and 2400 for exports.

Until 1920, the articles enumerated in the lists were set out in alphabetical order, though some " article " headings had several subdivisions whose grouping together represented the beginnings of a classification. Thus the heading " Corn, grain, and meal " in the 1871 import list had 17 subdivisions covering much the same field as the group " Grain and flour " in the current classification. It was followed in the alphabetical list by the headings " raw cotton," " cotton yarn," and then " cotton manufactures," which was further subdivided into four headings. In the *Annual Statements of Trade*, the statistics were presented in the same form as the import and export lists, *i.e.*, mainly in alphabetical order. However, summary tables with items grouped according to broad economic classes had been prepared for special purposes.[5] From 1899, summaries of imports and exports by three broad classes (similar to but not identical with the present classification) were included in the *Annual Statements of Trade*. In 1920 the division into " economic classes " first appeared in the import and export lists themselves; since that date the statistics have been presented solely in the " grouped " order. The main principles of the classification, which are described below, have since remained unchanged, but there were important detailed changes in 1933 and again in 1936.

USE AND APPRAISAL OF THE STATISTICS

Introduction. It is at no time possible to maintain complete continuity in the series of trade statistics—to achieve precise comparability over time. The statistics of the United Kingdom provide a good example of what is a fairly general feature of trade data—the occurrence of times of major change in the form and content of the statistics, with long intervening periods of stability when comparability is scarcely disturbed. In the past 100 years, there was a general change in the statistics in 1871, a major adjustment of the country designations about 1904, and a new classification by commodities in 1920. From 1920 until 1939, there was practically no disturbance in the continuity of the United Kingdom statistics. Indeed, on the matter of coverage alone, the statistics remained essentially unchanged during the first 40 years of the 20th century; the introductory notes to the monthly *Accounts* in 1939 differ only slightly in wording from those in the 1900's. World War II and the post-war years, however, form another period of change; problems have arisen, *e.g.*, in the programmes involving the transfer of military equipment, which have entailed adjustments in coverage. The process of change cannot yet

[5] See, for example, *The Report of the Royal Commission on the Depression of Trade and Industry*, 1886.

(1952) be regarded as complete, and the current description of the coverage and classification of trade statistics will not necesarily apply in 1953 and later years. The introductions to the current monthly *Accounts* should always be consulted for notes on changes; these changes are made as far as possible at the beginning of a year.

In many cases, adjustments can be made in past figures to allow for variations in coverage and form of presentation. In the monthly *Accounts*, which present statistics of imports, exports, and re-exports, in summary form, the presentation varies in detail from year to year, but as far as possible the current year's issues include comparable figures for each of the 2 preceding years. In the *Annual Statements of Trade*, which present statistics in much greater detail covering a period of 5 years, either each year's figures are shown on a comparable basis or discontinuities are noted. If statistics are used over longer periods, it becomes desirable to consult the *Monthly Digest of Statistics* (and its supplement on Definitions) and the *Annual Abstract of Statistics*. Although these publications show only abstract tables, they do cover longer periods and they give past figures adjusted as far as possible for changes in coverage, etc., with unavoidable discontinuities noted. The monthly *Report on Overseas Trade*, prepared by the Board of Trade, is also a useful supplement to the standard publications of trade statistics.

While past figures can often be adjusted, and are adjusted in the official statistics, to make them comparable with the current data, there remain discontinuities in the series and more gradual shifts in the data for which no allowance can be made. Examples are the appearance in the records of transhipment under bond since 1939 of certain goods previously recorded as imports and re-exports, and the changing borderline between re-exports and exports of domestic produce. These and other such examples are discussed in the following sections.

Coverage. The United Kingdom maintains its statistics on a general trade basis; re-exports are distinguished from exports of United Kingdom produce and manufacture. Statistics of goods in direct transit through the United Kingdom, transhipped under bond (*i.e.*, under Customs control) are separately maintained. These goods, which may be dutiable or free of duty, are mainly transferred from one ship to another at the same port, but they will also include goods entered in one port and conveyed under bond to another port for re-shipment.

A distinction is, therefore, made between goods imported and subsequently re-exported which are included in the trade aggregates, on the one hand, and goods transhipped under bond, which are separately recorded and not comprised within the total of imports or re-exports, on the other. The distinction, however, may be somewhat arbitrary from an economic point of view, and it can vary with administrative procedures and practices. For example, the value of goods transhipped under bond after the World War II is considerably higher relative to the value of re-exports, and contains a higher proportion of non-dutiable raw materials as compared with pre-war. One reason for this is the suspension in 1939 of facilities previously extended for some non-dutiable goods in transit through the United Kingdom on through bills of lading to be treated as imports and re-exports; they amounted to £9·1 million in 1938. It seems likely that most of the goods which would have been entered in this way are now transhipped under bond and, therefore, properly excluded from the import-re-export statistics.

The borderline between exports of domestic produce and re-exports is sometimes difficult to define and may be subject to change. For example, horses and greyhounds entering the country for breeding or racing are included as imports and, before 1950, they were shown as re-exports when they left. The attempt to separate re-exports from domestic exports of such animals is no longer made, and all exports of horses and greyhounds (whether previously imported or not) are recorded as exports of domestic produce. The reduction of the re-export total as a result of this change amounted to £1·0 million in 1948 and £0·6 million in 1949.

Apart from transhipments under bond, the general principle governing the coverage of the statistics is that all movements of goods into and out of the country are included; most temporary movements, including movements of goods for repair, are included under this principle. It is mainly the exceptions to this principle—some of them small, some of them of sufficient importance to affect comparison with the statistics of other countries—which are described in this and the succeeding section.

Among minor exclusions made mainly for practical reasons are passengers' private possessions,[6] works of art for temporary exhibition (but not exhibits for trade fairs, etc.), used clothing and other goods exported by charitable bodies, parcels to members of the armed forces, and some similar items. A more important exclusion is that of diamonds and other unset precious and semi-precious stones. Before 1949, some imports and re-exports were included in the statistics, but they were known to be incomplete, partly because the trade was largely conducted by registered post. Imports recorded in 1939 were only £0·1 million, whereas exports of rough diamonds from the main exporting countries to the United Kingdom were over £3 million; in 1946 recorded imports were as high as £8·7 million compared with the exporting countries' total of

---

[6] Goods charged to duty brought in by passengers were included as imports until May 1947.

some £13 million. From 1949, the diamond trade has been excluded altogether from the statistics.

Special types of transactions. The merchandise figures do not include *gold and silver bullion and coin*. A separate record is kept for both imports and exports of bullion and coin; the monthly accounts up to 1939 included a separate " Bullion and Specie Account," but since then the figures have appeared only in the *Annual Statements*.[7]

Coal and other fuel *bunkers*, shipped in the United Kingdom for use on board vessels (including fishing vessels) engaged in foreign trade, and for aircraft, are not considered an export. The quantities (not values) of such shipments are recorded and are shown in the published accounts. Coal bunkers are divided between vessels of British flag and foreign flag, but otherwise no country breakdown is available. *Ships' stores* for use on the exporting vessel are also excluded from the trade statistics and (except for certain dutiable items contained in the revenue accounts) no separate record is kept for this category.

Temporary movements of *aircraft and of sea-going vessels* to and from United Kingdom ports are excluded for obvious reasons; so also are deliveries from United Kingdom production of aircraft and vessels to the British fleet and airlines and old craft withdrawn from their service. For other aircraft arriving or departing, Customs entries are required so that all aircraft, whether new or secondhand, imported from abroad or delivered to a consignee abroad, should be included in the statistics; in practice aircraft flown out of the country on a temporary flight and subsequently sold abroad are probably not in all cases recorded; the difficulty of recording aircraft on their first flight to the United Kingdom after being purchased is obvious.

The treatment of sea-going ships differs from that of aircraft in that only new vessels departing on their first voyage for delivery to a consignee outside the United Kingdom, and arrivals and departures of old ships for breaking up or for use as hulks or moored training vessels are included. New sea-going ships acquired by the United Kingdom from owners abroad are excluded, and no attempt is made to include transfers of second-hand vessels to or from the British fleet. Craft other than sea-going are included in the statistics like any other commodity unless the movements are shown to be temporary.

Vessels and aircraft also provide an exception to the principle of including movements of goods for repair.[8] Export statistics do not include

---

[7] Until resumption of monthly publication in 1953.

[8] Before 1950, aircraft on regular flying routes were included at full value in the import and export statistics if they were entered for repair in the United Kingdom. The records of imports and re-exports of aircraft and their classification by countries were greatly affected by this practice.

the cost of repairs done to foreign ships or aircraft, even that part which is represented by raw materials, machinery, or equipment. Equally, import statistics exclude the cost of repairs to British vessels and aircraft abroad.

With the exception of military stores and equipment imported on government vessels, and British Government stores exported for British Government use abroad, *government imports and exports* have normally always been included in the statistics. All imports and exports by government trading departments are included; simplified recording procedures are used in some cases, but otherwise all such imports, whether or not under Lend-Lease, the European Recovery Programme (ERP), or other special programmes, are treated in the same way as imports by a private trader. Imports of military equipment under the Mutual Defense Assistance Agreement with the United States are, however, excluded.

Figures usually quoted for the years 1942–1945 exclude trade in " munitions," fairly narrowly defined; for this reason, and because of the difficulties of accurate recording under war conditions, the wartime figures need to be used with care. Another difficulty arises because of goods imported or exported by Allied Governments in exile, and by the agencies of other governments, in the United Kingdom. Imports by these governments and agencies for their official use or for their armed forces, are excluded from the statistics in the same way as imports by diplomatic representatives. Equally, any equipment so imported (and not recorded) is excluded from the statistics of exports if subsequently sold abroad. In addition, all purchases and sales (*e.g.*, of surplus equipment) within the United Kingdom by these governments and agencies are excluded, as are sales by the United Kingdom Government of surplus equipment held abroad.

The export figures of the years following World War II include a substantial amount of relief and rehabilitation supplies. All such goods are recorded, whatever the agency concerned with their export, with the exception that supplies landed for subsequent on shipment by UNRRA are completely ignored (even in the separate records of transhipment). In the same period, the export statistics include also stores exported to certain organizations (such as the Navy, Army, and Air Force Institutes) concerned with troops serving abroad.[9]

The need for secrecy has generally been met by the simple device of not showing particular items separately, or not giving country detail under particular headings, in the current accounts of trade published monthly. The full details do appear in the *Annual Statements*, but these are published

---

[9] During the war such stores were often consigned to military officers and so excluded from the export statistics.

at a much later date. An exception to this is the exclusion from the statistics of all records of trade in fissionable materials since January 1947.

Commodity classification. Unlike those of many other trading countries the commodity lists and classification used in the United Kingdom trade statistics are not based on tariff lists of headings but are designed primarily for statistical purposes. The import list has, however, been influenced to a certain extent by the form of the United Kingdom tariff. In some parts of the list tariff considerations have dictated the principle of classification. The distinction drawn between " sweetened " and " unsweetened " food preparations is, for example, associated with the fact that sweetened foods are liable to sugar duties. A single import list heading does not normally include commodities subject to different rates of duty, but the import list does not show all the subdivisions (for example into value ranges, or according to size) required for tariff purposes. It is thus not always possible to obtain detailed information for each tariff heading. The same difficulty may also arise in other trade studies. For example, lists of commodities in import and export licensing regulations, or in trade agreements are rarely related to, and are not always easily comparable with, import and export list headings.

The lists of headings are revised annually, a balance being kept as far as possible between the need for continuity and for an up-to-date system, and between the need for detail and what it is practical to require from traders. Since they are designed for statistical purposes and revised annually, the United Kingdom lists are free from many of the difficulties met with in those of other countries.

The onus of making the correct declaration is in all cases on the importer or exporter. Tariff headings or licensing headings and the technical or trade description of the goods are required to be shown on the entries in addition to the import or export list heading. These descriptions, which may be subject to a Customs check, are likely to ensure allocation to the correct statistical heading; and the accuracy is, in general, limited only by the amount of detailed knowledge of the goods possessed by the trader or his agent. On the import side, there is probably little likelihood of error; apart from the fact that entries may be checked for duty purposes, the foodstuffs and materials which form the bulk of the trade are less likely to be wrongly classified, and the manufactures headings are generally less narrowly defined, than on the export side. In the export list, over 2000 of the 2500 headings consist of manufactured goods. There may in a few cases be some incentive to declare exported goods under a wrong heading to evade duty or licensing regulations in the country of destination, but the greatest source of error probably arises from the difficulty of allocation to closely defined categories of manufactures by agents who may have insufficiently detailed knowledge for the purpose.

The commodity headings in the export and import lists are arranged:

Class I. Food, drink, and tobacco.
       II. Raw materials and articles mainly unmanufactured.
       III. Articles wholly or mainly manufactured.
       IV. Animals, not for food.
       V. Parcel post.

The bulk of the trade falls into the first 3 classes; these are further sub-divided: the first into 9 groups, the second into 14, and the third into 21. This arrangement into classes and subdivision into groups does not follow any one principle, but a mixture of several principles including classification by use, by degree of manufacture, and according to component material. In practice, the major difficulty in using figures grouped into classes probably arises from the fact that the manufactured goods class includes such commodities as refined petroleum and unwrought metals, as well as highly finished manufactures. In both 1938 and 1948 between 80 and 90 per cent of exports in the manufactured goods class consisted of advanced manufactures—items which, in the League of Nations Minimum List, are classified as " more elaborately transformed." For imports the proportion of total " manufactures " formed by these advanced manufactures is very much smaller than for exports—just over a half before World War II, rather less than a half in 1948. This difference in the composition of United Kingdom imports and exports is not indicated by the class totals and, since the principle of classification into groups within the manufactured goods class is mainly by component material or use, it is not even obvious from an analysis of group totals.

In 1936 the annual totals, by value, of imports, exports, and re-exports were first reclassified into the headings of the League of Nations Minimum List; the figures were published in this form for each year from 1936 to 1939. This reclassification was suspended during World War II, but with its resumption in 1946 some quantity information and a country analysis of trade in each chapter in the Minimum List added to the value of the reclassification. From 1949 the annual statistics are reclassified according to the United Nations Standard International Trade Classification.[10]

Units of quantity. Both monthly and annual statistics include a good deal of information on quantities as well as values of trade. Quantity particulars are given, in the *Annual Statements*, of commodities amounting to over 90 per cent by value of total exports, but in the monthly *Accounts*

[10] It is proposed to revise completely the main commodity classification (from January, 1954) and to base it on SITC.

the amalgamation of some headings reduces the number of commodities for which quantities can be shown. For imports both annual and monthly quantity figures are given for all but about 3 per cent of the total.

The quantity unit or units for each heading are set out in the import and export list; units of weight are most frequently used, but a variety of other units (*e.g.*, number, cubic feet, proof gallons) are employed, sometimes in addition to weight. The weights required to be declared are in all cases net weight exclusive of packing, and they may therefore differ considerably from shipping weight. Approximate factors for converting quantities shown in other units to weight are listed for a large number of commodities in the *Annual Statement*, but these factors apply to total trade and cannot be used for trade with individual countries.

Valuation. Imports are valued c.i.f. and exports and re-exports are valued f.o.b. The value of exports is defined as the cost to the purchaser abroad, including all charges accruing up to the point where the goods are deposited on board the exporting vessel or aircraft, or the land boundary in Northern Ireland. Although there is no more than a test check on the accuracy of the values as declared by exporters, there is no obvious reason for bias in the total values recorded in the statistics. The value required is probably that most easily supplied by the United Kingdom exporter, and there will be very few instances in which there is any incentive to " invent " an alternative to the actual f.o.b. cost, or in which this cost is genuinely unknown or cannot be estimated with fair accuracy. The only serious valuation defect in the export statistics is the treatment of parcel post, a defect which applies to both import and export figures for this category since the declared value system is difficult to apply.

Except for parcels on which duty (or drawback) is paid, exports and imports by parcel post are declared to Customs only in terms of numbers of parcels, and the values are obtained by multiplying by fixed estimated values per parcel. The last actual investigation into the value of parcels was by a sample census in 1928, and, although some adjustments have since been made to allow for price changes, the figures cannot represent with any accuracy the value of postal packages exported or imported. Some of the parcels will, of course, represent gifts or other " non-payment " items (such as commercial samples). On the export side, at least, an appreciable part of the trade in particular goods is conducted by parcel post; lace, hosiery, jewellery, books, and periodicals are thought to be the most important commodities concerned. On the import side, a larger part of the imports recorded under parcel post is probably non-commercial, and goods charged to duty are included in the appropriate headings in the accounts and not as parcel post. Only for a short period after World War II, when large numbers of Forces' parcels were admitted free of duty, did the official value of parcel post imports form more than 1 per cent of total imports, whereas for exports the proportion is about 2 to 3 per cent in most years.

The valuation of imports is in accordance with the statutory definition of valuation for the purpose of levying Customs duties; the same definition is applied to free goods and to those subject to specific rates of duty as well as to ad valorem dutiable imports. From 1935 until 1951 the value of imports was briefly stated in official descriptions as " the open market value " or the " price which the goods would fetch on sale in the open market at the time of importation," this being a summary of the statutory definitions of valuation for duty purposes contained in the Finance Act of 1935. Taken literally, this definition would have been difficult to apply rigidly to all imports, particularly under war and post-war conditions of trading, when for many commodities the government was the sole importer.

The concept of " the open market value " was, in fact, introduced for duty purposes and only appeared in the description of the value of imports included in the statistics after the introduction of a general ad valorem tariff by the Import Duties Act of 1932. Before this the values used in the statistics had been defined as the " cost to the importer, including insurance, freight, etc." In practice it is clear that the valuation of most imports has continued on this basis of cost to the importer. Goods which are not dutiable ad valorem amount to some 85 per cent of total imports, and there would be no reason for the Customs authorities to insist on an import valuation different from that actually paid or payable, *i.e.*, that most easily provided by the importer. In recent years there would have been appreciable differences, on account of timing alone, between prices actually paid, adjusted where necessary to a c.i.f. basis, and " prices in the open market at the time of importation." Comparison of changes in unit values of arrivals of important commodities as recorded in the statistics, with movements in market prices or government buying prices, confirms the conclusion that values are mainly based on prices which had actually been paid for the goods recorded.

For the remaining 15 per cent the values are those accepted for duty purposes. In order to bring the legal definition of import values for duty purposes formally into line with the Convention on the Valuation of Goods for Customs Purposes signed at Brussels in February 1951,[11] the 1951 Finance Act included an amended definition of the valuation of imports. This had the effect of giving formal recognition to the practice of accepting the c.i.f. price actually paid or payable for goods imported under a commercial contract negotiated in fully open market conditions,

[11] Published in the United Kingdom as Cmd. 8245.

and it implied no change in the actual basis of valuation used for statistical purposes. In the case of a sale not in the " open market " (for example, a transfer between associated companies in the United Kingdom and abroad), the value entered for duty (and statistical purposes) might, of course, differ from the actual cost to the importer. Although such differences may be important for some commodities, particularly certain manufactured goods, the effect on total imports is not likely to be appreciable. For the most part the total values recorded reflect fairly accurately the actual c.i.f. cost of imports.

Goods consigned for sale present a special problem which is met by entering provisional values which are amended when the final sale values are established; for some imported goods (for example, fresh fruit and vegetables), this procedure sometimes results in very substantial amendments to the provisional values entered in the monthly *Accounts*.

Values declared in foreign currencies are converted to sterling at the rate of exchange ruling at the time of entry; this is not necessarily the rate of exchange appropriate to the actual transaction. Thus, some of the sterling import values in the months immediately following the devaluation of sterling in 1949 were, as a result of this procedure, higher than those which had actually been paid, since some goods valued using the new dollar/sterling exchange rates had been paid for at the old rate of exchange.

Charges for freight, insurance, etc., have always been included in the import values (*cf.* the 1854 description of the valuation quoted above). In the current official estimates of the United Kingdom balance of payments, payments for imports are valued f.o.b., not c.i.f. The balance of payments figures represent transactions (not actual arrivals of imports), and there are also differences of coverage between the two sets of import figures. However, it is the different basis of valuation which accounts for most of the difference between the balance of payments and the trade figures and gives rise to the main difficulty in using trade statistics to arrive at estimates of payments. Freight and insurance charges included in United Kingdom imports have been variously estimated at from 10 to 13 per cent of the total c.i.f. value, but these charges show a very wide dispersion for different commodities and from different sources, and no single factor of this kind can be applied to total imports to give more than a rough adjustment to an f.o.b. basis.

Country designations. Imports are credited to the country of consignment, which is generally defined as " the place or country from which the goods were originally despatched to the United Kingdom with or without breaking bulk in the course of transport, but without any commercial transaction in the course of transport." Exports are similarly credited to the last destination to which the goods are actually consigned.

Normally this method of crediting United Kingdom imports and exports yields figures which are very close to those of trade classified according to the country with which the commercial transactions actually took place.

It was for this reason that the consignment basis was recommended by the committee which considered the method which should be adopted. The country of origin method for imports was considered but rejected, partly on practical grounds, but also (to quote the committee's report) because " the trader, for whose benefit primarily the statistics are obtained and published is mainly interested in the places with which the trade is carried on."[12]

Supplementary information was collected on imports by country of origin for some commodities as part of the League of Nations inquiry into the various methods of recording trade by countries in the 1930's. The difference between the origin and consignment basis revealed by this investigation were surprisingly small for most commodities. There may at any time be occasional transactions involving countries other than the country of origin, and under conditions of shortages and exchange control such as those following World War II these may be on a larger scale than before the war. However, there are few differences of any importance, among which should be noticed the consignment from European ports of produce of dependent overseas territories of the country concerned. Even these differences were generally quite small compared with the total trade in the commodities concerned. Consignments of unmanufactured tobacco from the Netherlands were among the examples revealed by the pre-war inquiry, and similar consignments are also included in post-war imports; these would not be included as exports in the Netherlands trade statistics, which are on a special trade basis. In some cases, however, it is not possible to detect such examples by comparison with the statistics of the country from which the goods are consigned; for example, dates from Tunis or Algeria, most of which are consigned from France, are recorded as special exports in the French statistics.

On the export side, the most important difference between statistics of trade credited to countries as recorded in the United Kingdom accounts, and trade credited to the countries with which transactions take place, probably arises from the treatment of ships. Exports of ships are normally attributed to the country of registration. Exports to Panama, for example, include all new ships registered under the Panama flag as exports to that country; in 1950 these amounted to nearly £4 million, 80 per cent of the total value of exports to that country, and resulted in the trade figures giving a very much higher figure than any estimate of transactions with Panama.

[12] *Report of the Trade Records Committee*, 1908. Cmd. 4345.

The list of countries distinguished in the United Kingdom statistics is, like the commodity list, revised annually to take account of frontier or Customs area changes. The current list of 178 countries includes the Channel Islands, which are not included in the area covered by the United Kingdom trade statistics. The Channel Islands are part of the United Kingdom monetary area and are so treated in the United Kingdom balance of payments statistics. They are generally included with the United Kingdom in other countries' statistics, but, with the possible exception of France, their trade with other countries is normally negligible.

The country list includes three special headings for landings of fish and of whale oil and products direct from the fisheries. British landings of fish are not recorded, but landings direct from foreign fishing vessels are recorded as imports from the " Deep Sea Fisheries." Whale oil and whale products landed direct from whaling vessels are recorded as from " Whale Fisheries, Foreign " or " Whale Fisheries, British."

Publications. United Kingdom trade statistics are first published in the monthly *Accounts Relating to Trade and Navigation of the United Kingdom* on or about the twentieth day of the month following that to which they relate. In addition to statistics for the month itself, cumulative figures are shown for trade in the expired part of the calendar year, together with the corresponding figures, both monthly and cumulative, for the 2 preceding years.

The monthly *Accounts* present statistics of imports, exports, and re-exports in summary form. The 1951 *Accounts* included some 750 headings for imports and nearly 1,200 for exports, with country information for commodity headings, or groups of headings, accounting for over 80 per cent of imports and nearly 70 per cent of exports. The commodity headings shown are groupings of the headings in the import and export lists and are considerably fewer than those of the detailed tabulations. Country particulars are given only for the more important headings or combinations of headings, and only the more important sources or destinations are shown. Country detail is, however, given for the total of each of the 46 groups distinguished in the classification, a large number of the countries distinguished in the country list being generally shown. A summary of the total trade with each country is not available at the time of publication of the main account for the month itself, but it was published in the same volume 1 month in arrear.

The inclusion of cumulative figures means that, within 3 weeks of the end of each calendar year, provisional annual totals are available in the same detail as in the monthly accounts. This form of monthly publication is designed to present the main features of United Kingdom trade with sufficient detail to show movements of the principal commodities, and the main sources or destinations for those commodities.   With cumulative as well as monthly figures, it provides a convenient and up-to-date summary. For any general study of the commodity composition of United Kingdom trade, the user is unlikely to need more detail than is included in it.

For country and detailed commodity studies, however, this form has a number of disadvantages.   The countries distinguished as sources or destinations under the various commodity headings are those which are most important for that particular commodity, trade in that commodity with countries not separately distinguished being shown for " Other Commonwealth Countries and the Irish Republic " and for " Other Foreign Countries."   Both commodity and country headings to be distinguished in the *Accounts* are revised at the beginning of the year;   they remain unchanged in each issue of the *Accounts* for that year.   Trade with the most important trading partners of the United Kingdom will always be shown for a sufficient number of commodities for a fairly complete picture to be built up of the pattern of trade with that country.   The process of extracting from the *Accounts* the figures for all the commodity headings for which the country is distinguished is, however, a rather laborious one;   for all but the most important sources, a substantial part of the trade will remain in commodities for which no country detail is given, or for which the particular country was not considered sufficiently important as a source or destination to be distinguished in the *Accounts*. For commodity group totals, however, figures will probably be shown for a sufficient number of countries to give a fairly complete summary of trade with all but the smallest trading nations.

A useful addition to the country and the area information in the monthly statistics is currently contained in a monthly *Report on Overseas Trade* prepared by the Board of Trade.   This includes an area by commodity group analysis of imports and exports for selected currency and political groupings of countries.   Another supplementary publication prepared by the Board of Trade[13] contains the provisional annual figures as shown in the December *Accounts* rearranged to form a set of country tables of trade with each of some 70 important countries;   although this publication consists only of a rearrangement of the monthly *Accounts* detail, it presents the available information in a much more convenient form for country studies.

For any more detailed information on either commodities or countries the user must either await the publication of the full detail of the year's trade in the *Annual Statement of Trade* (more than a year after the end of the year concerned), or make application to the Statistical Office of H.M. Customs and Excise for a special extract or tabulation.   The information

---

[13] *Trade of the United Kingdom with Selected Countries.*

is generally available on payment of a fee to cover the cost of the extraction. Monthly figures are tabulated (though not published) in full commodity-country and country-commodity detail, but, since these tabulations have not always been permanently filed, monthly statistics for past periods are sometimes not available in any more detail than in published sources.

The *Annual Statement* is now issued in four volumes, and the amount of information included is such that the difficulty in use may be because of an excess of detail rather than a lack of it. Each issue normally contains figures for a period of 5 years. The tables in Volume I include commodity statistics in the full import and export list detail for imports, exports, re-exports, and for retained imports. Volumes II and III contain tables showing sources or destinations for each commodity; the country break-down against each heading is not exhaustive, the less important sources or destinations being grouped together. In Volume IV are tables of trade with each country, the commodity headings being for " principal commodities." These headings are generally groupings of import or export list headings. For the most detailed commodity information on trade with a particular country, the user may need to refer to the com-modity-country tables in Volumes II and III as well as the country-commodity tables.

In addition, the annual volumes include tabulations of a kind not prepared on a monthly basis. These include analyses by country and by commodity of transhipments under bond, and a set of tables showing exports, imports, and re-exports through each port in the United King-dom. The *Annual Statement* also includes certain statistics of Customs revenue from import duties and, in a special revenue supplement, statistics of dutiable goods entered for home consumption, receipts of duty, and rates of duty charged.

A new annual publication presenting statistics of the nationality of vessels carrying the imports and exports of the United Kingdom was begun in 1938 with statistics for 1936 and 1937. This was suspended on the out-break of World War II, but similar figures have been compiled for 1938 and for the years 1947, 1948, and 1949; these have been published in summary form.[14]

Period covered; amendments. All the published statistics relate to calendar months and years, but the statistics do not, strictly, cover all shipments or arrivals during the calendar period. They include imports cleared by Customs officers at the ports during the month, and exports declared on documents received in the Customs Statistical Office during the month. Since the normal procedure for declaring most imports and exports allows some extension of time after the arrival or departure of the

[14] *Board of Trade Journal*, 25th August, 1951.

ship, there is a time lag before arrivals or shipments are actually recorded
as imports or exports; the difference between the period actually covered
by the statistics and the calendar period is probably about a week or ten
days, but this probably varies a good deal even over short periods.

Late entries received after the end of the month are included in the
statistics for the month in which they are received, not treated as amendments. The monthly figures as first published are, however, provisional
and subject to amendments arising from corrections received after the end
of the month to entries already included in the accounts. No separate
figures of amendments are published, but corrections are taken to account
in the cumulative figures for the expired portion of the year at the first
opportunity after notification of the correction. Amendments received
after the end of the year are included in that year's figures as they appear in
the December *Accounts* for later years and in *Annual Statements*. These
amendments are not generally made in the monthly or cumulative figures
for individual months published in later years. For a few important
dutiable commodities monthly figures of imports are corrected in later
years; otherwise only a few large corrections are allocated to the month
to which they relate. The sum of the monthly figures published for any
year or part of a year will therefore differ from the aggregate or cumulative
figures for the same period, and the annual totals for the latest year
included in the December *Accounts* will be liable to correction in the
corresponding *Accounts* of the following year and in the *Annual Statements*.

In official publications, quarterly figures are obtained not by addition of
three monthly figures but by deduction of the aggregate figures for the
first 3 months from those of the first 6 months, those for the first 6 months
from the aggregate of the first 9 months, and so on. The quarterly totals
derived in this way add to the totals shown for the year, but like the
cumulative figures they will differ from the sum of the monthly figures.
It follows that the figures obtained for one quarter will incorporate the
corrections made during that quarter in respect of figures of earlier
quarters, as well as the corrections to the figures for the current quarter
itself. On balance, it is thought that figures derived in this way give rise
to less error in use than quarterly figures derived by the addition of three
uncorrected monthly figures.

CHAPTER 15

The British Commonwealth

HERBERT MARSHALL, C. D. BLYTH,
AND L. A. SHACKLETON
Dominion Bureau of Statistics, Ottawa

HISTORICAL DEVELOPMENT

Australia. All the Australian colonies compiled trade statistics before their union in 1901, but differences in the methods prevent the aggregation of these records into a valuation of the trade of Australia as a whole. Indeed, until September 1903, defects in the method of recording exports and imports transhipped between Australian ports caused the statistics to underestimate actual trade. From the first the statistics were on a general trade basis and were compiled monthly. Annual figures were originally published for the calendar year, but the desirability of bringing the trade year into line with the seasonal pattern of agricultural and pastoral exports was soon recognized. When normal trading was disrupted by World War I, the annual period was changed; from 1914–1915 the year ending June 30 has been used. Monthly statistics have been published since 1907, since 1937 facilitated by the use of mechanical tabulation methods.

From the time of union the Commonwealth has controlled the noncontiguous territory of British New Guinea (Papua), and after World War I (1914–1918) the Trust Territory of New Guinea, Norfolk Island, and Nauru came under Australian administration. These territories are excluded from the Australian Customs area. Consequently, they are treated as foreign countries in Australian trade statistics.

Australian statistics at first listed commodities in alphabetical order. In 1907 the commodities were grouped into 24 categories based primarily on component material. Revisions of the categories in 1918–1919 and 1921–1922 reduced their number to 21, but over the years the number of commodities distinguished in the export and import lists was substantially increased. A further major revision of the classification was introduced in 1945–1946, but the same 21 categories were retained. Since 1929–1930 secondary analyses of Australian trade according to economic classes and degree of manufacture have also been prepared.

Australia at first credited imports to the country from which the goods were imported, and in 1905 introduced an additional record of imports by country of origin. The second of these records was found to be of greatest interest, and in 1921–1922 the record of country of consignment was discontinued. Exports are credited to the country of final destination of the goods, so far as this can be ascertained at the time of export.

The method of valuing imports was little changed until 1947. The f.o.b. port-of-shipment value was used, with an addition of 10 per cent for freight and insurance costs. This value was expressed in " British currency," and for Customs and statistical purposes all currencies expressed in pounds, shillings, and pence were treated as of equal value. Other currencies were converted to British sterling at first at their mint par of exchange, and, after November 1920, at the London market rate of exchange. Exports were valued in Australian currency at their domestic market value or at an equivalent value calculated from the overseas price of goods shipped on consignment less overseas freight costs. From 1929–1930 special adjustments to the export values of several commodities were made to allow for export subsidies or controlled prices. In 1937–1938 export valuations were changed to the actual f.o.b. price paid by the foreign importer, or its f.o.b. equivalent based on prices in the country to which goods were consigned.

On November 15, 1947, a major change in the method of valuing imports was introduced. Import values thereafter have been the f.o.b. value of the goods in the currency of the country of origin, converted to Australian currency at the Commonwealth Bank's official selling rate for the date of export of the goods. To obtain closer comparability with the new statistics, import values for earlier years were adjusted *in the aggregate* by the addition of 14 per cent to the earlier f.o.b. values in sterling on the old " British currency " basis.   Gold imports, however, were separately revalued at the average export price of Australian gold for each year.

For the period of World War II (1939–1945) the trade statistics are incomplete because of the partial or delayed inclusion of war material and supplies, Lend-Lease and Reverse Lend-Lease, and other special transactions.   However, for the years 1942–1943 to 1947–1948, civil and government trade were classified separately, and the civil trade figures for the war years are approximately comparable with earlier and later statistics.

Canada.   Trade statistics for Canada have been published since the union of the provinces of British North America in 1867, and earlier records for the individual colonies are also in existence.   Annual data were first published for the fiscal year, to 1906 the year ending June 30, and after that date for years ending March 31.   Fiscal year reporting was abandoned with the returns for 1938–1939, and from 1939 the annual data have been on a calendar year basis.   Quarterly returns (in somewhat less detail) were published from 1894–1895, and monthly data have appeared since about July 1899, although from April 1926 to December 1943 the monthly returns were published only quarterly.   A supplementary report for the calendar year giving the same detail as the monthly reports is also available from 1927.   During World War II the publications series was revised.   Data in full detail have been published since 1944 for months and annual periods on a commodity-by-country basis, and for quarters on a country-by-commodity plan.

Canadian trade statistics were originally on a general trade basis.   In 1917 import statistics were restricted to goods entered for consumption. Before that year both general and special import totals had been published, but due to Canada's minor entrepôt trade these had differed little.   In 1920 a similar change was introduced for re-export statistics; from this year they have excluded re-exports from bonded warehouses.

Another major change in the coverage of the statistics concerns gold. Difficulties were encountered in valuing gold after the general abandonment of the gold standard in the early nineteen-thirties, and further difficulties were experienced in distinguishing newly mined from other gold. After experimenting with various procedures, it was decided to exclude all movements of gold (except gold products) from the trade statistics. This has been done from 1939, and the trade statistics are now supplemented by a table of " net exports of non-monetary gold."   Gold coins and gold in concentrates were excluded from the statistics at the same time as bullion.

At first the trade statistics were published by the Department of Customs.   Before 1900 the Collector of Customs for each port prepared statistics for his port, and these were aggregated in Ottawa. Since 1900 all compilation has been done by a central staff. As long as the statistics were published by the Department of Customs, the classification of articles was basically alphabetical, although 7 categories based on industrial origin were distinguished in most tables. In 1919 the Dominion Bureau of Statistics was established, and it assumed the task of editing and publishing the trade statistics. A new commodity classification, featuring 9 main groups based on the component material principle, was introduced in 1920, and is currently in use (though with changes of detail). Work on a major revision of this classification is now (1952) in progress. The Bureau has also (from 1938–1939) undertaken the compilation of the trade statistics, in addition to the editing and publishing. This growth of centralization has facilitated the use of mechanical methods of tabulation, and has promoted uniformity of presentation of the statistics.

There has been no major change in the method of valuing or crediting Canada's trade since 1867. Imports are valued as at the inland point of purchase in the country from which they are consigned to Canada, and exports as at the inland point of consignment for export. The valuation definition for exports was clarified in 1939, and more uniform export valuations have resulted. Both imports and exports are credited to the country from which (or to which) the goods are consigned.

An important change in the coverage of Canadian trade statistics was introduced on April 1, 1949, because of the union of Newfoundland and Canada. From this date Canadian trade statistics include Newfoundland's imports from, and exports to, foreign countries; the important trade between Canada and Newfoundland disappears from the records.

Ceylon. Trade statistics for Ceylon first appeared in the *Ceylon Blue Book* for 1865. The data were supplied by the Principal Collector of Customs, and some trade information also appeared in his *Annual Administration Report* from a relatively early date. From 1881 annual Customs returns giving a detailed classification of trade by commodities and countries were included in this latter report, and in 1901 Ceylon began the monthly publication of her Customs returns. The general trade system has been in use throughout, and the calendar year is the basic reporting period.

The monthly Customs returns were quite detailed from the outset, and have remained basically unchanged to the present (1952). They provide, for the month and for the elapsed period of the year, quantities for total imports, imports for consumption, and for domestic exports and re-exports; and values for total imports, domestic exports and re-exports. Detail for the chief countries in trade is provided for each commodity. However, no summary figure for total imports or exports appeared until

1922. Tables showing trade by principal countries were not added until 1934. Exports are credited to the country of destination of consignment. and imports to the country of origin.

Ceylon's commodity classification has undergone only one major change in the period covered by the Customs returns. Until June 1921, the items were grouped under the 4 main headings of food and drink, raw materials, manufactures, and bullion and specie. After this month the classification was modified on the basis of the United Kingdom's classification and the suggestions of the Imperial Statistical Conference of 1919. Since that time the groupings have been: food, drink, and tobacco; raw materials and articles mainly unmanufactured; articles wholly or mainly manufactured; animals not for food; bullion and specie (the last grouping excluded from merchandise totals since 1923). At the same time the subgroups within the main groups were increased from 9 to 37. In 1923 summary tables of trade by main groups and subgroups were added to the returns, together with a page of explanatory notes.

The valuation of trade has been in terms of the rupee throughout. Exports have from the first been valued f.o.b. Imports were valued, until May 1948, at their wholesale market value in Ceylon less duties and trade discounts, or, where no such value could be ascertained, at their c.i.f. value. Wartime and post-war shortages and abnormal market conditions led to a growing divergence between market values and c.i.f. values, and from June 1948 all valuations have been on a c.i.f. basis.

British India. Trade statistics for British India were instituted in 1869, with the publication of a volume covering the year ending March 31, 1867. This volume, and the main trade accounts thereafter, covered only seaborne trade. Separate accounts were kept of trade by land, and publication of these began about 1878–1879. Airborne trade was included with seaborne trade from 1937–1938. Monthly publication of seaborne trade data began about 1869–1870; that for land trade also appeared monthly shortly after publication of statistics by land was instituted. The records were on a general trade basis.

The seaborne trade accounts were at first confined to the trade of the British provinces. The trade of the native states was relatively small, and was recorded separately. The trade of French and Portuguese possessions in India was also recorded; at first these data appeared as a supplement to the seaborne trade accounts, but from 1905–1906 were included in the regular seaborne trade publications.

The Indian accounts at first presented only an alphabetical listing of commodities, but in 1884–1885 a grouping under 7 main categories was introduced. Changes in the commodity classification occurred in 1912–1913 and 1922–1923; from the latter date 4 main classes of merchandise trade were distinguished and an additional class covered postal trade. Treasure, including gold and silver, was distinguished from merchandise trade as early as 1874–1875, and this practice continued throughout. Both exports and imports were credited by country of consignment. In the earliest publications the list of countries was restricted, but changes particularly in 1874–1875 and 1903–1904 greatly expanded the country classification in use. Exports and imports were valued on the basis of their wholesale market value less trade discounts and duties. For imports this resulted in valuations on an approximate c.i.f. basis, whereas exports were valued approximately f.o.b. The currency unit used for most of the period was the rupee, but from 1911–1912 to 1920–1921 the pound sterling was used as the currency of account.

A major change in the coverage of the statistics was instituted in 1937–1938, after the separation of Burma from British India. From this year until August 1, 1947 (when statistics for British India ceased), the records include the trade of India with Burma, and exclude that of Burma with other countries.

India and Pakistan. The independent states of India and Pakistan came into being on August 15, 1947. Since that date each country has compiled its own statistics. The major features of the trade figures of British India have been retained by each, pending revision. Exports are still valued approximately f.o.b., imports approximately c.i.f. Both countries have basically retained the old commodity classification. Also, the separate recording of seaborne and landborne trade has been continued. The rupee is used as the currency of account in both sets of records, but the value of the two rupees is, of course, not necessarily the same.

Initially the trade statistics of India covered only the trade of former British territory; they excluded the trade of India with Pakistan. Indo-Pakistan trade was not included in Indian records until March 1948. The territorial coverage of the Indian records was gradually extended as several formerly separate native states acceded to India. By April 1, 1949, the main Indian records included the seaborne and airborne trade of the provinces of West Bengal, Orissa, Madras, and Bombay; and, in addition that of the former states of Travancore, Saurashtra, Baroda, and Kutch. No adjustments, however, were made in the figures for earlier periods to increase comparability. India has initiated a revision of her commodity classification on the basis of the United Nations Standard International Trade Classification (SITC), with modifications to suit Indian conditions.

Pakistan has compiled trade statistics since becoming independent. Administrative problems were initially great, and improvements in statistical methods and administration have in some cases resulted in discontinuities in the figures. One important change in scope has featured

Pakistan's statistics: arms, ammunition, and munitions imported on government account are now excluded from the records, as are ships' stores.

New Zealand. From 1853, when a New Zealand Customs department was established, complete statistics of the country's trade have been kept. These were published in the *New Zealand Blue Book* on a calendar year basis. At first the records were primarily by ports, but by 1868 their scope had been extended and trade was presented for the country as a whole with detail of commodities by countries. In 1914 the compilations were centralized in the head office of the Customs Department with a consequent improvement in accuracy, and summary trade information by months was included in the new *Monthly Abstract of Statistics*. Mechanical tabulation methods were introduced in 1949, with a consequent improvement in the detail available. The general trade system has been used throughout, and the external trade of annexed islands is included in the totals.

In the early years the main trade tables presented only an alphabetical listing of articles. In 1914, influenced by the recommendations of the Dominions Royal Commission and by Australian example, New Zealand adopted a commodity classification which assembled homogeneous items in 23 main groups, with a number of additional subgroups some of which later received main-group status. Gold and silver bullion were treated as metals, but specie was segregated in a separate group. Specie was excluded from the merchandise trade totals after 1933. This classification is basically the one currently in use, although from 1921 a subsidiary summary commodity classification on the basis of the United Kingdom's groups has also been published to facilitate international comparisons.

Exports have been credited to the country of destination throughout, but as in the case of Australia the treatment of imports has changed. At first imports were recorded by country of consignment, but in 1914 country of origin was adopted as an additional record; from 1927 the country of consignment information was omitted from the detailed commodity tables. However, country of consignment records have been maintained for subsidiary purposes, notably for the computation of the balance of trade.

New Zealand has, from the first, used f.o.b. port of shipment values for exports, but for the considerable portion of trade represented by exports on consignment these values have had to be calculated from prices prevailing at the time of export. Imports have been valued at their domestic market value in the country of export of the goods, plus 10 per cent to cover freight, insurance, and similar costs. From 1868 export values were recorded in British currency, and a similar plan was followed for imports from 1880. When in 1930 the New Zealand pound departed from parity with sterling, export valuations were recorded in New Zealand currency, but as Customs duties were fixed in " British currency " terms, sterling remained the currency for the main import records (except that the Australian pound was treated as equivalent to sterling). Analytical tables were, however, converted to New Zealand currency, and in 1935 the main records were also changed to the local currency and the commodity detail for 1930–1934 was converted to this basis.

During World War II, New Zealand excluded Reverse Lend-Lease shipments from her exports statistics; in import statistics Lend-Lease and similar transactions are distinguished from other trade. However, the bulk of defence shipments were included in the trade statistics, and this leads to some incomparability with totals for peacetime trade.

Union of South Africa. Trade statistics on a uniform basis for the territories now included in the Union of South Africa are first available for the calendar year 1906. Earlier records exist for individual colonies and states—those for the Cape of Good Hope date back to 1826—but their coverage is incomplete and the methods used by various authorities differ. In July 1905, the South African Customs Statistical Bureau was established by the governments of the British South African territories to keep uniform records of the trade of the members of the South African Customs Union. Monthly and annual records on a general trade basis date from this time. When the Union of South Africa was created in 1910, the Customs Statistical Bureau was merged with the Union's Department of Customs and Excise.

The South African Customs area has always extended beyond the boundaries of the Union itself, and the scope and presentation of the Union's trade returns have varied with the changing nature of the relationship between the Union and neighbouring territories. The first statistics were for British South Africa as a whole and for the individual colonies, namely, Cape Colony, Natal, Orange River Colony, Transvaal, Southern Rhodesia, and Northern Rhodesia. After the establishment of the Union, the data for the first four colonies were merged, but the territorial coverage of the report was unchanged. Under the South Africa Act the protectorates of Basutoland, Bechuanaland and Swaziland were subject to the Union's Customs laws, and their trade was assimilated with that of the Union. When the territory of South-West Africa came under Union administration after World War I, tables on its trade were included in the statistics. Not until 1930 did the Union cease to publish the returns of the trade of Southern and Northern Rhodesia, and totals for British South Africa.

The information presented for the trade of the Union with other South

African territories has also differed from that presented for trade with other countries. The detail of Union trade with Northern Rhodesia has been excluded from the general tables throughout, and that with South-West Africa from 1922. Trade with these territories is represented in the main tables only by totals. Trade with Southern Rhodesia was similarly treated until 1935, when Southern Rhodesia left the Customs union, but from that year has been included in the main tables. The definition of " South African produce " used in the statistics has also differed from most countries' practice; exports of " South African produce " embraces not only the produce of the Union, but that of South-West Africa and the Zambesi basin of Northern Rhodesia as well. Before 1935 the produce of Southern Rhodesia was also included in the term.

At first the Union's trade statistics included all in-transit traffic, an important constituent of the country's trade. In-transit goods were removed from export statistics in 1923 and from imports in 1924. In 1924 also, a commodity classification was introduced; previously the detail of commodities had been arranged alphabetically, although sub-sidiary statements of imports (from 1910) and exports (from 1911) sum-marized the information under 5 main headings and several subgroups. In 1924 a 13-category classification was adopted; this continues in current statistics. However, within each category the commodities are still listed alphabetically. Under the commodity headings imports are credited to the country of origin, exports to the country of destination or consign-ment.

Both imports and exports are valued approximately f.o.b. by the Union. In the case of those export products for which there is no local market, values are based on the overseas price, with allowances for freight, insurance, and other charges. Until 1946, re-exports were valued at their import value; from that year the export value has been taken. Gold is of almost unique importance to the Union, and was originally included in the value of merchandise trade. To 1923 the quantity of gold exported was recorded in standard ounces and valued at the statutory price of £3. 17 per ounce. From 1923 the quantity was recorded in fine ounces, and until 1936 gold was valued at £4·24773 per fine ounce. For the years 1936–1938 the value of gold was based on the price ruling on the day of export or import. From 1939 gold bullion has been excluded from the trade statistics; instead, estimates of net gold movements are published by the Reserve Bank.

Southern Rhodesia. Beginning with 1930, statistics of the trade of Southern Rhodesia were compiled and published by the government of that territory, and several changes in their nature were made. The chief of these was in the coverage of the statistics. Before 1930 goods imported through Beira for Northern Rhodesia, which passed through Southern Rhodesia, were included in both the imports and re-exports of Southern Rhodesia. For 1930 separate columns in the statistics record the trade of Southern Rhodesia excluding this in-transit movement, the in-transit movement itself, and the total of the two. After 1930 the " old method " records were discontinued, and the published statistics are exclusive of this in-transit trade. A definition of domestic exports restricting this to goods of Southern Rhodesian production was also introduced. The Union of South Africa and Northern Rhodesia were treated as any other country in the general tables, except that goods of South African production were credited to the country whence imported. Other imports were credited to the country of origin of the goods; exports were credited to the country of final destination or consignment.

The valuation methods in use before 1930 remained basically unchanged. Imports are valued f.o.b. or f.o.r. at their place of despatch to Southern Rhodesia, and exports f.o.b. at the frontier of export. The commodity classification in use before 1930 was also continued, which maintains, to a large extent, comparability with the statistics of other South African countries.

USE AND APPRAISAL OF THE STATISTICS

Introduction. The countries of the Commonwealth vary considerably in their national backgrounds and in their historical development. Thus, although their records of trade have many objectives and features in common, and although all have been influenced in some degree by their close relations with Britain, nevertheless significant differences have developed because of the special problems which each Dominion has had to face. There has always been the need to compromise between purely statistical objectives (which are relatively uniform) and the needs of practical administration (which vary greatly). To quote only one instance, statisticians in all the Dominions would recognize the desirability of a consistent and uniform system of valuation, both over time in one country and as between countries. But in Canada, where a major proportion of both export and import trade passes across the long land frontier with the United States, the valuation problem has a different aspect than in those Dominions where the greater part of trade is seaborne. Similar factors account for other considerable discrepancies in statistical practice among the Dominions.

Coverage. The territory to which the statistics of the several countries relate has been influenced by differences in their problems. For Canada, Ceylon, India, and Pakistan, which have no detached dependencies or close administrative integration with neighbouring territories, the problem is relatively straightforward. In these countries the statistics relate to the whole area under the administration of the central government. Australia has, since its union, been entrusted with the administration of neighbouring but detached territories at a less advanced stage of development. These territories have never been regarded as part of Australia proper, and they have, therefore, been treated as foreign countries in Australian trade statistics. New Zealand, faced with a similar problem, chose to include the Cook Islands and Niue in her Customs territory and in her statistics. The problem in South Africa has been more complex; besides administering the territory of South-West Africa, the Union surrounds the British protectorates of Basutoland, Bechuanaland, and Swaziland, and has from the first been in a Customs union with neighbouring British dependencies. The Union's statistics have always included the trade of the three protectorates, and her definition of " South African produce " has been framed to include the produce of all territory administered by the Union government or included in the Customs union.

Important changes in the territory to which the statistics of individual Dominions refer have occurred, particularly after World War II. The most important was the disappearance of British India, and the establishment of separate governments in India and Pakistan. This has introduced entirely new series of statistics of foreign trade, and has seriously limited the extent of temporal comparisons for the trade of the subcontinent. The full scope and significance of the new tabulations are still difficult to appreciate, especially as the series are not yet (1952) settled into definitive form. The territory to which the new series refer has also changed; at first neither India nor Pakistan recorded its trade with the other, and the trade of the former Native States was only gradually incorporated into that of the new nations.

The separation of Burma from India in 1937 also affected the comparability of the statistics of British India. Similarly the union of Newfoundland with Canada in 1949 involved more than a simple amalgamation of two sets of trade records; export statistics relating to certain fishery, forest, and mineral products were noticeably affected. It is probably generally true that some commodity detail will show greater proportionate effects than trade totals, where such changes in territorial coverage occur. The detail shown in the main tables of the Union of South Africa's trade reports has also changed: first when South-West Africa became a mandate, and later when Southern Rhodesia left the Customs union. However, trade totals were largely unaffected by these changes, and supplementary tables in the reports supply commodity detail which can be used to fill out the main tables for analysis over time.

The " general trade " system is followed by all Dominions with the exception of Canada. The chief difference between " general " and " special " trade records, so far as the Dominions are concerned, is in timing rather than in coverage, since in-transit trade is of relatively little importance except to the Union of South Africa. Direct in-transit trade is excluded by both systems, but the one Dominion where such traffic is of importance, South Africa, keeps a special record of the total value of such trade, and publishes it as a supplement to the trade figures. All the Dominions publish statistics of imports, exports of domestic produce, and re-exports. These terms have the usual meaning except in the case (again) of the Union of South Africa. The special Customs relations between the Union and other British South African territories led to a definition of " South African produce " to include produce of these territories, as well as of the Union. Thus, for current accounts, " South African produce " must be taken to mean the " produce or manufacture of the Union of South Africa, South-West Africa, and the Zambesi Basin of Northern Rhodesia." [1] Prior to 1935 the produce of Southern Rhodesia was also included in the term; domestic export totals for the Union from 1935 are therefore not comparable with those before that year, although statistics for total exports were not affected by the change.

Special types of transactions. The inclusion or exclusion from their statistics of commodities of a special character causes some differences in the meaning of the various Dominions' trade totals. A good example is provided by gold. *Gold bullion and specie* are excluded from the merchandise trade statistics of all the Dominions except New Zealand and Southern Rhodesia (which exclude only specie), and Canada also excludes the gold content of ores and concentrates. The production of gold is of dominating importance in the Union of South Africa and of considerable significance in Canada; for a full analysis of these countries' trade, reference to supplementary material on gold production and net gold movements is necesary. Most of the Dominions publish series on gold movements, together with their merchandise trade statistics. Silver ore, bullion, and specie generally receive the same treatment as gold except for Canada and the Union of South Africa, which treat silver ore and bullion movements as merchandise trade.

Ships and aircraft are treated in varying fashion by many countries. All the Dominions, however, treat imports of ships in essentially the same fashion: seagoing vessels purchased abroad are not included in imports, but vessels for the coastal trade or for inland use are generally included. India's statistics include only parts of ships, and New Zealand's records show only ships not sailed to New Zealand under their own power; but

---

[1] *Cf. Annual Statement of the Trade and Shipping of the Union of South Africa*, 1946.

in effect these methods give largely the same results. The one real exception is Canada, which does not record ships for coastal or inland use if of British construction and registry. The treatment of ships in exports usually corresponds to that in imports, but Canada, which has developed a significant shipbuilding industry, includes in exports newly built ships and also old ships sold out of the country and transferred from Canadian to foreign registry. Australia and New Zealand treat aircraft in the same manner as ships, but the other Dominions regard aircraft as merchandise. However, Pakistan excludes defence stores on government account from imports, and aircraft for military use would therefore not be included in the statistics. The other Dominions normally include all government trade in their merchandise statistics, although some also provide separate analyses of this portion of trade.

The treatment of *bunker fuel and ships' stores* by the several Dominions differs widely. Canada does not record sales of these commodities to foreign ships as exports, but in the *import* statistics special items are provided for fuel ex-warehoused for bunkers and articles ex-warehoused for ships' stores. This is probably the most unusual treatment of these items. India and Pakistan exclude these supplies from merchandise exports, but Indian statistics provide the value of bunker fuel exported. Ceylon records as exports sales of goods for these purposes, but credits them as " for bunkers " or " ships' stores " rather than to a country. Australia excludes these items from merchandise totals, but provides the value of ships' stores and bunkers in a separate table. New Zealand and the Union of South Africa include them with merchandise, but South Africa provides detail of these transactions in a separate table in the same way as trade with Northern Rhodesia or South-West Africa is recorded. Variations in the treatment of bunker fuel and ships' stores generally affect the comparability of trade totals to a much lesser extent than variations in the treatment of, for example, ships, aircraft, or bullion.

Unusual transactions of a special character have been of significance in relation to trade totals in certain periods, notably the war years 1939–1945 and the immediate post-war years. Different Dominions applied varying treatments to the movement of war materials and of supplies under Lend-Lease and Mutual Aid agreements. The comparability of trade statistics as between the different countries was much disturbed in consequence. For example, the export statistics of Canada included Canadian production shipped as mutual aid and (in a separate item) supplies sent to Canadian forces.[2] In contrast, Australia excluded

---

[2] This resulted in the inclusion in the import statistics of military equipment returned to Canada from abroad, which distorted the records of Canada's imports from the United Kingdom in particular for the years 1945 (by about $19 million Canadian) and

materials for her forces overseas from the export statistics, and some mutual aid goods for civilian consumption were not recorded in imports. Australian trade was further affected by the practice adopted by the United Kingdom during World War II of purchasing in bulk Australia's production of wool, wheat, and flour, and of storing part of her purchases in Australia for strategic purposes. These stocks were later exported to the United Kingdom or other countries, and were recorded as exports in the month of shipment. Special care must be taken by the user of Dominions' trade statistics for the war and post-war years. Reference to supplementary material will often prove helpful.

Commodity classification. Two basic types of commodity classification are in use in the Dominions. The classifications of Ceylon, India, and Pakistan are based on that of the United Kingdom. They distinguish trade in foodstuffs in one group, and designate other groups chiefly by stage of manufacture. New Zealand also publishes a summary table of trade on this basis, but her primary classification and those of the remaining Dominions are based on component material. The component material classifications differ widely among themselves. Canada designates only 9 main groups of commodities, and arranges individual items in subgroups within these categories. The Union of South Africa and Southern Rhodesia use 14 major groups, Australia 21, and New Zealand 30. The statistics are published as arranged in their classifications by all Dominions except India. India prints group and subgroup totals at the front of its reports, but arranges the commodities alphabetically in the main trade tables.

The classifications in use in 1952 by the Dominions have been established for some time. This facilitates the comparison of summary information over a period of years. Important commodities can be distinguished in the records for even longer periods. Over the years, the demand for summary trade information on different bases has grown, and many of the Dominions have catered to this demand by providing summaries of their trade on alternative plans. Canada, for example, publishes annual data summarizing the trade items according to degree of manufacture, industrial origin, and purpose. As trade has grown more complex, more detailed information has also been needed, and the number of items included in the Dominions' trade statistics is continually being expanded. Although temporal continuity in a national classification is desirable, changes in the nature of trade can often render a classification plan

---

1946 (by about $60 million Canadian). With the outbreak of war in Korea it was decided to exclude shipments of goods to Canadian forces abroad from the export statistics, and of military equipment returned to Canada from the import statistics in order to avoid such distortions in the future.

obsolete. India has announced her intention to revise her classification on the basis of the United Nations Standard International Trade Classification (SITC); Canada, which has encountered many difficulties in applying her component material principle, is also working on a revision of the " standard " type.

One factor that must be kept in mind when using Dominions' statistics is that the import classification used for statistical purposes is often influenced by the Customs tariff classification. The range of detail shown, therefore, sometimes changes because of tariff alterations. This is particularly true of Canada. Although this relationship tends to circumscribe the development of statistics most suitable for economic analysis, nevertheless most major commodities in trade are clearly designated.

The treatment of articles imported and exported by post is variable, and leads to some difficulties in handling the detail of trade. For instance, in the statistics of Ceylon all exports of postal articles are classified in one item, whereas imports by post are assigned to their appropriate commodity headings (although from 1939 to 1948 these were listed as a separate item in the coin and bullion group). Although postal trade is only a small part of the total trade of most Dominions, nevertheless in the case of some commodities it is quite important; and care should be taken in using statistics of those commodities to allow for the national treatment of postal trade.

Valuation. Nowhere in the trade statistics of the Dominions is there greater variation than in the valuation of imports. Almost the only common feature is that all Dominions record in their statistics the value as determined for Customs duty purposes. Canada values her imports at their fair market value at the time and in the place whence the goods were consigned to Canada. This valuation thus excludes any inland freight and handling charges in the country where the goods were purchased. Australia, the Union of South Africa and Southern Rhodesia base their import valuations on the f.o.b. cost of the goods at the frontier of the exporting country, thus including inland freight and the costs of loading the merchandise on the exporting vehicle. New Zealand starts her valuations from the same principle as Canada, but adds to the " current domestic value " of the goods a flat 10 per cent to cover estimated freight, insurance, and other costs incurred in transporting the goods to New Zealand. India and Pakistan base their import valuations on current wholesale prices at the time and place of import, with allowances for trade discounts and duties. Only Ceylon uses a straight c.i.f. valuation, and that only from July 1948; previously her values were on the same basis as those of India and Pakistan. Four Dominions thus use f.o.b. or approximate f.o.b. values, and four use c.i.f. or approximate c.i.f. values. In the case of only four, however, can the description f.o.b. or c.i.f. be used without qualification.

All the Dominions use f.o.b. values or approximations to f.o.b. values for exports. Their methods of calculating these, however, differ. The Canadian practice again results in the lowest value: exporters are asked to supply the actual amount received or to be received for the goods exclusive of all charges. As with exports, this value excludes all inland freight and handling costs. The Union of South Africa and Southern Rhodesia value goods f.o.b. at the place of despatch from their territory, and Australia, Ceylon, and New Zealand use the usual f.o.b. port of export values. India values exports as imports; that is, on the basis of wholesale prices at the time and place of export with allowance for trade discounts. Pakistan used the same principle until 1951, but beginning January 1951 adopted the f.o.b. port of shipment value inclusive of all export duties. This is the only case in the Commonwealth of the inclusion of Customs duty in statistical values.

The wide variations in valuation practices are largely due to administrative considerations. Canada, for example, was influenced by practical considerations in the recording of trade with the United States. The greater part of the goods shipped between the two countries move at a through rate from their point of origin, to their point of destination. Shippers are not in a position to know what proportion of their freight charges apply to the movement of goods in one country or the other; it is therefore impractical to value goods at the border. It is, of course, possible to get information on the allocation of total freight charges between the two countries for balance of payments purposes; but this allocation is not possible either in time, or in detail, for records of trade. The only other Dominions faced by a similar problem, South Africa and Southern Rhodesia, likewise exclude a great part of inland freight charges on shipments to neighbouring territories from their valuations. The variability of ocean freight rates and the relatively long distances over which goods must move has presumably affected valuation practices as well. An accurate check on strict c.i.f. values would be difficult under these conditions, and most Dominions have preferred to use either f.o.b. import values or calculated approximations to c.i.f. values as being administratively more convenient. However, especially in the case of New Zealand (and of Australia before November 1947) the c.i.f. approximations must be recognized as approximations. If the rate of addition to foreign domestic values (10 per cent) is well chosen, this procedure may result in reasonably reliable totals for the c.i.f. value of all trade. Clearly, however, the accuracy diminishes when the flat rate is applied to the values of individual commodities imported from different sources at varying rates of freight.

The basic element of the valuation of imports is not always the actual cost of the merchandise. Most countries have a secondary valuation principle, and may use whichever of the two methods gives the higher value. In particular, the " fair market value in the country of origin of the goods " may at times vary from the cost of goods due to market discrimination or overseas dumping by producers. In addition to their regular Customs duties many Dominions may at times impose dumping duties to protect home industries from this type of competition. In such cases the goods in question are generally valued at above their actual cost for both Customs and statistical purposes. Canada, for one, made fairly wide use of dumping duties in the depression years 1930–1935, but since World War II this practice has not had significant results. Ceylon has used official prices to value small shipments of merchandise for which values were not declared, but no Dominion has ever made wide use of such a principle.

The countries which normally ship a considerable proportion of their exports " on consignment " or " for orders "—Australia, New Zealand, and the Union of South Africa—have also found it necessary to adopt special methods of valuing such merchandise. Generally the procedure is to estimate a value from the price of the commodity in the market to which it is consigned at the time of shipment, with allowance for transit charges and discounts. Where this type of transaction is less prevalent, exporter's estimations of value are generally accepted.

Considerable difficulty arises in matching Dominion statistics of export and import values in analysing inter-Dominion trade or in the aggregation of Dominion trade for comparison with other world aggregates. The difficulties are due both to the varying treatment of international transit costs and to the treatment of internal freight charges. In addition, valuation practices have varied over time, and often in the middle of a statistical recording period. Changes have occurred in Pakistan's valuation of exports (January 1, 1951), and in the valuation of imports by Ceylon (July 1, 1948) and Australia (November 15, 1947). Care must be taken that factors of this sort do not distort conclusions drawn from the statistics.

Currency conversions. The valuation of merchandise trade always raises the problem of how to convert to the domestic currency values expressed in other currencies. This is especially true under conditions of fluctuating exchange rates or at a time of widespread revaluation of currencies, but arises even under exchange control and stable rates. Ideally, the conversions should probably be made at the actual exchange rates appropriate to the settlement of individual transactions, but this is simply not practicable. Merchandise trade must be recorded at the time the goods move, and therefore the exchange rates used for conversion are generally those appropriate to this time rather than to the time at which payments are made. It is also the general practice to adopt official rates (though not necessarily arbitrary rates) which may differ from the actual rates used in particular payments.

Canadian experience provides a good cross section of methods in use, both because in the period when the exchange value of the Canadian dollar was fixed her practice corresponded closely to that of other countries under those conditions, and because she is presently facing the usual problems involved in a fluctuating rate. In the period of fixed rates, conversions for imports were made by Customs officials at the official selling rates for United States dollars or sterling, or at cross rates with these for other currencies. The rates used were those appropriate to the date of shipment of the goods. Subsequent to the unpegging of the exchange rate in October 1950, the conversion rates for imports were based on the noon (average) rate quoted by the Bank of Canada, for United States dollars or sterling, or appropriate cross rates with these currencies. Since November 1950 the rate with the United States dollar has been expressed only to the nearest half cent to eliminate the need for daily changes. As the value on export entries must be expressed in Canadian dollars, conversions in both periods (where necessary) have been made by exporters. During the fixed exchange rate period, the appropriate and generally used rates were the official buying rates for the currency in question but, since the freeing of the Canadian exchange rate, practice has been more variable. Many exporters adopted the practice of using an approximate rate, but others used forward rates or rates available from dealers. Some variation in the rates in use is likely to remain, especially since the rates available to the individual trader vary with the size of the transaction and his relations with dealers.

There were greater divergencies at some times during the inter-war period, particularly at the time of currency instability in the early 1930's. There was then a difference, sometimes appreciable, between the market rate and the proclaimed value of sterling; Canadian imports from the United Kingdom were overvalued in the trade records in some periods and undervalued in others.

Other variations can be found in Dominions' practices. For example, for a long period up to November 1947, Australia valued all imports in " British currency." Values not expressed in pounds, shillings, and pence were converted into sterling at official (to November 1920), then at commercial, rates of exchange. Other pound-shilling-pence currencies were accepted as the equivalent of sterling, even though these were at a discount (or premium) with sterling. Since November 1947, the valuations have been in Australian currency, and conversions of all other currencies have been made at official rates. Comparability with previous periods has been improved by adjusting the earlier records to approximate the new basis.

Country designations. Two basic principles are used by the various Dominions in the crediting of trade to countries. Exports are credited either to the country to which the goods are consigned or to the country of ultimate destination of the goods. Imports are credited either by country of consignment or to the country of origin of the goods. Canada and India use the consignment principle for both exports and imports; Pakistan uses it for exports. The ultimate destination-origin criterion is in use elsewhere, except that New Zealand maintains a secondary record of imports by country of consignment for the calculation of her balance of trade.

There is little real difference between the consignment and ultimate destination principles as applied to export statistics. The country of consignment is defined by Canada and India as the country to which goods are intended to pass without interruption of transit save in transhipment from one conveyance to another. At the time of export of goods an exporter would rarely if ever know that the goods he has sold to an importer in one country would be resold to another country; the country he would give as country of destination would be the same as that received if asked for country of consignment. Indeed, some Dominions specifically point this out: "A proportion of the goods declared to be for export to any one country may be distributed from that country to other countries, but as the ultimate destination is unknown when the consignment leaves South Africa the export figures are credited to the country declared on bills of entry (export)."[3] India uses the terms " country of final destination " and " country to which goods are consigned " interchangeably.

One important qualification to the accuracy of export-by-country information must be made. In all Dominions, especially before World War II, a large proportion of some exports were shipped on optional bills of lading, or " for orders." The country to which such goods were credited was either the most likely market (usually the United Kingdom) or the country of first port of unloading of the exporting vessel (again usually the United Kingdom). Comparison of Dominions' export statistics, particularly with the statistics of imports of Continental European countries from the Dominions, will often reveal wide discrepancies, due

[3] *Annual Statement of the Trade and Shipping of the Union of South Africa, 1946.*

in part to this factor as well as to genuine entrepôt trade through the United Kingdom.

Although the two principles for crediting exports are effectively one, there is a very real and important difference between the two principles used to credit imports. In all cases the country from which goods have been imported " without interruption of transit save in the course of transhipment " can be identified. It is usually also possible to discover the country in which the goods were actually grown or produced (primary products), or in which the manufacturing process is substantially completed (for manufactures). It is not unusual for tea from India or Ceylon to be shipped to a merchant in the United Kingdom for resale abroad. Tea imported in this way by the Union of South Africa would be credited to India (or Ceylon), but if imported by Canada it would be credited to the United Kingdom. Here the differing results of the crediting principles are obvious, and equally obvious is the possibility that India (or Ceylon) would present a different statistical picture of trade with South Africa than would be given by the Union's statistics.

Administration and publications. The primary source of information on which the import statistics of the Dominions are based is generally the entries used for Customs purposes. The information contained on these forms is prepared to comply with the national Customs law, and is generally verified by Customs officials at the time that the goods are cleared for consumption. As a result, statistics of imports can usually be evaluated with reference to a given set of standards, and with reasonable confidence in their accuracy. It should be remembered, however, that where duties are on an ad valorem basis, valuations will normally be subject to more intensive scrutiny than quantity measurements; the reverse is true where duties are specific.

In the case of exports, Customs entries are again the usual source of information, although Indian records are based on the quite different system of taking data from shipping manifests received in the recording period, together with notices of short shipment. As exports are less universally subject to duty than imports, the verification by Customs officials of export documents is generally less thorough than that of import documents, and there is greater possibility of error. India, for example, follows the general policy that goods should not be detained because of misdeclarations which affect only statistics (and not revenue). The problem of the variety of rates used by exporters in currency conversions as illustrated above by the Canadian experience likewise reflects the lack of thorough checking of export entries. Export records are thus much more dependent than import records on the good will of exporters.

In most of the Dominions, trade statistics were at first compiled and published by the Customs department.   The primary records were usually compiled by officials at individual ports and aggregated by a central staff. The tendency has been, however, for all compilation work to be concentrated in the hands of a central group, in order to increase uniformity of recording procedures and to facilitate checking of the data.   In some cases the work has been transferred from Customs to special statistical offices. The tendency towards centralization has facilitated the adoption of mechanical methods of tabulation.   In turn, this has permitted more speedy and detailed compilations.   It is probable that this factor will influence those Dominions still using decentralized methods, and will lead them in the direction of centralization.

The periods for which statistics are compiled vary among countries. Australian statistics are prepared on the basis of a fiscal year ending June 30.   India and Pakistan use the year ending March 31.   The remaining Dominions use the calendar year.   Within each year statistics are compiled for months, but the monthly records published are generally subject to amendment.   Only the annual tabulations are usually presented in final form.   Recording periods are generally not identical with the calendar periods whose name they bear: Canadian statistics for a given " month " relate only to the trade covered by forms processed by the Bureau of Statistics during that month; the annual statistics relate to trade covered by forms processed during the 12 months.   Australia, Ceylon, India, and Pakistan use similar " statistical " periods in their compilations, but New Zealand, the Union of South Africa and Southern Rhodesia hold open their books until all, or almost all, of the trade that actually moved in the calendar period is covered.   The few days' difference between " statistical " and calendar period coverage has little effect on the comparability of statistics over time or between countries, although it may have meaning for the analysis of national data.

No one trade statistics publication can meet all needs.   Detailed and bulky trade returns are essential as reference books, but there is also need for interpretive and selective data.   Publications of different types also permit the earlier issuing of summary information, before the time-consuming task of preparing the detail for release has been completed. All the Dominions follow the practice of either issuing monthly trade returns or publishing summary information in other bulletins.   But only Canada, Ceylon, and India issue monthly publications covering all, or almost all, of the range of detail provided by their annual tabulations.   As a result it is not always possible for the general user of trade statistics to make accurate inter-Dominion comparisons of monthly trade in specific commodities, because of a lack of published data.   It is likewise difficult to obtain values for all Dominions for approximately the same time periods (*e.g.*, calendar years), except over a limited range of totals.

Adaptation of statistics in use. However accurate and detailed the published records may be, statistics of the movement of goods are inevitably limited by the nature of the basic sources, the definitions, and the classifications in use. Not only do the different Dominions handle a common problem in different ways, but the treatment of a given aspect of trade in one country will often change over time. Thus, for temporal comparisons or for aggregations or analyses of inter-Dominion trade, the published data often require adaptation or adjustment. The adjustment may be a matter of allowing for a change in area, for the treatment of special transactions (such as Mutual Aid after 1939), for different valuation methods or inappropriate currency conversions, or for variations in country designations.

There is particular need for adaptation, and for caution in handling records of the movement of goods, when trade statistics are used in building up, supplementing, or checking a statement of international payments on merchandise account, or for national accounting purposes. Movements of goods do not always coincide in time with payment for the same goods, and trade statistics often record goods movements for which there is no corresponding financial transaction (for example, gifts, or settlers' effects). The statistics of the Dominions are further complicated by intricate inter-company and intra-company relationships among themselves, with the United Kingdom and its dependencies, and with the United States. These may have considerable effect on the valuation of trade in the commodities concerned, of which oil, base metals, and many manufactures are characteristic. Even under conditions of exchange control and Customs scrutiny, trade totals need close examination for analytical use.

It should not be felt, however, that the statistics of the Dominions are unique in their differences, or in the problems involved in their use. Their records are comprehensive, their publications adequate for most purposes, and, although in some cases there is a considerable lapse of time before complete annual records for a given year appear, their performance here is no worse than that of some wealthier and more prominent nations. No nation's trade statistics can be said to measure up to even its own ideals; there were, in 1952, no international standards for trade statistics at which all could aim. It is to be hoped that the United Nations work in this field will improve this situation.

CHAPTER 16

British Colonies and Dependencies

and Members of the Statistics Department,
*Colonial Office, London**

HISTORICAL DEVELOPMENT
Early history 330
Report of Colonial Office Committee, 1891 332
Conference of British Empire Statisticians, 1920 334
Conference of Colonial Government Statisticians, 1950. . . . 337

USE AND APPRAISAL OF THE STATISTICS
Characteristics of trade returns 338
Commodity classification 339
Valuation 340
Country designations 341
East Africa 342
Northern Rhodesia and Nyasaland 344
West Africa 345
Singapore and Federation of Malaya 346
Hong Kong 348
West Indies 348

TABULAR CHART AND NOTES 349
Tabular Chart 349
Notes on individual Colonies 349

HISTORICAL DEVELOPMENT

Early history. The first systematic attempt to persuade Colonial governments to make annual statistical returns to the War and Colonial Department [1] was made in the 1820's when the system of annual *Blue Books* was introduced. From this time onwards Colonial governments were expected to provide brief annual figures of their import and export trade by commodity, in quantity and value, although they did not always succeed in doing so. Statistics were, in general, scanty. In 1839, R. M. Martin wrote of the Jamaica *Blue Books:* " There is a slovenliness, a total want of decorum to the home authorities manifested in every document; almost invariably there is no summing up of the totals. . . . It is to be hoped that the authorities of Jamaica will in future pay more attention to the important subject of statistics." [2] The difficulties that obtained for

---

* By far the largest contribution to this chapter was made by Miss E. M. Hill when she was a member of the staff of this department.

[1] As the department concerned with the Colonies was then called.
[2] *Statistics of the British Empire*, 1839.

many years after this are referred to by the Parliamentary Under-Secretary in reply to a suggestion that all Colonies should render returns of the quantity and value of principal articles imported and exported. He wrote: " I am to add that the imperfect returns contained in the *Blue Books* have only been extorted by the most urgent injunctions, repeated year after year, and by order sent out to defer payment of salaries to officers charged with the preparation of the returns until they should have been furnished." [3]

Nevertheless, despite the difficulties encountered, it was possible for G. R. Porter of the Statistical Department of the Board of Trade to prepare brief tables of trade statistics for the year 1835 for all British Colonies of any importance.[4] Probably because the Colonies themselves provided no information on the way in which their figures were compiled, this excellent publication contains no notes at all on the subject. It appears that Porter reclassified the statistics obtained from the Colonies, since the same list of commodities, in alphabetical order, is used for all Colonies (other than Malta and Gibraltar for which Colonies the statistics were incomplete). For most Colonies there are tables of imports and exports showing a country breakdown by item, the figures for the various territories of the British West Indies being particularly full. In an article published in 1849, J. T. Danson stated that any declaration of the value of imports and exports " unconnected with the levy of an ad valorem duty, even if it be regularly enforced by law, is likely to be often made without care to say the least." [5]

Fragmentary information relating to Colonial trade statistics may be gleaned from the *Reports* which were made from the years 1845 onward by the governors of the British Colonies when transmitting their annual *Blue Books* to the Secretary of State.[6] During the period 1840–1860, a number of these *Reports* were very critical of the trade statistics presented in the *Blue Books*. The criticisms throw light on the way in which the statistics were prepared and indicate in many cases a lively awareness of statistical problems. There is no evidence that the statistics were more satisfactory in the 1860's and later, but for some reason frank commentary was no longer made in the *Reports*. The comments that were made suggest that imports were normally valued f.o.b. and not c.i.f., but some

---

[3] *Colonial Office Circular*, 22 August, 1860.
[4] *Tables of the Revenue, Population, Commerce, etc., of the United Kingdom and its Dependencies*, Part VI, 1836.
[5] " Some Particulars of the Commercial Progress of the Colonial Dependencies of the United Kingdom, 1827–1846," *Quarterly Journal of the Statistical Society of London*, November 1849.
[6] These reports were published by Her Majesty's Statistical Office as " *Reports exhibiting the Past and Present State of Her Majesty's Colonial Possessions, Transmitted with the Blue Books*."

governors were aware that a c.i.f. valuation would be more satisfactory (and would, of course, increase the yield from import duties). Thus in the *Report on Tobago* for 1848 it is stated that the opinion which prevailed in the mercantile community that declarations of import values should be based on the cost prices of the articles in the country whence they are imported appeared to be " an evasion of the real spirit and intention of the Import Duty Act." There is evidence also that for some Colonies dutiable goods only were included in the official statistics.

The valuation of exports was probably often very unsatisfactory. Thus the *Report on Jamaica* for 1848 stated that the value of exports was made up from the value put upon cargoes by the shippers, but that a committee of the House of Assembly estimated these values at one-third less. The *Report on St. Kitts* for 1850 said that the official returns of the value of exports were governed by no fixed rule, and the *Report on British Guiana* for 1851 suggested that Customs officers should be instructed to adopt some settled principle of valuing exports, instead of the purely hypothetical mode of valuation hitherto prevailing. In 1858 the Governor of Barbados commented that there was a tendency to overrate the value of exports, but in some other cases there was evidence of undervaluation.

The *Reports on Sierra Leone* for 1846 and 1847 were particularly illuminating on the detrimental effects of the Navigation Acts which caused foreign vessels to land in neighbouring rivers. The goods which arrived in these vessels were brought on to Sierre Leone by canoe and were not shown in the official statistics. The 1847 *Report* also mentioned that gold exports were omitted, as gold was not subject to duty in England and thus did not " in general appear in the manifest of the vessel in which it is shipped."

Report of Colonial Office Committee, 1891. It does not seem to have been until 1882 that any attempt was made by the Colonial Office to consider the question of the proper basis of valuation of imports and exports. A Colonial Office *Circular* (4 December, 1882) said that " a question has arisen in one of the Colonies as to the proper method of valuing imports and exports for statistical purposes," and sought information as to the practice followed in individual Colonies. Following the publication of this *Circular*, and the receipt of the replies, an official committee was set up to enquire into the compilation of import and export statistics and this Committee reported in 1891.[7] It reported that no general rules on the valuation of imports and exports had at any time been laid down for the guidance of Colonial officials and that " the system

---

[7] *Report of a Committee Appointed to Inquire into the Compilation of Import and Export Statistics in the Colonies*, Colonial Office, Miscellaneous Paper 83, October 1891. The Committee consisted of representatives of the Colonial Office, India Office, Board of Trade, and Board of Customs.

actually in force in each Colony has been independently developed, subject only to such modifications as may have been introduced from time to time by officers transferred from one Colony to another in the ordinary course of promotion."

On the valuation of imports the Committee found that three systems were common: (1) Value at the port of shipment; (2) value at the port of shipment plus a fixed percentage (the same for all classes of goods); (3) value at the port of entry. About half the total number of Colonies used method 1; the second method was used by South Australia, New Zealand, Natal, and St. Helena; and the third was adopted by Cyprus, Malta (where only goods subject to duty were valued), and the Straits Settlements. The Committee was of the opinion that the use of method 2 had its origin in two Acts of 1755 and 1833, which were concerned to regulate the trade of the British possessions abroad and which laid down that, in cases where the Customs office had reason to doubt the declared value, the value of goods for duty purposes should be the invoice price plus 10 per cent. Although the Committee found that in the great majority of cases a declaration was required from the importer, supported by production of the invoice, they reported that " in general terms it is not too much to say that while goods subject to an ad valorem duty are valued with considerable care and correctness, those liable to a specific duty are valued with but little care, and duty-free goods with no care at all."

With exports the Committee found that there was general agreement as to the principle on which calculations should be based, and that the value at the port of shipment was taken in every instance, except in four of the smaller West Indian Colonies. But on the " methods of making calculations " they found more variety. In the greater number of Colonies this was done by Customs officials either from local current price lists or from average values obtained from Chambers of Commerce. In several instances exporters' declarations were obtained. " But," they reported, " we gather from the correspondence that, in practice, values are given for the most part in a very loose manner." The Committee reported that another possible source of error had been pointed out to them by an ex-Customs official. " There was," he said, " a theory that a Colony to be flourishing must have a preponderance of exports over imports and if the unassisted figures did not show this they were duly ' rectified ' by the customs."

The main recommendations of the Committee were:

(1) that imports should be valued c.i.f., " as they lie in the port of entry, including the value of packages," and based on consignees' declarations (with penalties for making false declarations); in the case of imports consigned for trade, it was suggested that the best way to

ascertain the value would be " by an official computation from average prices obtained from the trade at frequent intervals and by carefully watching the markets ";

(2) that export values should be f.o.b., including the value of packages, and should be based on exporters' declarations; in the case of exports consigned for sale, values at the place and time of sale should be taken, less freight and insurance;

(3) that " weights and measures should be simplified as much as possible, Imperial standards alone being used " ;

(4) that values should be expressed (at least for totals) in pounds sterling;

(5) that both imports and exports should be classified under four uniform heads:

I. Live animals, food and drink, and narcotics.

II. Raw materials: (a) textile, (b) metal, (c) other.

III. Manufactured articles: (a) textile, (b) metal, (c) other.

IV. Coin and bullion.

With regard to recommendation (5) the Committee made it clear that they were not proposing the adoption of a detailed, uniform classification and they gave only the briefest indication of the distinction between Classes II and III.   They stated that " imports of raw material must include everything that is raw material to the importing country whether it may have already undergone a partial process of manufacture elsewhere or not." From this it followed that goods regarded as raw materials by one colony would not necessarily be so regarded by another.

On the question of the countries to which imports and exports should be credited, the Committee reluctantly decided to formulate no rules. They stated, however, that the aim should be " to show not the country of original production or ultimate consumption but the commercial transaction that takes place in an exchange of goods between two countries."

Included in the Committee's report is an account of the procedure followed in collecting the trade statistics of the United Kingdom.

The Secretary of State accepted the Committee's recommendations, and in a *Circular* (5 December, 1891) urged Colonial governments to give effect to them.   He said that the Committee had been set up as he " considered it desirable that an attempt should be made to arrive at as complete uniformity of procedure . . . throughout the Empire as the varying circumstances of its component parts may admit."   Special attention was drawn to the recommendations on the classification of goods, and it was stated that the United Kingdom proposed to summarize their external trade in the same way.

Conference of British Empire Statisticians, 1920.   It appears that between 1891 and 1920 such progress as was made in improving Colonial trade returns depended on the initiative of the individual colony. In February 1920, a Conference of British Empire Statisticians was held and their *Report* [8] made a number of recommendations on trade statistics. There was appended the *Report of a Committee* appointed to examine Colonial and Protectorate *Blue Books*, and this suggested model tables for statistics of imports and exports for the *Blue Books*. In a *Circular* (19 November, 1920) the Secretary of State informed Colonial governments that he agreed [9] with the recommendations of the Conference, and he submitted the recommended model tables for the *Blue Books*. He hoped that " in view of the great importance of uniformity in the compilation of Empire statistics " every Colonial government would conform to the model as closely as possible; and he anticipated that most of the larger Colonies would find it possible to adopt the new forms in their entirety either at once or in the course of a few years.

There were sixteen model tables, including those on rates of Customs duty and revenue. Four of these related to trade by principal country by class; three related to imports, domestic exports and re-exports of principal articles (and included figures for the 4 preceding years); one covered Customs revenue derived from principal articles; two were detailed tables for imports and exports, showing sources, and distinguishing total imports and imports for home consumption, and total exports and domestic exports; one table dealt with imports for home consumption, distinguishing goods according to whether they were subject to general, preferential, or other tariff rates; one table related to rates and amounts of Customs duty; two covered imports and exports of bullion and specie; one was designed to show the principal articles imported from and exported to each country (distinguishing re-exports); and the last table related to transhipment trade by article and country whence imported.

The other main recommendations made in the Conference Report were:

(1) that imports should be valued c.i.f. and exports f.o.b.;
(2) that " wherever possible imports should be classified under countries of origin or of consignment and exports under countries of final destinations ";
(3) that Colonies should use the Uniform List of Countries used by the United Kingdom;

[8] *Report and Resolutions adopted by the First Conference of Government Officers Engaged in Dealing with Statistics in the British Empire*, held at the Board of Trade 20th January–26th February, 1920, Cmd. 648, 1920.
[9] Except that the Conference had stated that they considered the *Blue Book* import and export tables should be available in the second week of February in the year following that to which they relate; the Secretary of State suggested the second week in March.

(4) that *sterling* values should be shown in all important totals and in summary tables;

(5) that the arrangement of items in the United Kingdom *Annual Statement of Trade* should serve as a guide on classification for the time being (the Conference not being in favour of the classification in the Brussels Convention of 1913);

(6) that it was of the utmost importance that all trade returns should be accompanied by prefatory notes explaining the basis on which the statistics are compiled;

(7) that Colonies should produce monthly trade returns, the amount of detail being left to each Colony to decide.

An examination of the *Blue Books* for the more important Colonies in the early 1920's suggests that the model tables were to a large extent adopted, though Colonies such as the Straits Settlements and Hong Kong which did not record re-exports or transhipment trade were naturally unable to conform.   There was great variation in the number of countries dealt with in the table concerned with trade by principal commodities with individual countries; the Gold Coast compressed the table to show 6 countries (or groups) only, but Jamaica covered 90 countries.   The table which related to imports for home consumption showing tariff rates was omitted by a number of Colonies, though it was presented in great detail by some of the West Indian territories.   In a good many cases the table relating to transhipment trade was omitted, as no records were kept.   Most of the other recommendations contained in the *Report* were adopted by the major Colonies, except that the use of sterling values in totals and summary tables was, and is, by no means universal, and that prefatory notes have continued to this day to be overbrief.

It was not found necessary to issue any comprehensive guidance to Colonial governments between 1920 and 1950, but two *Circulars* may be mentioned.   One (25 July, 1933) requested all Colonial governments to classify imports according to the country of origin, " since this system alone renders it possible to ascertain which countries are actually enjoying the benefits of the dependency's markets."   The other (8 August, 1939) related to the League of Nations Minimum List and stated that it was not desirable for Colonial dependencies to adopt the List as the primary classification " as the United Kingdom Government has not seen fit to do so, and it is necessary that for purposes of comparison Colonial trade statistics should be on the same general basis as those of the United Kingdom."   It was nevertheless considered that the Minimum List classification should be borne in mind in drafting new headings or subheadings. A few of the larger Colonial dependencies were requested to consider the possibility of publishing annual supplementary statistics based upon the Minimum List (corresponding to the statistics published by the United Kingdom); however, dependencies generally were advised that their volume of trade would not justify the labour involved.

The Colonial Economic Advisory Committee, reporting on colonial economic statistics in 1945, pointed out that the break in continuity brought about by World War II provided an excellent opportunity for changes in the basis of trade statistics. It recommended that Colonial governments should recast their commodity classifications on the lines of the League of Nations Minimum List.[10] Six colonies, of which three are the East African group, have adopted the Minimum List.

Conference of Colonial Government Statisticians, 1950. In March 1950, the first Conference of Colonial Government Statisticians was held, and in its *Report* [11] it made recommendations concerning statistics of external trade. At the time of the Conference, the final draft of the Standard International Trade Classification (SITC), later approved by the Economic and Social Council of the United Nations, was not available. Hence, in recommending the adoption of a standard classification, the Conference was not able to go further than to note that Colonial territories would necessarily be influenced by the attitude of the United Kingdom to the United Nations SITC.

The Conference did not feel able to make firm recommendations about any uniform layout of trade accounts but considered that the approach should rather be by way of the removal of existing anomalies, after which uniform summary tables would be easier to achieve. Some degree of regional uniformity was, however, regarded as more immediately desirable.

More definite recommendations of the Conference included those on publication of trade statistics. It was urged that high priority should be given to the printing of trade returns to minimize delays in publication, and that fuller explanatory notes and definitions than those usually provided should be included. Other recommendations were:

(1) that monthly and quarterly trade returns should be extended, where possible, to comprise statistics of the more important commodities by country;

(2) that the number of commodities recorded by value only should be reduced to the minimum;

(3) that quarterly index numbers of quantum and unit values of trade should be compiled in the larger Colonial territories.

[10] In the Committee's *Report*, C. M. 13, August, 1945.
[11] *Report on the First Conference of Colonial Government Statisticians*, 1950, C. O. 207, 1951.

USE AND APPRAISAL OF THE STATISTICS

Characteristics of trade returns. Although strict comparability for all territories is impracticable, two main systems of recording predominate: the " general " system (as used in the United Kingdom) and the " *Blue Book* " system recommended by the 1920 Conference (p. 335 above), a mixture of the " general " and " special " systems in that imports for home consumption are additionally recorded.   The " *Blue Book* " system is used in the Mediterranean territories and generally throughout West Africa and (with some exceptions) the West Indies.   The " general " system is adopted in East and Central Africa, in some Eastern and Pacific territories, and in some of the West Indian islands (*e.g.*, Bermuda and Jamaica). Exceptions to this broad classification are entrepôt centres like Malaya and Hong Kong which use the " general " system but do not record re-exports,[12] and Gambia and Nyasaland which use the " special " system of recording imports but the " general " for exports.

The section " Tabular Chart and Notes " at the end of this chapter presents some of the more important characteristics of the statistics of individual colonies[13]; for convenience of comparability the chart has been based on an analysis of the trade *Reports* for 1949.   Though some general instructions on the preparation of trade statistics have been issued by the Colonial Office, many detailed matters are left to the individual colonies and information on them may not always be currently available in London.

The first three columns of the tabular chart show the general nature of the returns and tabulations.   Tables of trade by commodity-country are usually given in detail, but practice on the other cross classification by country-commodity varies greatly, as indicated in column 3.   " Not available " in this column means either no country tables or tables which only show trade for countries by the broadest classes of goods.

Column 4 indicates whether import and export lists exist for use by traders when making declarations.   Colonial governments generally have not been urged to draw up such lists.   Indeed, in some Colonies lists are unnecessary, since trade is in the hands of a small number of traders who are familiar with the requirements on classification.   The existence of lists, however, reduces the amount of re-classification done by Customs.

Some special categories of trade are referred to in columns 5, 6, and 7, which indicate whether separate records are maintained or not.   These columns do not show whether the categories are comprised within the

---

[12] Aden's land trade also falls (to some extent) into this category.
[13] The table includes almost all the territories which are currently the responsibility of the Colonial Office; it does not refer (nor generally does this chapter) to countries which have assumed independent status.

figures of total imports or exports; almost all Colonies exclude transit and transhipment trade from their main statistics, but bunker exports (whether separately recorded or not) may or may not form part of merchandise exports; the bulk of the bunker trade is in re-exported fuel in most Colonies. The treatment of domestically produced gold also varies in the trade returns. Northern Rhodesia and Sarawak include gold as merchandise; other Colonies (East and West Africa, Fiji) show gold exported in the separate category of bullion and specie.

One other special category—the general entrepôt trade—needs particular mention. Entrepôt trade is considerable in many Colonies, and of dominating importance to Singapore, Hong Kong, and Aden. Neither Singapore nor Hong Kong maintains separate records of entrepôt trade (which would be a formidable undertaking), and each of them shows only total imports and total exports in the statistics; the effect of this is examined in more detail in later paragraphs. The bulk of the trade of Aden Colony is entrepôt or transhipment traffic, and Aden is a free port which does not levy import duties proper. Consequently the published statistics are not of the quality or relevance found in other Colonies, e.g., declared values are considered unreliable by the Aden authorities.

Titles of the annual returns, and of the monthly or quarterly returns where these exist, are quoted in the " Notes on individual Colonies " which follow the chart. The publications referred to are obtainable from the Crown Agents for the Colonies. Monthly and quarterly returns vary greatly, from Malaya, which issues very detailed monthly data some 2 months after the end of the month in question, to the small Colony producing two or three typescript pages. Substantial progress has been made in reducing delays mainly caused by lack of staff and printing difficulties in publishing returns.

Commodity classification. From 1891 onwards, most Colonies based their classifications of trade by commodities on practice and experience in the United Kingdom. For imports, many classifications currently in operation follow the United Kingdom pattern—sometimes in detail (as with Malaya, Cyprus, and Nyasaland), but sometimes with Class III manufactured imports condensed into three groups: textiles, metals, miscellaneous (as for West Africa, Barbados, British Guiana, and Mauritius). This grouping of manufactures is an example of the persistence of the classification system recommended in 1891. For exports, classifications are not generally so elaborate, since most Colonies have a highly specialized export trade; sometimes a simple listing suffices.

However, alphabetical listings still survive. Sometimes the alphabetical order is in one list (as Brunei, Sarawak, Bermuda, Tonga); sometimes it is within a few broad classes (as Malta, Bahamas, British Honduras,

Dominica, Grenada). Fiji shows 11 classes with items listed alphabetically within each.

Northern Rhodesia has a different but well-developed classification, which is divided into 13 classes broadly by the nature of component materials.

As noted in the historical account above, recommendations on practice have come to lay greater stress on international classifications. In 1947–1948, several important Colonies (four in East Africa, Hong Kong, and Jamaica) introduced the League of Nations Minimum List as their classification system. This, of course, was done before the adoption by the United Nations of the Standard International Trade Classification (SITC) which, since 1951, is coming increasingly into use in the colonial territories.

Valuation. The Colonies have been urged to base their trade valuations on c.i.f. for imports and f.o.b. for exports, and in general they do so. For imports, a change to c.i.f. valuation has been made only since 1939 for a few small Colonies, the latest being Seychelles in 1950; Bermuda still uses f.o.b. values. A few Colonies (*e.g.*, Barbados, Mauritius) continue to value imports f.o.b. for duty purposes, but record them c.i.f. in the statistics. The main exceptions to c.i.f. valuation are in Northern Rhodesia and Nyasaland, landlocked territories with special difficulties which are described later.

Within the c.i.f. valuation, however, the items of cost included vary from Colony to Colony. In most cases, declarations by importers are employed, usually with considerable checking by Customs (particularly for dutiable goods). Even so, adjustments often need to be made, *e.g.*, when the invoice values are inappropriate because goods are being sold to subsidiary companies below market prices. In checking, Colonies usually compare declared values with " open market values " in the territory, but some relate them to the prices ruling in the exporting country at the time of export (with insurance and freight added).

Evidence suggests that, for a few Colonies, import valuations are still somewhat unreliable. Sometimes a large proportion of the import business is handled by a small number of traders, and the Customs authorities must depend very much on these traders so far as accuracy of valuation is concerned. The peculiar difficulties of Northern Rhodesia and Nyasaland have led them to employ complex systems of valuation, and the import statistics must be handled with care. For example, imports from a particular country of origin may be valued differently according as they come by direct or indirect routes.

Imports of currency notes and coin are often large, since the whole of the Colony's requirements may be imported. Until 1950, many Colonies (other than those in the West Indies) followed the practice of recording them at *face value*, not as merchandise but under the heading of bullion and specie. No information was given on cost value, for addition to the merchandise records. Colonies were advised in 1950 to follow the United Kingdom practice of including the imports as merchandise at cost value.

The valuation of exports on an f.o.b. basis presents difficulties in many Colonies. The prices realized for produce exported are not always known at the time of export, and there may be no alternative specification of value to employ. Some produce is entirely for export with no local markets or prices. Again, the goods may be supplied to a parent company abroad at a nominal value. Further, export duties are quite commonly levied, and, in the past, these may or may not have been included in f.o.b. valuations. It was not until 1950 that Colonies were asked specifically to include duties in the value of exports; at that time some of the smaller Colonies (*e.g.*, Somaliland, Windward Islands) excluded them.

Very special problems have arisen since 1940 in the valuation of cocoa, palm oil, palm kernels, and other export produce of West Africa. These products have been marketed centrally, and local practice in preparing trade statistics was to record f.o.b. cost price rather than f.o.b. selling price (which was considerably greater). Other important cases of undervaluation of exports, at various times, have been minerals from Northern Rhodesia and iron ore from Sierra Leone. Further, until 1950 in Sierra Leone, exports of diamonds escaped valuation entirely since the trade was recorded only in carats. The effects of these undervaluations are examined in detail below.

Apart from these particular problems, export valuations may be regarded as fairly reliable in general. However, the difficulties in Colonial conditions of valuing produce accurately at the time of export must be recognized. The standard of accuracy achieved in recording, for both imports and exports, is being steadily improved with the aim of bringing it to a level comparable with that attained in more developed countries, with their greater experience of what is required.

Country designations. Since the 1920 recommendations it has been broadly true that Colonies credit imports, as far as possible, to country of origin. Some smaller Colonies find it difficult to follow this practice consistently, since many imports may not come direct and with only the country of consignment known. Indeed, Brunei, North Borneo, and Sarawak are so dependent on the entrepôt port of Singapore that they are unable to maintain any records by country. On the other hand, because of the system of Imperial Preference for goods of United Kingdom origin, most Colonies have reliable figures of imports of dutiable goods from the United Kingdom.

The definition of country of " origin " is generally that country in which the last process (*i.e.*, manufacture) is performed. Consequently, cotton goods woven in Japan and finished in the United Kingdom are credited to the United Kingdom; trade of this kind has been increasing in the period since World War II.

Exports are similarly credited to what is usually denoted as country of " final destination." This must often be qualified by " as far as is known " at the time of export. To some extent, moreover, it is inevitable that country of consignment is shown, particularly in small Colonies off the main shipping routes.

East Africa. The need to consider the area as a whole as well as the three individual territories gives rise to many special problems because of the large volume of inter-territorial trade both in local produce and in " transfers " (i.e. goods imported from outside East Africa and consigned from one territory to another). Different solutions of these problems resulted in changes in the method of recording trade statistics in 1949 and in 1950.

Prior to 1949 Kenya and Uganda were treated as a single unit and Tanganyika as another in the *Annual Trade Reports*, each treating the other as a foreign country. Goods imported from outside East Africa and subsequently transferred from one unit to another were recorded both as an import and a re-export of the transferring territory and again as an import of the receiving territory. Local produce exported to the other unit was included in domestic exports. The domestic exports of Tanganyika exported *via* Mombasa (Kenya) entered also into the import and re-export statistics of Kenya-Uganda. Trade was valued at the borders of each unit except that imports into Tanganyika *via* Mombasa were valued at that port.

In 1949, the trade statistics of the three territories were placed on a common basis and inter-territorial trade in local produce excluded. " Total Imports " (*i.e.*, all imports originating outside East Africa, whether received direct or by transfer from another East African territory) and " Re-exports (including ' transfers ') " were given for each of the three territories. From 1949 all trade is valued at the port of entry or exit irrespective of the territory to or from which the goods are consigned. Thus, for Uganda, imports are recorded at a slightly lower and exports at a slightly higher value than if the goods had been valued at the Uganda border. This applies also to that part of the external trade of Tanganyika which passes through Kenya. Domestic exports to countries outside East Africa are credited only to the territory in which they were produced even when they pass through one of the other territories before shipment abroad.

In 1950 there was a further change ; the trade of each territory was put on a net basis, *i.e.*, " transfers " of imported goods were deducted from the imports of the transferring territory and added to those of the receiving territory. It follows that " transfers " no longer enter into the re-export figures.

Although this elimination of " transfers " sometimes results in negative import totals, due to " transfers " of goods imported in the previous year or transferred at a higher value than when originally imported, this treatment does allow the net trade of East Africa as a whole to be easily calculated from the territorial totals, whereas in years prior to 1950 comparable figures can only be deduced by considerable adjustment. In 1949 (inter-territorial trade in local produce having already been eliminated) it is only necessary to deduct the value of " transfers " of imported goods from the recorded imports and re-exports to arrive at comparable figures. Prior to 1949 it is necessary to deduct from total imports all imports of the local produce of other East African territories and also all re-exports to those territories. Domestic exports must be adjusted by deducting exports to other East African territories and adding back any such exports subsequently re-exported outside East Africa. Re-exports must be adjusted by deducting both re-exports to other East African territories and also re-exports of their produce outside East Africa. All the totals required for these adjustments are given in the published reports with the exception of Tanganyika's re-exports of Kenya and Uganda produce. These, however, may be estimated by examining the main tables for re-exports of commodities originally imported from Kenya and Uganda (*e.g.*, butter, tea, hides and skins). In cases where another source is important, it is necessary to assume that Kenya and Uganda's share of the re-exports is proportional to their share of the imports.

It will thus be evident that it is possible to ascertain values of net imports, of re-exports, and of domestic exports for the whole area both in total and by commodity on a comparable basis. The same cannot be said for the imports and re-exports of the individual territories since Kenya and Uganda were treated as one unit before 1949. Separate totals for domestic exports were, however, given.

Since the country of origin of re-exports is not recorded it is not possible to deduce with any degree of accuracy, the countrywise distribution of a particular territory's net imports in the years prior to 1950. Similarly, an accurate direction of trade in respect of those domestic exports which were consigned to another East African territory and subsequently re-exported is not ascertainable from the recorded statistics prior to 1949.

One of the results of showing separate import statistics for Kenya and Uganda from 1949 onwards was to increase to a great extent the amount of duplication in the total East African figures, including " transfers." This fact should always be borne in mind when studying the change in pattern by country through time.

Northern Rhodesia and Nyasaland.   Both these territories lie inland. The valuation of imports and exports therefore presents special difficulties. For Northern Rhodesia, goods which are imported direct from overseas, *e.g.*, by the most direct route through Portuguese East Africa, are valued f.o.b. at the port of the country of supply.   Goods which originate in or are re-exported by other African territories, are valued f.o.r. (free on rail) at the place whence consigned.   Imports are recorded in the trade returns by countries of origin (so far as possible), and it is not therefore feasible, in all cases, to determine the basis of valuation of goods which originate overseas and which may or may not have been imported direct.   The December 1950 issue of the Northern Rhodesia *Economic and Statistical Bulletin* [14] includes estimates of the necessary adjustments for freight and insurance in order to arrive at " frontier " values for imports for the years 1945 to 1949.   In 1949 the necessary adjustment is given as £1,595,000 (total recorded imports being £21,266,000).   The comment is made that the adjustment is no higher because a very high proportion of all merchandise imports into Northern Rhodesia is accounted for by re-exports from Southern Rhodesia and the Union of South Africa.

Exports of metals, the bulk of Northern Rhodesia's export trade, are valued by various special arrangements.   Since the prices which will be received are often not known at the time of export, values based on past prices realized overseas or on market quotations (less insurance and freight charges) may be accepted.   Other exports are valued f.o.r. at place of despatch in Northern Rhodesia.   The issue of the *Bulletin* cited above states that mineral exports may have been undervalued by over £2 million in 1947 (total recorded exports in that year were about £21 million), and there is also doubt about the valuation in later years.   The matter is currently being investigated by comparing recorded exports with quantities of minerals produced, quantities railed, and company receipts from sales.

On the valuation of imports, Nyasaland's statistics are rather nearer to " frontier " values than Northern Rhodesia's.   Goods which are imported direct from abroad (*i.e.*, through Portuguese ports) are valued c.i.f. at the port of arrival.   Imports from contiguous territories are valued f.o.r. In order to allow for the greater cost of freight in respect of goods imported from non-contiguous African territories, valuation is the cost

[14] Published by the Central African Statistical Office, Salisbury, Southern Rhodesia.

of goods at the place of purchase plus 10 per cent. So far as is known no estimates, corresponding to those for Northern Rhodesia, have been made of the amount which should be added to arrive at true frontier values. The valuation of Nyasaland's exports on the basis of the price received has so far not proved possible owing to the geographical position of the territory and the fact that prices are often not known at the time of exportation. The values of principal exports, with the exception of tobacco, are fixed annually by a valuation committee acting on the advice of representative growers and exporters, and are based on market prices in the country of destination less costs of insurance and freight. This method of valuation is particularly unsatisfactory when prices are changing rapidly and there is reason to believe that the value of exports has been considerably underestimated.

West Africa. The main difficulty which occurs when using West African trade accounts from about 1940 onwards arises from the method of valuation used for certain exported agricultural products—commodities for the most part purchased and disposed of by Central Marketing Boards. These Boards stem from the West African Cocoa Control Board which was set up by the Colonial Office shortly after the outbreak of World War II. At a later stage this board, its name changed to the West African Produce Control Board, became also the sole purchaser of West African palm oil and oil seeds. This Board was situated in London, the actual handling of the produce being left to local merchants. It is this circumstance which was no doubt largely responsible for the method of valuation adopted.

After the war, the functions and the accumulated profits (about £25 million for cocoa and £18 million for palm oil and oil seeds) of the West African Produce Control Board were transferred at various dates to a number of newly created Marketing Boards operating in the individual West African territory.[15]

From adjustments and revisions which have subsequently been published,[16] it appears that these centrally marketed products were valued at what may be defined as an " f.o.b. cost price," *i.e.*, the price paid to the producer plus the costs incidental to placing goods aboard ship, and *not* at the f.o.b. selling price. The products principally affected were bananas, benniseed, cocoa, cotton, groundnuts, palm kernels, and palm oil (Nigeria); cocoa (Gold Coast); benniseed, cocoa, coffee, groundnuts,

---

[15] See W. L. Bloomfield, " West African Farmer and World Markets," *Journal of the Royal Society of Arts*, 2nd December, 1949, Vol. XCVIII, 4809, for information on the origin and objects of the Marketing Boards.

[16] Nigeria: *Annual Trade Report*, 1949; *Summary of Overseas Trade*, 1950. Gold Coast: *Annual Trade Reports*, 1947, 1948; *Supplement to Annual Trade Report*, 1949. Gambia: *Annual Trade Report*, 1949.

palm kernels, palm oil (Sierra Leone); groundnuts (Gambia). All these products are currently valued on the correct basis. The difference in these two valuations is in fact a large one. Account of it must, therefore, be taken when considering aggregates containing the unrevised values of these commodities.

Further undervaluation in the accounts of Sierra Leone should be noted: until 1950 the export of diamonds was recorded by carats only and the value omitted (subsequent reports include the value of diamonds exported in total tables).

Unless account is taken of these matters, and also of the former practice of recording imports of currency notes and coin at face value, a very misleading picture of the balance of trade of the territories with the world as a whole, and with individual countries is obtained.

Singapore and Federation of Malaya. The trade statistics shown in the monthly publication *Malayan Statistics—External Trade* relate to the Colony of Singapore and to the Federation of Malaya (the whole area being hereinafter referred to as Malaya). The main statistics relate to Malaya as a whole, and trade between the separate territories is not included. Brief summary tables relate to the direct imports and exports of Singapore and the Federation separately. However, as neither inter-trade nor re-exports are recorded, these tables give no indication of the size of the domestic exports or the retained imports of the two territories. In 1950 Singapore handled approximately 74 per cent of Malaya's total of direct imports and approximately 63 per cent of her total of direct exports, these percentages being somewhat higher than in 1939.

Before the war the Malayan trade registration area comprised the Straits Settlements, the Federated Malay States and the Unfederated Malay States, this being the same area as at present except for the pre-war inclusion of Labuan, which was of negligible importance, and the trade statistics were, as at present, on a Pan-Malayan basis. The publication of trade statistics was resumed at the end of the Japanese occupation in August 1946.

A substantial proportion of Malaya's trade is of an entrepôt nature, but separate records of re-exports have never been kept. Therefore, accurate statistics of domestic exports and of imports for local consumption are not available. Section IV of the chapter on the Straits Settlements in the *Economic Survey of the Colonial Empire* (1937) (His Majesty's Statistical Office, 1940) contains, for 1937, detailed estimates of the domestic exports and re-exports of the Straits Settlements and the Federated and Unfederated Malay States, as well as an estimate of the value of the trade among the three territories. At that time the value of re-exports was slightly in excess of the value of domestic exports (inter-trade being excluded in both cases). Estimates[17] suggest that in 1950 the value of domestic exports was slightly (13 per cent) in excess of the value of re-exports. In 1950 the value of Malayan retained imports was about 50 per cent of the total value of imports.

The most important commodities which are produced and exported by Malaya and also re-exported are rubber, tin, copra, coconut oil, and palm oil. It has been estimated that in 1950 domestic exports of rubber were approximately 56 per cent by quantity and 59 per cent by value of total exports of this commodity. The corresponding percentages for copra (and coconut oil) and tin were approximately 59 per cent by quantity, 49 per cent by value, and 88 per cent by quantity, 87 per cent by value, respectively. In making these estimates it was assumed that there were no retained imports of these commodities (and allowance was made for the greater value of the goods when re-exported than when imported).

Among the most important commodities which are imported and also re-exported by Malaya are fuel (and petroleum products), cotton piece goods, other textile manufactures, manufactured tobacco, and vehicles including parts. It has been estimated that in 1950 retained imports by value of fuel (and petroleum products), cotton manufactures, and other textile manufactures were approximately 31 per cent, 45 per cent, and 68 per cent of total imports (respectively). In making these estimates it was assumed that there were no domestic exports of these goods and allowance was made for the lower value of the goods when imported than when re-exported.

Since the Far Eastern territories of Brunei, North Borneo, and Sarawak are supplied almost wholly from Singapore, the Malayan trade statistics provide a fairly complete picture of the trade of these areas. But the value of the statistics is reduced by the necessary lack of data on the sources of Malayan re-exports and by the difficulty of adhering consistently to the aim of recording exports by country of final destination. For cargoes declared on optional bills of lading the first port nominated is taken as the country of final destination. Goods exported from Malaya to the United States of Indonesia and Borneo are, however, nearly all consigned direct to and consumed in those countries.

Imports are recorded so far as possible by countries of origin. From August 1949, a footnote in the *Trade Returns* records the value of imports of United States origin which were imported *via* Hong Kong. These statistics are of value for balance of payments purposes as these imports are not financed from the central dollar reserves of the sterling area.

The Malayan trade statistics are notable for the speed with which they are prepared and published. The bulky monthly report, with cumulative

[17] The National Income of Malaya, 1947–49 (Chap. VI) by Frederic Benham.

totals for the year, becomes available in London two months after the end of the month to which it relates. Special advance returns are prepared for important commodities such as rubber and tin. Any errors that may be discovered in earlier figures are corrected in the cumulative totals. All the value figures are given in Malayan dollars.

Hong Kong. The collection of trade statistics did not start until 1918; it was discontinued during the period July 1925 to March 1930 and again during the Japanese occupation, being finally resumed in April 1946. Post-war published statistics have been available from June 1948. Until the year 1940 annual trade statistics were contained in *Hong Kong Trade and Shipping Returns*. The post-war publication *Hong Kong Trade Returns* was on a monthly basis only until 1952 and annual totals could only be computed by the addition of the monthly figures. From 1952 cumulative totals are also given each month so that the December issue is tantamount to an annual report. It is intended to publish annual reports for the post-war years up to and including 1951 as soon as printing difficulties can be overcome. The monthly *Supplement* to the Hong Kong Government *Gazette* includes tables of imports and exports giving countries and (separately) principal commodities. These tables show monthly averages for the current year and the 3 previous years.

Imports and exports are now classified according to a revised list based on the Standard International Trade Classification of the United Nations. In the country classification there is considerable grouping of British countries—British East Africa, British Central Africa, British West Africa, and British West Indies each being shown as groups only. Values are recorded in Hong Kong dollars and local units of weight are largely used.

The prosperity of Hong Kong depends on its entrepôt trade. Though no separate records of its value can be kept, it probably represents the bulk of the total imports and total exports of the Colony.

West Indies. Although the various islands of the British West Indies (together with Bermuda and Bahamas and including the mainland territories of British Guiana and British Honduras) form a natural regional group, the separate statistics of trade present no more uniformity than is the natural consequence of the common historical development of the statistics of all the older British Colonies. An example of lack of uniformity is the fact that, whereas most of the territories record their values in West Indian dollars, three of them use sterling.

This lack of uniformity is being tackled in several ways. The *Report of the Commission on the Establishment of a Customs Union in the British Caribbean Area*, 1948–1950 (C.O. 268, 1951) has made many recommendations directly bearing on statistical matters, the most relevant of which are:

that a common commodity classification for imports and exports should be used for statistical as well as tariff purposes ; that the trade statistics for all the territories should be abstracted in Jamaica (from material sent daily by each territory); and that certain statistics of intercolonial trade should be prepared by each territory. This *Report* is being studied by the governments concerned. The Caribbean Commission is also urging the need for greater uniformity of trade statistics in the whole Caribbean area (including non-British territories). At a Trade Statistics Conference organized by the Commission in October 1950, it was recommended that territorial governments should consider the adoption of the United Nations Standard International Trade Classification (SITC).

A new classification of trade by commodities, based on the League of Nations Minimum List, was introduced in Jamaica in 1947; Trinidad adopted the United Nations Standard International Trade Classification in 1951. In each case the previous classification was similar to that of the United Kingdom.

TABULAR CHART AND NOTES

Tabular Chart. This section provides a tabular chart comparing some of the more important characteristics of the trade statistics of individual colonies and dependencies, based on an analysis of the *Trade Reports* for 1949.

A discussion of the several columns in the chart is found in this chapter in the section " Use and Appraisal of the Statistics—Characteristics of trade returns."

Notes on individual Colonies. The following notes indicate the sources of the data, area by area. Where the information for a given cell in the Tabular Chart could not be summarized satisfactorily by a code letter, an asterisk (*) was inserted, thereby keying the chart cell to the explanation in these notes.

EAST AND CENTRAL AFRICA

Somaliland Protectorate: Description of trade returns based mainly on *Annual Report* of 1939; returns resumed after World War II, with a brief *Report* for 1949; later *Reports* to be fuller.
*Column 5. Separate records of goods in transit to and from Ethiopia and Somalia, the Protectorate being one channel for the trade of these countries.
East Africa: Annual data in *Annual Trade Report of Kenya, Uganda and Tanganyika* (East African Customs and Excise Department); monthly data in *Trade and Information Report*. Prior to 1949, separate reports issued for Kenya and Uganda (combined statistics) and for Tanganyika.
*Column 3. Summary tables for imports distinguishing 22 countries or groups of countries.

TABULAR CHART

Trade Statistics of British Colonies and Dependencies

[Asterisk (*) denotes items explained further in " Notes on Individual Colonies."]

Colony or Dependency	CHARACTERISTICS OF ANNUAL TRADE RETURNS							
	Returns of		Country-commodity Tables	Import and Export Lists	Special Categories			Interim Trade Returns
	Imports	Exports			Transit Trade	Bunker Exports	Government Imports	
	(1)	(2)	(3)	(4)	(5)	(6)	(7)	(8)
East and Central Africa								
Somaliland Protectorate.	TH	DR	na	x	s*	n	n	X
East Africa								
Kenya								
Uganda }	T	DR	a*	P	s	s	n	Mp
Tanganyika								
Zanzibar	T	DR	a*	P	s	s	s	Mp
Northern Rhodesia	T	DR	a*	P	n	n	n	Mp
Nyasaland	H	DR	na	x	n	n	s	Mp
West Africa								
Gambia	H	DR	na	P	s	n	n	X
Gold Coast	TH	DR	na	} West {	s	s*	n	Mp
Nigeria	TH	DR	na	} Africa	s*	s	s	Mp
Sierra Leone	TH	DR	na		s	s	s	Mp
Eastern								
Singapore and Federation of Malaya	T	T	a	P	n	s	n	Mp*
Brunei and North Borneo	(See Notes on individual colonies.)							
Sarawak	T	T	na	x	n	s*	n	X
Hong Kong	T	T	a	P	n	n	n	Mp*
Mediterranean								
Cyprus	TH	DR	a	x	s	s	s	Mp
Gibraltar	(See Notes on individual colonies.)							
Malta	TH	DR	a*	P	n*	s	n	Qp
West Indies								
Bahamas	TH	DR	a*	x	n	n	s*	Q* .
Barbados	TH	DR	na	P*	n	s*	s*	Qp
Bermuda	T	DR	na	x	n	s*	n	Q
British Guiana	TH	DR	a*	P	s	s	s*	MQ
British Honduras	TH	DR	a*	P	s*	n	s*	Mp
Jamaica	T	DR	na	P	s	n*	s	Mp
Leeward Islands	(See Notes on individual colonies.)							
Trinidad	TH	DR	a*	P	s	s	n	Qp
Windward Islands								
Dominica	T	TDR	na	x	n	n	n	Mp
Grenada	T	DR	na	x	n	n	s*	Mp
St. Lucia	TH	TDR	na	P	n	n	s	M
St. Vincent	TH	DR	na	P	n	n	s*	Mp
Miscellaneous								
Fiji	T	DR	a*	P	n	s*	n	M
Tonga	T	T	na	x	n	n	n	X
Falkland Islands	T	T	na	x	n	n	n	X
Aden	T	DR	a	x	s*	s*	n	Mp*
Mauritius	TH	DR	na	x	n	n*	s*	X
Seychelles	(See Notes on individual colonies.)							

Notation: (1) T = Total imports; H = Imports for home consumption.
(2) T = Total exports; D = Domestic exports; R = Re-exports.
(3) a = available; na = not available.
(4) P = Printed list; x = no list.
(5), (6), (7) s = separately recorded; n = not separately recorded.
(8) M = Monthly returns; Q = Quarterly returns; X = No returns; p = published.

Zanzibar: Annual data in *Zanzibar Protectorate Annual Trade Report* (Comptroller of Customs); monthly data in *Trade and Information Report*.

*Column 3. Tables relate to groups of commodities for 48 countries or groups of countries (imports), for 38 countries or groups (exports), and for 29 countries or groups (re-exports).

Northern Rhodesia: Annual data in *Statement of the Trade of Northern Rhodesia*; monthly data in *Economic and Statistical Bulletin*.
*Column 3.   Detailed tables for 7 countries.
Nyasaland: Annual data in *Annual Report on the Trade of the Protectorate* (Customs Department); monthly data in the *Gazette*.

WEST AFRICA

Gambia: Annual data in *Report on the Trade and Shipping of the Colony* (Collector of Customs).
Gold Coast: Annual data in *Gold Coast Trade Report*; monthly data in *Monthly Accounts* relating to external trade.
*Column 6.   Oil bunkers only distinguished; no supply of coal customarily available for bunkers.
Nigeria: Annual data in *Nigeria Trade Report* (Department of Statistics); monthly data in *Trade Summary*.
*Column 5.   Details of transit trade to and from French territory and totals of transhipment trade at each port.
Sierra Leone: Annual data in *Trade Report* of the Colony and Protectorate; monthly data in *Trade Statistics*.

EASTERN

Malaya: All data from *Malayan Statistics* (Registrar of Malayan Statistics), a monthly publication from April 1950.
*Column 8.   Annual data provided in cumulative totals for 12 months in monthly reports.
Brunei: No annual trade report prepared; principal imports and exports in 1948 and 1949 shown in *Report on Brunei* for the year 1949 (Colonial Office).
North Borneo: No *Annual Report* (Customs Department) published after 1939 until 1948; no annual trade report currently prepared; total values of imports and exports (and a few main items) in years up to 1949 shown in *Report on North Borneo* for the year 1949 (Colonial Office).   Monthly data in supplements to the *Gazette*.
Sarawak: Annual data appear in the *Gazette* of the Sarawak Government, and include figures by ports and by divisions of the territory.
*Column 6.   Record of Diesel bunkers.
Hong Kong: Monthly data in *Hong Kong Trade Returns* (Department of Commerce and Industry).   No cumulative totals were given prior to 1952. Supplements to the *Gazette* do show trade data including monthly averages for current and past years (*Column 8).

MEDITERRANEAN

Cyprus: Monthly data in *Import and Export Statistics*, with cumulative figures. More detailed annual data in *Statistics of Imports, Exports and Shipping* (Comptroller of Customs and Excise).
Gibraltar: No trade returns are prepared.   Exports are negligible.   Import statistics are collected; summary available in *Report on Gibraltar* for the year 1949 (Colonial Office).
Malta: Annual data in *Malta Trade Statistics* (Collector of Customs); quarterly data in supplements to the *Gazette*.

* Column 3.   Summary table for imports (and exports in some cases) for 39 countries.
* Column 5.   Total imports include transit goods unless transhipped under bond.

WEST INDIES

Bahamas: Annual data in *Report on Customs*, last published issue for 1942 Unpublished quarterly data relate to imports; exports are small (*Column 8).
* Column 3.   Tables (some very detailed) for 50 countries for imports, and for exports where appropriate.
* Column 7.   Dutiable items only.

Barbados: Annual data in *Report of the Comptroller of Customs*, last published for 1948.   Quarterly data in *Report on Trade and Agriculture*.
* Column 4.   Traders are required to declare according to lists.
* Column 6.   Oil bunkers only.
* Column 7.   Dutiable items only.

Bermuda: Annual data in *Imports and Exports, Shipping, Aircraft, etc.* (Collector of Customs).
* Column 6.   Bunkers to H.M. and U.S. Forces.

British Guiana: Annual data in *Annual Report of the Comptroller of Customs*, last published for 1947, subsequently prepared in typescript.   Quarterly data in *Trade and Economic Report*.
* Column 3.   Tables (of varying detail) for 31 countries for imports, and for exports where appropriate.
* Column 7.   Dutiable items only.

British Honduras: Annual data in Customs Report;   monthly data in supplements to the *Gazette*.
* Column 3.   Tables for 14 countries for imports, and for exports where appropriate.
* Column 5.   Separate records being kept of transhipment trade (excluded from totals) from 1949 onwards;   previously trade included in total without separate record.
* Column 7.   Dutiable items only.

Jamaica: Annual data in *External Trade of Jamaica* (Central Bureau of Statistics); monthly data in Central Bureau of Statistics *Bulletin*.
* Column 6.   Bunkers neither recorded separately nor included in total exports.

Leeward Islands: No published data since *Blue Book* for 1945.   Statistics relate to group of islands as a whole, but trade of separate islands distinguished and interpresidency (internal) trade recorded.

Trinidad: Annual data in *Administration Report of the Comptroller of Customs and Excise;* quarterly data in *Quarterly Economic Report*.
* Column 3.   Tables for 12 countries.

Dominica: Annual reports not prepared since 1939 (when Dominica was one of the presidencies of the Leeward Islands), but brief statements published as supplements to the *Gazette*, which also contain monthly data.

Grenada: Annual data in *Returns of Imports and Exports;* monthly data in the *Gazette* Notices.
* Column 7.   Dutiable items only.

St. Lucia: Complete annual returns not published since 1941, but those for 1946–1949 are being printed.

St. Vincent: Annual data in *Imports and Exports*, but last published for 1947; principal imports and exports in 1948 and 1949 shown in *Report on St. Vincent* for the year 1949 (Colonial Office). Monthly data in supplements (Monthly Enclosure) to the *Gazette*.

* Column 7. Dutiable items only.

MISCELLANEOUS

Fiji: Annual data in *Trade Report*, the last for the year 1949 (Legislative Council Paper 8, 1950).

* Column 3. Principal articles imported for 18 countries.

* Column 6. Shown as re-exports of coal and oil for ships' stores.

Tonga: Annual data in *Statement of Trade and Navigation*, compiled from documents collected by the Department of Customs.

Falkland Islands: No published annual returns. Detailed statistics prepared in typescript for use in *Blue Book* until 1944. Brief statistics for 1946–1949 shown in *Report on the Falkland Islands* for the year 1949 (Colonial Office). Fuller reports from 1950.

Aden: Description of trade returns relates to statistics of Aden Colony published until 1946 in *Trade and Navigation Report;* the bulk of the trade is entrepôt and transhipment.

* Column 5. Transhipment trade recorded only by packages, and by countries of origin and destination.

* Column 6. By quantity only.

* Column 8. *Aden Port Trust Returns*, published in Government Gazette. Subsequent *Trade and Navigation Reports* for the Colony relate to 1947, 1948, and 1949, and show quantities only (except for dutiable goods) since declared values are considered unreliable. Eastern Aden Protectorate maintains summary records of trade by sea, as shown in *Report on Aden* for the year 1948 (Colonial Office). Western Aden Protectorate, largely supplied overland from the Colony, has no trade statistics.

Mauritius: *Annual Trade Returns*, last published for 1949.

* Column 6. Recorded but not included in trade returns.

* Column 7. Imports by government, local authorities, etc.

Seychelles: No published data since *Trade Report* for the year 1945.

CHAPTER 17

Continental Europe and Dependencies

H. VAUTHIER
Economic Commission for Europe, Geneva

HISTORICAL DEVELOPMENT

Early history. There have been some statistics of international trade in Europe for a long time. In France, for example, there are partial records going back to the beginning of the 18th century, though the first statistics of use in economic analysis date only from 1827. Several European countries began to collect and to publish regular trade statistics about the same time. France was followed by Belgium in 1831, and then by Sweden and the Netherlands. Some years later, there were published the first statistics of the German Confederation (1836), Russia, Austria, Norway, Denmark, and Spain. Italian statistics appeared about 1870, and those of Switzerland in 1885.

The early statistics are of varying usefulness, particularly as regards the valuation of merchandise and the crediting of trade to countries of provenance. At first, almost all countries used fixed official values for each item of merchandise (" valeurs officielles permanentes "), *i.e.*, values per unit of quantity which, once fixed, were not varied over time. Two countries (Germany, Norway) showed trade by quantities, but not by value; the German statistics became complete in 1880 only. It was about the middle of the 19th century that some countries followed the lead of

France and Belgium in adopting the system of official values revised periodically by a commission. Finally, following British practice, countries began to record trade according to values declared by importers and exporters. The different systems each had advocates, and a change from one system to another was often strongly resisted.

At the beginning of the 20th century (1901–1905) the position on valuation can be summarized as follows: [1]

Fixed official values: Greece (values fixed in 1889, after 1901 values revised periodically).

Official values revised annually: Austria, France (" valeurs actuelles "), Germany, Hungary, Italy, Norway, Rumania, Spain, Sweden.

Declared values: Bulgaria, Portugal, Russia.

Mixed systems:

Belgium—declared values for a few products, otherwise official values revised annually.

Denmark—official values with estimation of the cost of transport.

Netherlands—declared values for a few products, otherwise fixed official values.

Switzerland—declared values for exports and for a few imports, other imports by official values.

As regards definition of countries to which trade is credited, it is difficult to determine the system actually used by different countries. Almost all countries sought to classify imports by country of origin or production, and exports by country of consumption or final destination as far as known. Exceptions at the beginning of the 20th century include Greece, which recorded imports by country of immediate provenance, and the Netherlands, which followed the same practice for imports arriving across the land frontier. Spain showed imports classified both by country of origin and by country of immediate consignment. By 1913, Denmark, Norway, and Sweden indicated trade by countries of purchase or sale. Portugal also classified imports by country of purchase while specifying exports according to " real consignment "; Rumania used the converse procedure of showing the destination of exports by country of sale.

Changes since 1913. During and after World War I, there were many changes in the compilation and presentation of European trade statistics. For example, the change-over from official values to a valuation based on declarations by importers and exporters, which began before 1913, was accelerated during the post-war years. Fixed official values were elimina-

---

[1] The corresponding position in 1913 and in 1926 is shown in a table in a memorandum published by the League of Nations: *Memorandum on International Trade and Balances of Payments* 1912–1926, Vol. II (1928).

ted from the Netherlands statistics in 1917, and Austria introduced declared values in 1924. In France, the monthly publications showed imports by declared values from 1921 and exports from 1927 (but only from 1929 in the annual volumes). By 1926, all countries in Europe had adopted the system of declared values, with the exception of Rumania, Russia, and Spain (imports and exports), of France (exports), and of Germany and Norway (imports). In 1952 there were no exceptions to the declared-value system among those countries which publish trade statistics, though for a few specific commodities official quotations, as opposed to declared values, may have been used in some cases (*e.g.*, exports from Portugal).

The main changes after 1918 were in the political grouping and in the extent of the various national territories in Europe, and consequently in the Customs areas to which the trade statistics related. In particular, the new states created by the Versailles Treaty began publication of their trade statistics in the early 1920's. The position between 1912 and 1927 in this respect—and also as regards methods of compilation and presentation of the statistics—is fully described in the 1928 *Memorandum* of the League of Nations already cited.

There were further changes during the 1930's and particularly after World War II, including modifications in territories and Customs areas. The trade statistics of the USSR have not been published since the period before World War II, and subsequent to the war the statistics of countries in Eastern Europe were almost entirely suppressed. The publication of detailed Czechoslovakian figures, for example, ceased after December 1948, and even the value of total imports and total exports was not released after September 1950. Some details were published in late 1951 in quantity and value at 1937 prices without country breakdown by Poland, alone among the countries within the Soviet sphere. Estimates of the total value of trade between each of the countries of Eastern Europe, and between these countries and other countries, have been made for some postwar years by the United Nations Economic Commission for Europe.[2]

The statistics of Yugoslavia were again published (August 1951) and the first issue gives a summary of trade from 1945 onwards. The trade records of Germany have been completely reorganized since World War II, and they relate to a territory which is very different from that covered by pre-war data.

Otherwise, the changes arising from World War II have not been sufficiently great to affect comparability very seriously. Despite modifications in area and in methods of classification, it is true that statistics of trade,

[2] See *Economic Survey of Europe for* 1948 and the *Economic Bulletin for Europe*, particularly Vol. 2, No. 2, and Vol. 3, No. 2.

in total and for particular commodities, are broadly comparable from the early 1920's to 1952 for each of the countries of Europe publishing such data, apart from Germany.

Individual countries. The following sets out some of the more important features of the trade statistics of individual European countries and their overseas dependencies. Attention is concentrated on special characteristics which vary from one country to another, and on changes since 1920. No further reference is made to the USSR.

Austria. Up to World War I, the trade statistics relate to the Austro-Hungarian Empire as it was variously composed (separate statistics also exist for the Austrian part of the empire). The statistics for Austria proper date from the second half of 1919. Because of the Anschluss, trade between Austria and Germany was excluded from Austrian external trade in 1938, and from 1939 to 1945 inclusive the Austrian statistics were amalgamated with those of Germany. A revised commodity classification was introduced in 1925. It was based primarily on the nature of the component material. In 1951, this was supplemented by the use of the Standard International Trade Classification (SITC) as drawn up by the United Nations.

Belgium-Luxembourg. On 1st May, 1922, an economic union between Belgium and Luxembourg came into force. Since that date, the trade statistics relate to the two countries taken together and trade between Belgium and Luxembourg disappeared from the records. After World War II, a Customs agreement was negotiated between Belgium-Luxembourg and the Netherlands and came into operation on 1st January, 1948. The trade statistics of the two areas are still published separately but with greater conformity. One main change in 1948 was the introduction of a new commodity classification, adopted in common by Belgium-Luxembourg and by the Netherlands. This was designed to conform with the recommendations of the League of Nations on Customs nomenclature (1937). In 1951, all the " passive improvement " trade (and also since 1922, the " active," *i.e.*, the processing of goods on foreign account, so important to the Belgian economy) was included in the " special trade " of Belgium-Luxembourg. For a time, in 1945–1946, imports of cereals and some minerals were valued at the prices ruling on domestic (internal) markets instead of c.i.f.

Belgian Congo and Ruanda Urundi. Detailed statistics are published for this territory, both monthly and annually. The valuation of exports is based on conventional f.o.b. values adjusted periodically by the Customs; export duties are added to the valuation.

Bulgaria. The pre-World War II statistics were published in detail annually, and there was also considerable detail published each month.

Imports were recorded by country of purchase and exports by country of sale; these criteria were adopted in 1906, the statistics for earlier years being on an origin/consumption basis, as far as possible. From 1935, for certain commodities, country of origin was recorded as well as country of purchase. The last annual trade statistics (relating to 1944) were published in 1946; figures for total trade were published up to May 1948.

Czechoslovakia. Until September 1938 the Czech trade statistics relate to the territory of the Czechoslovak Republic, as settled at the end of World War I. From 1st October, 1938, certain territory transferred to Germany, Hungary, Poland, and Austria was excluded. From 16th March to 31st July, 1939, the returns related to the Protectorate of Bohemia and Moravia, and *excluded* trade with the remainder of the German Customs Area (*i.e.*, the old Reich, Austria, and the Sudeten Territories). Prior to 1st January, 1923, the trade statistics were based on the pre-World War I Austria system (*i.e.*, imports recorded by country of origin and exports by country of consumption). As from 1923, imports were recorded by country of consignment (though additional information on country of production could be stated by the importer), and exports were recorded by country of sale, or by country of ultimate destination, where this was different and was known by the exporter.

Denmark. Before 1938, the " general trade " system was used in Danish trade statistics. From 1938, this was replaced by the " special trade " system. Immediately before World War II, the commodity classification was revised to conform to the Minimum List recommended by the League of Nations (1937). A further revision was made in 1951 when the Standard International Trade Classification of the United Nations (SITC) was adopted.

Finland. In 1918, Finland introduced the declared-value system of valuation of trade; previously official values were used, and these were different for trade with Russia than for trade with other countries. From the same date, trade was designated by country of purchase or sale, but from 1935 a second classification (by country of origin for imports and consignment for exports) has been used in conjunction with the first. Since World War II, goods exported as reparations are excluded from the commercial statistics, but are shown separately.

France. The French Customs area excluded Alsace and Lorraine from 1871 to 1918. It included Monaco but excluded Andorra. The main variation since 1918 concerns the inclusion or exclusion of the Saar. This territory was included in the Customs area from 10th January, 1925, until 17th February, 1935, and was included again from 1st April, 1948, onward. Before 1930, imports included fish landed from deep-sea (far-distant) fishing grounds, but subsequently this item has been excluded from recorded imports. Before 1948, the commodity classification used was not elaborate enough to be satisfactory. Starting with 1948, a more detailed classification was adopted, derived at least in part from the League of Nations recommendations on Customs nomenclature (1937). To overcome the break in continuity to some extent, the monthly returns from 1948 onward show the quantities and values of some important commodities imported and exported in 1938, 1946, and 1947 by the new classification. Although exports have always been shown classified by countries according to final destination (as far as this is known), there has been a change in practice in the corresponding designation of imports. Before 1934, imports were credited to the country of immediate consignment (" provenance effective actuelle "). This was changed in 1934 to country of origin.

French Union. The different territories of the French Union have adopted various systems and classifications in their trade statistics. It has generally not been possible to obtain homogeneous aggregates from the separate records. However, for 1938 and for years from 1945, the statistical service of the Ministère de la France d'outre-mer has compiled and published summary tables of the trade of the component territories. This aggregation has been made more feasible by the adoption by the French overseas countries (in 1950) of commodity classifications based on those introduced in the metropolitan statistics of 1948. The most complete statistics of trade, within the French Union, are probably those of French North Africa and Indochina. However, even for Algeria, it is only since the end of 1947 that declared values, rather than official values, have been used. Moreover, imports from France are taken from the French export statistics. The statistics of Morocco do not include trade with Tangier and the Spanish Zone. Imports into Indochina have been given since 1947 by country of origin instead of by country of consignment; this involved substantial regroupings since much of the trade of Indochina is through Hong Kong and Singapore.

Germany. For the period after World War I, the trade statistics of Germany need to be handled with great caution. The territory covered after 1918 was quite different from that of 1914, and the new frontiers were not completely controlled by the German authorities, with consequent defects in the recorded trade statistics. Values of trade, as shown in the statistics, are particularly difficult to interpret in the early 1920's because of the inflation of the currency and also probably because of official distortion intended to hide capacity for reparation payments. Though the territory of the Saar was part of Germany at different times, trade between Germany and the Saar is actually shown separately with foreign countries. The German Customs area, until the collapse in 1945, was extended to include Austria from 1939 and the occupied part of Czechoslovakia from October 1938. The trade statistics of what is now the Federal Republic have been subject to many changes since 1945. At first, the statistics were issued separately for the three zones by the Allied military governments, then by JEIA (Joint Export-Import Agency) for Bizone and by OFFI-COMEX for the French zone. The first post-war trade statistics in German, *i.e.*, with a German classification and the German language, date from July 1948. Finally, from 1st October, 1949, the statistics were published for the whole of the Federal Republic (the three zones and Western Berlin included with the Bizone from 15th December, 1948). Up to mid-1948, therefore, trade was valued only in dollars, as established by the Allied military governments. Later, the valuation was both in dollars and in West German marks. It was only from the beginning of 1951 that a single rate of exchange was used and the trade valued almost exclusively in a single currency (marks).

Greece. Declared values have been used uniformly in the Greek statistics only from 1926. From 1921 to 1925 inclusive, 17 of the most important commodities were recorded at official values, and up to 1920 all trade was so valued, the same official values being used for a commodity irrespective of its origin or destination.

Hungary. Separate trade statistics for Hungary prior to 1919 were published, even though at that time Hungary formed part of the Austro-Hungarian Customs Area. From October 1938, certain territory was transferred from Czechoslovakia to Hungary, and there were further additions to the area as a result of adjustments made during the war. After World War II, Hungary reverted to its pre-1938 area. Imports were recorded by country of commercial origin and exports by country of commercial destination. The commodity classification was based on the Hungarian tariff, but summaries were also prepared by degree of manufacture and use. The last figures published for the value of trade were for 1948; these also give an analysis of trade by country.

Ireland. What is now the Republic of Ireland became independent of the rest of the British Isles, and responsible for her own trade statistics, in March 1923. Previously the trade of the whole of Ireland with the rest of the world (outside the British Isles) was comprised within the British trade statistics, and also shown separately in these statistics from 1904 to 1921. From 1924, trade statistics have been published in Dublin for an unchanged Customs area, known first as the Irish Free State, then as Eire and now as the Republic of Ireland. The system followed in the trade statistics has been closely analogous to that of the United Kingdom. For example, the British version of the " general trade " grouping has been maintained, *i.e.*, total imports, exports of domestic produce, re-exports. Since 1925, all exports of horses (an important trade item) have been classed as exports of domestic produce, even when the horses were previously imported. Imports were originally designated by country of consignment, but in April 1935 a change was made to country of origin.

Italy. The territory and Customs area of Italy was enlarged after World War I by the inclusion of parts of the Austro-Hungarian Empire. Following World War II, however, Trieste came under international control. Italian trade statistics exclude the trade of Trieste from 15th September, 1947, but the December issues of the monthly trade returns show separate tabulations for the trade of Trieste with the rest of the world (outside Italy) on an annual basis. Nowhere in mid-1951 was the trade between Trieste and Italy shown. The commodity classification was changed in 1921 and revised 30 years later in July 1951. The present classification is based on the results of the work of the Study Group on European Customs Union in Brussels.

Netherlands. The Customs agreement with Belgium-Luxembourg resulted in a new commodity classification, introduced on 1st January, 1948, on a common basis with the other partner to the agreement. Some items important in the trade of the Netherlands have been subject to changes in practice, both before and after 1948. In 1920, foreign bunkers, previously excluded from exports, were shown separately but included within the export totals in the trade statistics. Similarly, in 1941, ships' stores imported for Dutch vessels were included for the first time in imports. Trade in diamonds, both imports and exports, has always been subject to Customs returns, but the records are known to be seriously incomplete. Consequently, no analysis of this trade by countries has been shown from October 1949. The designation of trade by countries has been changed, first from 1917 when imports were credited by country of purchase and exports by country of sale, and then from 1927 when the country of consignment was adopted as the criterion for all trade.

Netherlands West Indies. The trade statistics are not always very detailed for these possessions. Good annual statistics are available for Surinam.

Norway. The trade classifications of Norway have been similar to those of Denmark. In 1939, the " general trade " system was abandoned, and from that year the trade statistics have been shown on the " special trade " system. The commodity classification was revised about the same time to follow the League of Nations Minimum List (1937). Norway is expected to introduce (in 1953) the United Nations Standard International Trade Classification (SITC) as the national nomenclature.

Poland. From 1922, the Polish statistics include the Free City of Danzig, which formed a Customs Union with Poland in that year; the free port area of Danzig was, however, outside the Customs Union. From October 1938 certain Czechoslovak territory was transferred to Poland. Imports are recorded by country of origin or production, and exports by country of probable consumption. For the years from 1934 up to World War II, the annual trade returns contain a summary on the League of Nations Minimum List classification. Certain foreign trade data are still published in the " Statistical News " of the Polish Central Statistical Office (total trade by weight, divided into 20 commodity groups, and values at 1937 prices). The last published statistics of trade by country relates to 1947 (published in 1948).

Portugal. The classification of Portuguese trade by countries, adopted in 1911, was by country of purchase for imports and of consignment for exports. This was changed in 1937, and from that year Portugal has grouped imports according to country of origin and exports according to country of consumption.

Portuguese Overseas Territories. Annual statistics of trade on a commodity-country basis are published by each separate territory, Macao, and Timor, with a delay of about 10 months for Angola and Mozambique, and much longer for the rest of them. Latest monthly statistics available are issued in the *Monthly Bulletin* of the National Institute of Statistics in Lisbon, an annual summary being in addition included in the *Overseas Statistical Yearbook* published by the same Institute. Direct and indirect transit trade is also shown.

Rumania. There were territorial adjustments between 1939 and 1947, and the trade figures appear to relate to the territory actually under Rumanian administration. Imports were recorded c.i.f. but exports were valued at officially fixed unit values up to 1937; from 1938, exports were based on values as declared by exporters. Imports were recorded by country of purchase and exports by country of sale. No official trade statistics have been published since World War II, though estimates of Rumanian trade have been given in various United Nations publications.

Spain. During the civil war (1936–1938) there were no published statistics of Spanish foreign trade. Up to 1921, valuation of trade was according to official values, which were established in 1912 and remained unchanged. From 1922, the values were revised periodically, and from 1931 declared values have been used. All values are still expressed in gold pesetas (with consequent ease of conversion into dollars). A double classification of trade by countries (by origin and by " immediate consignment " for imports) was in force for many years; this was given up in 1918 and from that year a single classification (by origin and " real destination ") has been used.

Spanish Possessions. The trade publications issued in Madrid, both monthly and annual, give separate data for the trade of the Canary Isles and of the two ports of Ceuta and Melilla in Spanish Morocco. There are also annual data, published in Tetuan, of the trade of the Spanish Zone of Morocco. The Ballearic Isles are comprised within the Customs area of Spain. There are no other trade statistics for individual Spanish territories.

Sweden. Declared values have been in use in Sweden since 1914, though some imports were at official values for some time thereafter. Sweden is one of the countries which classified trade by country of purchase or sale. However, from 1936, the grouping by country of origin or consumption has been used, and the old grouping (by country of purchase or sale) is now a secondary classification shown in the annual publications.

Switzerland. The Customs area of Switzerland was extended on 1st January, 1924, to include Liechtenstein; from that year the trade of this small principality with the rest of the world (outside Switzerland) has been included in the Swiss trade statistics. In 1940 and subsequent years, two special categories of trade have been excluded from the statistics— the " improvement " trade on foreign account, and repair work.

Turkey. From 1935, Turkey has adopted a classification of trade by country of origin or consumption; previously (1913–1934) the statistics showed country of purchase or sale.

Yugoslavia. The trade statistics relate to the political territory of the Kingdom of Serbia (before World War I), and later of the Kingdom of the Serbs, Croats, and Slovenes. After World War II, the first issue relating to the Federal People's Republic of Yugoslavia appeared in August 1951 and gave summary figures for the period 1945–1949 and detailed figures for 1950.

USE AND APPRAISAL OF THE STATISTICS

Introduction. Each country in Europe has designed the compilation of trade statistics to suit its own needs, and the tabulations, as published, have consequently varied very much from one nation to another. In part, the varying nature of the external trade of different countries has influenced the information collected; in part, the objects to be served by the statistics have been different. Some countries need the data primarily for fiscal and administrative purposes; others collect the figures more especially for the information of those engaged in external trading, or of those interested in general economic matters.

Two opposing tendencies are generally to be seen in the development of trade statistics. One is the need for continuity, to preserve comparability of trade data over time. The other is the need to keep the information in up-to-date form, to modify the methods of collection and classification according to changing requirements. The evolution of trade statistics in any country depends on which tendency dominates. In Switzerland, for example, the advantage of a long series of comparable figures offsets the inconvenience of an out-of-date classification; in Belgium, the position is exactly reversed.

In the following paragraphs, attention is directed first to the variation in the coverage and in the methods of compiling trade statistics within Europe, on such matters as scope, definition, and classification. Then, some account is given of the forms of publication of the statistics. This is particularly important since the presentation of the data varies greatly from one country to another in Europe, much more so than (for example) among the countries of the British Commonwealth.

The account relates to the 18 countries in Western, Northern, and Southern Europe which have been noted in the preceding section, together with Iceland and the overseas dependencies of European countries. Little or no reference is made to the USSR and countries in Eastern Europe. In some cases there have been frequent changes in trade statistics since World War II, and, when the present position is described, it is that at late 1951.

Coverage. The main reason for lack of comparability over time in European trade statistics is the change that has taken place over the years in political boundaries and hence in Customs areas. The time of greatest change was that following World War I when the map of Europe was so largely redrawn. The effect of this upheaval on trade statistics is adequately described in the 1928 *Memorandum* of the League of Nations already mentioned. There were further changes during and after World War II, but, except in one respect, these are more manageable in the statistical sense. It is possible to get a fair degree of comparison between pre-war and post-war trade statistics, as is evidenced by the various analyses made by the United Nations and other international organizations. The exception concerns the statistics of Germany and of countries of Eastern Europe, including the USSR. Little need be said about the latter countries since (at best) only incomplete information on the trade of these countries is currently obtainable. (Nevertheless, some estimates of their trade are given with geographical breakdown in the *Economic Bulletin for Europe*, Vol. 2, No. 2, Table XXI, and Vol. 3, No. 2, Table XXII, published by the Economic Commission for Europe, Geneva.) The recorded trade of Germany after the war (Federal Republic) is not comparable with any pre-war statistics. Changes in territory, both before the war (Austria, Sudetenland) and afterwards (Saar, Soviet Zone) make this inevitable. Strict comparability does not even exist for the territory of the Federal Republic in the period 1946–1949, since the reestablishment of

German trade statistics was by stages. At first the trade of the zones was compiled separately and valued in dollars. A progressive amalgamation, and valuation in marks, came later. However, in recent German publications, estimates are given of the trade in 1936 of the present area of the Federal Republic (and more detailed estimates were published at the end of 1951). These estimates, which utilized information in the 1936 industrial census of Germany, are shown in the same groupings of trade as in the quantum index number compiled since the war.

On the other hand, one of the reasons for imperfect comparability among the statistics of different countries is that the general scope of the information varies. All the countries considered (except Ireland, which follows British practice) use the " special trade " system, Denmark and Norway only since 1938–1939. Consequently, all transit trade (both direct and indirect) is excluded from the statistics. Imports relate to merchandise for consumption or to be " nationalized "; exports comprise domestic products and imported goods which have been " nationalized " (perhaps by no more than the payment of import duties). Everything turns, therefore, on the precise scope of " nationalized products " included in exports. This clearly varies from one country to another, e.g., according to the nature of the tariff. Sometimes the scope is so wide as to include fresh bananas or dates, as is the case for French exports.

Transit trade is large for many countries, and separate returns of such traffic are kept and published by most maritime countries (Belgium, Denmark, France, Italy, Netherlands, Portugal, Spain) as well as by Austria and Switzerland. The Scandinavian countries, apart from Denmark, do not show any tabulation of their in-transit trade.

There are also variations in the inclusion or exclusion of particular commodities. As indicated below, most countries, but not all, exclude gold bullion from merchandise trade. Fabricated gold, however, is generally included. In 1949–1950, there developed a world-wide trade in so-called fabricated gold which was, in effect, a disguised traffic in bullion, with consequent difficulties in interpreting the statistics of countries which include fabricated gold but exclude bullion. For example, in 1950, France records the export of fabricated gold (mainly to Switzerland) to the value of $43 million and Switzerland shows a corresponding export (mainly to Italy) worth $48 million. This is largely a speculative movement; the recorded amount bears no relation to the value of the work done on the gold.

Similar problems arise in the interpretation of the " entrepôt " and " improvement " trade so important to such countries as Belgium, Netherlands and Switzerland. Diamonds are a case in point. Belgium and Netherlands, among other countries, include trade in diamonds in their merchandise statistics. Since so much of the trade goes unrecorded, *e.g.*, that in the form of registered letters, it is generally recognized that the published figures have little significance. As has already been stated, the Netherlands statistics in 1949 ceased to give any " country analysis " of the incomplete figures of exports of diamonds. The processing of goods on foreign account (the " improvement " trade) is treated differently by Switzerland, which has excluded the trade since 1940, and by Belgium, which in 1951 included " passive improvement " trade in the category of " special trade." Repair work is also excluded by Switzerland but not by some other countries. As an example of the difficulties which can arise, the case can be quoted of railway wagons sent from the Bizone of Germany for repair in Belgium in 1949. These were included at full value equally as imports and as exports in Belgian statistics, but not in the German records, until the discrepancy was put right in the second half of the year.

Two other cases of difference in the treatment of commodities important in international trade are fish and electric current. Electricity supplies to foreign consumers are not always included in the trade statistics (as in Austria). Similarly, fish landed direct from the fishing grounds in foreign ports may or may not be counted as exports. Of the countries with large fishing fleets, Iceland includes direct overseas landing of fish from her vessels as exports, whereas Norway does not. The important export of whale oil from Norwegian vessels thus escapes record in the trade statistics (but is published in *Nasjonalbudsjettet*).

In any consideration of exclusions from trade records, it should not be forgotten that contraband is always of some importance and that the traffic can be quite large in difficult times, for example, in such portable items as watches or drugs. Even foodstuffs, for example, during periods of rationing, can escape record in great proportion at the frontier, *e.g.*, coffee brought out of Belgium or Switzerland in 1947–1948 by returning tourists or by those residing in frontier districts.

Special types of transactions. The merchandise tables in the trade statistics of European countries generally exclude *gold and silver bullion*, though this may appear as a separate tabulation. Only 4 countries (Finland, Germany, Greece, Spain) now include gold and silver in bullion form as merchandise. Belgium appears to have included bullion in the past, but the present practice is to exclude it.

Merchandise imports and exports almost always include *vessels and aircraft*. For example, Norway is a large purchaser of ships built abroad and shows them (as a distinct item) within total imports. The exceptions arise as a matter of practice rather than of principle; most ships bought and sold by Greece and Ireland escape record in their trade returns.

The practice on *bunkers and stores* for ships and aircraft varies greatly.

Foreign bunkers are included as merchandise exports of many maritime countries (Belgium, France, Germany, Italy, Netherlands, Portugal, Spain), but other countries, *e.g.*, those in Scandinavia, exclude them from the tabulations; generally, these countries exclude also from their imports statistics fuel imported for foreign bunkers, so that calculations of home consumption are not impaired. A few countries only, *e.g.*, Portugal, include stores purchased abroad by their own ships as merchandise imports. In the case of Germany, such stores are recorded as imports only to the extent that they are actually unloaded in German harbours.

The treatment of special categories such as relief goods, reparations, and supplies for occupation forces also varies considerably. UNRRA supplies have sometimes been excluded from merchandise imports (as in Austria). German export statistics do not include reparations, and this is true also of Finland, where the figures are shown separately. The items, however, may be comprised within the import figures of the receiving countries; France did not exclude them, for example, until July 1947. Germany does not record, in her imports, any supplies for the occupation forces. French exports include supplies to American and British forces in Germany (paid for in dollars and pounds), but not those to French forces. Danish exports being classified by country of sale, show supplies to American and British forces in Germany as going to the United States and United Kingdom, respectively. Finally, Austrian export statistics exclude goods moving to Eastern Europe from plants in Austria which are under Soviet control. Since all these categories of transactions are large at different times, there are serious difficulties in matching post-war data from different countries.

Commodity classification. There could scarcely be a greater diversity of practice than in the commodity classifications currently employed by European countries. Some have been in force for a long time; others have been revised to conform to modern requirements. Some are designed on statistical lines and others on the basis of the tariff. Some are sparing of detail, whereas others make very fine distinctions and run to upward of 5000 separate items. It is often quite impossible to match the exports from one country with the same item imported by the receiving country. This is so, even when great detail is provided, since the detail may depend on different (and changing) tariff structures in the two countries.

Many of the countries considered have classifications dating back to well before World War II. This is true, for example, of Germany; the old classification in great detail was reintroduced after the war with no more than minor modifications. (As from October 1951, a new tariff was adopted by Germany; it is based on the Brussels Tariff). The Spanish classification is also old and detailed, and has remained unchanged despite the fact that many headings now have nil entries, *e.g.*, items 758–772 which are devoted to different kinds of balloons under the group heading of vehicles for aerial transport. Greece has no more than a summary grouping of commodities, whereas Turkey's classification could almost be described as archaic. Switzerland also has maintained continuity at the expense of retaining an out-of-date grouping of commodities. Its classification, moreover, is scarcely on statistical lines, and it must have been designed for tariff and other administrative purposes; it distinguishes, for example, between flour imports in lots of less than 5 kilograms and larger lots, but not between wheat and barley flour.

Five countries have revised completely their commodity classifications since World War II. The joint classification adopted in 1948 by Belgium-Luxembourg and the Netherlands, following their Customs agreement, is very close to the Customs nomenclature elaborated by the League of Nations in 1937. It is quite modern, detailed, and precise. The new French classification, introduced about the same time and later extended to the French overseas territories, is also based, in part, though more remotely, on the same model. The commodity grouping used until 1950 by Italy was changed to a much more detailed one based on the work of the Brussels Study Group of the European Customs Union. Finally, following the adoption by the United Nations of the Standard International Trade Classification (SITC) in 1950, Denmark decided to change its classification in January 1951 to conform to the United Nations recommendations.

Most of the classifications mentioned are based on a grouping of commodities by nature of the component material. A few countries in Europe, however, have in use a different type of classification in which the primary distinction is by stage of manufacture. This is so for Ireland and Portugal, and the German classification is also on this basis.

A drastic revision of a commodity classification is not lightly undertaken by any country, because of the difficulties of making comparisons with earlier data. On the other hand, it is clearly undesirable that, when several countries change about the same time, they should adopt different classifications, as in fact happened from 1948 onward. Moreover, it seems probable that there will be two different models—those of the United Nations and of the Brussels Study Group—available for those countries proposing to revise their classifications from 1951 onward. Many may indeed adopt the United Nations standard, but some may follow Italy in basing their classifications on the tariff nomenclature devised by the Brussels Study Group which unfortunately is not a statistical classifiction useful for economic analysis. Nevertheless, a table of correspondence between the two classifications—the statistical one of the United Nations and the tariff one of Brussels—has been published (United Nations, August 1951).

On the other hand, the present prospects of a greater standardization of statistical information supplied by European countries are very promising. In fact, it appears from statements made at the second Regional Meeting of European Statisticians held at Geneva in September 1951 that the countries represented (amongst whom were the United Kingdom and the United States of America) realized the many benefits of such a standardization and have all practically decided to adopt the SITC nomenclature in one form or another, *i.e.*,

(1) as the basis of their national or published nomenclature (Austria and Denmark since 1951, Ireland in 1952, Norway and Yugoslavia in 1953); or

(2) as a subsidiary nomenclature and published by themselves (published monthly by Germany and quarterly by France since 1951); or

(3) as the basis of information supplied to the United Nations Statistical Office, which will publish it quarterly (Belgium, Finland, Italy, Netherlands, Portugal, Sweden, Turkey in 1951, Norway and Yugoslavia in 1952).

Only Switzerland appears to have difficulty in supplying figures according to the SITC at present, but a revision of Customs tariffs is foreseen and should certainly simplify her task.

Although the proposed use of the Standard International Trade Classification (SITC) varies from one country to another, it may be said generally that in the course of 1952 most countries made available, in one form or another, data for at least the principal SITC groups and items with a geographical breakdown. This represents a considerable progress as compared with the pre-war situation, when several European countries had adopted the League of Nations Minimum List (1937) as a subsidiary classification, but in most cases were only publishing annual tables for total trade without distinction by countries of origin and destination.

Units of quantity. The metric system is used in all the countries considered, except in the Irish statistics which employ the British units of weights and measures. This greatly simplifies comparisons between the statistics of different countries on trade in particular commodities. However, in any comparison of continental with British statistics, it must be remembered that the metric ton is slightly (but significantly) different from the long ton of 2240 lb.

A more serious difficulty, when data on different commodities are handled, arises from the fact that, though most products are given effectively in terms of weight, other types of measure are used, *e.g.*, fabrics in metres, drinks in hectolitres, shoes in pairs, automobiles by number, and so on. Even when weight is the measure, the unit employed can vary from one product to another, *e.g.*, tons and kilograms. The difficulty is partially overcome by two practices often adopted. One is to show the quantities of some important commodities in alternative measures, *e.g.*, automobiles by number and weight. The other is to show (as many countries do in their annual publications) the conversion factors between non-weight and weight in the form of mean weight per unit for the trade of the year in question. There remain a few commodities, such as penicillin and other drugs, for which an indication of weight is not useful.

The general practice, where weight is the measure used, is to record net weight, *i.e.*, weight net of crates and other bulk packing, but usually inclusive of any containers used in retail sale. In France, imports from and exports to French overseas territories are denoted in gross weight; otherwise, even where there is an ad valorem import duty on containers and contents alike, the weight is taken net of the packaging. In Italy, a distinction is drawn between products measured in tons and those measured in kilograms; those given in tons are given net in the usual sense, whereas those given in kilograms are recorded net in a stricter sense, excluding also containers for retail sale. Finally, a system of " net legal weight " is adopted for a few products, in which an arbitrary deduction is made from gross weight for recording purposes. It can be noticed that shipping and transit statistics are often in terms of gross weight.

Publications of trade statistics vary according to the extent to which the unit of measure changes from one item to another in the commodity classification, or is dropped altogether with value alone shown. The Italian publication, for example, is in great detail with many changes of unit from one item to another, the changes being clearly indicated. Sometimes, however, the indication of units is not always clear (as with the annual statistics of Rumania between the two World Wars) and there is a certain risk of error in using the statistics.

Valuation. There is equal conformity among the different countries on methods of valuation of trade. Imports are valued c.i.f. (before duties) and exports f.o.b., with only relatively minor variations. For example, exports of timber from Finland are valued f.a.s.—at the dock before loading on ship. Again, the Algerian records of imports from France are derived from French export statistics and valued f.o.b.; imports into Algeria from other sources are valued c.i.f. as declared. The c.i.f. value of imports has, of course, a clear economic significance. It is, however, important for certain purposes (*e.g.*, for balance of payments statistics) to have at least estimates of the f.o.b. values. European statisticians during their second meeting (Geneva, September 1951) promised their co-operation in providing data to facilitate such estimates.

The cost of the merchandise as declared is the basis of valuation. This has not always been so in the past; valuation of imports at domestic prices and of both imports and exports at " official " values have been quite common at different times. Indeed, a general change-over from official values (e.g., for purposes of assessing Customs duty and hence of recording imports) to declared values was made in European countries as late as the first quarter of this century. Only in exceptional cases, and for particular commodities, are official values now used in European trade statistics. For example, a few items in the Portuguese export trade are taken at official values.

It does not follow that all valuations are equally accurate. On the contrary, there is a general tendency for traders to declare false values, particularly when an ad valorem tariff is in operation.[3] Customs checks pick up many errors, e.g., undervaluations of goods subject to duty, and corrections are made in the statistics. No Customs authorities, however, are able to check all items. The accuracy of a country's import statistics can only be assessed in the light of the nature of its tariff and the extent of Customs control. Nevertheless, import values are generally more accurate than export values in which the Customs officials are genuinely less interested (except for exchange control).

There is also some tendency, at different times, for exports from Colonial territories to be understated in value. The statistical service of the Ministère de la France d'outre-mer (in the *Annuaire Statistique* for 1945) notes, in regard to Réunion, that " le calcul des valeurs était de toute tradition systématiquement faux " and that a correction amounting to an increase of 32 per cent had been applied to the value of exports (mainly sugar). A study of exports in 1944 from French Equatorial Africa led similarly to an increase of 63 per cent in their valuation. As is evident from the publications after 1945, the statistical service has since succeeded in effecting considerable improvement in the accuracy of the trade statistics of the French Union.

A few particular difficulties arise from time to time in interpreting recorded values. One example is the import of Lend-Lease goods, which are necessarily valued rather arbitrarily. Another example is the treatment of parcel post, which is often valued by number of packet times an arbitrary figure of value per packet. A rather different difficulty may arise in the handling of subsidies. The appropriate method is to value exports

[3] As a result of the general tendency toward higher prices in international trade. Customs duties increasingly are set ad valorem, e.g., the new German tariff which came into operation in October 1951 substitutes ad valorem rates for specific duties in respect of numerous commodities.

net of subsidies in the exporting country (as is done in the Irish statistics, for example) and imports before the deduction of subsidies in the importing country. France departed from the latter practice in the years 1946–1949 inclusive, when French subsidies were deducted from import values as shown in the monthly statistics. The annual figures for 1946–1949 were later adjusted upward to correct the valuation, and the corrections were sometimes quite large (*e.g.*, for imports of coal).

Conversion of currencies. Rates of exchange between currencies are relevant to statistics of international trade in two respects. In the first place, the statistics are generally published with valuations in the national currency. Nearly all international trade involves transactions or contracts between different nationals, and these may be denominated in the currency of the recording country or in another currency. The valuation of trade (imports particularly) depends largely on the conversion of foreign into domestic currency, as made in the traders' declarations to Customs.

Secondly, in handling the published statistics of different countries, there is often the need to translate values from one currency into another, *e.g.*, to value all trade in gold francs, pounds sterling, or United States dollars. For this, the usual practice is to use official rates of exchange if these are fixed, or mean rates of exchange over a period if the variations are relatively small. In the *Direction of International Trade*[4] a table is given of conversion factors (from 1937 to date) designed for use in trade statistics in converting values in different currencies into United States dollars.

There may often be differences between the rate of exchange used in a particular transaction and the market or official rate quoted at the time of import or export. These differences have been considerable and biased at different times, *e.g.*, during the inflation of the 1920's and the unsettled period of the 1930's. German trade statistics provide good examples. The figures recorded in the early 1920's became progressively less meaningful as the inflation of the currency developed. Later, the official manipulation of the mark in the 1930's made it difficult to assess the valuation of trade (for trade with Latin America, China, and Yugoslavia) from 1935 onward. The official rate of exchange was then 40 cents to the mark, whereas the effective rate is estimated to have been only 30–35 cents to the mark.

Particular conversions may be rendered difficult by special circumstances, *e.g.*, when countries have multiple rates of exchange or when there are large and rapid changes in rates over time. There were many such

---

[4] *Statistical Papers*, Series T, published jointly by the United Nations Statistical Office, the International Monetary Fund and the International Bank.

difficulties in the conversion of European currencies in the period since World War II.   The following are among the more important instances.

In Spain, there have been multiple exchange rates (for different categories of transactions), but the statistics of trade are published in terms of gold pesetas, with a fixed rate of conversion into dollars.

In 1948, France had rates of exchange which were changed twice in the year and which were different according to the nature of the products imported, and according to whether or not the currency of the export proceeds was available on the free market.   It is consequently difficult to convert the French statistics of 1948 into United States dollars or other currencies.   Moreover, as we have already noted, in the monthly statistics published about this time subsidies were deducted from the recorded values of certain goods imported.

Until the end of 1950, there was in fact no single official rate of exchange in the Federal Republic of Germany.   The foreign trade of Western Germany had been monopolized by Allied organizations intervening between the exporter and the foreign customers (until the monetary reform of 1948).   In this period there was no fixed relation between prices in marks (in the German domestic market) and prices in dollars ruling on world markets.   An official rate was progressively introduced until it became the sole rate in 1951.   The problems of conversion are simplified by the fact that the German trade publications (for a period to the end of 1950) gave all values both in dollars and in marks.   Somewhat similar difficulties have arisen in Italian trade statistics since World War II; here again, many items have been valued both in dollars and in lire.

The valuations of Greek imports since 1945 are peculiarly suspect.   The official exchange rate of 5000 drachmas to the dollar is used.   But it is known that some Greek Customs houses add, in Customs duties, the value of exchange certificates (10,000 drachmas to the dollar on top of the official rate) and other charges.   The valuations, moreover, are subject to revisions of an apparently arbitrary nature.

As a final example, the problem of allowing for any large devaluation of currencies can be illustrated by the devaluations of September 1949.   Here it is essential to know how the valuations in national currencies are established in each country's statistics.   The general practice, following devaluation late in September 1949, was to apply the new rates of exchange immediately, i.e., to goods passing through Customs in October and all later months.   For imports en route at the time of devaluation, this meant that the domestic valuation was set higher than the importers had anticipated when the goods had begun to move, i.e., more tax would be paid if the goods were subject to ad valorem duties, taking account also of the time lag in the Customs returns.   It is admitted that the new rates of exchange would in practice be applied after some time lag. In France a lag of about 2 months for imports and 1 month for exports is used in official studies.

Country designations. There is not a great variety in the methods of crediting trade to countries, since most national statistics designate imports by country of origin and exports by country of destination (consumption). A different system, by country of consignment, is used by Belgium-Luxembourg and the Netherlands, and also by Iceland; this makes it difficult to develop some important analyses of trade between European countries and the rest of the world. Similarly, there have been some changes in the past, *e.g.*, switches from imports by country of consignment to country of origin in France (1934) and in Ireland (1935); consequently some comparisons of the direction of trade over time are difficult to make.

The monthly statistics published by Denmark are based on the classification by country of purchase or sale of the goods.[5] This is an important point to be remembered when comparing Danish statistics with those of other countries. For example, Denmark credits some imports to the United Kingdom (as country of purchase) when they come in fact from other regions (mainly sterling area countries) and may not have passed through the United Kingdom. This appears immediately from a comparison of the Danish and British statistics by countries and commodities. Denmark also employs a classification according to country of origin or destination, but only as a secondary grouping in the annual statistics. The other Scandinavian countries (Finland, Norway, Sweden) and, since 1951, Germany adopt a double classification; trade is grouped both according to country of origin or destination and according to country of purchase or sale.

The trade of Western Germany with Eastern Germany is not included in the foreign trade statistics (separate returns are nevertheless available). Similarly, the trade between Italy and Trieste is treated as internal by Italy, *i.e.*, it is excluded from the Italian returns of trade and Trieste does not appear as a country of origin or destination. The territory of the Saar is handled differently by Germany, France, and other countries at different times. For example, from December 1947 to March 1948 inclusive, the territory was completely ignored in the French statistics; neither imports into France from the Saar nor imports into the Saar from the rest of the world were included; and similarly for exports.

Publications. All countries in Europe, except some eastern European countries, publish trade statistics for months and for calendar years. The returns are generally based on a calendar month, *i.e.*, items passed or

---

[5] This has also been true of other countries in the past.

cleared by Customs during the month. However, France records trade for a " statistical " period which differs according to imports (21st to 20th of month) or exports (26th to 25th of month). July imports relate to imports cleared (" prises en compte par le douane ") between 21 June and 20 July, inclusive. July exports similarly relate to the period from 26 June to 25 July, inclusive. All countries, with the exception of Yugoslavia issue monthly publications, varying greatly in the amount of detail shown. All countries, with four exceptions indicated below, publish annual data in separate volumes, usually in much more detail than can be obtained from the monthly publications.

Annual data on trade are needed usually for detailed information. The more detailed the tables, the longer it takes to prepare them for publication, even when mechanized methods of tabulation are used. The choice which must inevitably be made is between very detailed publications appearing after much delay, and rapid publication in less detailed form. Most countries in Europe stress the importance of detail at the cost of delay. But some, *e.g.*, Austria, Portugal, Germany, and particularly Switzerland do achieve rapid publication of their annual data. The best solution may be to issue several annual volumes, some published more quickly than others. Switzerland follows this method with great success.

Table 1 shows the approximate length of the delay (as at mid-1951) in publication of the annual data by those countries which issue separate annual volumes.

Table 1

Annual Data, Trade Statistics—Time Lag in Publication, Mid-1951

Country	Delay (months)	Country	Delay (months)
Austria	4	Portugal Vol. 1 . . .	4
Denmark	12–20	Vol. 2 . . .	6
Finland	11	Spain	12–15
France	20	Sweden: exports . . .	8
Germany, Vol. 1 . . .	6	imports . . .	10
Vol. 2 . . .	3	full tables . . .	18
Vol. 3 . . .	3	Switzerland, Vol. 1 . .	1
Iceland	30	Vol. 2 . .	3
Ireland	*	Vol. 3 . .	8
Norway	18	Turkey	†

* No post-war annual volume issued by mid-1951.

† Issued in three parts, of which the first is the monthly publication for December; Parts 2 and 3 for 1949 became available in Geneva in May 1951.

The main reason for reference to annual publications, in their full detail, is to obtain cross classifications of trade, *either* by each commodity for the various countries of origin or destination *or* by each country for the various commodities traded. The former can be described as a commodity-country classification and the latter as a country-commodity classification. The number of commodities whieh are, or could be, listed under each country may exceed 5000; and the number of countries which are, or could be, distinguished is generally between 100 and 200. The practical difficulties in the way of publication of complete detail on two cross classifications are clearly very great, and practice varies among the different countries in Europe. France, Iceland, Portugal, Sweden, and Switzerland succeed in giving a very complete analysis both on a commodity-country and on a country-commodity classification. The Swiss commodity-country analysis is so complete that the rubric " Other countries " is practically not used. Denmark and Finland also achieve complete or considerable detail on both classifications. In addition, they provide tabulations by country both on an origin-destination and on a purchase-sale basis. On the other hand, Austria, Portugal, and Spain provide reasonably complete detail only for the commodity-country classification, and not by country-commodity.

It can be noticed that the best may be the enemy of the good, and some annual tabulations are so detailed that information can often be got only after long and painful research. For example, suppose that the exports of machine tools from France are needed in some country detail. The annual volume of France shows 80 types of machine tools but with no grouping into totals for all types. Further, for each type, the analysis by countries is given, but always with a residual heading of " Other countries," which varies in content from one type to another. Aggregation is, therefore, difficult—if not impossible. An approximation to the required aggregates may, in fact, be obtained more quickly by reference to the tables giving country-commodity detail, *i.e.*, by taking each country in turn and seeing whether there are exports of machine tools to it.

Monthly data on trade are generally less detailed than the annual, and the publications appear after shorter time intervals than the corresponding annual volumes. The Swiss publication appears very quickly. For Sweden, trade in the current month is shown only in commodity detail, whereas trade by countries is given for the previous month. For some countries the delays are still inconveniently long. Table 2 shows the approximate position at mid-1951.

The 4 countries which do not issue separate volumes of annual data are Belgium-Luxembourg, Greece, Italy, and the Netherlands. Each of them relies entirely on monthly publications, and figures for a year are to be obtained from (and only from) the December issue of the monthly series. The monthly publications of Belgium, Greece, and Italy are given in great

Table 2

Monthly Data, Trade Statistics—Time Lag in Publications, Mid-1951

Country	Delay (weeks)	Country	Delay (weeks)
Austria	6	Iceland	9
Belgium-Luxembourg . .	10	Ireland	8
Denmark*	6	Italy	12
Finland	5	Netherlands (3 volumes) . .	10–15
France	7–12	Norway	8
Germany: Summary . .	4	Portugal	5–7
Commodity-country . .	7	Spain	10–14
Country-commodity . .	†8	Sweden	7
According to the SITC . .	6	Switzerland	2
Greece	12–20	Turkey	14

* Furthermore, the greater part of Danish exports is recorded and published weekly with a few days' delay.

† Quarterly publication, becoming monthly in 1951.

detail only on a commodity-country basis.   Country-commodity tables are given only for some important countries (Belgium, Greece) or only for a different (summary) grouping of commodities (Italy).   Although this may be sufficient for monthly data, it is not adequate for a full analysis of annual trade.   There is an unsatisfied need for separate and detailed annual statistics; this is recognized by Belgium who indicated in 1951 that annual volumes are to be issued in the future.

The position is different for the Netherlands and (from 1950) for Germany.   Their monthly publications are in full detail both by commodity-country and by country-commodity.   They have adopted the policy of issuing figures each month, not in summary form, but in exactly the same detail as for annual data.   The December issue of the publications gives the statistics for a year (Germany publishes also annual books with special tables); but each of the other issues gives the same detail for the current month and the elapsed part of the year.   The practice has obvious advantages, and perhaps one disadvantage.   It is to be noticed that the publications of the Netherlands appear after a time lag of about 10–15 weeks.   This means that, regarded as *annual* data, full details are issued rapidly, although, as *monthly* data, the publication is delayed.   It should also be noted that, for Germany, two supplementary publications exist monthly: imports under the ERP and trade by groups of the United Nations Standard International Trade Classifications (SITC).

The monthly publications of the other countries (issuing annual volumes) vary in the extent to which detail is suppressed.   Some give a cross classification based on about 50 groups of commodities (following the League of Nations Minimum List or now the SITC) and on principal countries;

these include Austria, Denmark, Norway, and Sweden. Some give a commodity-country classification only; this is detailed for Switzerland, more summarized for Spain. Others (Finland, Ireland) give no cross classification at all in their trade publications (details are given by Finland on wood and paper products in another publication). France gives some cross classification; though there is only a simple split of French territories—foreign countries in the commodity table, there is good commodity detail for trade with each of a limited number (43) of selected countries. In addition, from 1951, a summary table is given each quarter, both by commodity-country and by country-commodity, in which the commodity grouping follows the Standard International Trade Classification of the United Nations (SITC).

The usual practice is to show cumulative figures for the part of the year elapsed as well as monthly figures. Spain and Switzerland are exceptional in showing only data for the current month.

International publications. Figures for European countries may be found in international trade publications of different agencies. For Europe, special reference may be made to the OEEC *Foreign Trade Statistical Bulletin* and to the various publications of the Economic Commission for Europe: *Economic Survey of Europe* (annual) and *Economic Bulletin for Europe* (quarterly).

Errors and revisions. Although annual publications are (at least in principle) definitive, the monthly series published by European countries contain figures which are provisional and subject to later amendment. Apart from the correction of misprints, monthly figures can be revised for a number of reasons. The most usual are changes in valuation, country designations, etc., following detailed examination of declarations by Customs authorities. Another reason might be the decision to apply retroactively some change in classification or method of compilation. This was done, for example, in France at the end of 1949 in correcting for the previous deduction of subsidies for import values. Prices themselves are sometimes retroactively revised, as was the case in mid-1951 for German coal.

Corrections and revisions are usually made in the cumulative figures shown with the figures for the current month. Thus the figures for any given month may be corrected several times in the cumulative data published on several later occasions. This gives rise, naturally, to apparent anomalies when individual monthly figures (as originally issued) are compared with various cumulative totals. It is not generally correct, for example, to derive data for a period by subtracting cumulative totals one from the other. The cumulative total for March subtracted from that for June does not necessarily give the correct, nor indeed the unrevised, total for the second quarter.   Table 3 provides an illustration from Italian monthly statistics.

Table 3

Italian Exports to Malta, 1948—Monthly Revisions of Cumulative Data
(Thousand lire)

Month	Figures as Originally Issued		Cumulative Figures as Issued
	Monthly	Cumulative	
January . . .	109,097	—	—
February . . .	992,839	1,101,936	1,101,936
March . . .	169,470	1,271,406	1,271,424
April . . .	130,095	1,401,501	1,401,519
May . . .	189,483	1,590,984	762,743
June . . .	334,980	1,925,964	1,097,723

In Table 3 addition of unrevised figures gives 654,558 for the second quarter.   Subtraction of the cumulative figures gives a negative result: 1,097,723 minus 1,271,424.   The correct figure (as revised to the end of June) is not obtainable.   In this case, it can only be guessed that the original February figure was in error, and corrected in May.

Trade statistics in use.   Trade statistics must cater, or attempt to cater, to a great variety of users.   It is, therefore, not possible to judge any country's publications on one criterion alone;   there must always be a balance to be struck, e.g., between rapid and detailed figures.   The quality of the statistics of European countries is generally high; it is also improving rapidly as trade statisticians are brought increasingly in contact with each other, in particular, thanks to the meetings of European statisticians. Even the statistics of trade of the overseas territories, though not of the quality of those of the mother countries, have made notable if uneven advances since World War II.   The various statistics are not, and never can be, at all completely comparable; but the more is known about their differences, the more allowances can be made for them in practice.

In some cases—too many of them—the serious user of trade statistics is not sufficiently helped by the official publications.   The rules and methods followed, which may have been in force for so long that their object is forgotten, are not always adequately described in the introductory or tabular notes to the data as published.   This is particularly inconvenient when the user is handling the statistics of another country than his own.

It is becoming increasingly the practice to withhold some information in the published sources.   This may be for reasons of national security, as with fissionable materials.   It may also be for reasons of commercial confidentiality, for example, when a single firm is the sole producer of an export item, or in order to hide differential price treatment of different countries. In such cases, the value of the exports may not be published at all, or not shown by country of destination, as is the case, *e.g.*, with artificial fibres (Netherlands) and milking machines (Sweden), at least in provisional figures. Further, the internal trade of one company, or group of related companies, may cut across national boundaries, as it frequently does in Europe with such products as petroleum, whale oil, furs, and diamonds. The records of such trade, and particularly their valuations, may contain an arbitrary element. Port wine exported from Portugal to the United Kingdom, for example, does not necessarily change in ownership at the time of export, and the wine may then have no definite market value.

These facts may not greatly limit the use of the trade statistics for some purposes. They must, however, be borne in mind in many applications of published merchandise trade data to particular or general problems. One of them is of great importance, the use of trade statistics in the construction and analysis of the balance of payments (see Chapter 9). Here, it is not only the omission or inappropriate valuation of certain items which causes difficulty. Some of the classifications, and particularly the country designations, adopted in compiling trade statistics are no longer relevant. For payment purposes, country of origin or consignment is not the significant classification of imports, but rather country of purchase. An alternative grouping according to purchase or sale is available in the statistics of Scandinavian countries and Germany, thus facilitating their use in the balance of payments. It may be, however, that Denmark overstresses these advantages in making the purchase-sale classification the primary one, thus falling foul of other users of the statistics.

CHAPTER 18

Latin America

Amos E. Taylor and John B. Rothrock*
Pan American Union

HISTORICAL DEVELOPMENT

Early history. The development of foreign trade statistics among the countries of Latin America has been slow and irregular. The achievement of independence by these countries, which came in most cases during the second and third decades of the 19th century, was followed rather generally by prolonged periods of economic and political disorder. Such conditions provided neither the incentive nor the means for the development of statistical measures of economic growth at home and of commercial dealings with the outside world.

Mexico initiated the publication of basic economic data, including statistics on export and import trade as early as 1823, the third year of independence. The need for at least partial statistics relating to public revenues, taxation, and foreign trade gradually stimulated other newly established governments of Spanish America to undertake the collection and compilation of data. In 1831, a year after the division of Gran Colombia into three separate states, Venezuela began the publication of export and import statistics. Soon after the break-up of the Confederation of the United Provinces of Central America in 1838, Costa Rica and Nicaragua developed a more or less systematic compilation of basic

---

* *Note:* The authors are indebted to Mr. Lewis Ortega and Dr. Charles F. Carson of the Pan American Union for assistance in the preparation of this chapter.

economic data, including statistics on export and import trade. Following the development of foreign trade data in Chile to the point where they were reasonably complete by the 1840's, and consistent with the growing signs of political and economic order after the middle of the century, separate reports on foreign trade made their appearance in a number of countries, including Argentina, Brazil, and Peru. For a long time, these statistics were confined to the movements of goods through the principal ports; nor were they featured by any systems of classification designed to provide comparability from year to year.

Contrary to developments in some other major world areas, changes in national boundaries throughout Latin America have not been important factors affecting the comparability of national foreign trade statistics. The transfer of territory by Peru and Bolivia to Chile in 1883 and 1884, after the War of the Pacific, came at a time when reported official statistics were still relatively undeveloped. Colombia's loss of Panama in 1904 diminished the area of the former by nearly 30,000 square miles. This brought Panama into the family of Latin American nations as a relatively small member, but one whose foreign trade was destined to become a factor in the international economy because of geographical position and because of United States activity in the Canal Zone. The national areas affected by these events were thus few, and once altered have remained unchanged.

Although from time to time, since about 1920, disputes concerning national boundaries have arisen, no important trading areas were involved; in some instances the exact boundaries are not yet defined by mutual agreement.

Individual countries. The progress made thus far by the respective countries of Latin America in the development and publication of foreign trade statistics is briefly set forth here country by country.

Argentina. As in the case of many of the other Latin American countries, Argentina's earliest data on foreign trade were published jointly with statistics on public finance under the direction of the Ministry of Finance. Although originally the published data on export and import trade were limited to the port of Buenos Aires, the scope of the reported statistics was gradually expanded. With the appearance of the *Anuario del Comercio Exterior y de la Navegación* in 1892 the reported statistics assumed fairly bulky and detailed proportions. In 1915 the statistics on navigation were eliminated and the title was changed. Annual data now appear as Volume II of the *Anuario Estadístico* of the Dirección General del Servicio Estadístico Nacional. The structure of the official report on annual foreign trade data has remained virtually unchanged since that time.

Bolivia. Bolivia began the publication of foreign trade statistics in 1831, but for many years the published data were rather inadequate. The reported data on export and import trade have been somewhat expanded since 1928 when full statistics on the exportation of minerals were first published. The increasing attention given to the broader compilation and dissemination of economic data generally has strengthened trade data. The classification of foreign trade statistics has also improved, and progress has been made in the development of comparable series of data, as is evidenced in the Dirección General de Estadística's *Anuario* on foreign trade.

Brazil. The annual *Relatorio* of Ministerio da Fazenda, the publication of which dates back to about 1850, has since its beginning been a source of Brazilian finance and foreign trade data. In 1900 this was supplemented by various special reports on export and import trade under the direction of the Directoria de Estatística Comercial, a reorganized department of the Ministry of Finance. Although these special reports were subsequently suspended, the Directoria instituted the publication of a number of annual reports which dealt specifically with statistics on foreign trade. These reports were gradually broadened to provide considerable " product and country " detail on the country's foreign trade, and are parts of the *Comercio Exterior do Brasil* now issued by the Servico de Estatística Econômica e Financeira.

Chile. The Ministry of Finance of Chile began the issue of basic statistics on fiscal and related matters as early as 1823. With the appearance of the *Estadística Comercial de la República de Chile* in 1844 the statistics on export and import trade became gradually more and more complete. Several other publications, containing statistics on foreign trade, made their appearance beginning in 1873 and were consolidated in 1915. To date Chile has achieved a high degree of coverage and completeness in the development and compilation of foreign trade statistics and other economic data, and these are primarily published by the Dirección General de Estadística.

Colombia. Summary tables containing financial data, which originally appeared in Colombia in 1823, were gradually expanded to include data on foreign trade. About half a century later a special volume on foreign trade made its appearance and was continued until World War I when the present annual *Comercio Exterior* was started. After temporary suspension, the latter was revived and has been the principal source of annual statistics ever since; it is now issued by the Dirección Nacional de Estadística.

Costa Rica. The original data on the foreign trade of Costa Rica appeared in the *Memoria* of the Ministerio de Hacienda y Comercio, which contained various classes of economic data and started in 1844.

In 1883 a decree creating the Dirección de Estadística of the Ministerio required that its Director assume the responsibility for collecting, investigating, compiling, classifying, and publishing all official statistical data. Since that time, with the exception of a 12-year lapse at the turn of the century, detailed data on foreign trade have appeared in both the *Anuario Estadística* and the *Estadística de Comercio Exterior*.

Cuba. The colonial administration of Cuba gave considerable attention to foreign trade data as early as 1827, but did not succeed in the development of a continuous set of comparable statistics. Some progress was made during the period of United States military occupation after the Spanish-American war. Although various publications have long appeared at irregular intervals, the regular publication of annual figures on Cuban exports and imports dates only from 1923. This publication now is the responsibility of the Dirección General de Estadística and appears as *Comercio Exterior*.

Dominican Republic. Until 1905, the development of foreign trade data in the Dominican Republic did not follow any continuous or consistent pattern. The installation of the Customs Receivership that year coincided with the establishment of an Oficina de Estadística Nacional. For a number of years, however, progress was uneven and sporadic, especially until 1929. The work of the Customs Receivership and the Oficina de Estadística Nacional improved the situation, and in 1938 the Customs Receivership work on foreign trade statistics was unified with that of the Dirección General de Estadística, which office currently publishes foreign trade data.

Ecuador. Since 1889, when the first *Anuario de Estadística Comercial* appeared, figures on foreign trade have been made available at intervals in various publications for the issuance of which the Superintendencia de Aduanas (Customs), and later the Ministry of Finance, assumed responsibility. The Departmento de Estadística, organized in 1925, was succeeded by the Dirección General de Estadística y Censos in 1930, which undertook the issue of various compilations on foreign trade. These publications have frequently appeared only after a considerable lag. The same has been true in the case of the Dirección's annual *Comercio Exterior*. Current data appear in releases of the Banco Central del Ecuador.

El Salvador. The *Memorias*, of the Ministerio de Hacienda y Crédito público, contain data on foreign trade. Publication began in 1850 and the *Memorias* were gradually expanded in scope to include more detailed reports on exports and imports. These publications are now supplemented by the studies and compilations of the Dirección General de Estadística. The *Anuario Estadístico del Comercio Exterior e Interior* of the latter contains full data.

Guatemala. Until 1880, the compilation of statistical data in Guatemala rested largely with the respective government departments, each covering its particular interests in the respective segments of the economy. Upon the establishment that year of the Dirección General de Estadística, considerable space was devoted in its publications to the presentation of export and import data; the latest of these publications is that office's *Boletín.*

Haiti. Various statistical reports published after 1844 included statistics on foreign trade, but no comparable data appeared on a regular basis until the establishment of the Customs Receivership in 1915. At that time a consistent method for recording export and import statistics was adopted, largely as an aid to effective administration. Since 1924 an annual summary has been published, supplemented by a monthly bulletin.

Honduras. Scattered data on the export and import transactions of Honduras began to appear as early as 1847. In 1914 these statistics were placed on a more or less regular basis, and now regularly appear in the *Informe de Hacienda, Crédito Público y Comercio.*

Mexico. Partial data on export and import trade date back to 1823. These appeared in the *Memoria* of the Ministerio de Hacienda y Crédito Público, but gradually various special publications on foreign trade were issued. Statistics on foreign commerce were well developed by the end of the 19th century and represented by that time the most complete type of economic data. Soon after the beginning of the present century, the Dirección General de Estadística began the publication of a series of annual reports, *Importación* and *Exportación*, found currently in the *Anuario Estadístico del Comercio Exterior.*

Nicaragua. Although the development of economic statistics is not very far advanced in this country, the statistics on foreign trade are among the most satisfactory. Since 1845 the annual *Memorias* of the Ministerio de Hacienda y Crédito Público have included data on exports and imports which have gradually been presented in more and more detail. Since 1949 the annual data have been supplemented by monthly reports.

Panama. Panama was the last of the Latin American countries to achieve effective autonomy. During its existence of less than half a century (to 1952) as an independent state, its trade has been influenced by several important factors already mentioned. Statistics on foreign trade have been developed in detail and are compiled and published by the Dirección General de Estadística y Censo.

Paraguay. The slow progress in the development of economic data in Paraguay was long influenced by unsettled economic and political conditions and by the destructive war of 1865–1870. The principal source of foreign trade data, the *Anuario Estadístico*, dates from 1886, but it has appeared at rather irregular intervals. During World War I, publication lapsed entirely but was subsequently revived.

Peru. The first regular publication on Peru's exports and imports appeared in 1846 and was issued by the Ministerio de Hacienda. Various special reports which appeared subsequently from time to time included several detailed volumes prepared under the supervision of the Superintendencia de Aduanas. The regular summary has appeared since 1891; monthly releases date back to 1903.

Uruguay. Until 1874 the official data on the foreign trade of Uruguay appeared as part of a general compilation of economic data issued by the Ministerio de Hacienda. Since that time various agencies have issued special reports on the country's export and import trade. Currently, reviews and reports are issued by the Dirección General de Estadística as well as by several executive agencies of the Government, such as the Contaduría General, the Ministerio de Hacienda, and the Banco de la República.

Venezuela. The foreign trade reports of Venezuela were instituted in 1831. With the establishment of the Dirección General de Estadística in 1873 the official foreign trade data began to appear in *Estadística Mercantil y Marítima*, the principal source of annual data on exports and imports.

USE AND APPRAISAL OF THE STATISTICS

Introduction. A lesser degree of uniformity and comparability is reflected in the foreign trade statistics of the Latin American countries than in the statistics of the British Dominions and Colonies, or in the data of the European countries and their dependencies. The relatively small volume of trade among the Latin American countries, themselves, is in sharp contrast to the volume of trade under normal conditions within the British Commonwealth and among the countries of Europe, especially in view of the flow of manufactured goods which features the trade within Europe and among the Commonwealth. This relatively small volume of trade among the Latin American countries has been an important reason for the absence of uniform classification and statistical practices. One of the principal incentives to the development of uniformity and comparability stems from the direct interchange of goods in large volume.

The marked degree of progress in the diversification of the economies of many Latin American countries has been accompanied, however, by an increasing degree of attention to problems of uniform and comparable developments of foreign trade statistics. It may be expected, therefore, that the need for improvement will receive more attention in the future than it has in the past. The increase in trade among the Latin American countries during World War II, though still on a low level, provided special incentives toward the improvement of the quality of foreign trade data, as well as toward a greater degree of comparability.

Coverage—systems of trade statistics. The lack of uniform systems of reporting trade statistics can be important causes of discrepancies. The inclusion or exclusion of re-exports and the handling of "warehouse" trade, generally, are elements in the degree of comparability found in the respective countries. Among the Latin American countries the inherent difficulties are reflected in the varying systems employed, as indicated in Table 1. Eight countries employ the "general trade" system for both imports and exports. Nine countries use the "special trade" system for both classes of trade movements; and the other four adhere to a mixed system under which imports are shown according to either a "general" or "special" system and exports fall under a "semi-special" system according to which they are recorded as general exports less all re-exports.

The basic distinction between the definitions of re-export trade under the respective systems is determined by the point at which the import is recorded. Under the "general trade" system re-exports are, in effect, goods which have been received and recorded in the statistics as imports at the point of their entry into Customs control. Re-exports under the "general system" include "warehouse" trade. Under the "special trade" system re-exports do not include "warehouse" trade, because the point where the import is recorded is the point at which the goods move out of Customs control.

Table 1 (p. 388) does not make clear in every case whether the definition of re-exports is in conformity with the accepted interpretation. However, the statement relative to the system used by the respective countries is fundamentally accurate, despite a few apparent discrepancies in the relevant re-export definitions.

Coverage—miscellaneous. With very few exceptions, the Latin American countries report *gold bullion and specie* as a separate item, usually in the merchandise category. It is thus possible to isolate the item for purposes of trade analysis. Argentina, Brazil, Colombia, and Mexico are, however, the only countries which report monetary gold movements under a separate category distinct from merchandise trade. Brazil shows monetary gold and silver in a separate category, whereas Mexico places monetary gold and silver in a special "valores" category; this consists of a number of items, including bank notes, stamps, and similar items which are not shown as part of the merchandise trade. The countries employing a separate category for gold movements include, however, non-monetary items such as scrap, cubes, gold dust, and gold used for industrial or professional purposes as part of the merchandise classification.

Table 1

Trade Systems of the Latin American Countries

Imports—*General:* For consumption plus warehouse entries.
         Special: For consumption plus ex-warehouse for consumption.
Exports—*General:* Domestic goods plus all re-exports.
         Special: Domestic goods plus nationalized re-exports.
         Semi-special: General exports less all re-exports.

Country	Trade Reporting System	Definition of Re-Exports
Argentina	Imp: Special . Exp: Special .	No official definition given in trade publication. Goods having undergone minor transformation or simply having been entered for consumption are reported as ordinary exports upon later reshipment abroad.
Bolivia	Imp: Special . Exp: Special .	No definition available.
Brazil	Imp: Special . Exp: Semi-special.	No definition available. Re-exports are excluded from exports.
Chile	Imp: Special . Exp: Special .	Foreign goods reshipped abroad without having cleared Customs. They are not recorded. No mention of re-exports of Customs-cleared goods.
Colombia	Imp: General . Exp: General .	Customs-cleared goods leaving the country in the same condition as when imported. Re-exports are shown separately as a total figure in trade tables.
Costa Rica	Imp: General . Exp: General .	Principally goods involved in special transactions including temporary trade, returned empties, transit trade (presumably indirect), repair trade, etc.
Cuba	Imp: General . Exp: General .	No definition available.
Dominican Republic	Imp: Special . Exp: Special .	Customs-cleared goods leaving the country in the same condition as when imported.
Ecuador	Imp: General . Exp: General .	Customs-cleared goods leaving the country in the same condition as when imported.
El Salvador	Imp: Special . Exp: Special .	No definition available.
Guatemala	Imp: Special . Exp: Semi-special.	Customs-cleared goods leaving the country in the same condition as when imported.
Haiti	Imp: General . Exp: General .	No definition available.
Honduras	Imp: Special . Exp: Special .	Foreign goods reshipped abroad without having cleared through Customs. Customs-cleared re-exports are listed as regular exports.
Mexico	Imp: General . Exp: General .	Imported goods being re-exported without having been transformed.
Nicaragua	Imp: General . Exp: Semi-special.	No definition available. Re-exports are included in export figures.
Panama	Imp: General . Exp: Semi-special .	Goods previously imported (and recorded in the statistics) being re-exported without having been transformed. Re-exports are not published with exports.

Country	Trade Reporting System	Definition of Re-Exports
Paraguay . .	Imp: Special . Exp: Special .	Returned empties and other articles previously imported. Aggregate figure on re-exports published in trade tables.
Peru . . .	Imp: Special . Exp: Special .	No definition available. Re-exports are included in the export figures.
Uruguay . .	Imp: Special . Exp: Special .	No definition available. Re-exports are included in the export figures.
Venezuela . .	Imp: General . Exp: General .	No definition available.

Source: The basic source of this table is a paper prepared by the Inter American Statistical Institute for the first session of its Committee on the Improvement of National Statistics which met in June 1951. This paper was corrected according to the observations made by the various delegates at the meeting. This committee is composed of the chief statistical officer of each country and implements the general policy of IASI, which is the improvement of statistical methodology among the nations of the Western Hemisphere.

The other 16 countries, with the exception of Haiti and Paraguay, include all gold transactions as separate items under merchandise trade. The trade statistics of Hatii usually show movements of gold, silver, and platinum (combined) as a single item. Paraguay includes gold and silver in a " precious metals " item. The Chilean statistics show the movement of monetary metals under a separate section, Specie and Precious Metals, which is part of the total trade account. In the case of Ecuador it is not always clear whether gold transactions by the Central Bank are included in the trade statistics.

There are various minor deviations from the general practice. Colombia, for example, classifies imported gold coins as part of merchandise trade. In the statistics of the Dominican Republic, certain summary tables have at times made a distinction between " gold and coins " and merchandise proper.

Silver appears rather uniformly as a merchandise item in the Latin American trade statistics. As we have already noted, monetary silver appears in Brazilian and Mexican statistics as part of a separate non-merchandise category. Only in Haiti and Paraguay are silver movements combined with other metals; thus they are easily available for isolated examination. In the trade statistics of the Dominican Republic silver bullion has at times been lumped with gold manufactures as a single item under merchandise trade.

The official trade statistics of about one-half the Latin American countries include some indication as to the value of *bunker fuel* exports. In most of these cases, however, there is no segregation of value, but exports are included with other forms of merchandise. Peru and Uruguay report such exports under a separate category, Peru under " consumption of ships " and Uruguay under " mineral coal for ships." Chile includes bunker sales as part of ships' stores; Mexico includes bunker oil sales as separate items. El Salvador, Haiti, Panama, and Paraguay include bunker fuel data in the trade statistics. In all the remaining countries bunker fuel transactions are either omitted or included in some other item. There is virtually no information found in the official trade reports on fuel purchases abroad by domestic flag vessels, except in a few instances where it appears that such purchases are reported under the general category of ships' stores.

Most of the Latin American countries include transactions in *vessels and aircraft* in the official export and import data. The absence of specific items (for example, in Haiti, Nicaragua, and Paraguay) cannot necessarily be construed as evidence of omission, since it is possible that transactions appear in a broad or " miscellaneous " category. In other countries the reported data do not necessarily include all transactions. In certain countries, purchases of vessels and aircraft for military purposes are excluded, whereas in some the definitions relating to vessels entering into merchandise trade are restricted. The Chilean trade statistics include only the purchase or sale of vessels for harbor or inland navigation. Peru's trade statistics for 1948 define the trade item as consisting of ships exceeding 100 tons imported from the United States, together with certain other ships and boats.

Government transactions are usually included in the official trade statistics. It is not always clear, however, from the available data, to what extent exports and imports by governments are actually included. Apparently they are excluded entirely from the statistics of Nicaragua, whereas in Ecuador they are omitted in part. War materials are often excluded entirely. Since the groupings for ordinary commodities are almost invariably the same regardless of the importer, there is no basis for distinguishing between governmental and private transactions. In the statistics of Venezuela governmental transactions are usually shown within a general category of non-dutiable exports and imports, but even here the entries are not confined to such transactions.

In the treatment of *minor items* there is considerable lack of uniformity which is, however, not peculiar to the Latin American countries. Often the same countries are not consistent from one year to the next. In the case of *parcel post shipments* the list of Latin American countries which record only imports is much larger than that showing both imports and exports. Official statistics indicate that Argentina, Colombia, Costa Rica, and Guatemala report both export and import parcel post shipments and that El Salvador, Honduras, Nicaragua, Mexico, Peru, Panama, and Venezuela report imports only. Ecuador and Uruguay definitely exclude the item, and in various other countries it is either omitted or included in a miscellaneous category.

Exports of *ships' stores* are included in the statistics of Argentina, Chile, Ecuador, Peru, and Uruguay (from port of Montevideo). Argentina, Ecuador, Panama, and Peru include imports of ships' stores as and when landed for home consumption. The majority of Latin American countries indicate no information concerning this item.

Passengers' effects are normally excluded from the recorded imports, except in cases of long stay on the part of incoming passengers, an example of which is provided by Chile. That country records the item if the passenger entering the country stays more than 3 months and whenever personal effects are valued at more than $500. Recorded exports almost invariably exclude *personal effects* unless they are clearly in excess of what could be considered a normal amount. *Sample goods* are also usually excluded. *Secondhand machinery* brought in by mining companies and other types of business enterprise engaged in developmental work is often excluded from recorded imports, but available information relating to the extent of such omission is not very conclusive. Among miscellaneous types of operations which are occasionally reflected in foreign trade figures is the salvaging of wrecked vessels in connection with which Chile, for example, includes the goods salvaged in the trade figures without ascribing the imports to any specific country of origin.

In-transit trade. The explanatory notes accompanying the trade statistics of the Latin American countries do not make it possible in all cases to determine how in-transit shipments are handled. Among the 9 countries on a " special trade " basis for both exports and imports, transit trade is generally excluded. A partial exception is Uruguay, which includes goods in transit to Brazil. Though technically not an exception, in the sense that transit trade is excluded from the ordinary merchandise trade, Chile reports, in a separate category, the movement of foreign merchandise which enters Chilean ports and, without clearing Customs, is shipped to another countty. It should be noted in this connection that the major part of Bolivia's foreign trade by sea passes through the ports of northern Chile.

Since the methods of dealing with in-transit shipments are far from uniform they are often one of the principal reasons for lack of comparability of trade statistics. A country shipping goods in-transit through Panama, for example, to one of the countries of Central America may possibly show the goods as destined for Panama. In Panama the shipments may or may not be shown in the export and import statistics; and the country of actual destination may or may not show Panama, or the originating country, as a country of origin in its import statistics. Such

difficulties are still inherent in the statistics of most important transhipment countries and in the data of the " origination " and " destination "
countries involved.   In the River Plate area, such problems confront the
analyst in dealing with the trade statistics of Argentina, Uruguay, and
Paraguay.   Paraguay's exports through Argentina and Uruguay to what
are supposed to be other destinations are identified accordingly in the
official statistics, but they are considered as consignments without knowledge of final destination.   Argentina's trade statistics do not include
transit shipments.   Uruguay includes certain re-exports other than
nationalized products.

For an illustration of how the handling of in-transit trade in Latin
American countries may result in considerable lack of comparability, it
is not necessary to examine solely the trade statistics of such transhipment
countries as Panama, Uruguay, or Argentina.   In its May 26, 1951, issue
of *Foreign Trade*, the Canadian Department of Trade and Commerce called
attention to the lack of comparability between the Canadian statistics and
those of certain Latin American countries relating to Canada's trade with
such countries.   The discrepancies between Canadian and Mexican
statistics covering the movement of Mexican goods through the United
States to Canada are reflected in Table 2.

Table 2

Mexican Exports to Canada, 1948 and 1949

(In millions of Canadian dollars.   Mexican values are converted to Canadian dollars
by approximate annual average exchange rates.)

	1948		1949	
	Canadian Statistics	Mexican Statistics	Canadian Statistics	Mexican Statistics
Cotton, raw . . .	20·0	—	15·8	0·9
Cotton manufactures .	—	0·1	0·8	0·4
Sisal and istle fibre .	4·2	—	2·0	—
Vegetables, fresh .	0·1	—	2·9	—
Coffee, green . .	0·5	—	0·7	0·4
Nuts	0·1	—	1·3	0·5

Source: As reported by Canadian Department of Trade and Commerce, *Foreign
Trade*, May 26, 1951, issue.

The explanation of the wide discrepancy shown in Table 2 lies in the
almost certain fact that Mexican statistics recorded these shipments as
exports to the United States, whereas Canada recorded them as imports
from Mexico.

Commodity classification.   More than half the Latin American countries use, for both imports and exports, a commodity classification system based on their tariff classifications. In countries with highly diversified economies, these classifications have serious shortcomings for statistical purposes. In some countries, however, the commodity classification for both imports and exports consists merely of alphabetical listing without grouping into classes of commodities. Where only one or a few products are important in the trade, almost any commodity classification would be satisfactory if the important products were separately enumerated, regardless of whether the commodity classification provides for the grouping of products.

The Latin American countries are, nevertheless, giving considerable attention to the problem of standardizing international trade commodity classification especially since 1945. Mexico began retabulating its regular statistics in the form of the League of Nations Minimum List even before World War II, and Brazil made use of the Minimum List as a supplementary form of tabulation from 1943, retabulating data back to 1938. Shortly after 1943, Ecuador, Nicaragua, Costa Rica, and the Dominican Republic also began using the Minimum List as a supplemental classification, following the suggestion of the Inter American Statistical Institute (see below). Bolivia bases its commodity classification on that of the Brussels Convention of 1913, and Chile used it from the early 1920's to 1939. Uruguay adopted the Brussels International Nomenclature in 1942.

The publication by the League of Nations of its Minimum List of Commodities for International Trade Statistics in 1938 was the first important step taken toward dealing on a broad and constructive basis with the general lack of uniformity in commodity composition. The Inter American Statistical Institute, guided by the general objectives which had characterized the work of the Committee of Statistical Experts of the League of Nations during the 1930's, assumed the initiative in broadening the base of the League's Minimum List. To this end the Institute developed its Basic Classification Scheme of 1945, an initial step in a series of national indices to be used for converting the foreign trade statistics of each American nation into a common classification pattern for purposes of international comparison. The Convertibility Index for Foreign Trade Statistical Classification of the American States, which was published by the Institute in preliminary form in 1945, represented a forward step in adjusting the classifications of the Minimum List to the needs of inter American economic collaboration.

The application of the Basic Classification Scheme by the countries of the American Nations was suspended, however, when the United Nations made announcement in 1948 of its own plans for revision of the Minimum List. This step resulted in 1950 in the issuance by the United Nations of the Standard International Trade Classification (SITC) to replace the old Minimum List. The SITC contains cross references to the Minimum List and to the *Tariff Nomenclature* of 1950 as prepared by the European Customs Union Study Group in Brussels. Many of the Latin American countries have indicated a desire to retain, for their own use, their current national classification; but they have indicated, at the same time, a willingness to supply also foreign trade data within the framework of the SITC; in fact, Mexico did so in 1951.

In the statistical classification of foreign trade data, much remains to be accomplished before a high degree of comparability of national statistics can be realized. In many countries the statistical classification is still based on the tariff classification. Customs offices in many countries have traditionally been more concerned with fiscal control than with the requirements of full economic analysis. There is, of course, no ideal system of classification; the purposes for which data are used vary from country to country. Nevertheless, until the importance of uniformity and comparability is more fully recognized, the detail necessary to analysis will remain deficient. It should be noted that this problem is more pressing in connection with import classification than in the case of exports, largely because of the high percentage of exports covered, in the trade of many countries, by two or three basic products.

Valuation. The systems of import and export valuation employed by the countries of Latin America not only show marked differences, but in some countries changes have been so frequent that comparison of data over a period of years for certain commodities is exceedingly difficult.

In the *valuation of imports* 11 countries (Argentina, Brazil, Chile, Colombia, Costa Rica, El Salvador, Mexico, Paraguay, Uruguay, Peru, and Haiti) use a c.i.f. basis, often without clear indication whether on a landed or non-landed basis. The entry of livestock into Costa Rica from Nicaragua is on an f.o.b., point of shipment, basis. The system employed by Peru is a " calculated " c.i.f. system, with 20 per cent added to the f.o.b. value. Eight countries (Bolivia, Cuba, Dominican Republic, Ecuador, Honduras, Nicaragua, Panama, and Venezuela) use f.o.b. foreign port of shipment. Guatemala employs a mixed system. In that country, valuation for imports by land is usually on a c.i.f. basis (exclusive of duties) and for imports by sea on an f.a.s. (free alongside ship) basis, foreign port of shipment, plus 20 per cent to cover loading, insurance, freight, commissions, and other charges (exclusive of consular fees) incurred up to arrival in Guatemalan port. Uruguay employs c.i.f., officially appraised values. Mexico uses the f.o.b. basis in cases where it is impossible to determine the valuation on a c.i.f. basis.

In some instances countries employing the f.o.b. basis also determine a c.i.f. equivalent by adding an arbitrary amount in order to allow for such items as freight, insurance, and other charges. Nicaragua and Panama, for example, use a 10–12 per cent addition to cover freight, insurance, foreign export duties, consular fees, and buyer's commissions. Venezuela also makes certain arbitrary adjustments which apparently vary somewhat according to circumstances.

In the *valuation of exports* all the countries of Latin America use the f.o.b. basis, although there are many variations. In Costa Rica, for example, different bases are employed, namely, official f.o.b., declared (estimated) f.a.s., and declared f.o.b. The official values apply chiefly to coffee exports; they are assigned on the basis of net sales prices in San Jose, plus transportation to the port of shipment, loading, and other charges. The f.a.s. basis applies largely to banana exports the values of which are exporters' estimates. The declared f.o.b. values apply to other exports.

Many of the Latin American countries have followed more or less arbitrary methods in the valuation of exports. As discussed more fully in Chapter 5, " Valuation," Venezuela uses, for example, an official value, (f.o.b. excluding export duty) for the 10 per cent of its exports which consists of products other than petroleum. For petroleum exports the basis is a nominal value which has long had the effect of giving an over-all export value for Venezuela substantially different from a true f.o.b. value. The system employed by Peru has been clearly described by Woscoboinik, on the basis of a questionnaire inquiry, as follows:

The statistical values of exported commodities for a series of products (certain classes of metallic or non-metallic minerals, wool, coca leaves, cattle hides, rubber, etc.) represent weekly quotations based on the market prices in the United States, furnished to Customs by the Ministry of Finance. Rubber gums and " balata " values are based on British market quotations and these apply to the exports of British destination. For a number of other commodities, mainly forest and fishery products, the weekly quotations (furnished by the Ministry of Finance) are based on the prices of the commodities in Manaos, Brazil. Crude petroleum and gasoline quotations are based on United States market prices. Cotton, sugar, and flax statistical valuations represent the values shown in the sales contracts of those commodities in Peru. Values used for other products are those declared by exporters in the pertinent documents, following a check of the average values of those commodities in previous months.[1]

Mexico's basis for the valuation of exports, other than petroleum and metals, is f.o.b. port of shipment, exclusive of export tax. However, petroleum and metal exports have been valued since 1940 on the basis of

---

[1] *Survey of Foreign Trade Statistical Practices and Definitions in the American Nations, 1947,* a report prepared by Santiago Woscoboinik for the Inter-American Statistical Congress.

a complicated estimating process in which quotations in the principal foreign markets are used as a base from which various deductions are made to cover processing costs, wastes and losses, freight, and other charges. In Panama exports are valued f.o.b. port of shipment, except bananas, which are valued officially on the basis of production costs and selling prices in the principal foreign markets. Since many Latin American countries make exports on consignment, the value of the goods may not be known at the time of export; there are no doubt other instances in which more or less arbitrary valuations apply to particular export products.

Currency conversions. The various currencies in use in the Latin American countries, and the different rates at which some of them have depreciated, create a situation under which the trade statistics in some cases are only approximate measures of the trade movements. The existence of multiple exchange rates, and the allocation of exchange for particular countries or commodities at varying rates, complicate the difficulty of converting statistics, especially with regard to comparability over a period of time. A few cases may be cited as indicative. For example, in Argentina under the current (1952) exchange control system, exporters are required to surrender the proceeds of their exports at one of two rates, namely, 5 and 7·5 pesos per dollar, respectively, and at corresponding rates for other currencies, depending upon the commodity exported. Importers are required to buy the exchange needed to finance their imports at one of the same two rates, depending upon the commodity imported. The amount of pesos shown in the reported trade statistics is influenced by the multiple exchange rate structure. Exports are valued on the basis of domestic market prices, and although this procedure does not necessitate use of the exchange rates, such rates are reflected in recorded export values to the extent that they affect prices. Imports on the other hand are valued on the basis of foreign currency values which, in turn, are converted into Argentine pesos at the rates applicable to the respective transactions. This procedure may result in a fair approximation of the value in pesos of the country's trade, but conversion of Argentine trade statistics into dollars at the 5-peso rate results in overvaluation of items to which the 7·5-peso rate applies. On the other hand, conversion at the 7·5-peso rate tends to undervalue items to which the 5-peso rate is applicable. The value of the recorded statistics is limited accordingly for purposes of comparability.

Chile is an example of a country where the effect of multiple exchange rates is reflected in the foreign trade statistics in a somewhat different manner. The export and import values are expressed in " Chilean gold pesos of 6 pence." The United States equivalent of this is about 20·6 cents. Gold peso values of both imports and exports are based on commercial invoice values some of which are expressed in foreign currencies and some in Chilean currency. The rate used in converting foreign currencies does not in all cases correctly reflect the values of such currencies. After the devaluation of the British pound in September 1949, the rate for the pound remained unchanged. This resulted in some degree of overvaluation in gold pesos of trade values expressed in pounds steriing.

Country designations. In the Latin American countries, *imports* are generally credited to the country of origin but it is not clear that the meaning of the term is always the same. The term " procedencia," which applies particularly to Brazil, Costa Rica, Panama, Paraguay, Uruguay, and Venezuela is generally considered as " country of origin " but not necessarily so. Colombia is the only Latin American country using a double system for indicating the country to which imports are credited, namely, country of origin and country of purchase. Brazil, Chile, and Mexico credit their imports to country of purchase; Cuba uses country of purchase, except that, in the case of imports of certain commodities, a system is applied which credits also country of origin or country of consignment, depending on circumstances.

With regard to *exports*, the country of destination is stated in the majority of cases as the country to which the goods are credited, often with the reservation that it is not necessarily the country of *final* destination. As already noted, Paraguay identifies exports through Argentina and Uruguay as consignments without knowledge as to final destination. Colombia credits exports on the basis of country of sale. The basic products, such as sugar and coffee, exported from Latin America are frequently shipped on consignment. The result is that the country of destination is unknown at the time of export. In consequence, the distribution by countries of statistics on exports of these products tends to be inaccurate. In at least one Latin American country, namely, Cuba, a record is kept to show whether the country of destination shown in the statistics for export of sugar was based solely on country of consignment information.

Index numbers. Only a small number of Latin American countries have developed quantum and unit value indexes. In Argentina, monthly and annual indexes are compiled by the Banco Central. Brazil annually computes quantum indexes and in addition quarterly indexes on exports. Chile's Dirección General de Estadística calculates annually and monthly aggregate quantum indexes and also provides data for component subgroups; the Banco Central of Chile has also published quantum and unit value indexes employing different methods and base periods. Cuba compiles quantum indexes annually and monthly; the Dominican Republic and Colombia are also compilers of quantum indexes. In Latin

America the coverage of quantum indexes for exports is greater than for imports because of the limited number of individual commodities exported and the large number of commodities imported.   Usually the data are unadjusted for incomplete coverage.   Users of the index numbers should bear in mind the effects of varying import control regulations and the cases where an important export commodity has lost its foreign market. Index numbers of export and import unit values, or of the wholesale price of home produced and imported goods, are reported by the statistical offices of Brazil, Cuba, Costa Rica, Dominican Republic, Peru, and Venezuela.   At a meeting of foreign trade statisticians in Panama in late 1951, the matter of quantum and unit value index numbers was discussed, and some improvement is to be expected.

Publication; availability of data.   Although there is still a considerable lack of uniformity and comparability in the presentation of foreign trade statistics among the Latin American countries, the official reports reflect a noticeable degree of improvement.   For example, there has been progress in the concentration of statistical activities in a single statistical office. With few exceptions, consular invoices are now required, and documentation in general is becoming more satisfactory.   Progress is much slower in some countries than in others; there is still a large area for further improvement.

All but two of the Latin American countries employ the calendar year as the basis for reporting annual export and import data.   Haiti reports on a fiscal year basis beginning October 1 and Honduras on a fiscal year basis beginning July 1 (August 1 until 1938).   All the Latin American countries except Honduras and Paraguay issue some form of monthly or quarterly data.   In some instances, however, such short-term statistics are only partially reported.   For example, the *Boletin Estadístico Mensual* of Costa Rica shows only total trade figures.   In some countries (for example, in Bolivia, Colombia, Guatemala, and Venezuela) the Central Bank is the sole source of short-term data and the bulletins issued by these institutions, though usually accurate, are generally concerned with compilations designed primarily to reflect the country's balance-of-payments position rather than to show the detailed grouping of commodity trade.

Where countries export only one or a few products, data on such exports frequently are available more promptly, and with reasonable accuracy, from sources other than the official trade statistics of the country. Most of the Latin American countries allow public access to copies of manifests of vessels entering and leaving the ports of countries.   Many traders and steamship companies obtain information on the foreign trade of the Latin American countries from agents in the ports who compile summary statistical information from these manifests.   The information so compiled may be limited to one or a few products in which the user is interested.

One of the major difficulties in the use of trade statistics of the Latin American countries is the lack of promptness in the release of the official trade statistics. Of the annual reports available at the close of 1951, about one-half were published within 2 years of the close of the year to which the statistics relate, about one-fourth within 3 years, and the remainder after lags varying from 4 to 8 years. Among the countries in which summary annual data currently appears with reasonable promptness (usually within 6 months) are Argentina, Brazil, Chile, Colombia, Mexico, Panama, Peru, Uruguay, and Venezuela. Many of the countries which do not issue monthly or quarterly data (or do so on an irregular or partial basis) are among those which issue the complete annual statistics within a period of 2 years.

These delays may soon be relieved since countries have indicated a willingness to provide prompt summaries of foreign trade according to the SITC, to be published by the Statistical Office of the United Nations.

CHAPTER 19

Near and Far East

JOHN A. LOFTUS
U.S. Department of State

HISTORICAL DEVELOPMENT

Egypt and Anglo-Egyptian Sudan. Although the Sudan became nominally a condominium of Egypt and the United Kingdom, Egypt itself did not attain independence till 1936. Since 1907 the two sets of statistics have been more or less separate; the Sudan includes trade with Egypt in its statistics but Egypt compiles data separately on such trade, not aggregated with the regular trade statistics. Both in Egypt and Sudan the influence of British tradition and practices has affected the procedure of compiling trade statistics. As a result, the statistics of both of these areas are quite similar to those of the British Dominions and British Colonies.

Ethiopia. Prior to 1936, Ethiopian trade statistics were crude and irregular. During the period of Italian occupation, data were published from Rome, consolidating the statistics of Ethiopia, Eritrea, and Italian Somaliland. From 1941 through 1944 Ethiopia was under British administration, and such data as were available were released by the United Kingdom. The Ethiopian government resumed the publication of trade statistics in 1945. Until 1948, commodity data only were provided with no country distribution of exports and imports. From the Ethiopian year ending September 10, 1949, country totals were released, and also export statistics on coffee by country. Complete commodity-by-country statistics were initiated in the quarter ended March 9, 1951. The country distribution of exports is, however, heavily biased by the fact that a large part of the export trade is through Aden and no effort is made to determine the actual country of destination.

Israel (Palestine). During the period of the mandate for Palestine the British influence on the trade statistics of that area was very great. This influence has undoubtedly carried over into the statistics of the new state of Israel. Territorial changes, however, make the comparison of the statistics over an extended period of time very difficult. Data for 1947 and prior years refer to the whole of Palestine; until July 1941 trade with Trans-Jordan was excluded. Data for 1948 and subsequent periods cover only the new state of Israel; the balance of former Palestine has become part of Jordan.

Other Near East. For the remaining countries of the Near East (Jordan, Iran, Iraq, Syria, Lebanon, etc.) trade statistics have been very crude and in many cases non-existent. In addition, territorial and political changes make it very difficult to compare any statistics over a period of time. The Near East is virtually unrecognizable if the present territorial and administrative alignments are compared with the status of, say, 1910 or 1900. (Even place names, it might be mentioned, are different; what once was Persia is now Iran, what once was Mesopotamia is now Iraq.) The whole area roughly known as " the Arab world " was, prior to World War I, a component and an extension of the Ottoman Empire, subject to intrusive enclaves of British power or influence at Aden and other points around the periphery of the Arabian peninsula. Contact with the world outside was, on the diplomatic level, effected at the seat of Empire; on the commercial level, it was entirely *ad hoc* and, as regards large parts of the area, non-existent.

After World War I, mandates were established over much of the territory of the Near East. These were accorded to France and the United Kingdom; the French had the mandatory responsibility for Syria and Lebanon, the British for Iraq, Palestine, and Trans-Jordan. These various mandates had diverse histories and differing termination dates. Iraq became an independent kingdom in 1932, Trans-Jordan not until 1946 (it is now known as the Hashemite Kingdom of Jordan). When the British mandate for Palestine was terminated in 1948, the state of Israel emerged with jurisdiction over part of the territory; the remainder (loosely known as Arab Palestine) is now part of Jordan.

In Iraq and Jordan, the British, during the period of the mandates, introduced their concepts and traditions of civil administration; hence statistical practice in the foreign trade field now conforms, in a general way, to the main lines of British practice. The same was true of Palestine; and even the new state of Israel is preserving some of the British legacy.

Syria and Lebanon, during the period of the French Mandate, were administered as an integrated entity. After World War II, the two countries had, on the economic side, a council of common interests, a common currency and a Customs union; they could therefore be regarded as constituting, from the commercial point of view, an economic unit. The tie of the common currency has since been broken and the Customs union has been dissolved; the future is uncertain. In general, however, Syria and Lebanon reflect strongly the influence of French tradition and practice in the whole range of administrative procedure, including foreign trade, and other statistical, procedures.

The course of developments in the Arabian peninsula (the Kingdom of Saudi Arabia and Yemen, and the various semi-autonomous Skeikhdoms of the Persian Gulf from Kuwait to Aden) does not need to be described here, since these countries are not in fact discussed in the following pages. None of them publishes or even maintains foreign trade statistics in any organized form. Moreover, the total external trade of most of them is negligible. There are, of course, large exports of oil from Saudi Arabia and Kuwait; the oil companies release their own statistics and publish them in various trade papers.

Burma. There are no separate data on Burmese foreign trade prior to 1937 when Burma was part of India. During the period 1937 to 1941 there was a free trade regime with India, with the result that goods from other countries entering Burma by way of India were shown as imported from India, but with an indication that they were of foreign origin. There was no indication of the countries of ultimate origin. The pre-war figures included only sea- and airborne trade. During the period of Japanese occupation from 1941 to 1945, Burmese trade statistics were to all intents and purposes not compiled. Since 1945 statistics have been fragmentary except that more regular and prompt compilation and publication apparently started in 1951. The landborne trade of Burma has been included in the statistics only since 1947–1948.

China. The discussion of Chinese trade statistics is limited to Nationalist China, now Taiwan (Formosa). The coverage of trade statistics before World War II was subject to recurring change as the area under Japanese occupation expanded. Following the end of the war the coverage increased, but it was again diminished as the Communist Peoples Republic took over the mainland. The statistics for the mainland of China related only to ports under control of the Chinese Maritime Customs.

Current Nationalist China statistics show the trade of the island of Taiwan and are referred to in the publications as statistics on the trade of the " Taiwan District." The statistics include imports from China, but it is explained that these goods, although of Chinese origin, were imported direct from foreign countries and treated therefore as " imports from abroad " (1950 *Annual Trade Statistics, Taiwan*, Table 5). No exports to China are shown in the 1950 returns. Since Taiwan was Japanese-occupied prior to World War II, the current statistics are not comparable in any way with the pre-war Chinese statistics. Instead they are comparable in territorial area with the statistics on Formosan trade which were compiled and issued by the Japanese.

Indochina. Current Indochina trade statistics cover the combined trade of the three republics of Viet-Nam, Cambodia, and Laos with foreign countries. Figures on trade among the three countries are not available. Except for the present area occupied by the Communists, the territorial area of these three republics combined is comparable with the pre-World War II area of French Indochina. There was a break in the statistics of French Indochinese trade during the period of Japanese occupation during World War II.

Indonesia. The pre-war Indonesian trade statistics excluded the trade of (*a*) the free port of Sabang, a Customs exclave, and (*b*) the free port of Riau, insofar as trade in petroleum and petroleum products was concerned. There were no statistics on Indonesian trade during the Japanese occupation of World War II, and from 1946 to 1949 the trade statistics excluded the Republic of Indonesia. Beginning with 1950 the area refers to the United States of Indonesia, but coverage of the statistics is not yet (1952) complete. The area is essentially comparable with the pre-war area of the Netherlands Indies, except New Guinea.

Japan. A major change in the coverage of Japanese trade statistics is the post-World War II exclusion of Formosa and Korea from the Japanese Customs area. The Customs area previously included these territories and consequently Japanese statistics then excluded data on trade between Japan and Formosa and Korea. However, separate information on this trade was compiled. This pre-war trade was between one-fifth and one-third of the total Japanese trade. Most current use of the trade figures of

Japan, therefore, requires that the pre-war figures be adjusted to make them comparable to post-war Japan by adding the pre-war figures on trade between Japan and Korea and Formosa to the pre-war Japanese trade figures.

Korea. Southern Korea is the only post-war reporting area of the Korean peninsula. Because this represents only part of Korea, the data are not comparable with pre-war figures.

Philippines. The territorial coverage of the Philippines has remained unchanged for the past 50 years or so. There were no statistics on the trade of the Philippines during the period of Japanese occupation from 1942 to 1945.

Thailand. The very incomplete and spasmodic Thai trade statistics cover seaport foreign trade (Bangkok only until 1920–1921), land traffic with Malaya (since 1920–1921), land traffic across the Indo-China frontier at Aranya Prades (since 1931–1932), and land traffic crossing at various frontier points in the northwest as well as on the northeastern border (since 1942). There are no statistics on the foreign trade of Thailand by countries for the years 1942 to 1945, and the statistics for these years in the *Statistical Year Book* (No. 21 contains data through 1945) are in summary form.

USE AND APPRAISAL OF THE STATISTICS—NEAR EAST

Introduction. This discussion covers the following areas:

Egypt	Iran
Anglo-Egyptian Sudan	Iraq
Ethiopia	Israel
Jordan	Syria-Lebanon

These countries are each exporters of one or a few products and importers of a fairly limited range of finished manufactured goods. As in other countries with this type of trade, the statistics on the trade tend to be primitive in comparison with the standards of larger nations exporting and importing a wide variety of products. Information is usually available on exports of the one or the few products which are important in the export trade, but this information may frequently be obtained more promptly and with reasonable accuracy from sources other than the published government statistics.

Coverage. A major point to watch in the statistics of these countries is that relating to the inclusion or exclusion of what may be termed " government " trade or " government franchised trade."

Although this is not necessarily noted in the official explanations accompanying the statistics as nationally published, the 1950 *Supplement* to the *United Nations Monthly Bulletin of Statistics* states that " military imports " or " munitions " are excluded from the import statistics of Egypt, Iran and Israel; that statistics for Iraq exclude military stores for British forces; and that figures for the Anglo-Egyptian Sudan exclude stores of British and Egyptian armies. Jordan does not appear in the *Supplement*, and no mention is made of the exclusion of military items in the description of the statistics of Syria and Lebanon, but it seems likely that some similar exclusions exist for these countries. Since some items of military stores may consist of civilian-type goods, the commodity import statistics may be undercounted at some points. As far as is known, all government account items are reported in the statistics of Ethiopia, and government imports are indeed dutiable.

Perhaps more serious from the point of view of trade information on non-military-type items is the exclusion from the official statistics of Iran of imports and exports of the Anglo-Iranian Oil Company and the Irano-Soviet Fisheries Company (Shilat); the exclusion of pipeline exports of petroleum from the Iraq statistics (which are, however, reported separately by Iraq); the exclusion of petroleum exports from the Israel statistics; and the exclusion from the Syria-Lebanon figures of crude petroleum imported by pipeline from Iraq for refining in Tripoli.

In the Anglo-Egyptian Sudan where government imports of food, machinery, base metals, timber, etc., are substantial, information on such imports is included in the commodity import statistics without distinction. In addition, separate information is provided on how much of the value of total imports is for government account. A summary table is also provided showing the main commodity items imported by the Sudan Government. The figures on exports from the Sudan exclude camels; but the official statistics provide a separate estimate of the quantity and value exported, based on sales recorded in Egyptian markets. According to the estimate for 1950, the value of Sudan's exports would have been about 3 per cent higher if camels had been included.

All the countries except Ethiopia and Jordan are on a *special* trade basis (Iraq since 1940). Ethiopia is on a *general* trade basis, and the basis for the Jordan statistics is unknown. In-transit trade is recorded separately from exports and imports in all the countries.

In regard to the handling of *gold and silver* in the merchandise statistics, all the countries apparently exclude gold, except the Anglo-Egyptian Sudan, Iran, and Syria-Lebanon. Silver is included in the statistics of Egypt, the Sudan, Iran, and Syria-Lebanon. The explanations of statistics are not always clear on these points; it is to be suspected that whether such shipments are included in the merchandise statistics or reported separately, smuggling might make the figures incomplete. In regard to *bunkers and ships' stores*, it can only be determined that Egypt (and the Sudan) excludes such transactions from the merchandise statistics and presents separate information on loadings. Ethiopia provides fuel for the French railroad to Djibouti; this is not reported in the statistics. It is not clear what the other countries do. Somewhat the same observations apply to *vessels and aircraft*. Egypt, Iran, Iraq and Syria-Lebanon apparently include such items in the merchandise statistics. It is not clear whether the other countries do or not, but it can probably be assumed that trade in these items is trivial or non-existent.

Commodity classification. Of the countries in this area Egypt and the Sudan have the most refined commodity classification for their trade statistics. In addition to publication in terms of its regular commodity classification Egypt recompiles its statistics in terms of the League of Nations Minimum List of 1938. The other countries, with the exception of Jordan, use widely accepted classification bases.

Valuation. Import valuations for these countries are c.i.f. and export valuations f.o.b. There are a number of peculiar valuation practices in the region: Egypt includes export duties in its export values; the Sudan excludes export duties from its export values but they are official values revised monthly; Ethiopian import values are c.i.f. and c. (cost, insurance, freight, and charges) at the Customs station where reported for importation and therefore usually include inland freight to Addis Ababa. Customs duties and other taxes are not included. Export values are declared values plus Customs duties and other taxes at the Customs station from which exported, generally also an interior point. Iranian import and export values are subject to arbitrary adjustments.

An additional important problem with respect to valuation arises out of the existence of unrealistic exchange rates. The conversion of invoice values, where used, into national currency at such exchange rates tends to undervalue imports. Trade values from year to year, and sometimes even from month to month, tend to become non-comparable in terms of national currency. Also, because of the conversion problem, they tend to become non-comparable even in terms of a common denominator, such as the United States dollar. Careful adjustments therefore have to be made for these factors in interpreting the trade statistics of Near Eastern countries.

Country designations. Ethiopia and Egypt credit imports and exports to other countries on a consignment basis (the usual British practice), but Iraq and the Sudan use an origin-destination system. For the remainder of the countries in this area the method of crediting trade by country is not stated. In the published statistics it is not uncommon for countries in this region to indicate the direction of trade only by a selected list of countries with all other countries lumped together as " others."

Availability of statistics. It can be surmised from the discussion that the trade statistics of some Near East countries are not readily available in published form. The published statistics of Egypt and the Sudan are issued regularly and in good form. Statistics of Iran are issued regularly but not in the English language. Since dissolution of the Syria-Lebanon Customs union, trade statistics have been kept separately, and separate statistical publications are issued. In Syria the publication is in English as well as Arabic. For the other countries, issuance is irregular. All the countries are on a calendar year basis, except Iran which bases its annual statistics on a year beginning March 20, and Ethiopia which uses a year beginning about September 10 (though it varies slightly from one year to another).

As indicated in the discussion, information on the imports and exports of many of the products of these countries can be obtained from oil company trade press or other sources. Unpublished statistics may probably also be obtained on request prior to publication. Since the extra-regional trade of these countries is much more important than their trade with each other, the imperfections of the official statistical information can be overcome by using the statistics of the countries' trading partners outside of the region. Since most of the countries in the region obtain their imports from a relatively few sources, it is practicable to use the export statistics of the source countries to reconstruct the import trade statistics of the countries of the region. A similar procedure can be followed to arrive at information on exports from the countries in the region. Export statistics of a raw material supplying country frequently cannot provide accurate information on the destination of exports because of shipments on consignment, diversion after original export, etc.; hence a reconstruction of the exports of the country from the statistics of the receiving countries may actually provide more accurate information on destination than the country's own export statistics.

Conclusion. One generalization which can be made is that the quality of the foreign trade statistics available is low by United States and Western European standards. The quality deficiency most commonly takes the form of: (a) incompleteness of coverage caused by personnel deficiencies at the Custom House level; (b) irregularity and delay in the issuance of statistics; (c) very crude generality in the commodity classifications; (d) vagueness of definition with respect to the crediting of shipments, the treatment of government or other special categories of transactions, etc.; and (e) inadequate and confusing presentation.

Despite the difficulties with most of the trade statistics of these countries, the data are more comprehensive in scope and more systemized in collection and presentation than are the general economic statistics of the region. In many instances, the trade statistics serve in fact as a substitute for statistics on domestic economic activity.

USE AND APPRAISAL OF THE STATISTICS—FAR EAST

Introduction. This discussion covers the following areas:

Burma	Japan
Nationalist China	Korea
Indochina	Philippines
Indonesia	Thailand

Except for Japan, these countries are similar to those in the Near East in being suppliers of one or a few products and importers of a relatively limited range of manufactured goods. Although the trade statistics more or less follow the pattern of countries of this type, they are on the whole more adequate than the statistics of most of the Near East countries. This is despite the fact that the statistics are compiled by governments which for some of the countries (Burma, Indochina, Indonesia, Korea) are new and inexperienced. These countries attained independence, or passed through major political crisis, since World War II. However, these generalizations do not apply to the trade statistics of Japan. The Japanese statistics are of good quality, reflecting her importance as a nation trading in many types of manufactured products.

Coverage—government-type trade. A major point of difficulty with the statistics of a number of the countries discussed here arises from their method of handling certain types of shipments mainly of a government character.

Pre-war Burmese import and export figures presented separate data on trade on government account. Although Burmese trade statistics for 1945–1946 and 1946–1947 are noted as relating to " private trade " only, the statistics from 1947–1948 on include both private and government trade. However, the import statistics exclude imports of armaments and munitions on government account; whether they include civilian-type items is not known. Figures for exports of rice and rice products and timber during post-war years since 1946–1947 are those of the State Agricultural Planning Board and the State Timber Board.

China (Taiwan) in 1950 reported separately three types of imports: " General," " Military," and " ECA." (Military and ECA exports reported as " nil ".) Separate commodity information is provided for each of these types (country information is provided only for the first). It is noted on the table presenting commodity information on " Military " imports that " shipments imported at Taiwan with insufficient particulars for compilation of statistics * are not included.   No indication is given as to amount and type of such imports.

Indochina includes government stores in its statistics but excludes supplies for French forces in the country.   Indonesia excludes imports of the War and Navy Departments but does include United States surplus army supplies.

Reparations exports and imports for the occupation forces are excluded from the trade statistics of Japan.   Imports into Japan include aid supplied by the United States Government (approximately $2000 million from September 1945 through 1950), and goods diverted to the Japanese civilian economy from the occupation force located in Japan.   Despite its greater complexity by late 1951, non-commercial trade was apparently much more satisfactorily covered than in the 1930's.   At that time the Japanese trade statistics frequently omitted government transactions without indication of the extent of such omissions.

South Korean government figures included private trade only prior to the June 1950 hostilities with North Korea, but figures compiled by the United States ECA mission in Korea included government items.

Defense supplies, including all deliveries under United States defense and military assistance programs, are excluded from the trade statistics of the Philippines, as are United States surplus army supplies.   UNRRA supplies were included in the Philippine statistics if carried on merchant vessels, but they were excluded if carried on United States Army or Navy vessels—a haphazard distinction from the point of view of the effect of the shipments on the domestic economy.

Thailand includes government trade in its statistics.

The varying treatment of government trade among the countries of the Far East discussed here adds substantial difficulty in use of their trade statistics, particularly in the light of the importance of this trade.   Taken together with the exclusion of government trade by other countries in this region (for example, the exclusion of grain imports by India), the handling of government trade in the statistics accounts for one of the most important difficulties with the statistics of the region.

Coverage—miscellaneous.   In addition to the problem of government trade described above, there are other substantial difficulties with the coverage of the statistics of the countries in this area.   Some of the most important problems in regard to territorial coverage of the statistics were described in the section on historical development, above.   In addition, there are difficulties arising from the fact that smuggled goods are, of course, not included in the trade statistics.   The pre-war Chinese statistics were notoriously subject to this omission, and the Chinese Government from 1903 on attempted estimates of the amount of unrecorded smuggled goods. The estimates were based on the amount of trade with China recorded in the statistics of other countries (see Chapters 3 and 9).

The Far East countries are split 5 to 3 between the *general* and *special* systems of recording trade. Burma, Japan, Korea, the Philippines, and Thailand record their trade on the general trade system; Indochina, Indonesia, and China on the special trade system. China derives net import figures by subtracting re-exports from general imports.

Gold is included in the trade statistics of Indochina, the Philippines, and Thailand; and it is excluded from the trade statistics of Burma, China and Japan. The practice in Indonesia and Korea is to exclude gold from the trade data. In many of the Far East countries discussed here, gold has a premium value for hoarding purposes. To avoid gold restrictions, it is frequently traded in the form of articles only slightly fabricated. The dividing line between bullion and manufactured gold is therefore blurred. In addition there is the further difficulty that smuggling of gold is a widespread practice, and such gold movements go entirely unrecorded.

Silver is included in the merchandise trade statistics of Burma, Indochina, Korea, and Thailand, and excluded by China, Indonesia, and Japan.

For most of the countries the practice in regard to the inclusion or exclusion of *bunkers*, *vessels*, and *aircraft* is unknown. However, for these countries the practice in this regard is of little or no importance to the usefulness of the figures, since such transactions are probably unimportant. Certainly the usefulness of the data is more seriously influenced by the practice in regard to government trade as described above. Indochina, Japan, and Thailand include transfers of vessels and aircraft in their statistics. Bunkers are known to be included in the trade statistics of Indochina and Indonesia. Japan excludes bunkers from the regular import and export statistics, and presents separate information on such loadings.

There is one peculiarity of coverage in the Philippine import statistics which needs separate description. According to the 1948 *Foreign Commerce Yearbook* (page 520), issued by the Office of International Trade of the United States Department of Commerce, the Philippine import statistics prior to 1940 were recorded

on the basis of liquidation of Customs entries, *i.e.*, not until all duties and other charges had been paid and other Customs formalities complied with. Periods of up to 2 years were permitted and elapsed before import statistics were available. Beginning with 1940 . . . the method was changed to the recording of imports upon actual arrival, including imports intended for bonding. It is therefore obvious that import statistics prior to 1940 are not comparable with those of later years. Under the old system recorded imports of particular commodities may indicate a heavy decline for a period when actual arrivals increased, and vice versa. In making the change, no provision was made for recording imports which had actually arrived but had not been liquidated. The total value of such imports, lost so far as Philippine statistics are concerned, has been estimated by the United States Foreign Service at $25,000,000. Exports are recorded at the time of shipment.

Commodity classification. As might be anticipated, there is no uniformity in the commodity classifications of this group of countries. The Japanese system is the most refined and comprehensive. However, comparability of Japanese statistics during the years after World War II is somewhat handicapped by major changes in the commodity classifications. In April 1951, the United Nations Standard International Trade Classification (SITC) was adopted, with modifications to fit the Japanese import and export trade. Burma also adopted this classification with modifications in 1951. Indonesia substantially changed its import commodity classification from 1st January, 1948, and its export classification from 1st January, 1949. Indochina under French influence had a detailed commodity classification. Thailand has a reasonably detailed commodity classification in its annual publications, but it provides practically no commodity information in its current statistics.

Valuation. Except for the Philippines, which uses an f.o.b. valuation for both imports and exports, all the countries here being discussed use c.i.f. for imports and f.o.b. for exports. In Burma and China the market value at the port of importation or exportation is used as the basis of value, although invoice values substantially different from market values are sometimes used. Since 1946, the value shown in the Indonesian export statistics includes the amount of the export duties (pre-war export values did not). Indonesia sometimes uses an officially-determined value for exports, and the export value of rice and teak from Burma are set by government boards. Probably the most important difficulty with the value shown in the import statistics of the countries in the area is that resulting from the conversion of invoice values to domestic values. The import value shown in the trade returns may show the invoice value in a foreign currency converted to the domestic currency at the official rate of exchange, even though most imports may have been paid for at the market rate. Since the official rate normally overvalues the domestic currency, this understates the value of imports. In Thailand, and probably other countries in the area, the Customs may revalue the products when the value determined in this fashion is much too low in relation to domestic market value. Because the proportion of import trade carried on at official and market rates varies from period to period, the comparability of the value figures is limited by these practices in regard to conversion of valuations.

Country designations. Most of the countries in the Far East follow as far as possible the origin-destination method of crediting trade by country. However, Burma, and Thailand use country of consignment, and Indonesia uses consignment for its export statistics. Countries of the area face difficulties in getting information on country of origin or destination for goods moving through Hong Kong and Singapore, and this substantially limits the accuracy of the direction-of-trade information. Thailand, in its final annual reports, supplements the country of consignment information in its import statistics by a supplementary tabulation by country of origin for goods shown in the regular import statistics as consigned from Singapore or Hong Kong. A similar procedure is not followed for exports. Indonesia indicates by an " f.o." those cases where goods are sent to a country " for orders." Other countries in the area undoubtdely do not report the final destination for many important exports shipped on consignment, or with optional destinations, and the statistics may not indicate where this lack of information is important. This is a common weakness of statistics compiled under a " final destination " definition but it is a source of particular difficulty in raw material supplying areas.

Some of the countries do not regularly supply current information on direction of trade; others which do supply the information frequently combine many countries into an " other country " total, making use of the figures difficult. On occasion, the current figures released on import and export trade by commodities do not total to the same amounts as the figures released on trade by countries.

Availability of data: publications. As in the case of the Near East countries, and particularly in the period after World War II, publications of trade statistics in countries of the Far East have not generally been issued regularly. Some of the current information is not released for a year or more after the period covered, particularly in commodity or country detail. Current data not yet released in published form can frequently be obtained from the Customs authorities on request. These generalizations do not apply to the Japanese statistics which are released currently on a monthly basis in considerable commodity and country detail, with supplementary information on goods imported for occupation personnel, etc.

Because of the relatively disorganized state of the release of trade figures in published form by most of these countries, current statistics can frequently best be obtained from United Nations publications, such as the *Monthly Bulletin of Statistics* (totals of exports and imports) and *Direction of International Trade* (total value of trade with individual countries), which include information obtained from the individual countries directly even though not yet released in published form. The Mutual Security Administration (formerly the Economic Cooperation Administration) publishes a monthly *Far East Data Book* which incorporates much of the trade information shown in the United Nations publications noted, but also contains unpublished import and export commodity information obtained from the Customs or statistical offices of the countries by the United States Departments of Commerce and State.

It should be noted that the annual figures on trade for several of the countries are sometimes presented on the basis of the Buddhist year (April 1 to March 31). Thailand used the Buddhist year until March 31, 1940, and the Gregorian calendar year thereafter. Burma's statistics were on the basis of a Buddhist year before the war, but they are now compiled on the basis of a fiscal year ending September 30. Japanese and Korean trade statistics have consistently been on a calendar year basis, but the government fiscal year is from April 1 to March 31. Hence, economic programs and data are generally discussed on the latter basis and, in such contexts, trade statistics are also adjusted to the Buddhist year.

As for countries of the Near East, the gaps created by the lack of data on the trade of some of the countries of the Far East may be filled by use of the statistics of the trading partners of the countries. This in fact is the system used in the publications, cited above, to derive statistics on trade of some of the Far Eastern countries.

Efforts to improve Far East trade statistics. As indicated by the previous discussion, the trade statistics of Far Eastern countries, other than Japan, generally leave much to be desired. Efforts at improving the statistics are being made by all the countries. Burma reorganized the compiling operations of its trade statistics in 1951 and has introduced mechanical methods of compilation. The quality and timeliness of Burma's statistics should thereby be improved. Summary trade statistics for Burma covering the first quarter of 1951 were, in fact, available in published form in August 1951. Given reasonable political stability of the nations, trade statistics of these countries should become available in better quality than in pre-war and immediately post-war years. A meeting of foreign trade and balance-of-payments statisticians of the region was held in Rangoon in January 1951 and a meeting of foreign trade statisticians was held in Bangkok in December 1951, both under the auspices of the United Nations Economic Commission for Asia and the Far East. These efforts at solving common problems in regard to foreign trade and balance-of-payments statistics, together with projected future activities of ECAFE and the countries themselves, should result in a greater consciousness of the need for better statistics in these fields and improvements in the statistics compiled.

Appendix

APPENDIX

Primary National Publications of International Trade Statistics

This list sets forth the principal primary *national* publications of international trade statistics. Publications which reproduce or reassemble data from the primary publications are excluded. The list is based on the collection of publications available in the Statistical Office of the United Nations when the list was drawn up in January 1952. Countries may be unrepresented in the list because they do not publish their trade statistics for political reasons (*e.g.*, certain countries of Eastern Europe) or because their trade is not sufficiently important to warrant publication, or again because their publications were not available for a recent period at the time the list was compiled. In particular, certain small territories are not represented because their publications were either not available or too irregular in appearance. The list is therefore not exhaustive, and readers who wish to obtain the latest information for any country should communicate with the responsible authority in that country.

In general the titles of the publications are given in the language in which they are published. Where the publications are presented in two languages, the more common language has occasionally been used in the list.

Publication	Contents
Chapter 13. United States	

Annual

Foreign Commerce and Navigation of the United States Calendar Year.
United States Department of Commerce, Bureau of the Census, Washington, D.C.

Vol. I. Summary and detailed tables of trade by commodity subdivided by country and trade by country subdivided by commodity.
Vol. II. Summary and detailed tables of imports and exports by vessel, with value and shipping weight data, showing domestic port, foreign port, and commodity.
(No issues for recent years.)

Quarterly

Quarterly Summary of Foreign Commerce of the United States.
United States Department of Commerce, Bureau of the Census, Washington, D.C.

Summary tables, aggregates by country and trade by commodity.

Publication	Contents

Monthly

Report No. FT 110—United States Imports of Merchandise for Consumption, Commodity by Country of Origin.
United States Department of Commerce, Bureau of the Census, Washington, D.C.

Imports by commodity, subdivided by country of origin, current month. (*N.B.* Annual cumulative data available in special issue, once a year.)

Report No. FT 120—United States Imports of Merchandise for Consumption, Country of Origin by Subgroups.
United States Department of Commerce, Bureau of the Census, Washington, D.C.

Imports by country of origin, subdivided by subgroups of commodities, current month. (*N.B.* Annual cumulative totals available in special issue, once a year.)

Report No. FT 410—United States Exports of Domestic and Foreign Merchandise, Commodity by Country of Destination.
United States Department of Commerce, Bureau of the Census, Washington, D.C.

Exports of domestic merchandise by commodity subdivided by country of destination, current month; Re-exports of merchandise by commodity subdivided by country of destination, current month. (*N.B.* Annual totals available in special issue, once a year.)

Report No. FT 420—United States Exports of Domestic and Foreign Merchandise, Country of Destination by Subgroups.
United States Department of Commerce, Bureau of the Census, Washington, D.C.

Exports by country subdivided by commodity subgroups, current month; Re-exports, by country of destination, current month. (*N.B.* Annual totals available in special issue, once a year.)

Report No. FT 800—United States Trade in Merchandise and Gold and Silver with United States Territories and Possessions (except Alaska and Hawaii).
United States Department of Commerce, Bureau of the Census, Washington, D.C.

Exports by territory subdivided by commodity, current month; Imports by territory subdivided by commodity, current month. (*N.B.* Annual data available in special issue, once a year.)

Summary Report FT 900—United States Foreign Trade, Total Trade.
United States Department of Commerce, Bureau of the Census, Washington, D.C.

Imports and exports by months, last 2 years; Imports and exports by commodity groups, last 2 months.

Summary Report FT 930—United States Foreign Trade, Trade by Commodity.
United States Department of Commerce, Bureau of the Census, Washington, D.C.

Imports and exports by economic class divided by principal articles, last 2 months.

Summary Report FT 950—United States Foreign Trade, Trade by Country.
United States Department of Commerce, Bureau of the Census, Washington, D.C.

Imports and exports by country, last 2 months.

Chapter 14. United Kingdom

Annual

Annual Statement of the Trade and Navigation of the United Kingdom with British Countries and Foreign Countries.
Statistical Office of the Customs and Excise Department, London.

Vol. I. Trade by commodity.
Vol. II. Imports and re-exports, by commodity subdivided by country.
Vol. III. Exports by commodity subdivided by country.
Vol. IV. Trade by country subdivided by commodity.

Publication	Contents
Monthly	
Accounts Relating to Trade and Navigation of the United Kingdom.	Summary and detailed tables.
Report on Overseas Trade.	Summary tables.
Statistics Division of the Board of Trade, London.	

Chapter 15. The British Commonwealth

AUSTRALIA

Annual

Overseas Trade and Customs and Excise Revenue.	Summary and detailed tables.
Commonwealth Bureau of Census and Statistics, Canberra.	

Monthly

Monthly Bulletin of Oversea Trade Statistics.	Summary tables, trade by principal commodities, subdivided by country (exports).
Commonwealth Bureau of Census and Statistics, Canberra.	

CANADA

Annual

Trade of Canada Year Ended . . . Commerce du Canada année . . .	*Vol. I.* Summary tables, aggregates by country and by commodity groups. Trade by country subdivided by principal articles.
Department of Trade and Commerce, Dominion Bureau of Statistics, Ottawa.	*Vol. II.* Exports, aggregates by country of destination; Exports by main groups and items, subdivided by country of destination.
	Vol. III. Imports, aggregates by country; Imports by groups and items, subdivided by country of origin.

Monthly

Trade of Canada, Monthly Summary of Foreign Trade (No. 10–4110).	Imports, exports, re-exports, and balances of trade, by months;
Department of Trade and Commerce, Dominion Bureau of Statistics, Ottawa.	Summaries of trade with United States and United Kingdom.
Trade of Canada, Imports (No. 10–4030)	Imports by country, current month and cumulative;
Department of Trade and Commerce, Dominion Bureau of Statistics, Ottawa.	Imports by main groups, distinguishing United Kingdom and United States; Imports by articles, subdivided by countries, current month and cumulative.
Trade of Canada, Exports (No. 10-4020)	Exports and re-exports by country, current month and cumulative;
Department of Trade and Commerce, Dominion Bureau of Statistics, Ottawa.	Exports by main groups, distinguishing United Kingdom and United States; Exports by articles, subdivided by country, current month and cumulative; Re-exports by articles, current month and cumulative.
Trade of Canada, Imports for Consumption (No. 10–4130).	Imports by main groups of commodities, current month and cumulative;
Department of Trade and Commerce, Dominion Bureau of Statistics, Ottawa.	Imports by geographic areas and principal countries, current month and cumulative; Imports by articles, current month and cumulative;

Publication	Contents
Monthly	Imports by groups of commodities, distinguishing United Kingdom and United States, current month and cumulative.
Trade of Canada, Domestic Exports (No. 10–4120). Department of Trade and Commerce, Dominion Bureau of Statistics, Ottawa.	Exports by main groups, current month and cumulative; Exports by geographic areas and principal countries, same periods; Exports by principal articles, same periods.
Trade of Canada, Articles Imported from Each Country (No. 10–3050). Department of Trade and Commerce, Dominion Bureau of Statistics, Ottawa.	Imports by country from which shipped, subdivided by commodity.
Trade of Canada, Articles Exported to Each Country (No. 10–3040). Department of Trade and Commerce, Dominion Bureau of Statistics, Ottawa.	National exports by country subdivided by commodity.

CEYLON

Annual

Statistical Abstract of Ceylon. Department of Census and Statistics, Colombo.	Trade by commodity groups and aggregates by country.

Quarterly

Quarterly Bulletin of Statistics. Department of Census and Statistics, Colombo.	Trade by commodity groups and principal articles and aggregates by country.

Monthly

Ceylon Customs Returns. Customs Office, Colombo.	Trade by commodity subdivided by country.

INDIA

Annual

Statistical Abstract. Office of the Economic Adviser, Government of India, Delhi.	Trade by principal articles and aggregates by country.

Monthly

Accounts Relating to the Foreign Sea and Airborne Trade and Navigation of India. Department of Commercial Intelligence and Statistics, Calcutta.	Trade by commodity subdivided by country, and summary tables.
Monthly Abstract of Statistics. Ministry of Commerce, New Delhi.	Trade by principal articles and groups and aggregates by country.

NEW ZEALAND

Annual

Trade and Shipping Statistics . . Census and Statistics Department, Wellington.	Summary and detailed tables.

Monthly

Monthly Abstract of Statistics . . Census and Statistics Department, Wellington.	Trade by commodity and aggregates by country.

Publication	Contents

PAKISTAN

Monthly

Summary of the Statistics Relating to Foreign Sea-Borne Trade of Pakistan. Ministry of Commerce and Education, Department of Commercial Intelligence and Statistics, Karachi. — Trade by principal commodities subdivided by country and summary tables.

SOUTHERN RHODESIA

Annual

Annual Statement of the Trade of Southern Rhodesia with British Countries and Foreign Countries. Central African Statistical Office, Trade Division, Salisbury. — Summary and detailed tables.

Bi-Monthly

Economic and Statistical Bulletin of Southern Rhodesia. Central African Statistical Office, Trade Division, Salisbury. — Summary tables.

UNION OF SOUTH AFRICA

Annual

Annual Statement of the Trade and Shipping of the Union of South Africa and the Territory of South West Africa. Department of Customs and Excise, Pretoria. — Summary and detailed tables.

Monthly

Maandelikse Uitreksel van Handelstatistiek—Monthly Abstract of Trade Statistics. Department of Customs and Excise, Pretoria. — Trade by principal commodities and aggregates by country.

Maandbulletin van Statistiek—Monthly Bulletin of Statistics. Office of Census and Statistics, Pretoria. — Summary tables.

Chapter 16. British Colonies and Dependencies
EAST AND CENTRAL AFRICA

BRITISH EAST AFRICA

Annual

Annual Trade Report of Kenya and Uganda. Government Printer, Nairobi. — Trade by commodity groups and by country distinguishing principal articles.

Monthly

Trade and Revenue Report for Kenya, Uganda and Tanganyika for the Month of . . . The East African Customs and Excise Department, Government Printer, Dar es Salaam. — Trade by commodity and aggregates by country.

East African Economic and Statistical Bulletin, East Africa High Commission. East African Statistical Department, Nairobi. — Trade by commodity groups subdivided by country for each of the territories Kenya, Uganda and Tanganyika.

Publication	Contents
NORTHERN RHODESIA	
Annual	
Statement of the Trade of Northern Rhodesia. Central African Statistical Office, Salisbury, Southern Rhodesia, printed in Lusaka.	Summary and detailed tables.
Monthly	
Economic and Statistical Bulletin. Central African Statistical Office, Salisbury, Southern Rhodesia.	Trade by commodity groups and principal commodities subdivided by country.
NYASALAND	
Annual	
Annual Report on the Trade of the Protectorate. Nyasaland Protectorate, Customs Department, Zomba.	Summary and detailed tables.
TANGANYIKA (*see also* British East Africa, *above*).	
Annual	
Trade Report . . . . Comptroller of Customs, Dar es Salaam.	Summary and detailed tables.
ZANZIBAR PROTECTORATE	
Annual	
Annual Trade Report . . . Comptroller of Customs and Imperial Trade Correspondent, Government Printer, Zanzibar.	Summary and detailed tables.
Monthly	
Trade and Information Report Customs House, Government Printer, Zanzibar.	Trade by principal commodities.

WEST AFRICA

Publication	Contents
GAMBIA	
Annual	
Supplement to the Report on the Trade and Shipping of the Colony. Collector of Customs, Bathurst.	Summary and detailed tables.
GOLD COAST	
Annual	
Trade Report . . . . Government Printing Department, Accra.	Summary and detailed tables.
Monthly	
Gold Coast Gazette. . . . Trade Supplement, Government Printing Department, Accra.	Trade by commodity and aggregates by country.
NIGERIA	
Annual	
Trade Report . . . . Department of Statistics, Lagos.	Summary and detailed tables.

Publication	Contents

Monthly
Nigeria Trade Summary . .
Department of Statistics, Lagos.

Trade by principal commodities and aggregates by country.

ST. HELENA

Annual
St. Helena . . . . .
Colonial Annual Reports, HMSO, London.

Summary tables.

SIERRA LEONE

Annual
Trade Report . . . .
Government Printer, Freetown.

Summary and detailed tables.

Monthly
The Sierra Leone Monthly Trade Statistics, Freetown.

Trade by principal commodities and aggregates by principal countries.

EASTERN COLONIES

BRUNEI

Annual
Annual Report on Brunei by the British Resident, Malaya Publishing House, Singapore.

Imports and exports of principal articles.

HONG KONG

Annual
Hong Kong Annual Report . .
Government of Hong Kong.

Imports and Exports by commodity groups and aggregates by country.

Monthly
Hong Kong Trade Returns . .
Department of Commerce and Industry, Hong Kong.

Imports and exports by commodity, sub-divided by country.
Imports and exports by country, subdivided by commodity.

Supplement to the Hong Kong Government Gazette
Department of Statistics, Hong Kong.

Imports and exports by commodity groups and aggregates by country.

MALAYA (Federation) and SINGAPORE

Annual
Annual Report on the Federation of Malaya.
Government Press, Kuala Lumpur.

Trade by commodity groups and aggregates by country.

Monthly
Malayan Statistics . . . .
Trade Section (new title beginning April 1950).
Registrar of Malayan Statistics, Singapore.

Trade by commodity subdivided by country; trade by country subdivided by commodity.

NORTH BORNEO (BRITISH)

Annual
North Borneo. . . . .
Colonial Annual Reports, HMSO, London.

Trade by principal commodities, aggregates by country and exports by principal commodities subdivided by country.

Publication	Contents

SARAWAK

Annual

Annual Report of Sarawak . . Trade by principal commodities.
Government Printing Office, Kuching.

MEDITERRANEAN COLONIES

CYPRUS

Annual

The Cyprus Blue Book . . . Summary tables and trade by country
Cyprus Government Printing Office, subdivided by commodity groups.
Nicosia.

WEST INDIES

BAHAMA ISLANDS

Annual

Bahamas . . . . . Imports and exports by principal articles.
Colonial Annual Reports, HMSO,
London.

BARBADOS

Annual

Report of the Comptroller of Customs Imports, exports and re-exports, summary
on the Customs Revenue, Trade and and detailed tables.
Shipping of the Island, Supplement to
Official Gazette.

BERMUDA

Annual

Bermuda Blue Book . . . Imports and exports by commodity by
Hamilton Press, Bermuda. country.

BRITISH HONDURAS

Annual

Customs Report (*Customs Trade and* Imports, exports, and re-exports, summary
Shipping). and detailed tables.
Custom House, Government Printer,
Belize.

JAMAICA

Annual

External Trade of Jamaica . . Imports and exports, summary and
Central Bureau of Statistics, Kingston. detailed tables.

Quarterly

Quarterly Digest of Statistics . . Imports and exports by commodity and
aggregates by country.

TRINIDAD AND TOBAGO

Quarterly

Quarterly Economic Report . . Imports, exports, and re-exports, aggre-
Central Statistical Office. gates by country and principal articles.

MISCELLANEOUS BRITISH COLONIES

ADEN

Annual

Report on the Trade and Navigation of Summary and detailed tables.
Aden.
Government of India Press, Simla.

Publication	Contents

FIJI

Annual

Colony of Fiji . . . .
Colony Annual Report.
Government Press, Sura.

Trade by principal commodities and aggregates by country.

MAURITIUS

Annual

Annual Report of the Customs Department.
Port Louis.

Trade by commodity groups and aggregates by countries

SEYCHELLES

Annual

Seychelles . . . . .
Colonial Annual Reports, HMSO, London.

Summary data.

Chapter 17. Continental Europe and Dependencies

AUSTRIA

Annual

Statistik des Aussenhandels Oesterreichs.
Oesterreichisches Statistisches Zentralamt, Wien.

Summary and detailed tables.

Half Yearly

Statistik des Aussenhandels Oesterreichs für das erste Halbjahr.

Trade by countries subdivided by commodity groups, and summary tables.

Monthly

Statistische Nachrichten . . .
Monatsberichte des Oesterreichischen Institutes für Wirtschaftenforschung.

Summary tables.
Summary tables.

BELGIUM-LUXEMBOURG

Monthly

Bulletin Mensuel du Commerce Extérieur de l'Union Economique Belgo-Luxembourgeoise.
Institut National de Statistique, Bruxelles.

Trade by commodity subdivided by country and trade by country subdivided by commodity.

BELGIAN CONGO AND RUANDA-URUNDI

Annual

Statistique du Commerce extérieur de l'union douanière du Congo Belge et du Ruanda-Urundi.
Royaume de Belgique, Ministère des Colonies, 2 me Direction Générale.

Summary and detailed tables.

Monthly

Bulletin Mensuel des Statistiques du Congo Belge et du Ruanda-Urundi.
Congo Belge, Secrétariat Général, Section Statistique, Brussels and Léopoldville.

Summary and detailed tables.

Publication	Contents
DENMARK	
Annual	
Danmarks vareinförsel og-Udförsel—Importations et Exportations du Danemark. Det Statistiske Department, Köbenhavn.	Summary and detailed tables.
Monthly	
Vareomsaetningen med Udlandet—Commerce Extérieur Danmarks Statistik, Handels statiske Meddelelser. Det Statistiske Department, Köbenhavn.	Trade by commodity groups and trade by country subdivided by commodity groups.
FINLAND	
Annual	
Commerce Extérieur . . . Finlands Officiella Statistik, Helsinki.	Summary and detailed tables.
Monthly	
Commerce Extérieur de la Finlande . . Finlands Officiella Statistik, Helsinki.	Trade by commodity groups and principal articles; aggregates by country.
FRANCE	
Annual	
Tableau Général du Commerce extérieur Commerce de la France, avec la France d'Outre-Mer et les Pays Etrangers. Direction des Douanes et Droits indirects, Paris.	Summary and detailed tables.
Monthly	
Statistique Mensuelle du Commerce extérieur de la France. Direction des Douanes et Droits indirects, Paris.	Summary and detailed tables.
FRANCE (Union)	
Annual	
Annuaire Statistique de l'Union Française Outre-Mer. Ministère des Finances et des Affaires Economiques, Institut Nationale de la Statistique et des Etudes Economiques. Ministère de la France d'Outre-Mer, Service des Statistiques, Paris.	Summary tables of trade of component territories of French Union.
Monthly	
Bulletin Mensuel de Statistique d'Outre-Mer. Institut National de la Statistique et des Etudes Economiques, Paris.	Summary tables and trade by principal commodities for French overseas territories.
ALGERIA	
Annual	
Documents Statistiques réunis par l'Administration des Douanes sur le Commerce de l'Algérie. République Française, Gouvernement Général de l'Algérie, Direction des Douanes de l'Algérie, Alger.	Summary and detailed tables.

Publication	Contents

Annual
See also: Annuaire Statistique de l'Algérie.
Direction Générale des Finances, Service de Statistique Générale, Alger.

Quarterly
Bulletin Comparatif Trimestriel du Mouvement Commercial et Maritime de l'Algérie.

Summary tables.

Monthly
Bulletin de Statistique Général .

Trade by principal commodities with some country detail.

FRENCH EQUATORIAL AFRICA
Monthly
Bulletin d'Informations Economiques et Sociales Afrique Equatorial Française.
Statistique Générale de l'A.E.F., Brazzaville.

Trade by principal articles and aggregates by country.

FRENCH WEST AFRICA
Quarterly
Statistiques du Commerce extérieur de l'Afrique Occidentale Française Commerce spécial.
Gouvernement Général de l'Afrique Occidentale Française, Rufisque.

Trade by commodity and aggregates by country.

MADAGASCAR
Annual
Statistiques du Commerce et de la Navigation.
Ministère 'de la France d'Outre-mer, Haut Commissariat de la République Française à Madagascar et Dependances, Direction des Douanes, Tananarive.

Summary and detailed tables.

MOROCCO (FRENCH ZONE)
Annual
Statistiques de Mouvement Commercial et Maritime du Maroc (Zone Française et Zone de Tanger).
Gouvernement Cherifien, Direction de l'Agriculture du Commerce et des Forêts, Division du Commerce et de la Marine Marchande, Casablanca.

Summary and detailed tables.

Monthly
La Conjoncture Economique Marocaine
Gouvernement Cherifien, Service Central des Statistiques.

Summary tables.

TUNISIA
Annual
Annuaire Statistique de la Tunisie
Régence de Tunis, Protectorat Français, Secrétariat Général du Gouvernement Tunisien, Service Tunisien des Statistiques, Tunis.

Trade by principal commodities with country detail for exports.

Publication	Contents
Monthly	
Bulletin Economique et Social de la Tunisie. Résidence Générale de France à Tunis.	Summary tables.

GERMANY (WESTERN)

Annual

Der Aussenhandel des Vereinigten Wirtschaftsgebietes. Statistisches Amt des Vereingten Wirtschaftsgebietes, Wiesbaden.	Trade by commodity groups and by country subdivided by commodity groups.

Monthly

Der Aussenhandel der Bundesrepublik Deutschland, Teil 1, Zusammenfassende Übersichten. Statistisches Bundesamt, Wiesbaden.	Summary tables; trade by commodity groups and aggregates by country.
Der Aussenhandel der Bundesrepublik Deutschland, Teil 2, Der Spezialhandel nach Waren (Statistische Nummern). Statistisches Bundesamt, Wiesbaden.	Trade by commodity subdivided by country.

Quarterly

Der Aussenhandel der Bundesrepublik Deutschland, Teil 3, Der Aussenhandel nach Erdteilen und Ländern. Statistisches Amt des Vereingten Wirtschaftsgebietes, Wiesbaden.	Trade by country subdivided by commodity.

GREECE

Monthly

Bulletin Mensuel du Commerce Spécial de la Grèce avec les Pays Etrangers— Monthly Bulletin of the Special Trade of Greece with Foreign Countries. Ministère de l'Economie Nationale, Statistique Générale de la Grèce, Athens.	Trade by commodity subdivided by country and trade by country subdivided by commodity.

ICELAND

Annual

Verzlunarskyrslur-Statistique du Commerce. Hagstofa Islands, Reykjavik.	Summary and detailed tables.

Monthly

Statistical Journal . . . . Hagstofa Islands, Reykjavik.	Exports of principal commodities by country and imports by country subdivided by commodity groups.

IRELAND

Annual

Trade and Shipping Statistics . . Central Statistical Office, Dublin.	Summary and detailed tables.

Monthly

Trade Statistics of Ireland . . Central Statistical Office, Dublin.	Trade by commodity groups and principal articles and aggregates by country.

Publication	Contents

ITALY

Annual
Compendio Statistico Italiano . . Istituto Centrale di Statistica, Roma.

Trade by principal commodities and aggregates by country.

Monthly
Statistica del Comercio con l'Estero . Istituto Centrale di Statistica, Roma.

Summary and detailed tables.

Bolletino Monsile di Statistica . Istituto Centrale di Statistica, Roma (new series).

Summary tables.

NETHERLANDS

Annual
Statistisch Zakboek . . . Centraal Bureau voor de Statistiek, 'sGravenhage.

Trade by principal commodities and aggregates by country.

Monthly
Maandstatistiek van de In-Uit-en Doorvoer per Goederensoort. Centraal Bureau voor de Statistiek 'sGravenhage.

Summary and detailed tables by commodity subdivided by country.

Maandstatistiek van de In-Uit-en doorvoer per land.

Trade by countries subdivided by commodity groups.

NORWAY

Annual
Norges Handel-Statistique du Commerce Extérieur de la Norvège. Statistisk Sentralbyra.

Summary and detailed tables.

Monthly
Manedsoppgaver over Vareomsetningen med Utlandet-Bulletin Mensuel du Commerce Extérieur. Statistisk Sentralbyra.

Trade by commodity groups and principal articles and trade by country subdivided by commodity groups; Exports and principal articles by country.

POLAND

Annual
Statistical Year Book of Poland. Central Statistical Office of the Republic of Poland, Warsaw.

Trade by principal countries subdivided by principal articles.

Monthly
Wiadomości Statystyczne (Statistical News) Glowny Urzad Statystyczny. Warszawa.

Trade by principal commodities.

PORTUGAL

Annual
Comercio Externo-Commerce Extérieur

Summary and detailed tables.

Monthly
Boletim Mensal—Bulletin Mensuel Instituto Nacional de Estatistica, Lisboa.

Trade by commodity groups and principal articles with some country detail.

Publication	Contents

PORTUGAL (Overseas territories)

Annual

Anuario Estatistico do Imperio Colonial Annuaire Statistique de l'Empire Colonial.
Portugal, Instituto Nacional de Estatistica, Lisboa.

Summary tables and trade by principal commodities and groups for Cape Verde, Portuguese Guinea, Sao Tome, and Principe, Angola, Mozambique, Portuguese India.

Monthly

Boletim Mensal do Instituto Nacional de Estatistica—Bulletin Mensuel de l'Institut National de Statistique, Lisboa.

Trade by commodity groups and principal articles, with some country detail, for each Portuguese territory.

ANGOLA

Annual

Estatistica do Comercio Externo e da Navegacão.
Colonia de Angola, Reparticao Tecnica de Estatistica Geral, Luanda.

Summary and detailed tables.

Monthly

Boletim Mensal de Estatistica .   .
Reparticao Tecnica de Estatistica Geral, Luanda.

Trade by principal commodities subdivided by countries.

MOZAMBIQUE

Annual

Estatistico do Comercio Externo e da Navegacão, ano de . . .
Republica Portuguesa, Colonia de Mocambique, Reparticão Tecnica de Estatistica, Imprensa Nacional de Mocambique, Lourenço Marques.

Summary and detailed tables.

Quarterly

Boletim Trimestral de Estatistica— Bulletin Trimestriel de Statistique.
Colonia de Mocambique Reparticão Tecnica de Estatistica, Lourenço Marques.

Trade by principal commodities subdivided by country.

PORTUGUESE INDIA

Annual

Estatistica do Comercio Externo e da Navegacão.
Reparticão Central de Estatistica e Informacao, Reparticao dos Servicos Adnaneiros, Goa.

Trade by commodity subdivided by country.

Quarterly

Boletim Trimestral—Bulletin Trimestriel.
Reparticão Central de Estatistica e Informacao.

Trade by principal commodities with some country detail.

SPAIN

Annual

Estadística del Comercio Exterior de España.
Ministerio de Hacienda, Direccion General de Aduanas, Madrid.

Summary and detailed tables.

Publication	Contents

Monthly

Estadística del Comercio Exterior de España, Resumen Mensual.
Ministerio de Hacienda, Direccion General de Aduanas, Madrid.

Trade by commodity subdivided by country with separate data for Spain, Canary Isles, Ceuta, and Melilla.

MOROCCAN PROTECTORATE (SPANISH)

Annual

Estadística del Comercio exterior en la Zona del Protectorado Espanol.
Alta Comisaria de España en Marruecos, Delegación General, Servicio de Estadística, Tetuan.

Summary and detailed tables.

SWEDEN

Annual

Handel, Berattelse
Kommerskollegium, Sveriges Officiella Statistik, Stockholm.

Summary and detailed tables.

Sveriges Varuinforsel fran olika Lander (preliminary annual).
Appears as supplement to: Kommersiella Meddelanden Kommerskollegium, Stockholm.

Imports by commodity groups and imports by country.

Sveriges Varuntforsel till olika Lander (preliminary annual).
Appears as supplement to: Kommersiella Meddelanden Kommerskollegium, Stockholm.

Exports by commodity groups and exports by country.

Monthly

Manadestatistik over Handeln .   .
Statistiska Meddelanden Serie C, Kommerskollegium, Stockholm.

Trade by commodity groups subdivided by country.

SWITZERLAND

Annual

Jahresstatistik des Aussenhandels der Schweiz—Statistique Annuelle du Commerce Extérieur de la Suisse.
Eidgenössische Oberzolldirektion—Direction Générale des Douanes Federales, Berne.

Summary and detailed tables.

Monthly

Monatsstatistik des Aussenhandels der Schweiz—Statistique Mensuelle du Commerce Extérieur de la Suisse.
Eidgenössische Oberzolldirektion—Direction Générale des Douanes Federales, Berne.

Trade by commodity subdivided by country.

TURKEY

Annual

Statistique Annuelle du Commerce Extérieur et Statistique Mensuelle du Décembre.
Office Central de Statistique, Ankara.

Summary and detailed tables.

Publication	Contents
Monthly	
Statistique Mensuelle du Commerce Extérieur. Office Central de Statistique, Ankara.	Summary and detailed tables.
Statistique du Commerce Extérieur, Resumé Mensuel. Office Central de Statistique, Ankara.	Summary tables.

Chapter 18. Latin America

ARGENTINA

Annual

Anuario Estadística de la Republica Argentina Vol. II, Comercio Exterior. Ministerio de Asunto Tecnicos, Direccion Nacional de Servicios Tecnicos del Estado, Direccion General del Servicio Estadistico Nacional, Buenos Aires. — Imports and exports, summary and detailed tables.

Monthly

Servicio Estadístico Oficial de la Republica Argentina. — Imports and exports by commodity groups, and aggregates by country.

Sintosia Estadística Mensual de la Republica Argentina. — Imports and exports by commodity groups, and aggregates by country.

BOLIVIA

Annual

Comercio Exterior . . . Ministerio de Hacienda, Direccion General de Estadística, La Paz. — Summary and detailed tables.

Monthly

Revista Mensual . . . . Direccion General de Estadística y Censos, La Paz. — Exports, principal articles.

BRAZIL

Annual

Comercio Exterior do Brasil, por Mercadorias. Ministerio de Fazenda, Tesouro Nacional Servico de Estadistica Economica e Financeira, Rio de Janeiro. — Imports and exports by commodity and aggregates by country.

Comercio Exterior do Brasil, por Mercadorias Segundo os Paises. — Imports and exports by commodity, subdivided by country.

Comercio Exterior do Brasil, Resumo por Mercadorias. — Imports and exports by commodity and aggregates by country.

Comercio Exterior do Brasil . . — Separate publication for trade with each country.

Comercio Exterior do Brasil . . — Separate publication for each principal group of imports.

Monthly

Comercio Exterior do Brasil, Resumo Mensal. — Imports and exports of principal commodities, aggregates by country.

Comercio Exterior do Brasil, Exportacao do. . . . — Exports of principal commodities, separate issues for each commodity.

APPENDIX 433

Publication	Contents

CHILE

Annual

Comercio Exterior . . .
Direccion General de Estadística Chile, Santiago de Chile.

Imports and exports, summary and detailed tables.

Estadística Chilena Sinopsis . .

Imports and exports of principal commodities and aggregates by country; trade with each important trading partner by commodity.

Monthly

Estadística Chilena . . .

Imports and exports by commodity groups and certain commodities, aggregates by country.

COLOMBIA

Annual

Anuario de Comercio Exterior . .
Contraloria General de la Republica, Direccion Nacional de Estadística, Bogota.

Summary and detailed tables.

Quarterly or Half Yearly

Anales de Economia y Estadística .

Imports and exports of principal commodities and summary tables.

Monthly

Revista del Banco de la Republica Bogota.

Imports and exports of principal commodities by country.

COSTA RICA

Annual

Estadística de Comercio Exterior, Importacion y Exportacion por Artículos. Direccion General del Estadística, San Jose.

Imports, exports, and re-exports detailed tables.

Estadísticas de Importacion, Resumen

Imports by commodity; imports and exports aggregates by country.

Estadísticas de Exportacion, Resumen

Exports and re-exports by commodity and aggregates by country.

Monthly

Series Estadísticas . . .
Direccion General de Estadística, Ministerio de Economia y Hacienda, San Jose.

Imports, exports by month, value.

Boletin Estadística Mensual . .
Banco Central de Costa Rica, San Jose.

Imports and exports by groups of commodities.

CUBA

Annual

Comercio Exterior . . . .
Ministerio de Hacienda, Direccion General de Estadística, Habana.

Imports and exports, summary and detailed tables.

Monthly

Valor de la Importacion y Exportacion durante el mes de. . . . Comparado con Igual Mes del Ano Anterior.
Ministerio de Hacienda, Direccion General de Estadística, Habana.

Imports and exports by country.

Boletin de Estadísticas . . .

Imports and exports by commodity and aggregates by country.

Valor de la Importacion detallada por paises, etc.

Imports, exports and re-exports by country, with some commodity detail.

Publication	Contents
DOMINICAN REPUBLIC	
Annual	
Importacion de la Republica Dominicana. Direccion General de Estadística, Seccion de Publicaciones, Ciudad Trujillo.	Imports, summary and detailed tables.
Exportacion de la Republica Dominicana.	Exports, summary and detailed tables.
Bi-Monthly	
Revista de la Secretaria de Estado de Economia Nacional. Ciudad Trujillo.	Imports and exports, summary tables with certain commodity detail for exports.
Irregularly	
Exportacion de la Republica Dominicana. Direccion General de Estadística, Ciudad Trujillo.	Exports, summary and detailed tables.
ECUADOR	
Quarterly	
Boletin del Ministerio del Tesoro . Quito.	Imports and exports of principal articles and aggregates by country.
Monthly	
Boletin . . . . . Banco Central de Ecuador, Quito.	Imports and exports by groups of commodities and aggregates by country.
EL SALVADOR	
Annual	
Anuario Estadístico del Comercio Exterior e Interior de la Republica de El Salvador. Ministerio de Economia, Direccion General de Estadística, San Salvador.	Imports and exports, summary and detailed tables.
Half-Yearly	
Boletin Estadístico	Imports and exports, aggregates by country.
GUATEMALA	
Annual	
Sintesis Geografico-Estadística . . Direccion General de Estadística, Guatemala.	Imports and exports by commodity and aggregates by country.
Monthly	
Boletin . . . . . . Direccion General de Estadística, Guatemala.	Imports and exports by commodity groups and principal articles.
MEXICO	
Annual	
Anuario Estadístico del Comercio Exterior de los Estados Unidos Mexicanos. Secretaria de Economia, Direccion General de Estadística, Mexico.	Imports and exports, summary and detailed tables.
Monthly	
Revista de Estadística . . .	Imports and exports, principal commodities and aggregates by country.

Publication	Contents

PANAMA

Annual

Extracto Estadístico de la Republica de Panama, Vol. I, Comercio Exterior.
Contraloria General de la Republica, Direccion de Estadística y Censo.

Summary and detailed tables.

Monthly

Estadística Panamena   .   .   .

Exports, principal articles; Imports and exports aggregates by country.

PARAGUAY

Annual

Anuario Estadístico de la Republica del Paraguay.

Imports and exports by country, subdivided by commodity groups; Imports by groups; exports of principal articles by country.

PERU

Annual

Anuario del Comercio Exterior de la Republica Peruana.
Ministerio de Hacienda y Comercio, Superintendencia General de Aduanas, Departmento de Estadística, Lima.

Summary and detailed tables.

Quarterly

Boletin de Estadística Peruana .   .
Ministerio de Hacienda y Comercio, Direccion Nacional de Estadística.

Imports and exports summary tables.

Monthly

Boletin del Banco Central de Reserva del Peru.
Lima.

Imports and exports by commodity groups and aggregates by country.

URUGUAY

Monthly

Informativo .   .   .   .   .
Ministerio de Hacienda.

Imports and exports of principal commodities and groups, and aggregates by country.

Boletin de Hacienda, Supplemento .
Contaduria General de la Nacion, Montevideo.

Import aggregates, exports of principal commodities and aggregates by country.

Supplemento Estadístico de la Revista Economics.
Banco de la Republica Oriental del Uruguay, Departamento de Investigaciones Economices, Montevideo.

Imports and exports by commodity groups and aggregates by country.

VENEZUELA

Annual

Estadística Mercantil y Maritima .
Ministerio de Fomento, Direccion General de Estadística, Caracas.

Summary and detailed tables.

Anuario Estadistico de Venezuela .
Ministerio de Fomento, Direccion General de Estadística, Caracas.

Imports and exports of principal articles and aggregates by country.

Publication	Contents

Monthly
Boletin de Estadística . . .
Ministerio de Fomento, Direccion
General de Estadística, Caracas.

Exports of principal articles, imports by commodity groups and aggregates by country.

Chapter 19. Near and Far East
NEAR EAST

ANGLO-EGYPTIAN SUDAN

Annual
Foreign Trade Report . . .
Department of Economics and Trade,
Khartoum.

Summary and detailed tables.

Monthly
Foreign Trade and Internal Statistics .
Department of Economics and Trade,
Khartoum.

Trade by commodities with some country detail.

EGYPT

Annual
Annual Statement of Foreign Trade .
Ministry of Finance, Statistical Admin-
istration, Cairo.

Summary and detailed tables.

Monthly
Monthly Summary of Foreign Trade .
Ministry of Finance, Statistical Admin-
istration, Cairo.

Summary tables and trade by commo-dities with country detail for principal articles.

ETHIOPIA

Monthly
Monthly Letter . . . .
State Bank of Ethiopia, Addis Abbaba.

Summary tables.

IRAN

Annual
*Statistique Annuelle du Commerce Ex-
térieur de l'Iran.*
Ministère des Finances, Administration
Générale de Douanes, Teheran.

Summary and detailed tables.

Monthly
Bulletin Mensuel . . .
Administration Générale de Douanes,
Teheran.

Trade by principal commodities sub-divided by country.

IRAQ

Annual
*Foreign Trade Statistics for the Calendar
Year . . .*
Ministry of Finance, Department of
Customs and Excise, Baghdad.

Summary and detailed tables.

Statistical Abstract . . .
Ministry of Economics, Principal
Bureau of Statistics, Baghdad.

Trade by principal articles subdivided by country.

ISRAEL

Monthly
Statistical Bulletin of Israel . .
Central Bureau of Statistics, Jerusalem.

Trade by commodity groups and aggre-gates by country.

Publication	Contents
JORDAN	
Annual	
Administrative Report Customs, Excise, Trade and Industry. Department of Customs, Trade and Industry, Amman.	Summary tables and exports by principal articles.
LEBANON	
Annual	
Recueil des Statistiques Générales . Ministère de l'Economie Nationale, Service de Statistiques Générales, Beyrouth.	Trade by principal commodities and aggregates by country.
Quarterly	
Bulletin Statistique Trimestriel . . Ministère de l'Economie Nationale, Service de Statistique Générale, Beyrouth.	Trade by commodity groups and aggregates by country.
Monthly	
Bulletin Mensuel . . . Ministère de l'Economie Nationale, Service de Statistique Générale, Beyrouth.	Trade by commodity groups and principal articles.
SYRIA	
Annual	
Al-Majmua Al-Jhsaiya As-Suriya (The Statistical Collection of Syria). Ministry of National Economy, Department of Statistics, Damascus.	Trade by commodity groups and aggregates by country.

FAR EAST

Publication	Contents
BURMA	
Annual	
Annual Statement of the Sea-Borne Trade and Navigation of Burma. Collector of Customs, Rangoon.	Summary and detailed tables.
Monthly	
External Trade Statistics . . Ministry of National Planning, Rangoon.	Imports and exports of principal commodities and aggregates by country.
INDOCHINA	
Annual	
Annuaire Statistique de l'Indochine . Haut Commissariat de France en Indochine Affaires Economiques, Statistique Générale de l'Indochine, Saigon.	Trade by principal articles and groups; Trade by principal countries subdivided by commodity.
Monthly	
Bulletin Statistique Mensuel . . Haut Commissariat de France en Indochine Affaires Statistiques, Saigon.	Trade by principal articles with certain country detail.
Viet-NamThong-Ke Nguyet-San—Bulletin Statistique Mensuel du Viet-Nam. Institut de la Statistique et des Etudes Economique, Saigon.	Imports and exports by principal commodities.

Publication	Contents

INDONESIA

Monthly

Warta Bulanan, Impor dan Ekspor dari Indonesia, 1, *Ekspor Djawa dan Madura* (Exports of Java and Madura).
Penerbitan Kantor Pusat Statistik, Djakarta.

Exports by commodity groups subdivided by country.

Warta Bulanan, Impor dan Ekspor dari Indonesia, 2, *Ekspor Sumatra, Kalimantan, Indonesia Timor* (Exports of Sumatra, Borneo, and Indonesian Timor).

Exports by commodity, subdivided by country.

Warta Bulanan, Impor dan Ekspor dari Indonesia, 3, *Impor Djawa dan Madura* (Imports into Java and Madura).

Imports by commodity subdivided by country.

Warta Bulanan, Impor dan Ekspor dari Indonesia, 4, *Impor Sumatra, Kalimantan, Indonesia Timor* (Imports into Sumatra, Borneo, and Indonesian Timor).

Imports by principal articles, subdivided by countries of origin.

Warta Bulanan, Impor dan Ekspor dari Indonesia, 5, *Ekspor dari Indonesia Statistik Pelabuhan dan Negeri.*

Indonesian exports of principal commodities subdivided by country.

Warta Bulanan, Impor dan Ekspor dari Indonesia, 6, *Impor di Indonesia Statistik Pelabuhan dan Negeri.*

Indonesian imports by commodity subdivided by country.

Warta Bulanan Impor dan Ekspor dari Indonesia, 7, *Ekspor Indonesia.*

Indonesian exports by states subdivided by commodity groups and by country of destination subdivided by commodity groups.

Warta Bulanan, Impor dan Ekspor dari Indonesia, 8, *Impor Indonesia.*

Indonesian imports by states subdivided by commodity groups and by country of provenance subdivided by commodity groups.

JAPAN

Annual

Japan Statistical Yearbook
Statistics Bureau of the Prime Minister's Office and Executive Office of the Statistics Commission.

Trade by principal commodities subdivided by country, and summary historical tables.

Monthly

Detailed Import and Export Statistics of Japan by Country and Commodity.
General Headquarters, Supreme Commander for the Allied Powers, Economic and Scientific Section, Programs and Statistics Division.

Trade by commodity subdivided by country and trade by country subdivided by commodity.

Monthly Return of the Foreign Trade of Japan.
Minister of Finance, Tokyo.

Summary and detailed tables, aggregates by country, trade by commodity, trade by principal commodities subdivided by country.

Survey of Economic Conditions and Foreign Trade.
Mitsubishi Economic Research Institute, Tokyo.

Trade by principal commodities and aggregates by country.

Publication	Contents
KOREA	
Annual	
Economic Review . . . . Bank of Korea, Seoul.	Trade by principal commodities subdivided by country.
Monthly	
Monthly Statistical Review . . Bank of Korea, Seoul.	Trade by commodity groups and aggregates by country.
PHILIPPINES	
Annual	
Foreign Trade Statistics of the Philippines. Office of the President, Bureau of the Census and Statistics, Manila.	Trade by commodity subdivided by country.
Quarterly	
Statistical Bulletin . . Central Bank of the Philippines, Department of Economic Research, Manila.	Trade by principal commodities with some country detail.
THAILAND	
Annual	
Statistical Yearbook Thailand . . Central Service of Statistics, Bangkok.	Trade by principal commodities and trade by country subdivided by principal commodities.
Monthly	
Current Statistics . . . . Bank of Thailand, Bangkok.	Summary tables.

INDEX

I Subjects and Authors (Parts I and II)

II COUNTRIES

	PARTS I AND II	PART III
Andorra	—	358
Argentina . . .	69, 94, 136, 147	382, 387–8, 390–2, 394, 396–7, 399
Australia. . . .	86, 100, 197	308–10, 318, 320–6, 328
Austria	41, 94	354–7, 365–7, 369, 375–8
Belgium-Luxembourg .	46, 65, 69, 92, 94, 140, 145, 149–51, 197, 200	354–5, 357, 364–9, 374, 376–7
Belgian Congo . .	37	357
Bolivia . . .	40, 94, 118	382–3, 388, 391, 393–4, 398
Brazil . . .	41, 67, 197	382–3, 387–9, 391, 393–4, 397–9
Bulgaria	147	355, 357–8
Burma	40, 130	313, 318, 402, 408, 410–3
Canada . . .	10–1, 14, 16, 17, 19, 32–3, 37, 39, 42, 69, 86–7, 92, 100, 197, 200–1, 218–20, 226–8	310–1, 317–28, 392
Ceylon . . .	—	311–2, 317, 320–4, 327–8
Chile	34, 94, 101, 113	382–3, 388–91, 393–4, 396–7, 399
China . . .	20, 40, 166, 257	403, 408–11
Colombia . .	95, 101, 113	382–3, 387–90, 394, 397–9
Costa Rica . .	32, 33, 78, 112	381, 383–4, 388, 390, 393–5, 397–8
Cuba . . .	—	384, 388, 394, 397–8
Czechoslovakia .	39, 41, 65, 94, 118, 147, 197, 201	356, 358
Danzig	—	361
Denmark . . .	32, 64, 67, 69, 94, 185, 202	354–5, 358, 365, 367–9, 374–8, 380
Dominican Republic .	95, 201	384, 388–9, 393–4, 397–8
Ecuador . . .	41, 69, 94	384, 388–91, 393–4
Egypt . . .	35, 40, 67	400, 405–7
El Salvador . .	—	384, 388, 390, 394
Ethiopia . . .	86	401, 405–6
Finland . . .	30, 39, 86, 94, 182, 197, 199, 201	358, 366–7, 369–70, 374–8
France . . .	15, 32, 39, 41, 46, 65, 67, 71, 94, 96, 132, 134, 135, 140, 197, 201, 241, 248	303, 354–6, 358–9, 365, 367–70, 372–8
French Union . . (*See also* Indo-China).	95, 126	303, 312, 359, 368, 370–1
Germany . . .	39, 42, 65, 94, 140, 201, 241	354–7, 359–60, 364–9, 371–5, 377, 380
Greece . . .	34, 39, 94	355, 360, 366, 368, 373, 376–7
Guatemala . .	169	385, 388, 390, 394, 398

445

	PARTS I, II AND III
United States . . .	Balance of payments ; national income, 158, 181, 183–4, 219, 221
	Classification, commodity, 52, 70, 73–5, 78, 273, 277–80
	country, 118, 120–3, 283–5
	Coverage, 31–2, 34, 37–9, 41–4, 47, 273–7, 285–6
	Customs area, 126–7, 132, 134, 274–5
	Documents and codes, 10–3, 15, 279, 283
	History of statistics, 241, 269–73
	Index numbers, 197–8, 200, 201
	Machine tabulation, 19, 272–3
	Publications, generally, 141–5, 147, 149–51, 286–7
	Foreign Commerce and Navigation, 76, 141–5
	Reports (F110, 120, 410, 420), 141–5, 149
	Summary of Foreign Commerce, 141–5
	Survey of Current Business, 219, 226
	Statistical Abstract, 226
	other publications, 36, 226, 279, 410, 413
	Shipments, low-value, 26, 280–1
	Trade Agreements and Tariff Acts, 73, 75, 272, 282
	Valuation, 86–7, 93–6, 98–9, 169, 269–70, 282–3